A Foreign
Kingdom

A Foreign Kingdom

Mormons and Polygamy
in American Political Culture,
1852–1890

CHRISTINE TALBOT

UNIVERSITY OF ILLINOIS PRESS
Urbana, Chicago, and Springfield

Library of Congress Cataloging-in-Publication Data
Talbot, Christine, author.
A foreign kingdom : Mormons and polygamy in
American political culture, 1852–1890 / Christine Talbot.
pages cm
Includes bibliographical references and index.
ISBN 978-0-252-03808-2 (hardcover : alk. paper) —
ISBN 978-0-252-07957-3 (pbk. : alk. paper) —
ISBN 978-0-252-09535-1 (e-book)
1. Polygamy — Religious aspects — Church of Jesus
Christ of Latter-day Saints – History — 19th century.
2. Church of Jesus Christ of Latter-day Saints –
History — 19th century. 3. Church of Jesus Christ of
Latter-day Saints — Controversial literature — History
and criticism. 4. Mormon Church – History — 19th
century. I. Title.
BX8643.P63T35   2013
289.3'7309034—dc23   2013015222

Contents

Acknowledgments

Many people have helped this manuscript come to fruition, and I owe all of them gratitude. First, I thank the professors at the University of Michigan who nurtured this project through its beginning stages. María E. Montoya's faith in me and the project, her outstanding feedback, her straightforward advice, and her general goodwill have made this project much better than it otherwise would have been. Richard Cándida Smith ameliorated my journey through the beginnings of this project with astute guidance, superb criticism, encyclopedic knowledge, and a gentle sensibility. June M. Howard honed my theoretical and literary voices with encouragement, sharp advice, and good humor. Martha S. Jones offered the right thoughts at the right times, precisely the critiques that made me rethink everything.

Archivists, too, have proven priceless resources. Walter Jones and Peter Kraus at the University of Utah provided answers to endless questions and generosity in finding and lending materials. Stan Larson and Greg Thompson also offered valuable support in navigating University of Utah holdings. David Whittaker and Russ Taylor at Brigham Young University Special Collections were tireless in answering my many questions. However, I owe Larry Draper at BYU my special gratitude for acting well beyond his call every time I needed his assistance. His encyclopedic knowledge of the L. Tom Perry Special Collections and of Mormon and anti-Mormon sources more generally has been invaluable.

Archivists and volunteers at the LDS Church History Library were also helpful in finding rare materials.

I have been fortunate to receive generous grants for portions of this research from the Charles Redd Center for Western Studies and the Joseph Fielding Smith Institute of LDS History, both at Brigham Young University; the Friends of the Marriott Library at the University of Utah; and Rackham Graduate School at the University of Michigan. Chapter 2 appeared in slightly different form in the *Journal of Mormon History*, volume 37, number 4, Fall 2011, under the title "The Church Family and the American State: Mormonism and the Public Private Divide." It is published here with their permission. Portions of chapter 6 appeared in different form in the *Journal of Law and Family Studies*, volume 8, number 2, Summer 2006, under the title, "'Turkey is In Our Midst': Orientalism and Contagion in Nineteenth-Century Anti-Mormonism," and are reprinted here with their permission.

Numerous people have been generous with their time and thoughts in commenting on pieces of this work. Elizabeth Clement, Martha Ertmann, Margaret Toscano, and Dawn Anderson have been particularly kind in this regard. My thanks as well to Irwin Altman, John Carson, Brian Cannon, Kathryn M. Daynes, Jill Mulvay Derr, Laura DuPaix, Amy Farrell, Paul Finkelman, Sarah Barringer Gordon, Aaron Haberman, Hendrik Hartog, Erin Jordan, Laura Kessler, Ann Little, Michelle Low, Lorie Sauble-Otto, Donald Strassberg, Nicholas Syrett, Laurel Thatcher Ulrich, Diane Vecchio, John F. Wilson, Dan Wotherspoon, and the anonymous reviewers for the University of Illinois Press for their helpful and astute feedback. I also thank my family and friends who have read and commented on drafts and helped with editing, proofreading, compiling, fact checking, and the rest of the endless work of completing a manuscript. I am indebted as well to my many professors, mentors, colleagues, and friends at the University of Utah, the University of Michigan, Dickinson College, the University of Northern Colorado, and elsewhere who have offered friendship, advice, and sometimes commiseration.

I owe significant gratitude to my father, who endured constant interruptions that I might exploit his extensive lay knowledge of LDS Church history and doctrine. He has tolerated my invasions not only into his time, but into his rather large personal library of Mormon studies monographs. One person, however, has spent more time with this manuscript than anyone besides me—my mother. Her steadiness, ear, and editorial ruthlessness have made this project better than I could by myself. In these respects, my parents have indeed brought forth the best robe, put shoes on my feet, and killed the fatted calf in celebration of me, their prodigal daughter.

Introduction

In the 1830s, a young American named Joseph Smith founded a new religion that would come to be called The Church of Jesus Christ of Latter-day Saints, commonly known as the Mormons. As the Church developed, the practice of plural marriage became central to Mormon theology. Mormons practiced "the principle" in secret from the 1830s until 1852, when its public announcement launched Mormonism onto the national stage. This book explores the national controversy following that announcement. It maps two parallel and opposed ideological paradigms—Mormon and anti-Mormon—during Mormonism's most controversial period, from 1852 to 1890, when Mormon Church leadership publicly endorsed plural marriage.[1]

Polygamy generated decades of cultural conflict that contemporaries referred to, broadly, as "the Mormon question." The conflict was more than a simple condemnation of sexual and marital practices unacceptable to Victorian norms. Rather, it was a contest over the very meaning of Americanness. Advocates on both sides formulated what it meant to be American, each in very different ways. The Mormon question generated national discussions about gender, family, and the nature of citizenship that would define the parameters of membership in the late-nineteenth-century American body politic.

Essential to understanding the Mormon question are the conceptual categories of public and private. Over the nineteenth century, white middle-class northern Protestants regarded the separation of public and private spheres as central to the meaning of Americanness. They invested considerable political capital in distinguishing between private citizens and public government as well as between the private home and the world outside it. Polygamy destabilized these public/private divides in ways that dissociated family and gender relations from American citizenship. For Mormons, citizenship did not depend on the proper ordering of public and private. The Mormon question itself denaturalized and demonstrated the vulnerability of the public/private divide. Mormons subverted this and still claimed membership in an American body politic. This endangered the middle-class grounding of Americanism in the separation of public from private in family, gender relations, and government. The Mormon subversion of the public/private divide, I argue, was at the center of the Mormon question. Anti-Mormons responded virulently, asserting and reaffirming the public/private divide over and against one of its most powerful challenges.

Many nineteenth-century utopian and religious movements experimented in various kinds of communitarian living similar in many respects to the Mormons. These movements experimented with a variety of alternative economic, sexual, and filial structures that also challenged contemporary gendered structures of power. For example, John Humphrey Noyes experimented in group marriage and conceived of his community in Oneida as an "enlarged family," while the Shakers lived in celibate communities of adults they too called families.[2] Later in the century, free love advocates such as Mary Nichols and Victoria Woodhull critiqued marriage from the standpoint of individual sexual rights and experimented with a kind of sexual libertarianism based on pursuing individual happiness.[3] However, most of these movements remained national annoyances and none attracted the attention and vehement cultural and legislative campaigns the Mormons did. The Mormon question became a national question because Mormons occupied a western territory and exercised real political power. They dominated government in Utah. Moreover, Mormons were a much larger and more rapidly growing community than other utopian experiments. For these reasons, only Mormonism became a "question" worthy of the significant national attention that permanently altered both its character and the key role of public and private in shaping the American body politic.

The relative isolation of the American West was another factor that allowed the Mormon question to become a national question. Because of the geographic distance between the actual practice of polygamy and its detractors, anti-Mormons often made wild and unfounded claims about the nature of plural marriage. Moreover, because the federal government had unprecedented jurisdiction over western territories, the region was of particular importance in the consolidation of national and political culture.[4] In the immediate aftermath of the Civil War, the South had been central to national debates about the meaning of citizenship.[5] In an era of political conflict over states' rights and national loyalties, Reconstruction had asserted the power of the federal government over the states and established that the shape of the body politic would be "determined by the authority of a sovereign people, a community of citizens, that formed a single, united nation."[6] As the disenfranchisement of black men resolved the "Negro question" in the South, debates over national definitions of citizenship shifted westward during the 1870s, and new questions emerged as the nation wrestled with the political status of Mexicans, American Indians, Chinese immigrants, and Mormons. Some historians have characterized the Mormon question as a continuation of the processes of Reconstruction in the West.[7] In this regard, the West provided a federalized location for the consolidation of national political culture and a place to work out questions of national belonging. The West also provided a place in which the Mormons could determine the role of plural marriage in their communitarian project. As Mormons articulated the theological and political paradigms that encircled the practice of plural marriage, they staked new ground—theological, political, and filial—that reconfigured relations among the individual, the family, the kingdom of God, and the nation.

At the same time, with remarkable uniformity, anti-Mormons—mostly white middle-class Protestant Americans—espoused a contrary view of Mormonism and national identity that took shape in part over and against Mormons. Perhaps the most powerful mechanism through which these Americans asserted their sense of national identity was their formulation of categories of public and private which anti-Mormons understood to be inherently gendered. Nineteenth-century anti-Mormons asserted that it was through the proper maintenance of the gendered public/private divide that people qualified for membership in the American body politic. Anti-Mormons believed that Mormons, because of their improper domestic and political relations, should be denied the rights of American citizenship and expelled from the American body politic.

Citizenship is an artificial, unstable, fluid, shifting, and culturally constituted concept. It is an empty signifier into which ideas about political rights, national identity, and the constitution of the body politic are poured, and in which they are stirred and sometimes shaken. In broad terms, citizenship is composed of at least three elements: formal rights, participation in the polity, and a sense of cultural belonging. In the context of the Mormon question, the meaning of American citizenship was always in dialogic relationship with some notion of national identity. That is, in Carroll Smith-Rosenberg's terms, American subjects must "experience themselves as national subjects, that is, as integral parts of a collective 'people,' no matter how artificially constructed that collectivity and sense of belonging are."[8] The nature of Americanness has always been vigorously contested by culture-makers of divergent perspectives. The dynamics of social power make some players in this definitional game more successful than others—that is, some Americans have always been more "American" than others in their ability to deploy themselves at the center of a constructed national identity.

With all of this in mind, I use the term "American" recognizing the problematic exclusivity and artificiality of the term, but also recognizing the strategic historical and political work the term performed in nineteenth-century debates over the Mormon question. In disputes over polygamy, particular sorts of Americans posited themselves as "truly" American and thus could identify Mormons as un-American. Those who asserted cultural power through the Mormon question were, by and large, white middle-class Protestant Americans much more likely to be from the Northeast than the South or the West and much more likely to be Republicans than Democrats. The unprecedented popularity of anti-Mormon literature and, later, the success of anti-polygamy legislation show the success of those Americans at situating themselves on one side of a manufactured binary that opposed Mormonism to true Americanness.

Central to anti-Mormons' vision of true Americanness was the public/private divide. Feminist scholars have argued at length about the nature of the public/private distinction, and their work informs my understanding of these categories. But no one has ever seriously challenged the centrality of the distinction, however framed, to nineteenth-century white middle-class American political culture.[9] Public and private have always been conflicted and contested terms in feminist history. Historical and historiographical contests over what, exactly, was private or public show that, in June Howard's terms, the categories themselves "have fuzzy boundaries . . . but strong centers."[10] Moreover, as Linda Kerber astutely points out, historians must understand the metaphor of separate spheres not as a description of men's and women's lives, but rather as a "trope that hid its instrumentality even from those who employed it."[11] Most feminist scholars would agree with Patricia Uberoi that "there are as many feminist 'takes' on the private-public distinction as there are versions of feminism."[12] For my purposes, though, two contexts in which Americans formulated the public/private divide are most significant: first, the classical and revolutionary republican political theories in which American government was rooted and second, the evolving political culture of middle-class Americans.

Since the American Revolution, American political theorists have invested great political capital in the protection of the private individual and his property from government intervention. The ownership and independence of the self, initially constituted in part by the ownership of property, qualified an individual for membership in the body politic. As Gordon Wood shows, the American Revolution revolutionized not only politics but the family as well. In monarchical society, he argues, "The household, the society, and the state—private and public spheres—scarcely seemed separable." Personal relationships structured social and political dependencies. Moreover, "sometimes colonial communities seemed to be only enlarged families. Inbreeding and intermarrying . . . often created incredibly tangled webs of kinship. Some of these kinship networks grew in time to permeate or encompass entire villages, counties, or even colonies."[13] Embedded in some of these kinship networks were the public duties of gentlemen patriarchs in monarchical society. As gentlemen, heads of eighteenth-century genteel households were expected to provide political leadership, and, Wood argues, government "was regarded essentially as the enlisting and mobilizing of the power of private persons to carry out public ends."[14] Gentlemen patriarchs of notable genteel families owed public service "because of their talents, independence, and social preeminence."[15]

Over the latter half of the eighteenth century, family dynamics shifted from hierarchical, patriarchal families to more "republican" families in which "the family core of father, mother, and children became more distinct . . . and affection became more important than dependency in holding the family together." In keeping together, "families cut some of their ties to the outside world and became more insular."[16] Jay Fliegelman also points to a new contractual model of family voluntarily established by the mutual consent of husband and wife. Indeed, women were supposed "to find . . . 'liberation' through marriage," and their primary act of liberty, under this model, was to choose whom they would marry.[17] The revolutionary family became more privatized in its revolution against patriarchy, a revolution Wood calls "a century-long affair at least" that "was never complete, never undisputed, never final."[18] Despite revolutionary changes in the family, older models of patriarchal families endured into the nineteenth century. Particularly in genteel families, patriarchy and relations of dependence continued alongside and in tension with the newer middle-class models of "republican" or "contractual" families.[19] That is, even among white, middle-class Americans, the shift to the privatized, republican family was never complete.

In the decades immediately following the American Revolution, religious conscience was added to the list of political "privates," as legal theorists and courts alike embraced religious disestablishment. As Sarah Barringer Gordon states, American disestablishmentarianism maintained Protestant Christianity as a national value. By the 1830s, matters of faith had become private and voluntary at the state level as well as the federal, as long as they were also Christian.[20] Gordon contends that by the 1840s, American law, though "far . . . from advocating a separation of religious principles from government," had become increasingly committed to disestablishing religion, i.e., formally separating church from state. She shows how antebellum jurists "reconfigured the relationship of religion to American law and government," contending that "disestablishment itself became a Christian concept. Liberty of conscience and its corollary, uncoerced belief, were central to Protestantism as they were to free will as a political matter."[21] The separation of church and state made religious conscience a private individual matter. "Disestablishment was a practice, but not a rule, nationwide by 1850," Gordon observes, and further argues that only in the wake of the Mormon question "did Americans discover that separation of church and state was a fundamental component of all republican government."[22]

As feminist political theorists have pointed out, however, not just anyone could be counted as a private individual entitled to his or her private conscience. A common law principle inherited from Britain, the concept of coverture, constituted the legal unity of the family such that upon marriage, husband and wife (and children, by extension) became a single legal person under the law, represented in public government by the husband. Ruth Bloch has argued, "[M]en theoretically possessed . . . rights not as individuals, but as heads of households that subsumed the members of . . . disadvantaged groups—the 'dependent' servants, slaves, women, and children for whom they supposedly stood as representatives before the law."[23] Hence, from its beginnings, American legal theory linked the private individual, private property, and the private household into a single triumvirate of privacy that translated into men's eligibility and capacity for formal citizenship.

The private family was at the center of American national identity from the outset. As Bloch points out, the principle of coverture foreshadowed nineteenth-century understandings of the domestic private sphere. Early Americans "attach[ed] private rights to the household as a whole, rather than to each person within it."[24] Nancy Cott's study of marriage emphasizes its importance in "sculpt[ing] the body politic." Cott claims that because they formed households, "[t]he laws of marriage must play a large part in forming 'the people.'"[25] Moreover, "a commitment to monogamous marriage on a Christian model lodged deeply in American political theory."[26] Marriage, then, was a fundamental aspect of nineteenth-century citizenship and the privacy of a husband's household upheld his participation in public life. Women, children, slaves, and servants could not be citizens because they had no private interests to protect or represent; rather, they *were* part of those interests for male citizens.[27]

In the nineteenth century a new and loosely defined American middle class emerged in the wake of broad historical changes historians have called the market revolution. At the same time, the shift from domestic production to wage labor made the separation of the household from the outside world more imaginable.[28] Now, besides being the repository of private property, the home came to the center of American political culture in a new elaboration of the public/private divide. The market revolution produced a new middle class who, seeking an identity distinct from the wealthy and the poor, seized upon the home as the location from which that identity emerged.[29] Domestic fiction and prescriptive literature pictured the boundaries of the home as though the domestic realm could cleanly be set off from the rest of the world. By mid-century, white middle-class Americans imagined their world in bifurcated terms: a public sphere outside the home in which men carried out the business of political and economic life, contrasted to a private sphere in which women maintained the home as a "haven in a heartless world."[30]

In addition to separating the home from the world outside it, nineteenth-century white middle-class culture also manufactured sexual and political difference in terms of separate, gendered spheres of power. Superimposing separate spheres over public and private grounded the masculinity of the public sphere and produced a set of gender ideologies historians have called the "cult of true womanhood."[31] According to Cott, "By stipulating civic and political statuses of husbands and wives . . . marriage has been a cardinal—arguably the cardinal— agent of gender formation and has institutionalized gender roles."[32] Americans invested marriage with the cultural work of associating public and private with the separate spheres of men and women.[33] Catharine E. Beecher, in her best-selling 1842 *A Treatise on Domestic Economy*, quoted Alexis de Toqueville in defense of the relegation of women to the private sphere as protective: "If on the one hand an American woman cannot escape from the quiet circle of domestic employment, on the other hand she is never forced to go beyond it."[34] Although both the division itself and the gendering of public and private were always contested and incomplete, white middle-class Americans nonetheless fantasized that what women did was private and what men did was public. In reality, as June Howard points out, "when we speak of 'separate spheres' we are not describing a fact of social life but an organizing pressure within it."[35] This pressure was most deeply exerted by white middle-class Americans, the demographic from which almost all anti-Mormons emerged. The public/private divide and the ideology of separate spheres were limited, to be sure, and did not serve as an organizing pressure for all Americans.

Anti-Mormons operated with a conception of Americanness shaped by the centrality of the family and the increasing separation of public from private, and they believed that Mormonism threatened the ground upon which the American republic was built. Their portrayals of Mormonism attempted to shore up a particular vision of American national identity against a powerful nineteenth-century alternative, polygamy. While some anti-Mormons had occasion to observe Mormon life firsthand in Utah, their interpretations, often misinterpretations, almost invariably reflected a white northern middle-class Protestant world view anti-Mormons brought with them from the Northeast. The way anti-Mormons (mis)understood Mormonism betrayed intentions beyond the simple condemnation of polygamy. In Mormonism, anti-Mormons saw a grave challenge to their vision of national identity, a challenge that circulated around gender, family, and the public/private distinction. They mobilized to bar Mormons from the rights of citizenship, deny statehood to Utah, and expel the Mormon people from the body politic. Through the Mormon question, anti-Mormons worked to establish the marital qualifications of the citizen, settle the structure of the American family, and frame the gendered, sexual, and political limits of the body politic in the crucible of the public/private divide.

The projections upon which anti-Mormon visions of Americanness rested, however, had no stable foundation. Indeed, as Kathleen Flake has pointed out, "with the benefit of hindsight . . . we know that [marital and family] norms were not as stable or even as traditional as they seemed at the time."[36] Recent feminist scholarship has shown quite clearly that despite the rhetorical force of invoking the separation of public and private spheres, any division between them is necessarily incomplete; the categories are always dependent upon and inseparable from one another in at least two major ways. First, the home became a central location "in which individuals [could] exercise their choices freely and create a subjective moral vocabulary" that, theoretically, upheld their participation in the political public sphere.[37] Thus, the public depended on the private. Second, Mary P. Ryan, Linda K. Kerber, and others have convincingly shown that early republican women asserted a vision of republican motherhood and wifehood which credited women as the ones who exacted civic virtue from their husbands and reared the future citizens of the nation in the home.[38] Marriage also established the proper context for the political instruction of future citizens, carried out by republican mothers at the hearth. By the early nineteenth century, civic virtue had come to depend on "true women's" domestic influence in the private home. Men's public political life relied on women in the private sphere.[39]

Feminist scholarship has also shown that public and private were never so straightforwardly gendered as previous scholars and their nineteenth-century counterparts imagined. Men crossed into the private sphere of the home and engaged in domestic activities, and they sometimes manifested characteristics of a domestic sentimentality often marked as feminine.[40] Moreover, feminist historians in search of what Estelle Freedman has called the "female public sphere" have shown that women entered the fray as reformers and activists, although they did so in the name of their roles as wives and mothers expressing their political voices in the interest of their families.[41] Nevertheless, while women participated in various reform campaigns that thrust them into political conversations, the mechanisms of public government and citizenship remained a male-only province throughout the nineteenth century.[42]

So while all nineteenth-century men and women were subject to the divide between the home and the world outside it, they were never fully restrained by it—public and private were subject to cooptation, resistance, and subversion. Many Americans, even some white middle-class Protestant Americans, carved out domestic, social, community, and political lives that contested and subverted the realms of public and private. Clearly, despite the nineteenth-century ideological separation of public and private, the categories were always already contested, fluid, and blurred. Nineteenth-century Americans, as much as the historians who study them, disagreed about the nature of and distinction between what and who were properly public and what and who were properly private. Yet there was widespread agreement at the time that a distinction did exist between public and private, that the maintenance of the private home was central to national culture, and that the polity and political sphere were properly "public" and separate from the "private" home.

These visions of public and private were not uncontested, of course, but they were widely espoused, especially among northern white middle-class Protestants. Anti-Mormons embraced these ideals wholeheartedly and were consequently deeply disturbed by the peculiar marriages occurring in Mormondom. They deployed the categories of public and private in ways that most helped them critique the practice of plural marriage. The private that mattered most to them was the household, juxtaposed at times to the public world outside it, and at other times to public government. Anti-Mormons viewed the private home as the ground upon which public government was built and as an arena which qualified people for participation in the public polity. Mormons, anti-Mormons argued, should not be citizens for two reasons: they had no individual political consciences unaffected by Church politics, and they had no private home in which to develop that conscience.

This book offers a cultural history of the projections Mormons and anti-Mormons made about Mormonism, Americanness, citizenship, and the public/private divide. Yet these terms have no essential meaning; they are inherently unstable and contested concepts filled with meaning through political conflict. The contests over those meanings are precisely what I intend to examine through the Mormon question. I trace out the theological and ideological configurations that undergirded Mormon and anti-Mormon understandings of Mormonism and Americanness and the ways each side freighted those understandings with either robust potential for resistance or tremendous disciplinary power.

The historiography of polygamy is too deep and wide to cover here and has been well analyzed elsewhere.[43] By and large, studies of Mormon polygamy during the Utah period have focused on the social history, legal history, demography, and sociology of Mormon polygamy. Important to the historiography of plural marriage have been historians of Mormon women, who have debated the position of women in plural marriages. Some have argued that plural marriage subjected women to a patriarchal order, limiting women's access to power in the Mormon community.[44] Others have claimed that plural marriage allowed women more independence than traditional marriage, enabling women to participate in economic and political spheres much wider than did their eastern monogamous sisters.[45] My work builds on this discussion, arguing in chapter 3 that while polygamy subordinated women to men's ecclesiastical authority, it opened up space for women to engage in public and community affairs, limiting women's access to one form of power, but opening their access to another.

The two most important recent monographs examining plural marriage during the Utah period are Kathryn Daynes's *More Wives Than One: Transformation of the Mormon Marriage System, 1840–1910*, and Sarah Barringer Gordon's *The Mormon Question: Polygamy and Constitutional Conflict in Nineteenth-Century America*. Daynes's is a study of the Mormon marriage system in Sanpete County, Utah. She seeks particularly to examine the role of law and religion in how people in Utah made decisions about marriage and divorce.[46] She shows that plural marriage affected not only those who practiced it, but all of Mormon society. Daynes's most important historiographical contribution is her claim that "The nineteenth-century Mormon marriage system was actually a system; that is, it had its own rules governing the establishment and dissolution of marriage" despite its short-lived history.[47] With Daynes's analysis in mind, this study looks at the implications of the theological and ideological place of plural marriage within Mormon society and at how the Mormon marriage system challenged emerging middle-class American norms in ways that anti-Mormons found un-American.

Like Daynes's work, much of the study of plural marriage has remained isolated from the study of larger national narratives. An important exception to this historiographical oversight, Gordon's legal history argues that controversies over polygamy shaped nineteenth-century constitutional law, particularly in terms of debates over religious freedom, the separation of church and state, and the extension of federal power over claims to local sovereignty. While Gordon's central goal is to examine the implications of the polygamy controversy for the development of constitutional law, she casts a wide net, making forays into an analysis of anti-polygamy novels in the 1850s. Through the Mormon question, she illustrates that "marriage became a central social and spiritual issue of constitutional conflict in the second half of the nineteenth century."[48] In many respects, my work is a second, cultural side to the legal coin Gordon has tossed, complementing her legal analysis of the polygamy controversy with my examination of cultural conflicts between Mormons and anti-Mormons over the meaning of citizenship. A cultural history of the Mormon question shows that conflicts over the cultural meaning of citizenship, especially as it was shaped by the public/private divide, were as important as the legal questions Gordon investigates.

My analysis of Mormonism is rooted in the multitude of sources Mormons produced during the nineteenth century—sermons, Church books and periodicals, histories, biographies, and religious tracts. I have supplemented these sources with broad readings in Mormon archival sources that aimed to explain Mormonism to the rest of the nation and to defend their unique domestic and political arrangements against anti-Mormon onslaughts. I approach these sources as texts that contain not only religious, but also social, political, and cultural ideals. I read them as sources that show how Mormons, especially religious authorities, used religious beliefs and frameworks to make sense of their broader worlds. This is particularly true of Mormon sources because Mormons incorporated broader social, political, and cultural agendas and worldviews than did most American religions. All of the texts I used are readily available at a number of archives accessible to general readers, and many are currently available online.

Scholars have also given considerable attention to anti-Mormon portrayals of Mormons and polygamy in literature and popular culture. They have recognized that much in anti-Mormon discourse was factually inaccurate and grossly misrepresentative. Early studies of anti-Mormonism placed it in the context of polemic campaigns against Mormons, Catholics, and Masons.[49]

Another early study focused on how polemical literature against Mormons revealed "much about America's attitudes towards sex and the relationship of sex to family life."[50] Yet another argued that the isolation of Mormons in the Utah Territory made them excellent targets for "a myriad of jokes, myths, and distortions which would long go uncorrected by the schooling hand of familiarity and firsthand knowledge."[51] Davis Bitton and Gary L. Bunker have looked at graphic images of Mormons in popular literature during the nineteenth and early twentieth centuries and established a basic typological framework for subsequent studies of anti-Mormon literature.[52] Still another study examines the ways Victorian pornographic imagery informed anti-Mormonism.[53] Most of these analyses have located the source of anti-Mormonism in religious prejudice, paying scant attention to the larger national context that surrounded and shaped the meaning of anti-Mormon discourse. They have also divorced the study of anti-Mormonism from the study of Mormonism, hence missing the ways anti-Mormonism was a response to the profound ways Mormonism challenged middle-class American political culture. In these analyses, Mormons become the victims of the same kind of intolerance and oppression as "other" minorities, and the historical particularities of the Mormon question vanish behind Americans' many prejudices.

It is clear that Americans did not like Mormons, but to leave it at that is to neglect the question of why. One study of anti-Mormonism that tries to answer that question is Terryl L. Givens's *The Viper on the Hearth: Mormons, Myths, and the Construction of Heresy.*[54] Focusing particularly on the representation of Mormonism in fiction, Givens's book devotes surprisingly less attention to polygamy than previous work. Givens begins with the claim that the problem Americans had with Mormons was religious, rooted in the heresy of Mormon materialism—the faith's refusal to separate the sacred from the profane. He argues that anti-Mormon fiction had to reconstruct Mormon heresy into a target "out of the sphere of religion" and hence more amenable to social censure in a society valuing religious pluralism.[55] For Givens, the conflict over polygamy was merely a ruse that gave shape to a conflict not about plural marriage or domestic relations, but about heresy. Ultimately, Givens returns his readers to the place earlier scholarship began: with the apologetic claim that anti-Mormonism was fundamentally rooted in religious intolerance and Mormons were the victims of American religious bigotry. I depart from Givens in my analysis of the very nature of the Mormon question itself and its relationship to polygamy. I view the theological heresies anti-Mormons found in Mormonism as a smaller aspect under a larger umbrella of social, economic, and political challenges Mormonism posed—challenges that centered around the practice of polygamy and the public/private divide.

A more successful analysis of anti-Mormon fiction is Sarah Barringer Gordon's essay, "'Our National Hearthstone': Anti-Polygamy Fiction and the Sentimental Campaign against Moral Diversity in Antebellum America." Gordon's work argues that "the central theme of anti-polygamy novels . . . was marriage, the laws that defined it, and the central problem of its protection."[56] Gordon's analysis connects early anti-polygamy fiction to broader national developments, most notably a national call for "the legal reinforcement of monogamy as the only form of marriage across the country."[57] My work builds on her analysis by emphasizing how the categories of public and private were central to the white middle-class understandings of monogamous marriage upon which citizenship rested.

One recent monograph on anti-Mormonism, Patrick Q. Mason's *The Mormon Menace: Violence and Anti-Mormonism in the Postbellum South*, focuses on the ways southern anti-Mormon rhetoric and behavior upheld southerners' visions of honor and the Christian home, sometimes through vigilante violence against Mormons. Mason argues that anti-Mormonism provided a location at which southerners could make peace with northern reformers in a truly national crusade against plural marriage. The campaign against polygamy thus provided a kind of healing balm for the nation in the postbellum era.[58] Mason's description of southern anti-Mormonism echoes some of the more national themes I discuss here—the threat to the Christian family and the political menace of Mormon theocracy—but with a much different focus. His work places southern anti-Mormonism in the context of healing regional tensions between North and South, while my work locates anti-Mormonism in the context of more national debates over the public/private divide and the very meaning of American citizenship itself. Moreover, Mason's analysis fails to consider systematically the ways Mormonism undercut the public/private divide, leaving his examination of polygamy's threat to the family unconnected to the actual theology and practice of plural marriage among Mormons.

The most recent study of anti-Mormonism, J. Spencer Fluhman's *"A Peculiar People": Anti-Mormonism and the Making of Religion in Nineteenth-Century America*, examines the role of nineteenth-century anti-Mormonism in defining the boundaries of what counted as "religion." Fluhman's analysis of pre-1852 anti-Mormonism locates it in debates over claims to religious legitimacy in a newly religiously disestablished republic. Early anti-Mormonism, he argues, served as a kind of mirror against which American Protestants defined their religion as "true Christianity" against the "delusion" of Mormonism.[59] After 1852 when the Saints began publicly practicing polygamy, Mormonism was understood as a religion, but as an alien one.[60] By the early twentieth century, Mormonism was begrudgingly accepted as an American religion.[61] My work in chapters 4, 5, and 6 complements Fluhman's analysis by showing more precisely how and why anti-Mormons used the public/private divide to cast Mormonism as an un-American foreign faith. I argue that anti-Mormons saw Mormonism as an un-American faith because they believed it undercut the categories of public and private. According to anti-Mormons, because of Mormonism's refusal to separate public from private, the faith denied believers the right to consent to both marriage and government. It is against this backdrop that I explore more thoroughly how and why anti-Mormons relied on tropes of race and class to cast Mormonism as fundamentally foreign.

Some of the oversights in many studies of anti-Mormonism are rooted in limitations in source base or region. The complexities of anti-Mormon discourse can only be understood as the sum of its parts, and studies limited by genre or region, as most have been, neglect broad ranges of the available anti-Mormon literature. By and large, they have not successfully engaged anti-Mormon literature with broader trends in American history, especially regarding the centrality of marriage and the public/private divide to conceptions of citizenship and national identity. Only when the multiple sources of anti-Mormon discourse are examined together can the cumulative and multivalent meanings of the Mormon question become clear. I read together multiple sources of anti-Mormon rhetoric that combined and cross-pollinated each other in significant ways. My analyses are based on extensive readings of fiction, popular magazines, newspapers, books, speeches, pamphlets, political cartoons, and broadsides produced by any number of historical subjects: travelers, novelists, government and military officials, their wives, reporters, editorialists, ministers, scientists, ex-Mormon apostates, and anyone else inclined to produce such a document.[62]

Anti-Mormonism must be viewed in light of the ways Mormonism contested an identity anti-Mormons posited as American. Anti-Mormonism resonated with a broad sector of an American public who recognized the challenge Mormonism posed to their ideas about citizenship, Americanness, and the public/private divide. Indeed, for anti-Mormons the problem with Mormonism was that it pointed to the impossibility of making the diversity of Americans into an "imagined community," a cohesive, coherent idea of a nation to which both Mormons and non-Mormons could sensibly belong.[63] The ferocity of the conflict over polygamy demonstrated the conviction with which Mormons clung to their utopian visions of plural marriage despite its attendant political challenges. It also shows the determination with which anti-Mormons worked to hold in place their vision of themselves, America, citizenship, and the public/ private divide. Tempers ran hot on both sides of the Mormon question; the very meaning of American citizenship was at stake.

• • •

This book is in two parts. Chapters 1 through 3 articulate the radicalism of the Mormon project with respect to the fundamental categories of American political thought becoming increasingly normative in middle-class political culture. These chapters offer a new interpretation of Mormonism that places plural marriage at its center and analyzes the cultural implications of Mormonism's theological commitments to the practice of plural marriage. Chapter 1 traces the development of some of the fundamental theological turns that made Mormonism so unique among, and in some sense so disquieting to, nineteenth-century Americans. I examine the doctrinal place of polygamy from the founding of the Church in 1830 through the Mormons' exodus to Utah in the late 1840s. In part because contemporary Mormons dispute the centrality of polygamy to nineteenth-century Mormon theology, I treat at some length my sense of polygamy's theological and political centrality to early Mormon theology. Lastly, I interrogate Mormonism's complex theological understanding of the special role of the United States and its Constitution in facilitating the institution of God's kingdom on earth.

Chapter 2 explores Mormon communitarian practices in Utah after the public pronouncement in 1852 that Mormons practiced plural marriage. I show that Mormons made little distinction between the home and the community outside it, but rather constituted that community as a kind of broad, privatized family they juxtaposed to a broader American "public" polity and state. Mormons attempted to "live together as one great family," constituting a privatized community governed by God through His government.[64] Polygamy also accompanied a communitarian economic vision of communal property ownership that undermined notions of private property. In arguing for the compatibility of polygamy and Americanness, Mormons attempted to construct a vision of American citizenship and polity unrelated to marital structures. This entailed dissociating Americanness from the monogamous family and claiming that Church government itself was a perfection of American political principles.

Chapter 3 confronts one of the paradoxes that has vexed the historiography of Mormon women since its inception: activist Mormon polygamous women who claimed access to citizenship in the name of women's rights. I examine how and why a community rooted in ecclesiastic patriarchy was, in 1871, among the first to enfranchise women. While polygamy marked woman's ecclesiastical subordination to men, it enabled her civic equality. By undermining the concept of marital unity, plural marriage facilitated women's political equality. Mormons, women especially, claimed that plural marriage was compatible with American citizenship and facilitated woman's citizenship because it made her "more the companion and much less the subordinate" of man.[65]

From 1852 to 1890, middle-class white Americans struggled to mobilize their visions of citizenship to respond to Mormon claims, deploying ideas about Mormonism and Americanness. Part two of this project sorts out the ways in which anti-Mormon discourse manufactured knowledge about Mormonism, citizenship, and Americanness in the interest of holding in place the categories of public and private. Chapter 4 examines anti-Mormon literature from its beginnings in domestic fiction. Polygamy, anti-Mormons contended, undermined the central institution of American life and the birthplace of Americanness itself, the American home. Polygamy was, in short, "the utter destruction of the home circle."[66]

Chapter 5 elucidates the connections anti-Mormons made between private and public in Mormonism. They contended that the institution of polygamy was inseparable from the practice of political theocracy in Utah and that polygamy replaced the marital contract with male tyranny in the household. That tyranny, by extension, replaced the fraternal contract of a republican social order with patriarchal political despotism that flew in the face of American political values. Because of polygamy, anti-Mormons claimed, the structure of government in Utah was imbued with Church authority and constituted the invasion of an illegal polygamic theocracy into republican government.

In bolstering arguments to prohibit Mormon membership in the Republic, anti-Mormons used not only moral and political epithets and associations but racial ones as well. Chapter 6 examines the ways that the interrelated practices of polygamy and theocracy motivated cultural campaigns to remove Mormons from the body politic. Anti-Mormons used racial, particularly Orientalist, tropes to mark Mormons as nonwhite. Anti-Mormons also employed a rhetoric of social class to illustrate Mormonism's danger to the body politic. They argued, for example, that Mormon converts from Europe were "ignorant, almost pauper emigrants of the Old World" who threatened to degenerate the racial stock of America.[67]

These cultural campaigns against Mormons compelled and informed the reform and legal campaigns of the late 1870s and 1880s that resulted in Mormonism's capitulation to national demands. Chapter 7 shows how anti-polygamy legislation emerged from a particular imagining of the meaning of America. The

Edmunds and Edmunds-Tucker Acts of 1882 and 1887, respectively, mobilized a particular vision of the nation to drive into submission Mormonism's challenge to American political culture. Overall, the controversy over polygamy helped formulate the multiple meanings of citizenship and national identity as the Mormon question became a location at which the gendered, marital, and religious limits of the body politic were tried.

CHAPTER 1

"That These Things Might Come Forth"

Early Mormonism
and the American Republic

In the spring of 1820, a fourteen-year-old New England farm boy retired to the woods to seek guidance from God. The fervent religious sentiment stirred up by the Second Great Awakening had confused young Joseph Smith, Jr. God answered his youthful prayer with a series of visions over the next several years—visions that gave rise to the largest religion ever founded on American soil.[1] Before his death in 1844, Smith would articulate a broad cluster of controversial doctrines and practices that placed Mormons at odds with other Americans throughout the nineteenth century. In 1852, eight years after Smith's death, his most controversial doctrine—plural marriage—would set the nation alight with debate. Polygamy, central to early Mormonism, fueled early anti-Mormon sentiment and accusations of political theocracy, which became more virulent as the century progressed. Yet despite conflicts with other Americans that led to the expulsion of Mormons from New York and Ohio, then Missouri, and finally Illinois, Mormons retained a special place for the United States in their theology. In fact, Mormons believed they had a divine mandate to uphold religious freedom as guaranteed by the Constitution.

This chapter delineates how a New England farm boy changed the religious landscape of America and lays the groundwork for understanding the ideological battle known as "the Mormon question" in the nineteenth century. Three years after his first divine encounter—an event known among Mormons as the

"First Vision"—seventeen-year-old Joseph received a second divine contact in a series of visions revealing to him the location of ancient buried golden plates that he would eventually obtain, translate, and call the *Book of Mormon*. While translating, he received a number of revelations that were later compiled and published first as the *Book of Commandments* and later with further additions as the *Doctrine and Covenants*, accepted by Mormons along with the Bible and the *Book of Mormon* as scripture. In May of 1829, John the Baptist conferred upon Smith "the Priesthood of Aaron, which holds the keys of . . . baptism by immersion for the remission of sins."[2] A higher priesthood, the Melchizedek, would come later. The next year Smith received a "Revelation on Church Organization and Government," which "regularly organized and established *agreeable to the laws of our country*" the structure of priesthood authority and responsibility.[3] Smith, then twenty-four years old, organized the Church of Christ on April 6, 1830, in accordance with that revelation. The initial organization had six members, though others joined the fledgling religion that same day. Over the next several years, Smith established the essential doctrines that governed priesthood offices, Church organization, and leadership in the young religion. Beginning almost immediately, local persecution of the Mormon community drove a series of migrations that would eventually lead the Saints to Illinois, where locals were temporarily more tolerant.[4]

In the relative safety of western Illinois, the Saints gathered their resources, purchased land, and purchased the town of Commerce, later changing the name to Nauvoo. In 1840 the Illinois legislature approved their application to be recognized under state law. The Nauvoo Charter incorporated the city and granted the Mormons an unexpected measure of self-government. The creation of a city council, courts, a city police force, and even a militia marked the beginning of the Church's commitment to self-government and isolationism. Through the Nauvoo Charter, Mormons imagined they were securing local power to protect themselves against abuses of democracy and to shore up the true intentions of the American Constitution—religious liberty and self-government. Mormons viewed the Nauvoo city charter as a sort of Constitution in miniature, granting them broad powers of local control more consistent with republican principles. Previously, the law had not been friendly to Mormons, especially in Missouri, where the governor had issued an "extermination order," in effect equating the Mormon settlements with an infestation. Presumably, with a city charter, things would be different. According to one Mormon historian, "By invoking primary bases of law, [Smith in Nauvoo] attempted to avoid what he termed rapacious and evil misuses of the law."[5]

Plural Marriage and the Nauvoo Doctrines

In the relative quiet of Nauvoo in the early 1840s, Smith devoted more of his energy to the development of Church doctrine. Though initiated before 1840, the full doctrine of polygamy evolved during this period. Smith anticipated resistance from both Church membership and America at large, so at first only the highest Mormon officials were taught the doctrine and allowed to live its principles. Scholars of early Mormonism have hotly debated the place of polygamy in Mormonism for decades. But despite its being officially abandoned by the contemporary mainstream Church, polygamy fits in too neatly with other aspects of early Mormon theology, aspects which only make sense as part and parcel of each other, to be considered incidental to the overall theological system. Plural marriage was a key element within that system. While absolute secrecy surrounded plural marriage in Nauvoo, an air of mystery also enveloped the rest of the constellation of theological claims that surrounded polygamy, now known among scholars as the "Nauvoo doctrines."[6] The doctrine of plural marriage cannot be understood outside the following interrelated doctrinal concepts: the plan of salvation; priesthood and the powers of sealing, adoption, and ordinance work for the dead; and, of paramount importance, eternal increase.[7] Smith taught these interconnected ideas mostly in private sermons and conversations, and no single doctrine took shape without the others; they were inextricably connected.

The "plan of salvation" outlined God's divinely ordained agenda for His children. Smith taught that during a pre-mortal existence predating the creation of earth, human "intelligences" (roughly equivalent to the traditional Christian concept of "soul") existed. Through divine processes, large numbers of intelligences were "spiritually born" as children of God the Father and endowed with a kind of "spirit matter" beyond mortal comprehension.[8] After their spiritual birth, these spirits lived with God as his spirit children, before venturing into earthly mortality.[9]

Smith taught that God's plan required a sojourn in mortality for two reasons. First, only a mortal body allowed participation in the physical ordinances and rites necessary for Mormon exaltation—baptism, the gift of the Holy Ghost through the laying on of hands, temple endowment, and sealing in the temple. These were physical ordinances not available to spirit beings. Second, mortal separation from God allowed agency and moral choice. By their choices all humankind would be judged and rewarded in the afterlife. Smith posited that nearly all humans would be saved by the grace of God, but he made a clear distinction between salvation and exaltation. Salvation meant eternal life, while exaltation meant becoming like God, indeed, becoming *a* god. Only the most righteous would be exalted in the celestial kingdom. Exaltation was attained, Mormons believed, through righteous living combined with sacred priesthood-administered ordinances. God's power, flowing only through divinely ordained chains of priesthood authority, validated these ordinances.[10] Mormons believed that the chain of priesthood authority had been broken during a period they called the "Great Apostasy," approximately a century after Jesus's ministry until its restoration to Joseph Smith and his associate Oliver Cowdery. Ordination to priesthood empowered men to perform rituals and ordinances that prepared Mormons for exaltation and also endowed them with the spiritual power to occupy positions in Church government. All worthy male Church members older than twelve could participate in priesthood at some level.[11]

The most important function of the priesthood at its highest levels was the authority to perform sealing rituals in the temple.[12] Sealing, perhaps Smith's most unique religious innovation, figured centrally in his vision of God's plan for humanity; in the Mormon doctrine of exaltation, communion and equality with God depended on sealing. In sacred rituals, kept secret and carried out in the Mormon temple, priesthood administrators sealed Church members to one another in several ways. Temple marriage sealed men and women together and special sealing ceremonies sealed children to parents. Sealings enabled members to "procure to themselves an eternal exaltation" and live with God as part of his divine family.[13] Temple sealings made marriage bonds sacred and eternal, and no one could be exalted outside the celestial marriage covenant.

To be legitimate, the ability to perform a sealing had to be traced back through human history all the way to biblical patriarchs ultimately to Adam, who received the priesthood from and was sealed directly to God.[14] Only through legal priesthood sealings could one be "adopted into the family of heaven, becoming an heir with the Saints that have formerly lived upon the earth, and heir with the Prophets and with Jesus Christ, and being numbered with the children of the Most High."[15] The challenge for early Church members was to ensure the divine legitimacy and continuity of the chain of sealing that bound them by priesthood across human history. Mormon theology facilitated two approaches to this enormous challenge: the law of adoption and ordinance work for the dead.

The law of adoption played a much more central role in the early Church than it does in contemporary Mormonism. Much confusion and debate surrounded the law of adoption in the nineteenth century.[16] Mormons espoused the traditional Christian notion that a convert is adopted by baptism into a community of believers, becoming "fellow citizens with the saints, and the household of God."[17] But for Mormons, adoption was also about earthly family relationships and was no metaphor. It provided one means through which every member could be "'grafted' into the patriarchal order, thus becoming 'legal heirs,' and acquiring the 'fathers in the priesthood' necessary to link each one to the chain of families built up in the days of the patriarchs."[18] Although the absence of a functioning temple in Utah from 1846 to 1877 meant that adoption was not practiced during that period, it retained its theological salience for much of the nineteenth century.[19] In 1894, Church president Wilford Woodruff essentially discontinued the practice and it became much less central to twentieth-century Mormonism.[20]

Ordinance work for their deceased ancestors, however, provided Church members a second means by which to ensure the validity of their priesthood sealings. This practice took on a new urgency after 1894 that continues in the contemporary Church.[21] If exaltation required priesthood sealing, the Church required some mechanism by which to provide sealings for the millions who, by accident of birth, had missed the blessings of priesthood. Contemporary Church members must seal themselves to the ancient priesthood by sealing themselves to their ancestors (located through genealogical research) and establishing an unbroken chain of sealings back to biblical times. The rituals of sealing, referred to as "temple work," must be done by the living on behalf of the dead by proxy.

In yet another controversial doctrine, Mormonism also held that God possessed a physical, although perfected immortal body. Smith said, "That which is without body, parts and passions is nothing. There is no other God in heaven but that God who has flesh and bones."[22] This doctrine had two implications that other nineteenth-century Americans found blasphemous. First, the commitment to a God of flesh and bones meant that Smith held God and Jesus to be physically separate beings, each possessing a perfected mortal body. Second, a God of flesh and bones suggested a relationship between God and man that was closer than most Christians imagined. According to Smith, "God himself was once as we are now, and is an exalted man."[23] Furthermore, given men's pre-mortal state as God's spirit children, this view of the nature of God suggests that men are gods in embryo.[24] In the resurrection, human spirits would also be reunited with perfected immortal versions of their own physical bodies.[25]

Under this theological framework, the importance of sealings for early Mormon men and women can hardly be overestimated. For Smith, becoming "like God" was inextricably tied to the doctrine of eternal increase. Men as gods would spiritually reproduce—birthing intelligences into spirits as had God the father—and would govern the progression of their spirit children through a mortal experience. If a man's spirit children were themselves exalted and attained godhood, that man's glory increased. For this reason, until polygamy was officially abandoned, some Mormon men sought to swell their potential kingdom of glory in the afterlife by sealing multiple wives and children to them on Earth.[26]

The logic of eternal increase led Smith to believe that more than one god existed. If God was once a man in precisely the position of Smith and all humankind, then God's mortal sojourn must have been supervised by another God, and that God's mortality by yet another, *ad infinitum*. Smith publicly outlined the biblical backdrop for his polytheism in the "King Follett Discourse," a sermon at the funeral services of prominent Church member King Follett.[27] Smith's emerging belief in polytheism, however, did not prefigure its practice—Mormonism retained its monotheism because, as Smith claimed, "the heads of the Gods appointed one God for us."[28]

Smith's most controversial Nauvoo doctrine was unquestionably that of plural marriage, a practice which originated well before Nauvoo. Smith's curiosity about polygamy had likely been piqued by his study and re-translation of the Old Testament, in which biblical patriarchs Abraham, Isaac, and Jacob all took more than one wife. Smith enquired of God the proper situation under which polygamy might occur.[29] Most Mormon scholars agree that Joseph Smith probably received the revelation regarding plural marriage in 1831, while working on the Joseph Smith Translation of the Bible in Kirtland, Ohio.[30] Evidence suggests that Smith was sealed to at least one plural wife, Fanny Alger, in the early to mid-1830s.[31] In 1843 in Nauvoo, Smith first wrote down, but did not publish, the revelation supporting polygamy, and by the end of that year the women to whom he had been sealed numbered about thirty.[32] During the early 1840s, about twenty-nine Church leaders secretly practiced polygamy. Early polygamy did not necessarily imply public recognition of the marriage, nor co-residence (although some of Joseph Smith's wives lived in the Smith home as domestic servants), and wives did not assume husbands' last names. Early polygamy was thus a religious practice, more than a temporal lifestyle choice.[33]

By the Utah period the practice of polygamy was openly accepted by those who had chosen to migrate west. The precise theological role of plural marriage has been the topic of much doctrinal and historical consternation, however, troubling any attempt to finally establish the place of polygamy in early Mormon theology. Was it or was it not a requirement for exaltation? In the "Revelation on Celestial Marriage," which later became Section 132 of the *Doctrine and Covenants*, Smith made it quite clear that Mormon theology centered around celestial marriage, that celestial marriage was always eternal, and that entrance into God's kingdom required celestial marriage of all Mormons. But he failed to clarify the terms "celestial," "eternal," and "plural" in relation to marriage, leaving unclear whether the *celestial* qualities of marriage were derived only from the eternality of temple sealings or from their plurality as well. On the one hand are scholars such as B. Carmon Hardy who claim that "celestial" marriage was synonymous with "plural" marriage; thus celestial marriage (sometimes also called "patriarchal" marriage) meant polygamy and not monogamous eternal marriage.[34] On the other hand, Kathryn Daynes and, more recently, Craig L. Foster, argue an opposing view—a view the contemporary Church would endorse—claiming that polygamy was only one possible kind of celestial marriage. It was not plurality but eternality that made a marriage celestial.[35]

Unfortunately, Church leaders were not uniform in their pronouncements requiring plural marriage for exaltation. In 1880, at the height of the Church's official promotion of polygamy, Church leader George Q. Cannon declared that "there are men probably in this world now, who will receive exaltation, who never had a wife at all, or probably had but one." However, his examples of such men were "young men who die before they have had the opportunity to obey that law." For Cannon, "proof of willingness on their part, if they had the opportunity" to practice plural marriage was required for celestial exaltation.[36] Even given that the term *celestial marriage* might refer either to a monogamous or to a plural marriage, most nineteenth-century Church leaders simply equated celestial marriage with plural marriage.[37] Certainly, before 1890 no use of the term *celestial marriage* precluded its being polygamous; that is, celestial marriage was never *only* monogamous.

Questions about the doctrinal centrality of plural marriage cannot be resolved by turning to Joseph Smith. Conclusive documentation of the precise role the Mormon prophet imagined for plural marriage in his eternal schematics does not exist. Likewise, we will also never know if he intended the practice to be Church-wide or restricted to only the most righteous members. The scant documentation of Smith's Nauvoo doctrines is understandable.[38] His untimely death and the secrecy surrounding polygamy leave much of his doctrinal thinking on this topic unrecorded. As Larry C. Porter and Milton V. Backman, Jr., suggest of the Nauvoo period, "Many outside the Church and some within it were kept by that official silence from comprehending the full significance of several discourses delivered by the Prophet [Joseph Smith] between 1842 and 1844."[39] Porter and Backman point out, however, that the temple-related teachings of the Nauvoo doctrines clearly imply a central role for polygamy.[40]

Whether regarded as prophetic inspiration or as doctrinal speculation on Smith's part, the collection of doctrines arising from Smith's theological explorations in Nauvoo formed the basis of Mormon theology thereafter and grounded Mormon discussion of polygamy following its public announcement in 1852. Brigham Young, Orson Pratt, and other Church officials later explained the centrality of polygamy while explicating the Nauvoo doctrines. The terms "celestial" and "plural" had generally become synonymous by the late 1850s. Smith's intentions aside, under Brigham Young's forceful leadership, plural marriage was cast as a required celestial practice as well as an earthly one. In the first public sermon on polygamy, not coincidentally titled "Celestial Marriage," Orson Pratt stated the role of plural marriage in Mormonism: "[I]t is incorporated as part of our religion and necessary for our exaltation to the fullness of the Lord's glory in the eternal world." Plural marriage is "essential," Pratt went on to say, "to our fullness of happiness in the world to come."[41] In 1870, Brigham Young reaffirmed the centrality of plural marriage to early Mormon doctrine. Using the equivalent term *patriarchal marriage*, Young quoted Joseph Smith as saying, "'There is no question but it will be the means of damning many of the Elders of Israel; it is nevertheless true and must be revealed; ... and they will retrograde if they do not embrace more of the celestial law than they have yet.'"[42]

In the early 1840s, not all Church leaders accepted the Nauvoo doctrines. Internal opposition to polygamy and the doctrine of the plurality of gods, plus an Illinois government that had turned against the Mormons, ultimately led to the assassination of the Mormon prophet in 1844. That year, several influential members of the Church became antagonistic to members of the Mormon hierarchy, whom they accused of exploiting their political power to immoral ends, particularly the secret practice of polygamy. In their opinion, Smith was a fallen prophet. Smith and other Church officials responded harshly by excommunicating Smith's accusers. The group of dissenters then printed what turned out to be a single issue of a newspaper entitled the *Nauvoo Expositor*. The *Expositor* trumpeted the dissenters' belief that Smith had strayed from the true gospel during the Illinois period, specifically condemning the newer doctrinal developments, polygamy and the plurality of gods.[43]

Dissenters denounced plural marriage as the centerpiece and source of immorality that had ensnared Church leadership within a complex web of deceit and depravity that stood between Church members and the "salvation of the Human Family." The *Expositor* foreshadowed the ways later anti-Mormons would place polygamy at the center of broader claims against Mormonism. The anonymous writers married thinly veiled accusations of secret "abominations and whoredoms" (the practice of polygamy) to Church "tyranny and oppression" and Smith's un-American leadership.[44] Moreover, the authors of the *Expositor* rooted the authority of their claims explicitly in American citizenship. The voice of patriotic duty required their opposition to "new codes of morals" and "a new administration of the laws by ignorant, unlettered, and corrupt men," practices which "must be frowned down by every lover of his country."[45] According to the authors of the *Expositor*, by introducing polygamy, Smith had not only deviated from the true principles of Mormonism but the fundamental principles of Americanism as well. Defining those fundamental American principles became a main focus of the debate surrounding the Mormon question over the next fifty years. The *Expositor* called upon "all, who prize ... the sacred rights of American citizenship, to assist us" in objecting to the practice of plural marriage and the political power of the Church.[46]

Political power had become an important issue, something the Illinois residents who had taken pity on the straggling, impoverished band of refugees had not foreseen in 1839. Heeding the call to gather to Zion, converts flowed in—many from England—and in a mere five years, the rapid growth of Nauvoo had made the Saints a formidable political front. Not surprisingly, Illinois locals had become increasingly suspicious of the legal power of the Nauvoo Charter. Where the Mormons saw self-government and self-defense, other Illinois residents saw local authority usurping federal and state authority in an attempt to create an independent municipality not subject to laws governing other cities.[47] These charges foreshadowed tensions that would also emerge regarding Church government in Utah over the next fifty years.

For many Illinois locals, the breaking point was Smith's 1844 presidential campaign. Church leader John Taylor published an article in a February edition of the Church periodical, *Times and Seasons,* titled "Who Shall Be Our Next President?" expressing the reasons behind Smith's presidential campaign.[48] Smith's presidential campaign, however, simply convinced Illinois locals that their suspicions of political theocracy were warranted.[49] In the wake of Mormon growth, of the increasing power of the Nauvoo city government, and of Smith's presidential campaign, the controversy over the *Expositor* provided Illinois state officials a pretext to rid themselves of the Mormons. Shortly after the publication of the *Expositor*, the Nauvoo City Council, over which Smith presided, declared the paper a public nuisance and ordered the press destroyed. Subsequently state officials arrested Joseph Smith, his brother Hyrum, and other Mormon leaders on charges of riot and treason. Governor Ford of Illinois scheduled a trial at Carthage, and in a series of events still lauded as spiritual martyrdom among Mormons, a local mob in Carthage broke into the jail and assassinated Smith and his brother, Hyrum.[50]

The assassination of Joseph and Hyrum Smith finally convinced Mormon leadership that the American Republic in which they had so much faith was corrupt and either unable or unwilling to back up the Constitution's promise of religious liberty. While the idea of moving westward to a distant frontier had circulated in Mormon circles for years, it was not until Smith's assassination that Mormon leaders enacted a large-scale migration. In 1845, after the Illinois legislature repealed the Nauvoo Charter, and several local non-Mormon newspapers demanded a Mormon exodus, Brigham Young, having assumed leadership (though not without contest) prepared to remove the Saints from Nauvoo to a remote desert location in the western wilderness. In early 1846, the bulk of the Saints departed from Nauvoo and various companies headed westward.[51]

The first group of Saints arrived at an overlook above the Salt Lake Valley in late July 1847, and Brigham Young made the famous declaration, "This is the right place."[52] In 1849, Congress made Utah a territory, and the building of Zion in the West began with remarkable dispatch. That first year, Mormons built housing, roads, and fences, planted crops, and began one of the most accomplished irrigation systems ever built. By 1849, Young had filled vacancies in Church organization, organized the Saints into geographically determined areas called wards and stakes (to be governed respectively by bishops and stake presidents), and established the Perpetual Emigrating Fund Company "for the gathering of the [Mormon] poor from the nations of the earth."[53] In March 1849, the Saints adopted a Constitution and established a provisional civil government. President Millard Fillmore appointed Brigham Young governor and Fillmore and Young filled other state offices with both Mormon and non-Mormon officials. A Church-controlled weekly newspaper, the *Deseret News Weekly*, began circulation in June 1850. In only a few years, Salt Lake City had become a vibrant, self-sustaining western outpost.

Mormonism and American History

Mormonism is a faith steeped in history. As Richard L. Bushman has pointed out, Mormons rooted their faith as much in a belief in history as in Church doctrine: "The test of faith was not adherence to a certain confession of faith but belief that Christ was resurrected, that Joseph Smith saw God, that the Book of Mormon was true history, and that Peter, James, and John restored the apostleship. Mormonism was history, not philosophy."[54] Moreover, perhaps no religion places more spiritual emphasis on the narrative of its own early history than Mormonism. Jan Shipps has noted that it is impossible to separate Mormon history from theology.[55] Not only did Church doctrine evolve within

a particular historical context, but, Shipps observes, the theological development of Mormonism is inseparable from its own historical tale. The history of
early Mormonism recapitulates the biblical narrative of God's chosen people.
The institution of Abrahamic polygamy, persecution for religious belief, the
story of exile and wandering in the wilderness, and the establishment of a new
Jerusalem in a western, God-given land all parallel Old Testament history.[56]

Historical context shaped Mormon belief in other ways. Perhaps most importantly, Mormons viewed Joseph Smith's "first vision" in New York as signal-
ing God's plan to restore early Christianity, intending not another Protestant
denomination but a return to original Christianity after nearly two thousand
years of apostasy.[57] Because Smith understood God's word to be continuing as
well as restorative, Mormon theology left space for religious and theological
development over time. Mormons believed in a dynamic God who interacted
with human history and would guide every aspect of the developing Church by
directly communicating with His chosen prophet, the president of the restored
Church. They expected eternal religious truths to be continually unfolding
throughout human history as people prepared to receive God's word more fully.

The *Book of Mormon* is understood to be an example of this divine intervention in history. Mormons claim that God intended the *Book of Mormon* to add
to biblical doctrine and to correct long-standing biblical misinterpretation,
thereby restoring original truths and updating their relevance to a new dispensation. Joseph Smith's discovery and translation of the book represented God's
direct intervention into human history to ensure the restoration and renewal
of His word. The *Book of Mormon* tells a story of descendents of an ancient
prophet named Lehi, who sailed with his family and a few others to America
under the guidance of God around 600 B.C.E. to avoid the biblical destruction
of Jerusalem. Lehi's progeny divided into two groups, the Nephites and the
Lamanites (descendents of Lehi's sons, Nephi and Laman). In the narrative,
each clan varied in adherence to the word of God, but both were often mired
in warfare with each other. Eventually, both groups diverged from God's commandments, and one group, the Nephites, was completely annihilated, except
for one righteous man, Moroni, who "seal[ed] up these records" and laid the
book to rest in a hillside that would later lie in upstate New York.[58]

Not only did the narrative of the *Book of Mormon* take place on the American continent, but certain passages indicated that the United States was fundamental to God's plan for humanity and the restoration of the gospel. Smith
argued that the restoration of the gospel required the religious freedom only
the American Constitution embodied.[59] As the *Book of Mormon* prophesied,
God himself had foreordained that America be "set up as a free people by the

power of the Father that these things [the *Book of Mormon* and the restoration of the Church] might come forth."[60] Mormons believed that American religious freedom provided the only context in which God's plan for the Church and the future of humanity could unfold.

Despite persecutions, Smith always believed in the divine origins of the United States Constitution, proclaiming that it "is a glorious standard; it is founded in the wisdom of God. It is a heavenly banner."[61] The *Doctrine and Covenants* records a revelation given to Smith that God Himself "established the constitution of this land, by the hands of wise men whom I raised up unto this very purpose."[62] Yet Mormons' faith in the Constitution did not in any way include faith in government officers. For Mormons, the failures of American government to redress wrongs or protect Mormons marked the leadership of unrighteous and corrupt men. During his presidential campaign in 1844, Smith expressed his dissatisfaction with the officials of the U.S. government, stating that leaders who "meanly pander with demagogues, [lose] sight of the interest of the nation, and sacrifice the Union on the altar of sectional interests." They rendered themselves "unworthy of the dignified trust reposed in [them]."[63] Persecutions in Ohio and Missouri showed Smith and his followers that despite the divine purpose they attributed to American government, it was not God's will that they should be sheltered beneath it. They reconciled America's repeated failure to protect them with their unwavering faith in its political institutions by claiming that American politicians betrayed the legacy of the Constitution.

The contradiction between Mormonism's faith in constitutional government and their sense of betrayal by it perhaps convinced Smith that Mormons had a special call from God to champion and protect the Constitution. Church Elder James Burgess recorded Smith's prophesy that "the time would come when the Constitution and Government would hang by a brittle thread and would be ready to fall into other hands but this people the Latter Day Saints will step forth and save it."[64] Early Church leaders cast Mormonism as the principle institution standing against the violation of First Amendment freedoms. In 1843, an editorial in the *Nauvoo Neighbor* called the persecutors of Mormonism "recreant to the principles of republicanism; ... they are striking a secret but deadly blow at the freedom of this great republic; and their withering influence ... is like a worm gnawing the very vitals of the tree of liberty." The article then affirmed that "We shall always contend for our religious rights."[65] Later that year, Elder Wilford Woodruff claimed that "All the power that I desire or have sought to obtain has been the enjoyment of the Constitutional privilege for which my fathers shed their blood, of living in peace in the society of my wife and children, and enjoying the society of my friends and that religious liberty which is the right of every American citizen, of worshiping according to the dictates of his conscience and the revelations of God."[66] As persecutions increased, so did statements like these. Mormons became convinced that it was their divine task to uphold the bases of American religious freedom and toleration, protecting the First Amendment against the unconstitutional assaults of religious persecution. Ardent Constitutionalism would become the central premise of the Mormon defense of their right to practice plural marriage.

Not only did Smith believe that God had given the Mormons a divine role to play in American history, but he also held that the American continent was central to God's plan for the second coming of Jesus. One of the first events heralding the second coming, Smith prophesied, was the gathering of the pure in heart to the land of Zion, which "will be built upon this continent."[67] Smith envisioned that as the Saints gathered under the protective fold of American constitutionalism, they would be carrying out God's plan to establish the kingdom of God by building Zion in America, a sacred landscape divinely ordained for that purpose.

Joseph Smith used the term "kingdom of God" "with some lack of precision," according to Klaus J. Hansen. In Nauvoo in 1844 Smith had established the Council of Fifty, intending it to be the political arm of the kingdom of God.[68] The Council of Fifty, composed mostly of Mormon leaders but with three non-Mormon members, was thought to be a precursor to and model of God's perfect government which would fulfill American principles as established in the Constitution. It made decisions only by unanimous vote. No timeline was established, but Smith believed that the government of God would supersede and perfect American government and eventually all world governments to form a more perfect divinely ruled worldwide kingdom of God.[69] In theory, Church authorities understood the Church itself to be separate from the institutions of God's government; even in the future worldwide kingdom of God, the Church was not to serve as the government of God.[70]

In actuality, both in Nauvoo and later in Utah, the Church did govern. As D. Michael Quinn has pointed out, the Council of Fifty was "only infrequently active," and its primary role was "to symbolize the other-worldly world order that would be established during the Millennial reign."[71] Quinn notes that despite non-Mormon members, "In theory, theology, and reality, the LDS Presidency and apostles always governed the Council of Fifty when it was functioning."[72] That is, the Church often functioned as the political arm of the kingdom of God, regardless of the existence of the Council of Fifty. Church officials embraced the multiple functions of the Church at ecclesiastical, social, economic, familial, and political levels and sometimes equated the Church with the kingdom of God. Brigham Young declared in 1875 that "with regard to the kingdom of God on the earth—Here is the Church of Jesus Christ of Latter-day Saints, organized with its rules and regulations and degrees, with the quorums of the holy priesthood, from the first presidency to the teachers and deacons. . . . This is what we are in the habit of calling the kingdom of God."[73] Mormons understood the Church to be both a religious and a political institution—both a church and a kingdom.

Layered over these meanings, Mormons also used the term *kingdom of God* to describe both the literal reign of Jesus during the millennium, and the celestial kingdom established for the most righteous after the post-millennial day of judgment. These varying usages reflected not entirely different conceptions of the meaning of the kingdom of God, but rather stages or steps in Mormonism's eschatological vision of the history of the end of the world. Mormons envisioned the kingdom of God not as a singular event that occurred before, during, or after the coming of Jesus, but rather as a staged process that emerged as Mormons and the rest of humanity approached divine perfection. Smith's vision of the kingdom of God pre-wrote the future history of Mormonism, America, and the world, which would follow a divine plan for the political redemption and perfection of the Earth and its righteous inhabitants.

Zion was a separate concept. The community of Zion played a special role within the kingdom of God. Zion would "constitute a *standard* which will put an end to jarring creeds and political wranglings, by uniting the republics, states, provinces, territories, nations, tribes, kindred, tongues, people," unifying the entire world "in one great and common bond of brotherhood; while truth and knowledge shall make them free, and love cement their union."[74] Through the power of persuasion, the example of Zion would work to uplift all of humankind and prepare it to embrace a united divine order. As the political superiority of the kingdom of God became self-evident, the rest of the nation, and eventually all of humanity, would behold the truth of God's political institutions and elect to become subject to them.[75]

The unity of the world with the will of God would mark human preparedness for the second coming of Jesus. World unity under God, Smith argued, was the political plan for the community of Zion, "the only thing that can bring about the 'restitution of all things spoken of by all the holy Prophets since the world was'—'the dispensation of the fulness [*sic*] of times, when God shall gather together all things in one.'"[76] Under this millennial system, the world would live under Jesus's political rule in perfect peace, equality, and unity. The establishment of Zion and the development of the kingdom of God by the Saints would prepare the way, Smith believed, for the return and literal reign of Jesus on earth. Unsuccessful at establishing Zion in Ohio, Missouri, or after a promising start in Illinois, the Mormons would fare better in Utah under Brigham Young's leadership.

. . .

While Smith himself never connected polygamy explicitly to his vision of Church governance, as both Mormons and anti-Mormons later would, the Nauvoo doctrines he formulated in the early 1840s indicated a necessary role for polygamy in Mormonism's unfolding. The theological and political concepts Smith outlined in the early years of the Church, including the plan of salvation, sealing and adoption, and eternal increase, intimately tied gender, plural marriage, and the family to the building of Zion and the advent of the kingdom of God in all its phases. In Utah, the Saints' thriving Zion community posed a direct challenge to the premises of family and political life in which middle-class Americans grounded American political culture. After the Saints settled and established civil government in Utah, Brigham Young deemed August 1852 the right moment to publicly announce the Church's belief in and intent to openly practice plural marriage. At a special conference of the Saints, Brigham Young charged Church apostle Orson Pratt with delivering the first public discourse on plural marriage. From then on, Church leaders publicly endorsed the practice as a fundamental, even defining, aspect of Mormonism and integrated the practice into a broader vision of Mormon political philosophy. The open practice of plural marriage added new dimensions to Mormon doctrine that, combined with earlier controversies, produced an insurmountable distance between Mormon and white middle-class Protestant Americans. The ensuing "Mormon question" inaugurated decades of national conflict over the political meaning of gender, marriage, sexuality, and religion in shaping the meaning of American citizenship.

CHAPTER 2

"We Shall Then Live
Together as One Great Family"
Mormonism and the Public/Private Divide

Orson Pratt's public announcement in 1852 that Mormons practiced polygamy unnerved Americans.[1] Pratt was one of the Church's most voluble officials and over the next few decades would become the most ardent advocate of polygamy. In the wake of Pratt's sermon, Mormonism became a national "question" almost at once. The thousands of anti-Mormon novels, tracts, essays, exposés, and speeches indicate the vehemence of national responses; with few exceptions, American opinion makers passionately condemned the practice. Over the next forty years, anti-Mormon reformers embarked on unprecedented discursive and legal campaigns against polygamy, vilifying and eventually outlawing the practice. In the 1880s, the federal government moved to deny practitioners of polygamy many of the rights of American citizenship.

Clearly, polygamy deeply disturbed the nation. Pratt's announcement exposed a deep ideological divide between Mormons and the rest of the nation, a chasm perhaps even greater than the geographical distance between them. By consistently articulating the centrality of polygamy to the Mormon project, Mormons produced a significant challenge to emerging middle-class political culture. No other racial or religious community in the nation provoked such a prolific, vitriolic national response. Anti-Mormons objected to polygamy not simply because they found it offensive to their sexual mores and wished to protect women from its evils but also because the practice threatened some of the most central categories of nineteenth-century American political culture—public and private. Anti-Mormons contended that polygamy led to "the utter destruction of the home circle"[2] so completely that the Mormons "can not [sic] exist in contact with republican institutions."[3]

Mormonism troubled the public/private divide in three central and contradictory ways, disavowing, reinventing, and inverting the categories of public and private. First, Mormons disavowed the public/private divide by amalgamating religion, family, civic life, economics, and government as a single entity under God's kingdom. Plural marriage was central to that unity and situated the family in God's political order, not the nation's. What middle-class American political culture attempted to keep separate the ideals surrounding the practice of polygamy brought together. Ideally, the Mormon community "publicized" individual families; Mormons made little distinction between the private family and the broad Mormon community.

Second, while Church leaders made no distinction between public and private life within their own community, they reinvented the divide by imagining their whole community as a kind of private sphere writ large, the family of God, tied together by the bonds of priesthood and plural marriage. They juxtaposed this communal "private" to both a broader American "public" and to the "public" institutions of American government.

True to their disavowal of the public/private divide, Mormons also imagined God's family as a polity—God's polity—in the kingdom of God, building what I call the privatized kingdom of God in the West. An entire system of theo-political thought accompanied the practice of plural marriage in God's privatized kingdom, and the Mormons built an entire alternative political culture, complete with its own privatized political institutions. In this way, they troubled the public/private divide in a third sense, inverting its meaning. Figuring the entire community as God's family (as well as His polity) at once publicized the family, equating it with the broad Mormon polity, and constituted Church authority over the Mormon community as a private affair. In Utah, the publicized family of God was governed by a "privatized" government, the Church. Because God's government was private, Mormons argued, it could and must coexist with American public government embodied by the U.S. state. Mormon attempts to lay claim to American citizenship required them to position themselves as citizens in both the privatized kingdom of God and the public U.S. state.

Ordering the Kingdom: Priesthood and Polygamy in the Kingdom of God

Polygamy played as central a role in ordering the kingdom of God as monogamous marriage did in ordering American political culture. The practice established community boundaries, ordered God's family, and shaped social, civic, political, and economic relations. The contemporary LDS Church argues that polygamy was incidental to nineteenth-century Mormonism. By and large, they claim first that polygamy compensated for a demographic imbalance between men and women, and second that an insignificant portion of Mormons actually engaged in the practice. More recently, it has become apparent that the second of these claims holds much more water than the first, as no numerical imbalance existed between men and women in nineteenth-century Utah. Historians point out that never more than between 15 and 40 percent of Mormon adults actually practiced plural marriage.[4] However, a focus on practice fails to provide an accurate vision of the centrality of polygamy to Mormonism. Even though many Mormons did not actually practice plural marriage, it was still ideologically central to how they understood themselves and their communitarian millennial project. Nineteenth-century American white middle-classes enacted the ideology of separate spheres at least as incompletely, variously, and contentiously as Mormons enacted polygamy. Mormons were at least as committed to plural marriage as the demographic from which anti-Mormons were largely drawn, white middle-class Americans, was to the separation of public from private.

Polygamy was inseparable from nineteenth-century Mormon theology; its extrication from the very fabric of nineteenth-century Mormonism is impossible. First, as argued in the previous chapter, polygamy fits in too neatly with the entire theological system to be considered incidental or peripheral to Mormon theology. Orson Pratt's public announcement of polygamy laid out God's plan for humanity and situated the practice of plural marriage squarely within it. Moreover, as Kathryn Daynes has shown, over the course of its practice, those Mormons who engaged in polygamy were most likely to believe in its centrality to exaltation, and it was they who set the terms of Mormon belief from the pulpit.[5] Furthermore, the vehemence with which Mormons defended plural marriage over the nineteenth century and the myriad costs of that struggle suggest that historians cannot understand polygamy as theologically or culturally superfluous. Fortunes lost, beloved families left, years of violence and harassment, the psychological toll of extensive and often mean-spirited anti-Mormon campaigns, lives lived in hiding from federal officials, and systematic political disenfranchisement seem an inordinately high price to pay to maintain a peripheral principle. Lastly, although Mormons' commitment to the practice of plural marriage waxed and waned over time, and their rhetoric escalated during a period of religious revival in 1856–57, leaders' commitment, if not their exhortation, to the principle remained consistent from 1852 to 1890.

Among Mormons, marriage was especially important for women. In addition to the sealing function marriage played for both men and women, marriage also tied women to the patriarchal order of the priesthood.[6] It linked them to the priesthood leadership that enabled their exaltation. Women needed that priesthood direction because, as Church official Lorenzo Snow declared, "women have not the degree of light and knowledge that their husbands have," and the priesthood leadership of their husbands led them in the correct direction.[7] Brigham Young claimed that "it is in their [women's] nature to confide in and look to the sterner sex for guidance."[8] He also declared that "Every virtuous woman desires a husband to whom she can look for guidance and protection through this world. God has placed this desire in woman's nature. It should be respected by the stronger sex."[9] Though these attitudes toward women were common in the nineteenth century, Mormonism added religious duty to the justification for women's dependent status. Church leaders like Jedediah M. Grant, for instance, clearly established that they "want[ed] the women to understand, when they have a good husband, one that does his duty, that he is president over them."[10] Mormons held husbands responsible for the instruction of wives (and children) in the ways of the Lord, while wives' (and children's) responsibility was to submit to men's divine leadership.

Plural marriage also addressed the spiritual demographics of the Mormon community. While no numerical gender imbalance existed in Utah, Church leaders pointed to an imbalance in *worthy* Church members that necessitated the practice of polygamy.[11] Young claimed that "women are more ready to do and love the right than men are."[12] Church official George Q. Cannon as well declared, "There are but comparatively few men among the family of mankind who are capable of leading the daughters of Zion into the Celestial Kingdom of our God."[13] If exaltation hinged upon participation in celestial marriage to a worthy man, and single men worthy of celestial union were scarce, women must find their exaltation among the already married. In a ringing endorsement of the benefits of plural marriage for Mormon women, Cannon claimed, "I would rather my daughters . . . be the fiftieth wife to a good, faithful man, who had kept the commandments of God and unto whom promises had been made . . . than that they should be allied to a man unto whom the promises of God had not been made."[14] Polygamy incorporated a surplus of *righteous* women into filial networks of spiritual support, affording all *worthy* women the rare opportunity and "privilege of being honored matrons and respected wives."[15]

A man's exaltation also depended on his attachments to women, though in less clear ways. True, men's access to priesthood authority did not depend on women, but their exaltation did: "It takes a man and a woman to make a man; without woman, man is not perfect; God so ordained it."[16] While husband and wife needed each other to constitute a spiritual unity, the unity they constituted was in many respects more his than hers. Orson Pratt claimed that "the marriage ordinance [was] instituted to restore to man that part which was taken from him, without which he could not be perfect."[17] Nonetheless, the hierarchical family ties established among men through priesthood, and between men and women through marriage, linked both men and women to the spiritual authority required for exaltation and united them into the spiritual oneness that constituted God's kingdom.[18]

Besides structuring relationships between men and women, polygamy demarcated community boundaries and defined its spiritual and economic structure as well. Much evidence suggests that belief in plural marriage, even absent its practice, constituted membership in the Mormon community, defining the boundaries of the kingdom of God and ensuring the loyalty of its members. An 1853 editorial in the Church magazine, *The Latter-day Saints' Millennial Star*, announced that the Saints must either "take sides with the mother of harlots, and with her monogamy, and celibacy, and prostitution, or take sides with the Almighty, and with His holy law of polygamy, and sexual purity."[19] Mormons sometimes argued that disbelief in plural marriage was simply a first step in apostasy. Brigham Young remarked, "You take a woman in this church who does not believe in the doctrine of celestial marriage or plurality of wives, and she does not believe anything at all about the gospel, and she will soon manifest this by her unwise course, and by and by she drops off and away she goes."[20]

Polygamy also functioned as a measure of righteousness among the faithful, indicating a man's worthiness in the kingdom. Church Elder Joseph F. Smith said in 1878 that if a man "remain faithful with only the one wife, observing the conditions of so much of the law as pertains to the eternity of the marriage covenant, he will receive his reward, but the benefits, blessings and power appertaining to the second or more faithful and fuller observance of the law, he never will receive, for he cannot."[21] Only the most worthy of men and women qualified to participate in plural marriage, as plural marriages had to be approved and sanctioned by Church authorities before performed. According to Brigham Young, the "reward" for taking only one wife was eternal isolation and loneliness, as one would become unwed in the afterlife. Single men and women, Young claimed, could never achieve exaltation and would serve merely as angels in the Celestial Kingdom.[22] Plural marriage in this life marked one's anticipated status in the next.

Over the nineteenth century, the correspondence between priesthood rank and plural marriage indicates that plural marriage also structured men's qualifications for participation in Church government.[23] Men's standing in the Church hierarchy correlated to the practice of plural marriage, and while not universal, almost all Church leaders practiced polygamy. [24] According to Church president John Taylor, "A man obeying a lower law [monogamy] is not qualified to preside over those who keep a higher law [polygamy]."[25] In nearly all cases, Church authority came wedded to plural marriage. Hierarchies of ecclesiastical office, priesthood authority, and plural marriage linked the ecclesiastical, priesthood, and filial functions of Church leaders tightly together, interlocking the filial and spiritual roles of the priesthood with the political leadership of Church authority.

The practice of plural marriage also distinguished the wealthier from the poorer.[26] Presumably, wealthier men could more easily provide for plural wives, and the extent of a man's participation in polygamy generally corresponded with his economic status. The actual practice of plural marriage, then, seemed contingent upon both righteousness and financial considerations, though more on the former than the latter.[27] Thus polygamy conferred economic and religious status by indicating the Church leaders' evaluation of a man's ability to provide for women spiritually and economically.

Correspondingly, polygamy benefitted women by integrating them into networks of economic support. Plural marriage functioned as a kind of community assistance for economically disadvantaged women.[28] In 1869, Church official George Q. Cannon declared that "Patriarchal marriage [has] a tendency to elevate the entire [female] sex.... There are no refuse among us—no class to be cast out, scorned and condemned; but every woman who chooses can be an honored wife."[29] Plural marriage incorporated single and widowed women into the marital networks of God's kingdom, and economically disadvantaged women were significantly over-represented among plural wives. As Daynes concludes, "Mormon women undoubtedly believed in the principle of plural marriage, but women who needed economic help disproportionately practiced it."[30]

Despite its limited practice, the importance of plural marriage in shaping the kingdom of God is difficult to overestimate. Alongside priesthood, polygamy shaped filial, community, economic, and political life in the kingdom of God in profound ways.[31] Moreover, plural marriage, central not only to Mormon theology but also to ordering Mormon communities, was the ground upon which the unity of all things in the kingdom of God was built. Plural marriage upheld the structure of what I have termed the "privatized kingdom," a kingdom, church, polity, and family, that was at once political, religious, civic, and filial. Polygamy shaped a communitarian ethos that extended religion and family into all areas of Mormon life and disavowed, reinvented, and inverted the public/private divide.

Plural Marriage and the Church Family:
Publicizing the Family and Privatizing
the Kingdom of God

On January 12, 1868, Brigham Young described his conception of the ideal Mormon community:

> I have looked upon the community of latter-day saints in a vision and be-held them organized as one great family of heaven, each person performing his several duties in his line of industry, working for the good of the whole more than for individual aggrandizement; and in this I have beheld the most beautiful order that the mind of man can contemplate . . . , and the grandest results for the upbuilding [sic] of the Kingdom of God and the spread of righteousness upon the earth. . . . Are [the Saints] now prepared to live ac-cording to that patriarchal order that will be organized among the true and faithful before God receives His own? . . . [W]hen our spirits have returned to God who gave them, we will be subject to every requirement that he may make of us, that we shall then live together as one great family; our interest will be a general, a common interest. Why can we not so live in this world?[32]

This statement epitomized Young's vision for social, economic, political, and familial order among Mormons. Pursuing that vision, Mormons attempted to unite the entire community under the rubric of family, dissolving the boundary between the private home and the world outside it. Moreover, by understanding this broad family organization as synonymous with the political kingdom of God, Mormons at once privatized politics and undercut the private individual that Americans placed at the center of good government.

At its root, the Mormon challenge to public and private was grounded in the most fundamental of the faith's theological premises—a profound belief in the unity of all things. This unity, not a mystical or existential oneness, but a divinely commanded social order, was perhaps the most defining characteristic of life in the kingdom of God. God required that the Saints be "united according to the union required by the law of the celestial kingdom."[33] In its quest for unity, the Mormon community attempted to bring together the very things various configurations of the public/private divide insisted should remain separate. In ideal terms, Mormonism made no distinction between the domestic private and the world outside it and subsumed the private individual, private property, religious and political conscience, and the private home into a broad, commu-nitarian spiritual-political order.

The dissolution of public/private boundaries among Mormons also arose from the broad, all-encompassing nature of Mormon religious belief.[34] In 1830, Joseph Smith received a revelation that declared, "all things unto me are spiritual, and not at any time have I given unto you a law which was temporal."[35] In effect, this doctrine implied that all temporal matters fell within the purview of religion. Mormon theology and practice shaped family relations and structure, community order, the ownership and management of property, and the practice of politics among Mormons. Church leaders deeply influenced individuals' choices about how and with whom to transact their property, for whom to vote, whom to marry, and with whom to associate.[36] The extension of Church authority into the most intimate of the individual lives of Church members convoluted the borders that American revolutionaries had carefully constructed between public politics and the private individual. To Mormons, the multiple functions and authority of the Church were the unity of all things under God, while to more mainstream Americans, Mormonism looked like the absence of any semblance of a domestic private.

Polygamy prefigured and embodied the principle of unity in all the ways Mormons believed their God required. Ideally, the practice of polygamy united God's people and remade Mormon society as a broad, community-wide family that was also a political community—God's polity. In a sense, Mormons at once "privatized" the kingdom of God by making it a family and "publicized" the family by making it a polity. As such, Mormons divorced ideas about marriage and family from American civic contexts and reconstituted them in the unique terms of the kingdom of God. In effect, polygamy placed marriage in the service of the privatized kingdom of God. In the same way that middle-class Americans imagined monogamous family life to prefigure and enable virtuous American citizenship, polygamy prefigured and enabled political unity in the kingdom of God. In their refusal to separate private life from public, Mormons untied the moorings of the private American home, demonstrating its contingency and vulnerability in ways that deeply threatened middle-class visions of American national identity.

Polygamy created the feeling and experience among Mormons that their community was a family writ large. The practice both informed and, to a certain extent, actualized a view of the Church as an intermixture of family and community that constituted the polity of God as a kind of extended family. Church leader Heber C. Kimball was fond of referring to Mormonism as "a household of faith," over which Brigham Young, God's representative on earth, presided: "[T]his is his [Young's] house, and this is his people, and he is our leader, our Governor, he is our Prophet, and he is our Priest."[37] Wilford Woodruff remarked that a bishop "is called to be a father to the people of his ward."[38] As Jill Mulvay Derr, Kenneth W. Godfrey, and Audrey M. Godfrey state, "Mormons were a community of believers, a literal household where members addressed one another as brother and sister. Those who were outside the covenant were clearly outside the family, a separation apparent to Mormons and non-Mormons alike."[39] One non-Mormon observer, U.S. Army Captain J.W. Gunnison, travelling in Utah in 1849–50, noticed the familial privatized flavor of Mormon society: "The influence of their nomenclature of 'brethren and sisters' is apparent in their actions, and creates the bond of affection among those who are more frequently thrown together. It [filial affection] is impressed on infantile minds by the constant repetition and induces the feeling of family relationship."[40] As Gunnison noted, Mormonism understood all Mormons to be part of its divine family, extending filial relationships well beyond the private home. For practitioners of plural marriage, the nomenclature of early Mormonism also had some grounding in real, practical plural family relationships. Among those Church members whose lives most approximated the millennial kingdom, complex plural marriage relationships tied the community together, since male leaders were sealed to one another's sisters, daughters, mothers, widows, and sometimes even ex-wives.[41] These marital relations created complex networks of extended kin relations among polygamous Mormons.

In extending the domestic private into the public, plural marriage constituted a powerful alternative to the romantic, companionate models of marriage then emerging among middle-class Americans, models dependent on notions of personal and family privacy. In *Searching the Heart: Women, Men, and Romantic Love in Nineteenth-Century America*, Karen Lystra observes that "love appears to be at the core of Victorian family culture."[42] Arguably the most complete and authoritative study of nineteenth-century romantic love, Lystra's work explicates an idealized defining model of the romantic relations between men and women to which white middle-class Americans aspired. Both romantic love and domestic privacy depended on a sense of interiority that could only emerge out of the separation of the private home from the world outside it. Victorian romantic ideologies rooted romantic love in a vision of a true and essential private self that all men and women possessed. The private sharing of the self's truest and deepest expressions with another marked the meaning of intimacy and defined the private meaning of nineteenth-century marriage: "Privacy was essential to nineteenth-century middle-class romantic love because the meaning of love was so deeply rooted in acts of protected and exclusive self-revelation."[43] Public prudery served to deepen private love, making its expressions all the more intimate, romantic, and sacred. Those expressions "attained a special and privileged meaning in private precisely because of the public prohibitions."[44] Allowing the outside world into the private sanctity of the marital relation would violate the very essence and meaning of romantic love, intervening in the sacred, intimate sharing of private selves between lovers.

This vision of romantic love preconditioned nineteenth-century middle-class Americans for particular ways of approaching the self and the beloved. Romantic love, Lystra argues, bolstered the emergence of nineteenth-century American individualism because it "enriched and sharpened [the] separate subjectivities" of its participants.[45] Romantic relationships helped formulate "identity distinct from social roles."[46] Moreover, for its most impassioned advocates, "romantic love contributed to the displacement of God by the lover as the central symbol of ultimate significance." Nineteenth-century Americans in love "made deities of each other in the new theology of romantic love."[47] In the scheme of romantic love, children were understood to be tokens or symbols of a couple's love for one another. Children were not the end of sexual expression, but rather the badges that marked its import. "Sex was seen, not primarily as the ultimate gift of heirs, but as the ultimate gift of themselves."[48]

In at least some instances, this model of love translated into the private relations of plural marriage. Early in the history of polygamy, nineteen-year-old plural wife Emmeline B. Woodward Whitney (later Emmeline B. Wells) wrote to her fifty-two-year-old husband, Newel K. Whitney, that "like as a vine entwineth itself around an aged tree, so do my affections entwine about thy heart."[49] Martha Hughes Cannon, also a plural wife, frequently expressed similar sentiments to her husband, Angus M. Cannon, in the 1880s. In one letter she wrote, "Now, my *own loved one*, imagine yourself kissed, hugged, and a piece taken out of your ear, for were I near you right now I would *bite* you."[50] A few weeks later, Martha wrote, "I love you—you are my champion and if you took 40 others, I'd still love you."[51] Clearly, plural marriage did not proscribe or prevent romantic sentiments between husbands and wives.

Although plural husbands and wives often expressed romantic feelings for each other in private, as a culture Mormons resisted the romantic, companionate visions of sex relations emerging in middle-class nineteenth-century American culture. Downplaying the role of romantic love in marriage, Mormons ideally married more out of love for God than for each other.[52] Theirs were often marriages of spiritual economy and purpose, means to spiritual ends more than ends in and of themselves.[53] The Church actively discouraged the "gentile custom" and one-on-one dynamics of romantic self-disclosure, hoping that plural marriage would work against the bonds of intimacy that constituted romantic love in nineteenth-century formulations.[54] Polygamous wife Mary Isabella Horne frankly told a female visitor to Utah that "plural marriage destroys the oneness, of course."[55] Despite her private declarations of love, Martha Hughes Cannon also admitted that a polygamous woman was not as "completely absorbed as one wife is in her husband."[56] Zina D. Huntington Young declared that "a successful polygamous wife must regard her husband with indifference, and with no other feeling than that of reverence, for love we regard as a false sentiment; a feeling which should have no existence in polygamy."[57] Marital love, Mormons believed, was not to be based on the mutual private sharing of self that nineteenth-century Americans prized, but on mutual commitment between husbands and wives to righteous living as part of God's privatized kingdom/family. Plural marriage, as Flake points out, was to purify the Saints and render them priests and priestesses unto God through temple rituals and covenants.[58] Choosing a mate, for Mormons, was choosing someone worthy to participate in sanctifying temple rituals. Nancy Abigail Clement Williams found her future husband "to be a true Latter Day [sic] Saint, and had great respect for him." When he proposed a plural marriage, she "sought unto the Lord earnestly to know if it was his will." Apparently it was, for Williams accepted the proposal the next evening.[59] Marital success hinged not upon finding one's soul mate but on joining a broader Church family and tying oneself to someone righteous enough to ensure eternal exaltation. Ellis Reynolds Shipp, whose autobiography and journal are filled with tender and often passionate declarations of love for her husband, subjected that love to the higher purpose of plural marriage. When her husband took a third wife, she was determined, she wrote, to "not allow myself to become low spirited," for "I know there is but one way to be happy in polygamy and that is to keep burning in our hearts the spirit of God."[60]

While most Mormon marriages were probably not entirely devoid of romantic love (though some seem to have been), Mormon love was, as Kathleen Flake argues, "a love subordinated to religious devotion and ordered by religious, not romantic, ideals."[61] Many Mormon women's private reflections indicate that they entered plural marriage for religious, not romantic, reasons.[62] Martha Cragun Cox, for example, wrote in her autobiography:

> When the final decision [to enter plural marriage] was made known to my family that I could not recede from my purpose the storm broke upon my head. It was not a marriage of love, they claimed and in saying so they struck me a blow. For I could not say that I had really loved the man as lovers love, though I loved his wives and the spirit of their home. I could not assure my

family that my marriage was gotten up solely on the foundation of love for man. The fact was I had asked the Lord to lead me in the right way for my best good and the way to fit me for a place in his kingdom. He had told me how to go and I must follow in the pathe [*sic*] he dictated and that was all there was to it.[63]

Another Mormon woman, Mary Lois Walker Morris, married her second husband because she had pledged to her first on his death bed that she would marry his brother. She knew that his brother "Elias was worth all of the confidence and love that his brother had reposed in him."[64] Mormon marriage solidified one's membership in the family/polity of God more than it established a private household. In other words, polygamy connected its participants to the broader Mormon community rather than establishing a couple's privacy and intimacy; thus it more effectively established community boundaries between the broad Mormon family and non-Mormons than it did between the nuclear family and the world outside it.[65] On the whole, Mormon marriage shaped and served the ends of God's polity more than the individual, making the marriage relation more public than private—but public only within the context of God's private family.

While Mormons, like other Americans, left scant records of their sexual desires and erotic experiences, from the sources we do have it seems relatively clear that for Mormons, sexuality was also more religious than romantic. The purpose of sexuality, though likely not devoid of expressions of love, was first and foremost the production of children in service to the kingdom of God. As Orson Pratt declared, sexual desire existed, "namely, that the human species might be propagated on this creation, that the earth might teem with population."[66] Belinda Pratt agreed, in her *Defense of Polygamy, by a Lady of Utah*: "What then appears to be the great object of the marriage relations? I answer: the multiplying of our species—the rearing and training of children."[67] Hence Mormons viewed children not as tokens of sexual love, but as its final and divine end, gifts to the kingdom. Sexuality served the purposes of God first and romance only secondarily, if at all.

In effect, Mormon marriage "publicized" the self, even in its most intimate relations, by rooting the purpose of sexuality in reproductivity and making the home subject to God's government (the Church) within the privatized familial kingdom. For Mormons, imagining the whole community as a family prefigured their ultimate perfection and unity with God, the Father of the Mormon family. Speaking of the last days, Brigham Young asked, "Will the time ever come that we can commence and organize this people as a family? . . . Do you think we will ever be one? When we get home to our Father and God, will we not wish to be in the family? Will it not be our highest ambition and desire to be reckoned as the sons of the living God, as the daughters of the Almighty, with a right to the household and the faith that belongs to the household, heirs of the Father, his goods, his wealth, his power, his excellency, his knowledge and wisdom?"[68] Following Young's lead, Mormons viewed the privatized kingdom of God as a family contingent upon and shaped by plural family relations: the kingdom was a community that was also a family, a state that was also a home.

The ideal visions of plural marriage described by Church leaders were often quite different, as ideals often are, from the ways polygamy was actually lived. The ways plural marriage might have undermined the public/private divide were never fully realized since practitioners of plural marriage approximated the ideal only in limited ways. Perhaps this is because plural marriage was practiced only for a few generations and, as Jesse Embry points out, "Mormons did not have time to establish rules on how husbands, wives, and children should relate to each other."[69] Plural families had a variety of living arrangements that varied from circumstances in which wives shared living spaces to each wife having her own home. Most husbands housed each wife in her own home and created various ways of rotating visits. Moreover, Mormon husbands were frequently away on business or on missions, so husbands were often absent from Mormon homes. Some women were relatively untroubled by the absence of their husbands while others experienced significant heartbreak. Ellis Reynolds Shipp's autobiography and journal, for example, details missing her husband terribly when they were apart.[70]

Moreover, some Mormon women established good marital relations between wives, while others experienced jealousy. Some loved their sister wives as sisters. For example, Shipp wrote in her diary: "I truly believe our embraces [between Shipp and her sister wife, Maggie] and caresses linked our hearts in an indissoluable [*sic*] union. Maggie and I have lived together for years—our aims, desires, thoughts, and interests have been the same, and although there has been an occasional discord in our feelings I truly believe the holy relationship existing between us causes us to feel a sympathy and love for each other that two souls under other circumstances could never experience."[71] Other plural wives experienced significant tension and struggled to keep jealousies at bay. Mary Jane Mount Tanner wrote in letters to her family that polygamy "is a severe trial to our fallen nature" and that "there is some jealousy and many weaknesses to overcome."[72] However, like many Mormon women, Tanner sought to rise above those weaknesses and "rejoice[d] that I am counted worthy to suffer for Christ's sake, that I may receive a glory and exaltation in the celestial kingdom of our God."[73] Dr. Romania Pratt Penrose declared that polygamy "will prove the one thing needful to cleanse and purify our innermost soul of selfishness, jealousy, and other mundane attributes."[74] Mormon women who struggled with jealousy most often saw that struggle as indicative of personal weakness, not a problem with polygamy itself.

Despite some Mormon women's private misgivings about plural marriage, most defended it passionately in public. Emmeline B. Wells, for example, often bemoaned in her diary the lack of attention her second husband Daniel H. Wells paid her. Nonetheless, she wrote in the *Woman's Exponent*, a women's newsletter that Mormon women published from 1872 to 1914 and among the first of its kind, that plural marriage "gives women the highest opportunities for self-development, exercise of judgment, and arouses latent faculties, making them more truly cultivated in the actual realities of life, more independent in thought and mind, noble and unselfish."[75] Women defended plural marriage not only in the *Exponent* but also in a series of mass meetings in opposition to anti-polygamy legislation and sometimes in conversations with nonmembers. On a train ride from Salt Lake City to Omaha, Louisa Barnes Pratt met some men who "generally railed me about our peculiar doctrines. The principle of polygamy they were loud in condemning." Pratt answered them with biblical arguments, claiming that David and Solomon's plural marriages sanctified the practice. She "found it the better way to avoid argument as much as possible, but would testify boldly to what I knew to be true," specifically in this case the practice of plural marriage.[76]

How Mormon ideals of plural marriage may have played out, given more time, is impossible to know, but there are indications that ideals surrounding plural marriage undercut public and private spheres with important consequences for Mormon women. Perhaps the Mormon undermining of public and private translated most conspicuously into women's lives by upsetting nineteenth-century notions of woman's place arising from separate spheres ideology. Polygamy allowed Mormon women to participate in the public sphere much more than did the Victorian ideology of their eastern sisters. Brigham Young, for example, called on Mormon women to work outside the home: "Women are useful not only to sweep houses, wash dishes, make beds, and raise babies, but that they should stand behind the counter, study law or physic [*sic*], or become good book-keepers and be able to do the business in any counting house, and all this to enlarge their sphere of usefulness for the benefit of society at large."[77] Susa Young Gates asserted that polygamy would usher in a "millennium of usefulness and happiness" for women because it allowed each woman, "at the end of her child-bearing period," to "launch out into her chosen vocation, ready to add the mite of her experience to the great problem of humanity." Unlike monogamous wives, Gates asserted, "the plural wife may, from her own threshold, look out into the broad world and choose such enterprise as she feels herself adapted to."[78] By 1874, one observer noted that women in Utah constituted a "respectable class of professional and highly literate women."[79] Another claimed that "they close no career on a woman in Utah."[80] By these accounts, plural marriage enabled women's activity in the public sphere, loosening the associations between women and domesticity. In God's kingdom, women's influence, with the blessing of Church hierarchy, stretched beyond the domestic.

The kingdom of God also had an economic dimension that worked against nineteenth-century American notions that private property, at least in part, constituted the private individual. Mormonism's alternative communitarian economic vision was set forth in Joseph Smith's 1831 revelation, "The Law of Consecration and Stewardship." Smith's vision began with the assertion that all property belonged to God. According to the revelation, consecration first required each Church member to "consecrate" (donate) his or her property to the Church. Mormon bishops would then redistribute property in "steward-ships" to each male adult "every man equal according to his family, according to his circumstances and his wants and needs."[81] Property redistribution, however, would not be totally equal, for, as Brigham Young declared, just as "our features will differ from one another," so would "our acts, dispositions, and efforts to accumulate, distribute, and dispose of our time, talents, wealth, and whatever the Lord gives to us."[82] Stewardships would, under the discretion of bishops, differ from member to member. Ideally, each adult priesthood holder received a stewardship of "as much as is sufficient for himself and family."[83] In conjunction with their priesthood authority, male saints functioned as stewards over God's property by keeping and tending it on behalf of the community of Zion. Nineteenth-century Church leaders were fairly clear that stewardship was not the same as ownership.[84] Orson Pratt clarified the nature of stewardship: "What is a steward? Is he a bonafide [sic] owner of property? No. If I were called upon to be a steward over a certain farm or factory, the business is not my own, I am only as an agent or steward to take charge of the concern, and act upon it, as a wise steward, and to render up my account to somebody."[85] Mormon men managed God's property on behalf of His kingdom/family and rendered up their account to God through His agents on earth, priesthood authorities. Ideally, as Pratt declared, "each person in the church possess[es] the whole," constituting among God's kingdom a "union of property."[86] Mormons believed that in the last days they would all live the law of consecration under what Joseph Smith and later Brigham Young called the United Order or the Order of Enoch (an important prophet in one of Mormonism's four books of scripture, the *Pearl of Great Price*).[87]

Just as plural marriage undercut the privacy of the individual and the home, consecration worked against American middle-class notions of private property and the heads-of-household who possessed it on behalf of the private family. As Mormons intended it, the law of consecration would institute equality among its participants, and under a system of social cooperation, poverty and inequity would vanish.[88] Consecration intended to create relationships of interdependence and mutual economic interest among God's people. Mormons saw themselves as a broad, collective, private family that was also at once a political community. Consecration further integrated that community under a communitarian economic system. As Orson Pratt declared, "These laws, if adopted, were calculated to make this people of one heart and mind, not in doctrine alone, not in some spiritual things alone, not in a few outward ordinances alone, but to make them one in regard to our property."[89] Ideally, in God's kingdom there could be neither private families nor individuals with interests separate from the interests of the kingdom; the two mutually comprised one another.

In many senses, the law of consecration constituted a radical critique of the excesses of private property under capitalist individualism. One proclamation from Church leaders warned: "The very liberties for which our fathers contended so steadfastly . . . are endangered by the monstrous power which this accumulation of wealth gives so few individuals and a few powerful corporations."[90] Consecration sought in part to remedy at a local level the problem of massive individual property accumulation by rejecting the notion of private property altogether. From its inception, Smith had intended the law of consecration to end private property ownership among the Saints, commanding that "in your temporal things you shall be equal."[91] However, the Saints as a community lived the law of consecration to greater or lesser extents in response to a number of social, historical, spiritual, and economic variables. Consecration in most respects remained a utopian ideal Mormons found quite difficult to put into practice; most attempts to live the Order collapsed, and significant inequalities among Mormons remained in place throughout the nineteenth century. For Mormon officials, these failures marked the unfortunate unpreparedness of the Saints for the millennial coming of Christ.[92] Although most Mormons never lived the United Order, and those who tried frequently failed, Church leaders nonetheless expected plural families to live the law of consecration on familial levels. Thus polygamy functioned as a central organizing metaphor for Smith's communitarian economic vision. The polygamous family served both as training for the economic cooperation of a millennial future and as an economic model for living under the United Order. In *Building the City of God: Community and Cooperation among the Mormons*, Leonard J. Arrington, Feramorz Y. Fox, and Dean L. May argue that polygamous families "strove to perfect the art of cooperation, both in organizing the labor to sustain the household and in sharing the collective product of household production."[93] Some families were particularly successful at living the law of consecration; Martha Cragun Cox, for example, declared: "We had in our home an almost perfect United Order." She described labor and resource sharing among wives, such that "whoever needed most was served first."[94]

The plural family was intended to draw its members into economic cooperation in God's kingdom. As middle-class Americans increasingly relied on heads of household for economic support and attempted to isolate the home from the competitive capitalist market, the family economics of life in plural marriage necessitated precisely the opposite, a kind of consecrated economic cooperation involving all family members. It required that each family member contribute to the sustenance of the whole and that economic resources be shared among wives and children. Moreover, a man married to multiple wives had to consecrate more of himself to a number of women, more of his priesthood to their spiritual maintenance, and more of his stewardship to their temporal sustenance. Larger families also allowed economic and labor specialization among family members. In these ways, polygamous families especially lived a kind of family-based practice of consecration, a prototype of the ideal United Order that would be realized in the kingdom of God.

The connections between plural family economics and the law of consecration became increasingly clear over the 1870s as Brigham Young began instituting United Order communities in Utah. Young called several Church members and their families to begin living consecration in small communities that he wished to "live as a family."[95] Church leadership instructed that the Order should "be conducted on the system of a well-regulated family."[96] Under the United Order, Young declared, "A city of one hundred thousand or a million people could be united into a perfect family. . . . Why, we could organize millions into a family under the Order of Enoch."[97] United Order communities like those in Kanab and Orderville referred to the community as "the little family," "the big family," or "the family order"[98] and described their experiment in terms of "living as a patriarchal family, and in common, [where all] according to their circumstances fare alike."[99] Under the Order, every participant was considered a member of the family, and divisions between family and civil society became meaningless.

Those who lived the United Order took the polygamous family as their model. As Arrington, Fox, and May argue, "the ideal Order as described by the president [Brigham Young] bore a striking resemblance to his own family. The perfected Mormon society would possess the social dynamics, the economic structure, and the physical appearance of his own sizeable domestic establishment. Mormon society was to be his family writ large."[100] Put simply, Young modeled his vision of United Order communities on the workings of his own plural family. Even Young's prescriptions for the physical structures and domestic arrangements of the United Order bore a striking resemblance to his household. In one sermon he declared,

> I will tell you how I would arrange for a little family, say about a thousand persons. I would build houses expressly for their convenience in cooking, washing and every department of their domestic arrangements. Instead of having every woman getting up in the morning and fussing around a cookstove or over the fire, cooking a little food for two or three or half a dozen persons, or a dozen, as the case may be, she would have nothing to do but to go to her work. Let me have my arrangement here, a hall in which I can seat five hundred persons to eat; and I have my cooking apparatus—ranges and ovens—all prepared. I have not time to map it out before you as I wish to. But here is our dining room, and adjoining this is our prayer room, where we would assemble perhaps five hundred persons at one time, and have our prayers in the evening and in the morning.[101]

Young's ideal was much like his own home, with large common rooms for eating and prayer, but on a much larger scale.

While many polygamists preferred to house each wife in her own home, a few Church leaders—especially wealthy ones—lived in homes specially designed for polygamous living. These families produced a "distinctively Mormon architecture that became a genuine source of wonder to contemporary travelers."[102] With rooms for several wives who shared common spaces, these communally run households enacted Young's United Order ideal. Especially under the United Order, ideal Mormon architecture ideally served to unite family with community, not separate it.[103]

Despite Mormons' repeated attempts and failures to establish a sustainable communal social order, the United Order nonetheless remained an ideal central to their conception of themselves and their millennial project. In economic and architectural senses, the United Order was the polygamous household functioning at the level of God's kingdom. Economically and spatially, consecration, along with plural marriage, extended the private sphere into the public, creating a family and a marketplace that encompassed the whole community of Zion. Together, these undercut any notion of the private—be it the private individual, private property, or the private home. Ideally, priesthood and plural marriage constituted God's polity as a family, while Mormon economic cooperation united the economic interests of the individual with that of the community. This unification of public and private within Mormondom paved the way toward a form of divine politics that consolidated the individual political consciences of the community under the direction of Church leaders.

Political Dualisms:
The Private Kingdom in the Public State

When the Mormons planned their move to Utah in the mid-1840s, they intended to build the kingdom of God in the West. They carried with them a well-developed political philosophy they rooted in their eschatological vision of God's literal kingdom on earth. As a participatory utopian faith, Mormonism taught from the outset that human history would move inevitably toward the establishment of a literal political kingdom of God that would emerge to govern the entire world as human society perfected itself under divine tutelage. The Mormon Church regarded itself as the partial fulfillment of this divine political future, and Church leaders worked diligently throughout the late nineteenth century to gather Zion together, speed the world along its millennial political track, and usher in God's reign over His kingdom.

After the public announcement of plural marriage in 1852, a cacophony of anti-Mormon literature articulated middle-class Americans' multiple objections to the privatized kingdom of God in the West. Not the least of these was the observation that Mormons understood themselves as citizens of God's kingdom first and of the United States second. Chapter 4 delineates the ways that anti-Mormons used the practice of polygamy as proof that, despite their patriotic rhetoric, Mormons' loyalties to the kingdom of God precluded good American citizenship. Although wrong about Mormons in a number of ways, anti-Mormons were especially astute at connecting the various social, economic, and marital unities Mormonism tried to enact to what anti-Mormons saw as treasonous political theocracy. They saw in plural marriage an incipient political despotism resulting from the undercutting of the private individual. They also understood that the expansion of the domestic private to include the entire kingdom violated in several ways the very premises of American political virtue. Mormons, they argued, simply did not, could not, and must not be allowed to persist as members of the American body politic. They were, quite simply, un- or even anti-American.

As anti-Mormon rhetoric became increasingly acerbic and Congress became increasingly committed to legislating against the multiple evils they saw emerging from the Utah Territory, Mormons were increasingly pressed to defend themselves against both discursive assaults and federal political intervention. They employed a series of practical political tactics, including filling territorial government offices with Church leaders and relying on Church government to officiate their affairs. At the same time, Mormons struggled to articulate their unique political philosophy in ways solicitous of political acceptance in an American body politic. Mormons outlined a kind of political dualism through which they tried to demonstrate the compatibility of the kingdom of God with American political institutions. They defended the kingdom as a privatized government that could, and indeed must, be allowed to exist under American ideals.

In practice, the line between Church government and Utah's territorial government was thin. By electing Church leaders to territorial government positions, Mormons captured much of the political force of territorial government, infusing Utah's federal agencies with the Church's political agenda. In particular, they filled the territorial legislature with Mormons and passed legislation that protected plural marriage and facilitated Church government in Utah. For most of the latter half of the nineteenth century the Church had its own political party, the People's Party, and the Mormon polity voted nearly unanimously for its candidates. In 1849, in the wake of a failed campaign for Utah statehood, Stephen A. Douglas, Illinois democratic senator and local sovereignty advocate, helped the Mormons petition the federal government for explicit permission to elect their own territorial officials. The petition failed, and the federal government appointed their own representatives to many government positions, many of whom were hostile to Mormonism.

The Mormons' first act of defense was the passage of legislation in 1851 that gave the Church broad governing authority in Utah to make laws and punish and forgive offenses consistent with its own doctrines and "not inconsistent with or repugnant to the Constitution of the United States or of this State." The legislation also granted the Church "the Constitutional and original right ... to solemnize marriage compatible with the revelations of Jesus Christ, ... that the pursuit of bliss, and the enjoyment of life in every capacity of public association and domestic happiness, temporal expansion, or spiritual increase upon the earth may not be legally questioned."[104] The act placed marriage largely under Church authority. Mormons understood celestial marriage to be solely under Church control, even though a parallel legal system of marriage existed in Utah. These state-sanctioned marriages were, for Mormons, peripheral to the Church-regulated celestial marriage system.[105]

As Church representatives occupied the territorial Congress and nearly all elected offices, the Church itself filled significant political roles in Utah, directing public opinion and enacting political practices such as managing natural resources and resolving social conflicts that Americans elsewhere thought better and more appropriately served by public government.[106] The Church managed public and community affairs and regulated relations between its members. Perhaps most egregiously, however, the Church evaded federal judicial authority by instituting an ecclesiastical court system that established the Church as the foremost judicial authority in Utah. Church courts essentially supplanted significant portions of federal territorial court authority, raising the hackles of mainstream America; nowhere did the Church more clearly usurp the sort of political authority Americans required to be public.[107]

Tremendous political tensions wracked territorial government in Utah as the Mormon Church and Mormon elected officials contended with federal appointees. For Mormons, federal interventions in Utah government constituted a perversion of Constitutional principles, and they viewed federal officials, in the words of Brigham Young, as "some of the most corrupt, damnable, mean curses . . . that have ever disgraced the earth."[108] This sensibility increased Mormons' faith in Church government over civil government, and Church administration of political affairs in Utah flourished. One Utah Supreme Court Justice, James McKean, a federal appointee, called the Church an "*imperium in imperio*," an empire within an empire, and in many respects he was right.[109] In essence, Utah had two governments—the Church and the territorial government.

The institutions of God's government and the Church's exercise of political authority in Utah extended the religious into the political, a mixture of church and state that flew in the face of both the public/private divide and American disestablishmentarianism. Mormon political philosophy articulated a political dualism that facilitated the existence of a privatized kingdom within a public republican state. This dualism hinged on the construction of the kingdom of God as a privatized family/church (that was also a government) juxtaposed to a public American government. In an early articulation of this duality, Church elder Heber C. Kimball claimed that "as President Buchanan, the President of the United States of America, holds the keys of the government of this whole nation, so Brigham Young holds the keys pertaining to this Church and people."[110] To Mormons, the privatization of the kingdom of God made sense out of the institutions of God's government in American terms. As Mormons understood it, priesthood and plural marriage, together with consecration, constituted the kingdom of God as a sacred, private context in which, as long as Mormons followed the laws of the United States, American civil government had no right to intervene. They saw no problem with being subject to two governments at once. In the wake of the 1857 Utah War, John Taylor gave a sermon in which he declared, "It is true we have had a church government, church laws, church discipline, and by the holy Priesthood associated with this Church we have governed the people." He proceeded to defend such a government against federal intervention, arguing that the kingdom of God, "both Church and State, to rule both temporally and spiritually," could and must exist within U.S. boundaries: "The kingdom of God is higher and its laws are so much more exalted than those of any other nation, that it is the easiest thing in life for a servant of God to keep any of their laws; and, as I have said before, this we have uniformly done."[111] Mormonism reconstituted public and private into a consolidated private sphere, the privatized kingdom, all under the rubric of a private family that was also at once both a church and, although the expression is oxymoronic in American terms, a private state. Orson Pratt argued, the U.S. Constitution "gives every class of people, whether few or many, the privilege of organizing themselves, and establishing whatever laws they please to govern them in a Church capacity."[112] Mormons thus situated the privatized kingdom in juxtaposition to the public American state and contended that the two not only could but must coexist, at least until God saw fit to replace the latter with the former.

Ultimately, Mormons argued, not only was the kingdom of God compatible with and a perfection of American government, but the two political systems worked toward the same goal—government by the people. Mormons understood the meaning of government by the people in communitarian terms. They intended government by the people to unite the Mormon community, molding individual consciences together as one through a divinely inspired and ordered consensus. Joseph Smith had established the principle of consent very early. The first revelation on Church government in April 1830 established that "No person is to be ordained to any office in this church, where there is a regularly organized branch of the same, without the vote of that church."[113] Smith commanded that all canonized doctrine, advancements in the priesthood, and Church callings be sustained by the affected Church body. Mormons believed that in a community in which all individuals had unmitigated access to the divine, consensus would emerge organically as God's will became clear to all. The more perfect and unified the Saints became, the more accessible God's will would be, until God's desires became apparent to all citizens of God's kingdom, naturally replicating God's political order. As the Saints modeled God's perfected government to the people of the world, they would see its advantages and eventually unite in one great, worldwide kingdom under God.

In the meantime, Mormons reconciled their political separatism with their membership in an American polity by contending that the political arm of the kingdom of God, the Council of Fifty, was now and would always be a perfection of American political principles. For Mormons, the Government of God indicated by its similarity the essential validity of American government. Brigham Young imagined that the Council of Fifty utterly embodied American principles: "The Kingdom of God will protect every person, every sect and all people upon the face of the whole earth in their legal rights."[114] Young claimed that "Even now the form of the Government of the United States differs but little from the Kingdom of God."[115] While Mormons touted their belief in the superiority of American political institutions (if not the officials who filled them), arguing that the American Constitution represented humanity's highest political achievement, they maintained that in the last days God's government would supersede it. Orson Pratt suggested that the American Constitution figured as "a stepping stone to a form of government infinitely greater and more perfect—a government founded upon divine laws."[116] The Church's "theodemocracy" brought together republican ideas and divine order, and Mormonism's millennial government would perfect American Government. Parley P. Pratt, Orson Pratt's brother, embraced a vision of theodemocracy, claiming that "it is because of the ignorance that is in the world that two terms—'political government' and 'religious government,' are used."[117] For Parley P. Pratt, God's government in the last days would be both political and religious—indeed the two would be inseparable—and, with God's assistance, Mormonism would give perfected government to the world at large. The kingdom of God was a sanctified and perfected America that would govern the entire world.

Accommodating human weakness, Mormons believed that the role of Church hierarchy was to reveal God's political truth to his polity, directing and bringing about community consensus. While to "direct" consensus may seem counterintuitive to a modern reader, to Joseph Smith, Brigham Young, and their followers the concept made perfect sense. Mormons believed that the Church was an instrument of millennial purification, and its leadership lent order to the chaos of personal freedom and showed the direction in which divine personal revelation ought to point. Consequently, Mormons' vision of the kingdom of God prefigured and presupposed the absence of dissent. In Young's understanding, community consensus could occur only in unity with

God, and those outside of community consensus would mark themselves out of sync with divine will. Only repentance, faithfulness, divine revelation, and alignment with inspired consensus could bring them back into the fold.[118] Mormons contended that nearly universal agreement with Church leadership indicated not the absence of individual conscience, but the unity of God's kingdom.[119] Only a community driven wholly by the will of God, modeled on divinely ordained patterns, could avoid social discord, legal corruption, and the kind of political missteps that had, in Mormons' estimation, led even the most perfect of human governments, American democracy, astray.[120] According to Mormons, Church government represented popular government at its very best.

Despite their best attempts, the nineteenth-century Saints never completely realized their vision of the kingdom of God; human imperfection proved remarkably resistant to Smith's millennial vision. Perhaps Mormonism naively overestimated human capacity for cooperation and consensus. Church doctrine may have placed too much stock in the knowability of God's will, or perhaps leaders misjudged the interest and willingness of individual Church members to align themselves with it. Indeed, a long history of apostasy attests that members did disagree over the meaning of the will of God, and consensus failed not once but many times. Perhaps, too, the Church attempted too communitarian an experiment in a national milieu grounded in individual liberties. The vision of the kingdom of God as a perfected American Republic often lay over the institutions and practices of Church government uncomfortably in Utah because Mormon government was never as free of its coercive aspects as Smith imagined it would become. Yet despite its failures, Mormon political philosophy cannot be properly understood outside the context of Mormonism's vision of the unity of the kingdom of God. To take seriously Mormonism's perception of itself is to understand the theocratic aspects of Church government as attempts to accommodate the divergence between heavenly ideals and human weaknesses. For Mormons, theocracy and democracy were cut of the same cloth.

While Mormons articulated their compatibility with and importance to American politics, they also defended Church government with two conceptual tools that had great political clout in nineteenth-century America: first, that "the right to worship God according to the dictates of their own conscience . . . is the broad platform upon which our government has been founded," and second, that local self-determination in Utah was necessary to ensure all of the freedoms American government was designed to protect.[121] Strikingly, the issue at the center of both of these claims was the most reviled institution of Mormonism, plural marriage. Mormons took the position that marriage in Utah was a private religious practice, as opposed to a civil union (which may or may not also be religious). As such, it was rightfully placed under Church control, enfolding marriage in the domain of religious freedom. Casting plural marriage as a religious practice protected by the First Amendment, Mormons stripped marriage of its civic role in republican thought, even while they emphasized the role of polygamy in ensuring both religious freedom and local sovereignty.

Mormons went to great lengths to demonstrate the symbolic importance of Mormonism to the preservation of religious liberty under what they saw as an increasingly repressive federal government. In the words of Brigham Young, "Whenever the iron hand of oppression and persecution has fallen upon this people, our opposers [*sic*] have broken their own laws, set at defiance and trampled under foot every principle of equal rights, justice, and liberty found written in that rich legacy of our fathers, The Constitution of the United States."[122] Mormons contended that polygamy in particular occupied a special place in the American legacy. Opposed by other Americans on nearly every front, polygamy signified the religious liberty that needed protection by American government. In defense of their absolute religious freedom, most often couched as the right to practice plural marriage, Mormons claimed they were more American, even, than Americans. Pointing to the legacy of America's forefathers who revolted in the name of religious freedom, Church leaders identified freedom of religion as the genius of the American experiment. Accordingly, Brigham Young announced that "we believe that the Lord has been preparing . . . a place upon His footstool where sufficient liberty of conscience should exist that His saints might dwell in peace under the broad panoply of constitutional law and equal rights." He further stated that "we consider that the men in the revolution were inspired, by the Almighty, to throw off the shackles of the mother government, with her established religion."[123] Mormons claimed similarity with the revolutionary patriots: "We have the spirit of '76; we are patriots and we are true to our cause," the preservation of religious liberty.[124] For Mormons, the establishment of Zion in the West preserved religious liberty against a corrupt American government that refused the very principles that made it so exceptional.

Important as polygamy was to Mormonism's articulation of religious freedom, the practice also served as a kind of symbolic site upon which the Church ensured its right to privatized self-government over the family/polity of God. By claiming virtually everything about Mormon life as religious practice, Mormons asserted the Constitutionality of private Church government. If religion encompassed all of life, the Church should be protected by the First Amendment in its management of affairs in Utah. True American principles, grounded in religious freedom, should support privatized Church government of God's family, not undermine it. At the same time, Church control over marriage became a kind of test case for Church control over broad affairs in Utah and a symbolic nexus upon which Mormons justified privatized local self-determination.

Mormons claimed that American political traditions justified in the name of local sovereignty the role of Church government in the privatized kingdom of God. In the early republican and antebellum periods, the most powerful national incarnation of arguments favoring local sovereignty came couched in the discourse of states' rights. The Constitution had left ambiguous the balance between state and federal power, and debates about states' rights and federal powers persisted throughout the nineteenth century.[125] However, early Constitutional law placed jurisdiction over the legal category known as "domestic relations"—those laws regulating relations between masters and servants or slaves, parents and children, and husbands and wives—firmly in the jurisdiction of state governments. Early Americans considered domestic relations, in the words of Sarah Barringer Gordon, "matters for local debate and local disposition."[126] Early republicans reasoned that placing domestic relations under the decentralized control of the states offered domestic privacy and the private individual the most protection from government intervention. Leaving an institution as important as marriage under local control demonstrated both the importance of the domestic private sphere and the power of local self-determination in antebellum America.

The problem for Mormons was that Utah was a territory, not a state, and thus subject to as much authority as the federal government wished to exercise. Nevertheless, Mormons mobilized arguments for local sovereignty, claiming that despite its territorial status, Utah nonetheless had the right to select its own government.[127] The claim to self-government in the territories smacked of the contested idea of "squatter sovereignty." Southern Democrats contended that in Western territories, the "squatters" who settled the area should decide whether slavery should be allowed. Arguing for self-determination in Utah thus allied Mormons with slaveholders. As Newell G. Bringhurst shows, in the 1850s Mormons had an ambivalent relationship to slavery, expressing antislavery and anti-abolitionist positions concurrently.[128] A handful of southern Mormons had migrated to Utah with their slaves, and in 1852 the territorial legislature passed an act officially allowing slavery.[129] Despite this legal recognition, however, most Mormons had migrated from non-slaveholding areas of the United States and Europe and basically disliked slavery.[130] Yet the institution persisted in Utah until 1862, when Congress outlawed slavery in the territories.

As the Civil War approached, national debates over states' rights and local sovereignty became more contentious, especially as the concepts harbored the practice of slavery. After 1856 when the national Republican platform yoked polygamy and slavery together as the "twin relics of barbarism," Mormon anti-abolitionist rhetoric was motivated in part by the defense of Mormonism's own peculiar institution, plural marriage.[131] After a failed military campaign in 1857 to subdue Mormon "treason," the federal government asserted much more control over territorial government in Utah, placing its own appointees in many positions. On one hand, these events enabled Mormons to point to the tyranny of federal government in prohibiting popular government in Utah. On the other hand, the inflammatory political rhetoric linking slavery and polygamy that had prompted federal intervention in 1857 subsequently made plural marriage much more difficult to defend. Anti-Mormon reformers and government officials contended that polygamy enslaved white women as slavery enslaved black Americans and so justified federal intervention. The first legislative intervention specifically targeting plural marriage came in 1862 when the Morrill Act declared "bigamy" a crime and formally made Mormon family structure illegal.[132]

As the end of the Civil War settled the issue of slavery, Mormons increasingly relied on the idea of local sovereignty to defend Church government. If domestic relations were deemed matters of local concern, but territorial government was under federal control, all the more reason that the privatized kingdom of God should institute its own private, extralegal marriage regulations. This protected domestic relations from federal authority by bypassing territorial government. Moreover, in the interest of promoting self-government more broadly, Mormons contended that a local population inherently possessed the right to submit to a government of their own choosing, even if that government was also a church. Was not the right to select one's own government the legacy of the American Revolution? Mormons contended that if members freely opted to submit their affairs to an authority that was completely separate from and irrelevant to civic government, the consent of the governed protected that choice as long as it was also consistent with the U.S. Constitution.[133] Moreover, as a government (theoretically) guided by common consent and guided by the will of the people as directed by Church authorities, Mormons argued, Church government was consistent with American principles, even if it was private.

Despite the political role of the Church in Utah, as the century unfolded, Mormons increasingly maintained that the establishment of a privatized Church government did not preclude their participation in a public American state. Orson Pratt declared: "We came here as a religious people. We had a civil government, and a religious government; we had civil authority and ecclesiastical authority, before the gentiles came here in any numbers."[134] Mormons imagined Church government to be entirely compatible with civic government and argued, as did Wilford Woodruff, that "Church government and civil government are distinct and separate in our theory and practice, and we regard it as part of our destiny to aid in the maintenance and perpetuity of the institutions of our country."[135] While Mormons believed in the unity of church and state in the privatized domain of God's kingdom, they also embraced the more immediate need for a public civil state. In a sense, Mormon political dualism provided for a private government, the Church, to operate alongside a public one. Mormons located the boundary between public and private at the division between the privatized family/church/state and the public institutions of U.S. government. Mormons did not find it particularly problematic that the former performed many of the same delegated functions of the latter; they saw their right to Church government as a constitutionally protected republican right.

For much of the nineteenth century, Church leaders dominated the ranks of elected local government. Until the late 1850s, Mormons commanded appointed positions as well, from the territorial governor (Brigham Young) to cabinet positions to justices in the civil court system, until federal appointments made Church hegemony less possible. Despite their near monopoly over local elected offices, Mormons maintained that church and state were separate in Utah, that the nearly universal election and appointment of Mormon officials was merely a local particularity emerging from a Mormon majority. As Orson Pratt claimed in 1853, "The Latter-day Saints, in Utah, have no more liberties or privileges granted to them by the civil power, than any other denomination who may choose to settle there. If they constitute the majority of population, they can elect such individuals as they see proper to the legislative departments: this is not oppression, but is precisely according to the practice of all the other Territorial and State governments. The majority rules—the majority elects. This is the very essence of our national institutions."[136] As Pratt claimed, Mormons viewed the phenomenon of Church leaders in government offices as not only a happenstance of local democracy but a demonstration of its greatest strength: in Utah, public government would represent its people, the citizens of the kingdom of God. For Mormons, that the private Church predetermined the officers of public government was as it should be, not only because majority ruled, but also because the common interests of the Church family could only be appropriately represented by Church representatives in the public government.

Here again, Mormonism transposed American political concepts to Church contexts: in the same way that citizens filled public governmental roles representing private families, Church leaders in civic positions represented the common interests of the privatized Church family in civic life. The Church family paralleled the private family and, like the family, must be represented in civic government. While ordinary Americans were "apostatizing fast from the principles that the fathers of this nation instituted," John Taylor declared, "A republican government . . . in the hands of the righteous . . . is everlasting, while its power reaches to heaven."[137] As George Q. Cannon asked rhetorically, "what better people can be found . . . to take charge of the affairs of mankind in the earth and establish righteous principles and maintain laws under which all men can dwell in peace and be entirely free from oppression and everything of this character . . . than the men who understand the principles of truth?"[138] Mormons argued that Church leaders in civic roles represented the interests of the righteous, which were also the interests of the Church, which were also the interests of the nation.

Demonstrating the essential compatibility of Mormonism and republicanism, nineteenth-century Mormons constituted themselves as citizens of both the kingdom of God and the American Republic. They articulated a model of dual citizenship, in both church and state polities, one private and one public. They saw nothing incongruous about concurrent membership in the polity of God and U.S. citizenship and, by extension, nothing problematic about the integration of polygamy with Americanness. This viewpoint enabled them to claim access to political Americanness even as they asserted a divine political role for the Church. They found the privatized kingdom of God and the public American state not only fundamentally compatible but necessarily contingent upon each other. So central was this vision of government and family to Mormons that they endured decades of persecution, the passage of several antipolygamy laws, fines, arrests, and lives on the lam to maintain it.

• • •

Mormon women particularly articulated a vision of the compatibility of polygamy and Americanness in their defenses of Mormon woman suffrage. The next chapter will discuss one of the most intriguing and important implications of Mormon political culture, Mormon woman suffrage. Absent a stable, singular private sphere that could be represented by a citizen in the public sphere, Mormons saw no reason women should not vote, and in 1870 Utah was the second territory to enfranchise women, preceded by Wyoming only a few months earlier. They did so without a major suffrage movement—it simply made sense to them.

CHAPTER 3

"More the Companion and Much Less the Subordinate"

Polygamy and Mormon Woman's Citizenship

"Utah is the land of marvels. She gives us, first polygamy, which seems to be an outrage against 'woman's rights,' and then offers to the nation a 'female suffrage bill.' . . . Was there ever a greater anomaly known in the history of a society?"[1] With this statement a writer for the *Phrenological Journal* articulated what most nineteenth-century Americans understood to be the paradox of Mormon woman's suffrage, a paradox with which scholars have been wrestling ever since. How did a community which understood itself to be avowedly patriarchal, instituted a marriage system it called "patriarchal marriage," referred to itself as a "patriarchal family," and subjected women to the leadership of a male-only priesthood give rise to such a gesture toward women's equality?

This chapter looks at perhaps the most radical aspect of Mormon citizenship claims—Mormon woman's suffrage and its startling offspring, a polygamous republicanism. After receiving the vote in 1870, Mormon women increasingly entered the fray of the national woman question to construct alternative visions of independent women's citizenship—visions to which polygamy was central. In a curious twisting of patriarchy, woman's suffrage emerged naturally out of Mormon patriarchy. As Mormon women saw it, their ecclesiastical subordination cleared a path for their civic equality, as the avowedly patriarchal institution of polygamy empowered women's participation in the formal polity. Mormon women went to great lengths to show that plural marriage not only facilitated women's independence but developed her capacities for citizenship as well. By resisting, undermining, and disavowing categories of public and private, Mormons, especially women, both opened a space for woman's equal citizenship and also articulated broad critiques of American marriage structures and the visions of citizenship that emerged from the separation of public and private.

"To the Rights of the Women of Zion": Mormon Woman Suffrage

The idea of woman suffrage in Utah had its origins in the federal Congress. Between 1867 and 1869, several bills urged experimenting with woman suffrage in the territories, since if disastrous, federal sovereignty over the territories would allow Congress to repeal it. Some of these bills were particularly directed at Utah and had anti-polygamy reform in mind. For years anti-Mormons considered polygamy tantamount to women's enslavement and supposed that, given the chance, Mormon women would cast off the chains of their polygamic bondage. Following up on the suggestion of reformers, Indiana Representative George W. Julian proposed to Congress that it enact Mormon woman suffrage as a remedy to plural marriage. A day later, Senator S. C. Pomeroy of Kansas introduced similar legislation in the Senate. The problem for Congressional anti-polygamists, however, was that William Hooper, Delegate of the Utah Territory, welcomed the suggestion, as did the local Mormon press in Utah. With full faith in the loyalty of Mormon women, Mormon Church leaders demonstrated enthusiasm for the proposal, leading Congress to quickly abandon the idea, and neither bill ever came to a vote.

However, the suggestion did not go unnoticed among Mormon women who had a history of voting within the Church. Scholarship has demonstrated that Mormon women were not simply given political suffrage by Mormon leaders who hoped to expand their political base in the wake of increased non-Mormon settlement. Lola Van Wagenen shows that Mormon women were activists "in their own behalf." They acted as proponents of their own political equality before they received the vote in February 1870, though they were careful to "make sure the hierarchy never felt threatened or interpreted the women's goals as inconsistent with the goals of the church."[2] At a mass meeting in January 1870, the president of the Relief Society, the Church's women's organization, Eliza R. Snow said, "Although as yet we have not been admitted to the common ballot-box, to us the right of suffrage is extended in matters of far greater importance."[3] From the Church's inception, women members had voted equally with men to "sustain" Church officials.[4] Opposing votes were rare and were responded to by a conversation with the bishop, but because Mormons understood priesthood nominations to be directly inspired by God, leaders were almost always universally sustained. In the nineteenth century, as today, the vote to "sustain" Church leaders was largely a formality for both men and women. Nonetheless, because Mormon women voted alongside men to sustain their Church leaders, Snow contended in the 1870 mass meeting that "we, the ladies of Utah, are already in possession of a privilege which many intelligent and high-aiming ladies in the States are earnestly seeking; *i.e., the right to vote.*"[5] The assemblage of Mormon women then voted on and passed a resolution requesting the right of political franchise from the territorial governor. Apparently Mormons saw no reason God's intent for women's religious franchise should not translate into national civic contexts; Church leaders heard the demands of women and encouraged the territorial legislature to pass a woman's suffrage law.[6] With surprisingly little resistance, the legislature responded quickly, and one month later, on February 12, 1870, acting Governor S. A. Mann signed the woman's suffrage bill into law.[7] At the behest of Mormon women, Utah became the second territory (preceded only a few months by Wyoming) to grant women the vote.[8] In just a few months, Utah had presented the nation with the anomaly of Mormon woman suffrage.

Within a year and a half, Mormon women began publishing one of the first women's newspapers in the nation, the *Woman's Exponent,* founded by Lula Green Richards with the support of Brigham Young. From 1871 until 1914, the *Exponent* served as the unofficial voice of the Relief Society and dedicated itself to any and all topics it thought of interest to women. While not devoted entirely to supporting woman suffrage, the *Exponent* devoted many of its pages to endorsing women's right to vote and advocating women's broad civic equality. From 1879 to 1896, the masthead of the *Exponent* declared its allegiance to "The Rights of the Women of Zion, and the Rights of Women of All Nations." As though Mormon women recognized the paradox of their political equality, foremost on the *Exponent*'s agenda was the complementary public defense of both plural marriage and woman suffrage. It was in these defenses that Mormon women revealed how women's civic equality emerged organically from the practice of plural marriage and the ecclesiastical subordination that attended it.

In defending suffrage, Mormon women placed their activism within a Mormon context. While the national movement dated its origins to the first national woman suffrage convention at Seneca Falls in 1848, the *Exponent* could boast, "The women of the Latter-day Saints date the period of a new movement for the higher elevation of woman still farther back."[9] Prominent Relief Society leader Sarah Kimball claimed that "the sure foundations of the suffrage cause were deeply and permanently laid" in 1842 when Joseph Smith had established the Relief Society.[10] Most Mormon women agreed, contending that a "new era" for women had begun in Nauvoo, and that without the Relief Society the women of the territory "never would have had the ballot" and "would not have been so well qualified to step forward and exercise the privilege it gives them."[11] After 1870, Church leaders increasingly encouraged the Relief Society to take on a new expressly political purpose. In May 1874, Church apostle George Albert Smith called the organization to "meet together and discuss all questions that are calculated to interest or benefit the community . . . [and to] make yourselves thoroughly acquainted not only with the politics of the country, but with every principle of local government . . . and then you will be enabled to vote intelligently."[12] The women of the Relief Society commenced quickly with civic education efforts, holding formal and informal classes and meetings at which women taught each other various aspects of territorial and national political systems, discussed issues of local and national importance, and formulated political opinions. Over the next few decades, local Relief Societies would become hotbeds of women's political activism, advocating both woman suffrage and the practice of plural marriage.

The phenomenon of polygamous woman's suffrage in Utah put national suffrage advocates in an awkward position.[13] They responded to the curious blending of polygamy and suffrage in Utah in mixed ways that reflected other dissensions in the movement. By the time Mormon women received suffrage in 1870, the national suffrage movement was fracturing. The Reconstruction amendments enfranchised black men and failed to include women. Disagreements over the enfranchisement of black men divided the suffrage movement into two rival organizations, the National Woman Suffrage Association and the American Woman Suffrage Association. Those in the National Association opposed black men's suffrage as, in the words of Elizabeth Cady Stanton, "an additional weight to [woman's] enfranchisement," and they lodged their campaigns for woman suffrage within larger claims to education, economic independence, and broad-based equality for white women based on natural rights.[14] The American Association narrowed their approach to focus solely on the vote as the most powerful agent of women's equality. Concerns about respectability also separated the two factions. The American Association was, in one historian's terms, "anxious to keep out all those it considered undesirable," while the National professed to welcome any woman who supported the suffrage cause, Mormon women included.[15]

The National Association's platform of tolerant membership policies, advocacy of women's economic independence, critiques of the institution of marriage, and support for a national amendment facilitated their tendency to overlook the practice of polygamy in forging political alliances with Mormon women. Elizabeth Cady Stanton contended that Mormon women were, in one historian's terms, "no more deluded than any women who accepted the biblical concept of woman's inferiority and patriarchal marriage."[16] The American Association, however, strenuously objected to the Mormon practice of polygamy—for example, Henry Blackwell, husband of Lucy Stone and an Association founder, condemned polygamy outright as "the slavery of sex." The *Woman's Journal*, the official publication of the American Association, added: "The ballot to Mormon women in Utah is only another brand of shame upon their brows."[17] The American Association found the practice of plural marriage analogous to slavery and avidly supported anti-polygamy reformers.[18]

Although beset with "personal and political dilemmas" over plural marriage, in 1871 Stanton and a second prominent leader of the National Association, Susan B. Anthony, met with a variety of Utah women voters, many of whom were polygamists. Stanton and Anthony were invited to Utah by a new group of apostates known as the New Movement or the Godbeites. The New Movement had split from the official Church out of dissatisfaction with Brigham Young's isolationist economic policies. The Godbeites supported women's equality, however, and asked the National leaders to spend a few days in Salt Lake City on their way to the West coast. Not to be outdone, before the suffragists arrived, Young invited the pair to speak in favor of women's equality before Mormon women in the tabernacle. By Stanton's and Anthony's arrival, both the New Movement and the mainstream Church "were attempting to articulate an ideology that accommodated polygamy and woman's equality."[19] While neither Stanton nor Anthony supported polygamy, Anthony, in an article in *The Revolution*, lodged her criticisms of plural marriage within a larger critique of the entire institution of marriage and concluded that "woman's work in monogamy and polygamy is one and the same—that of planting her feet on the ground of self support. . . . Women here, as everywhere must be able to live honestly and honorably without the aid of men."[20] Though somewhat alienated by Anthony's refusal to support plural marriage, Mormon women could nonetheless support Anthony's demand for women's economic and political rights, and these meetings are perhaps what prompted Stanton and Anthony's subsequent decision to support, though tenuously, woman suffrage in Utah. Utah women, however, not especially satisfied with Anthony's claim that polygamy worked as much against women's rights as monogamy, were lukewarm about maintaining formal ties to the National suffrage movement.

Nevertheless, nine years after Utah women received the vote, notable Mormon women Emmeline B. Wells and Zina Young Williams visited Washington

D. C. to attend the annual conference of the National Woman Suffrage Association. The visit was preceded by correspondence expressing Mormon women's gratitude that the National Association had protested increased attempts in Washington to disenfranchise Mormon women. While in Washington, Wells and Williams defended Mormon woman's suffrage and the practice of plural marriage to national suffrage advocates and U.S. government officials; they even secured an audience with President Rutherford B. Hayes. This visit cemented the informal ties between Mormon women suffragists and the National Association, and Wells and Williams returned home to a grateful and encouraged Mormon community.[21]

The national visibility of campaigns for Mormon woman suffrage also added new dimensions to anti-polygamy campaigns at local and national levels. Anti-polygamy resistance to Mormon woman suffrage began the moment Acting Governor Mann signed the suffrage bill into law. As historian Beverly Beeton points out, "[T]he fortunes of female franchise in Utah would rise and fall . . . with the battle over plural marriage," in part because Utah was a territory and subject to federal intervention.[22] Within a few years of the bill's passage, when it became clear that Mormon women did not intend to exercise the ballot against polygamy, anti-Mormons quickly came to view the granting of woman suffrage as simply part of a larger Mormon agenda to seal off their Western polygamous stronghold from national influence. For anti-Mormons, the only reasonable explanation for the apparent complacency of Mormon women was that Church authorities controlled their votes and had enfranchised women to multiply their electorate with votes they could easily control. Mormon women quickly moved to disabuse anti-Mormons of that notion, articulating a flexible and sometimes contradictory logic of the compatibility of plural marriage with women's citizenship.

Plural Marriage and the Woman Citizen

Discussions of disenfranchising Utah women abounded throughout the 1870s. In 1872 Congress, firmly set against plural marriage, debated the first of several bills attempting to strip Utah women of the vote. Earlier that same year, Utahns had embarked on an extensive campaign for admission to the Union as a state. Initially, anti-Mormons had felt optimistic that women would vote plural marriage out of the proposed state constitution. However, when the proposal to hold a state constitutional convention carried, Mormon women dashed those hopes. While the number of women voters at the state constitutional convention had elated national woman suffragists, it had deeply concerned Utah anti-

Mormons who then clamored to oppose statehood. They had appealed to the federal Congress, and in 1872 Representative William Wheeler introduced the first of several legislative attempts to disenfranchise the women of Utah.[23] From then on, Mormon women endeavored to defend their suffrage from various onslaughts driven by anti-polygamy sentiment. They consistently defended both woman suffrage and plural marriage arguing that polygamy and woman's rights complemented each other. In fact, Mormon women viewed woman suffrage as a natural outgrowth of the practice of polygamy and claimed that both practices worked toward the same purpose: God's design for the fairer sex. Despite what seemed to nineteenth-century anti-Mormons an obvious clash between polygamy and women's rights, Mormon women placed plural marriage at the center of claims to suffrage that were uniquely Mormon. They contended that woman suffrage and polygamy worked together, justifying and reinforcing one another, to facilitate the higher development of woman and to extend her sphere of influence.

To be sure, Mormon women borrowed arguments from woman's rights advocates of the late nineteenth century, liberally reprinting in the *Exponent* articles from suffragist publications in the East. Mormon women agreed with many of their more radical eastern sisters of the National Association that woman deserved a political voice because she was, quite simply, man's civic equal. Mormon women believed it "unjust for [woman] to be deprived a claim for recognition by the right which men citizens enjoy, viz. the elective franchise." Appealing to republican principles, they argued, "The American people profess to believe in a representative government; then if all classes are to be represented, why not women represent themselves?"[24]

Like many nineteenth-century suffragists, Mormon women also rooted their claims to suffrage in women's essential virtue, contending that women's difference from men, their roles as wives and mothers, facilitated woman suffrage. Mormon women lamented the corruption and deceit they found in contemporary politics. Absent women's influence, they contended, men had not behaved well in the political sphere. One incriminating essay declared: "It would almost lead one to think that there was so much intrigue and deceit practised [sic], that men were afraid of exposure, else why are they unwilling that women should mingle in politics?"[25] Mormon women were in consensus that, as a general rule, "the motives of women are purer, their sentiments more refined and elevated than those of men," so women's purity alone "should be sufficient testimony that the right of suffrage ought to be conceded to them."[26] One Mormon woman, Isabella Pratt Walton, for example, argued: "Woman can diffuse the elements of peace and good will that must necessarily benefit any people or nation, and in no way can she do so as efficiently as having a voice in the public weal."[27] Like their sister suffragists in the East, Mormon women firmly believed that women, empowered by the franchise, could and would better serve as guardians of filial and national morality. In fact, after only a few years of woman suffrage in Utah, the *Exponent* hailed its success, claiming in 1874 that "the influence of women in politics is just what its advocates have maintained that it would be, elevating and purifying."[28] For Mormon women, suffrage extended women's natural wifely and motherly virtues to refine the political sphere.

Mormon woman suffragists joined the national woman suffrage movement in arguing that woman suffrage would work not only toward more virtuous politics, but social purity as well. Woman's political voice could eliminate the sexual double standard that held women much more responsible for immoral acts in which both women and men equally participated. Mormon women observed this inequity in the larger American culture: "Faults which are excused in men become crimes when committed by women, for which the supreme court of society finds them guilty and deserving of banishment for life."[29] Suffragists condemned the injustice of the double standard and saw woman's rights, and suffrage in particular, as a remedy. In 1880, Mary Ann Pratt called upon Mormon women to exercise their suffrage against men's immorality in Utah. She urged her sisters, "Raise your voices on high to abolish law that sustains grog-shops and billiard saloons to make drunkards of your husbands, sons and brothers. That make possible, yes lawful, houses of ill-fame, that lead women onward to shame and destruction and screen men from it while women are branded with infamy and total ruin, body and soul."[30] Mormon women believed that, armed with the vote, Mormon and gentile women alike could eliminate the legal structures that permitted men's sexual libertinism.

Mormon women also imagined a special place for the practice of plural marriage in instituting social purity and liberating women from "social disease" (a nineteenth-century euphemism for venereal disease) resulting from men's sinful sexual behavior. As Mormon women understood it, plural marriage paralleled woman suffrage in eliminating licentious sexuality. As Eliza R. Snow conjectured, "Here in Utah, through his servants and handmaidens, [God] is establishing a nucleus of domestic and social purity, confidence and happiness, which will, so far as its influence extends, eradicate and prevent, in future, all those blighting evils." She further claimed that "God loves purity, and he has introduced the principle of plurality of wives to restore and preserve the chastity of woman."[31] Like many Mormon women and men, Snow reasoned that men with plural wives would not need to look outside their marriages for sexual gratification during one wife's menses, pregnancy, or simple disinterest. For Mormons, polygamy enveloped men's presumed greater sexual drive into a divine plan that mitigated the social effects of male licentiousness and held men accountable for their presumed greater sexual propensities. In purifying the local and eventually the national community, redeeming women from prostitution, social disease, and poverty, plural marriage and woman suffrage served the same purpose.

In this sense Mormon women moved past the claims of their counterparts and cast plural marriage, like suffrage, as a woman's right in and of itself. They linked marital and political rights together, arguing that polygamy created marital equality between men and women, thus facilitating women's political equality. Mormon women contended that the power American men exercised in politics extended into the monogamous marital economy, undercutting women's marital rights. Mormon women claimed that "above all [woman] should enjoy the right to a home and a husband, to have a voice in the choice of the man with whom she unites her destinies."[32] Under monogamy "the supply of husbands falls so far short of the demand" that men selected freely from a broad pool of single women. Monogamy, Mormon women contended, denied women their most sacred rights to marriage and motherhood if men deemed them undesirable. One Mormon woman claimed that according to the U.S. census "seven hundred and fifty thousand women . . . must, unless they migrate to Utah, be debarred from this mansion of happiness."[33] A woman lucky enough to marry, despite unfavorable odds, too often married the first man who proposed, no matter how unworthy, subjecting her to the tyranny of a bad husband.[34]

Plural marriage, on the other hand, expanded the right to be wives and mothers to all women, not just those able to ensnare a man with youthful charms. Moreover, plural marriage shifted significant power in the marital economy from man to woman, giving her more voice in selecting the mate to whom she would tie her eternal fortunes.[35] Mormon women argued that while traditional marriage often subjected woman to the tyranny of unworthy men, "plural marriage . . . is the beginning of her freedom; it is the door of her emancipation from slavery to man."[36] It allowed every woman, even the least desirable, to select her mate from the whole array of men in the community: "An unmarried woman may fall in love with and marry whom she pleases, whether he has a wife or not."[37] Plural marriage liberated younger and older women alike to weigh their marital options carefully, select their mates more deliberately, and demand the best from men.[38] Mormon women hoped that all American women "will claim the freedom of choosing and marrying honorable husbands who will not be ashamed to own them before the world as wives, though they may have a plural number."[39] Selecting a worthy mate was a fundamental right that monogamy, in Mormon women's estimations, could not provide.

The radicalism of Mormon women's citizenship claims can only be seen clearly against the backdrop of American legal and cultural understandings of women's relationship to the body politic. Marriage laws and legal definitions shaped American citizenship status from its earliest origins. Key among these was the legal doctrine of marital unity, namely, that a man and woman constituted a single entity before the law, an entity represented by the husband. Thus until mid-century, under coverture, a husband assumed ownership of the couple's private property upon marriage and represented the couple and their children through his citizenship in the public realm.[40] In this sense, coverture was at once both a civic and a material concept, and marriage both a civic and material contract. Between 1839 and 1895, several states passed laws collectively known as the Married Women's Property Acts. Although they varied by state, these Acts allowed women to maintain ownership over property they brought into marriage, inherit property independently of their husbands, and sometimes even keep any wages earned while in the marriage. The Acts thus posed legal challenges to coverture. However, most historians contend that the statutes were designed primarily to protect estates from seizure for the payment of debts and also to insure wives against the expenditures of improvident sons and sons-in-law. Moreover, the legal flexibility of the construct of marital unity blunted antebellum feminists' attacks on coverture.[41] While the Acts had potential to dismantle aspects of coverture, as Norma Basch argues, "basic elements of that patriarchal construct [coverture] underpinned all of Anglo-American domestic relations law, and they continued to exist long after the enactments of the Married Women's Property Acts."[42]

After the Civil War, "the [U.S. Supreme] court bound women ever more securely to the family, restructuring and revamping the familiar elements of coverture even while state and territorial laws in the nineteenth century were granting women greater property and voting rights."[43] In 1875, the U.S. Supreme Court clarified that women were part of the "persons [who] originally associated themselves together to form the nation, and [who] were afterwards admitted to membership." However, national belonging did not necessarily entail the right to vote.[44] At federal levels, women were left to rely on their husbands for political representation. Furthermore, legal constructs had social ramifications. As Basch points out, "Non-lawyers construed the legal fiction not as a specific legal device, but as a broad metaphor for relations between the sexes."[45] That is, a husband and wife *should* function as though they were one public person, and that person was the husband. Both legally and conceptually, in nineteenth-century America, women's citizenship existed primarily in and through marriage.

Mormon women expressed deep concern for single women under the system of coverture held in place by monogamous marriage. Emmeline B. Wells perhaps expressed Mormon women's concerns best: "There are thousands of women who never have the opportunity of proving whether they possess domestic worth; they have no fireside to sit by, no table to preside over, and no husband to provide them with the shelter of a home. . . . If woman cannot radiate beyond the domestic sphere, then thousands are created for no purpose whatever."[46] The logic of coverture, Mormon women argued, left single women without purpose, making them utterly dependent upon marriage in a system that left many women without access to marriage.

While plural marriage marked Mormon women's spiritual unity with and subordination to men's priesthood, it established no necessary legal or economic unity or subordination. Until the 1890s, dual marriage systems operated separately throughout territorial Utah, one under civil law and one under Church jurisdiction. For Mormons, marriage was a religious covenant and only tangentially and sometimes a civil contract between husband and wife. Some marriages in Utah were only legal contracts, others solely religious contracts, and still others both.[47] A husband, then, could not legally "cover" a wife with whom he did not have a legal contract, so the legal and economic obligations between husband and wife did not take effect in every marriage.

Mormons, however, replaced the legal obligations of coverture with religious codes that unified husbands and wives under God but displaced marriage from its central role in defining women's political status in relationship to American law. In sidestepping the legal structure of coverture, Mormon marriage facilitated an understanding of woman in independent relationship to the state unmitigated by marriage or husband. While the legal status of women in plural marriage remained ambiguous under federal law, plural wives for the time being operated legally as single women. Unfettered by a concept of marriage that cast husband and wife as a legal unity, Mormon women, almost by default, could be understood as men's equals in the public sphere. Mormons, especially the women, simply rejected coverture both as a metaphor for relations between women and men and as a legal concept.

Mormon women's rejection of coverture rested upon a polygamous communitarian ethos that rejected the discourse of separate spheres that linked women to the private and men to the public. Mormon women argued that despite the best efforts of Victorian Americans to separate the sexes each into her or his domain, woman "never can form nor have a world of her own, where 'horrid man' will not be found."[48] Or to state it without the barb, "Men and women were not made to dwell separate, but in the society of each other."[49] One article in the *Exponent* specifically attacked the language of separate spheres, declaring, "We have long heard the man's sphere is the world; woman's is home. But women have a part in the world, while men are not ciphers in the home circle."[50] By and large ignoring their ecclesiastical inequality, Mormon women contended that, at least in temporal affairs, "woman should be side by side, a co-worker with, and helpmate for man. They belong to the same great family and their interests are identical and mutual."[51]

Eliza R. Snow, expressing the sentiments of more moderate Mormon woman's suffragists, reflected that "to think of a war of sexes which the woman's rights movement would inevitably inaugurate . . . creates an involuntary shudder."[52] While Snow's cautious endorsement of Mormon woman suffrage steered away from the more defiant language of the woman's rights movement, other Mormon women followed Sarah Kimball when she declared herself a "woman's rights woman" in 1870.[53] However, the differences in language between these two women and others like them were more a matter of tone than substance. Despite women's ecclesiastical subordination, matters were different in the family of God where, as Hannah T. King explained, "Man is the brother of woman, her co-partner; she is his sister, and they must be co-operatives in the grand business" of God's work.[54] For Mormon women, suffrage facilitated that partnership.

Central to Mormon women's rejection of separate spheres was a notion of the positive influence of the sexes upon each other. One writer suggested, for example, that "men who are habitually associated with women of refined natures, are themselves superior to other men. They lose their rude, declamatory and pedantic ways, and become more chivalric, courtly and elegant in mind and heart, as in manner and dress. The woman, too, who becomes accustomed to the society of educated, honorable men, so that she is at ease and enjoys freedom of thought and speech in such associations, becomes also superior to her sex in general."[55] For Mormons, a community that refused the separation of women's sphere from men's, in which the sexes labored together in household, community, and polity as one, elevated both sexes. By extension, a community that facilitated women's participation with men in political life produced better citizens of both women and men and so, in the long term, better government. Mormon woman suffragists contended, "That is always highest, best and most complete in which man and woman both participate, and the highest political and general good will be attained when men and women work harmoniously for the interest of the human family; politically as well as morally, socially and religiously."[56] Women's participation alongside men in the public sphere served God's purpose not only in perfecting Zion, but also in perfecting politics among humanity at large.

Mormon women also argued that polygamy, more than monogamy, facilitated civic equality between men and women. Mormon women lodged indignant and sometimes mocking critiques of the ways monogamous marriage confined women to the private sphere. In the East, woman's rights advocates like Elizabeth Cady Stanton, Lucy Stone, and Victoria Woodhull equated marriage with slavery, contending that marriage denied women the basic rights of property and self-ownership.[57] Mormon women voiced similar critiques of traditional monogamy but added more specific censures in regard to woman's personal development in marriage. In traditional marriage woman was confined to the household, destined to become "simply a necessity in his [man's] establishment, to manage his house, to cook his dinner, to attend to his wardrobe, always on hand if she is wanted and always out of sight when not needed."[58] Mormon woman suffragists claimed that monogamy made most American women "[d]omestic drudges, ignorant, low and vulgar.... They have no opinions, they are not in possession of intelligence, isolated and kept in subjection, required to fulfill only menial relations even in marriage."[59] Perhaps Mormonism's most vocal critic of monogamy, Emmeline B. Wells, chided American women: "Is there nothing worth living for, but to be petted, humored and caressed by a man? That is all very well as far as it goes, but that man is the only thing in existence worth living for I fail to see. All honor and reverence to good men; but they and their attentions are not the only sources of happiness on the earth, and need not fill up the every thought of women."[60] Under polygamy, however, woman broadened her sphere. "When woman's highest incentive is to attain to the most superior excellence in the disciplining and refining of the faculties of the soul," and not merely to marry a man, then and only then was she fully developed.[61] In other words, only in removing marriage from the centrality of women's lives did women become full persons qualified both to vote and to marry.

Moreover, Mormon women claimed that polygamy, much more than monogamy, facilitated women's equality and freedom. Wells contended, "Plural marriage makes woman more the companion and much less the subordinate than any other form of marriage."[62] Mormon women also believed that the "peculiar exigencies, and experiences of Mormon life have had a tendency to make women self-helpful, and self-reliant, and have given them indomitable energy, and undaunted courage."[63] Polygamist Helen Mar Whitney declared that she "could say truly that [polygamy] had done the most towards making me a Saint and a free woman in every sense of the word . . . it has proven one of the greatest boons—a blessing in disguise."[64] Running households more often absent male leadership than not, many Mormon women exercised broad decision-making power on behalf of themselves and their children. In requiring her broad contributions, "Celestial marriage . . . does not narrow, but widens woman's field for usefulness."[65] Because of this wider scope, Mormon women argued, they were better suited to political equality than other American women.

As Mormons understood it, polygamy also opened at a practical level the compatibility of women's domestic duties with their capacity for a public life. Like most Victorians, Mormons believed a woman's first responsibility was to her home and family. Eliza R. Snow explained, however, that although "the care of the children is a mother's first duty . . . it is not *all* her duty."[66] The women of Zion were bound to "find time for social duties because these are incumbent upon us."[67] For many women, their association with networks of sister-wives freed time for pursuing social and political activities. Polygamy consolidated domestic work, freeing wives to occupy their minds with other pursuits, giving "women more time for thought, for mental culture, more freedom of action, [and] a broader field of labor."[68] Indeed, according to one *Exponent* article, "In no other marriage covenant is there such perfect freedom for woman to pursue any pursuit or avocation she may choose."[69] In this sense, polygamy trained women for a sphere of influence outside the home; Mormon women framed their suffrage as the legal recognition of what they were already doing under polygamy.

One important piece of what Mormon women were already doing, and had always done, was owning property. Until 1872, Utah had no formal laws regulating women's right to own property. Prior to 1872, to the extent that Mormons acknowledged property ownership at all, they acknowledged women's property ownership equally with men's. Even legally married Mormon women owned property de facto, in the absence of any explicit territorial law prohibiting them to do so. In 1872, the Utah Legislature passed an act that decreed that "all property owned by either spouse before marriage, and that acquired afterward by gift, bequest, devise or descent, with the rents, issues and profits thereof, is the separate property of that spouse by whom the same is so owned or acquired." Besides declaring each spouse an independent agent of her or his property, the law also stated: "Either spouse may sue or be sued, plead or be impleaded, or defend and be defended at law."[70] Hence, as one woman exclaimed in the *Exponent*, "In Utah, woman holds her own property—her husband cannot touch it."[71] Moreover, Mormons also believed that women, single and married alike, "should have the right to work, and receive fair pay for it."[72] Young's economic vision, especially after 1869, combined with the discretionary time opened up by domestic cooperation among wives, meant that Mormon women often did work outside the home and kept their own wages.

As chapter 2 showed, Mormon notions of property ownership must be understood in the context of the law of consecration. In the strictest sense of Mormon theology, no one could be said to own anything at all; all property belonged to God, and individuals only managed it on His and the community's behalf. While Mormons behaved in the national polity as property owners, theology demanded that they see themselves as stewards of God's property. In this sense, consecration led Mormon women to understand themselves to be as equally divested of property ownership in God's kingdom as men, but also equal to men as stewards of God's goods on behalf of His Church. Mormonism opened up possibilities for women's material equality with men, both in the legal right to own property and in the spiritual surrender of it to the community.

For Mormon women, the equation between women's property ownership and woman suffrage rested on a rather simple maxim familiar to most Americans. Because woman, like man, paid taxes on her property, "she should enjoy representation with taxation."[73] In short, Mormon women by virtue of paying taxes deserved to vote. They also needed full citizenship to safeguard their property. The removal in Utah of marriage's legal and economic functions required woman's full membership in the American civil polity to protect her property interests.

Mormon women were explicit in their rejections of the material as well as civic implications of coverture. This was especially true in the early 1880s when controversy surfaced over Mormon women's right of dower. American law under coverture protected a woman's livelihood under her right of dower in the event of her husband's death. Dower entitled a woman to use a portion of her husband's estate to sustain her livelihood until the end of her life. In 1872, the Territorial Property Act officially did away with the right of dower in Utah, and anti-polygamists interpreted that law to be another repression of woman under polygamy. Senator Samuel Hoar claimed in 1884 that Mormons dissolved the dower in order to "give the husband the power to punish the wife for disobedience, by depriving her of a home and of the means and support."[74] Government official Shuyler Colfax agreed, contending that the Utah Legislature abolished the right of dower "so as to render a polygamous wife slavishly dependent on a husband's favor for any share of his property after his death."[75] Mormon women, however, declared that the repeal of the right of dower represented their equality, not their subordination. They reasoned, "In regard to the right of dower . . . it is only fair to state that women in Utah are citizens equally with men." They owned their own property which, to them, "removes the necessity of the right of dower."[76] In an unequivocal rejection of coverture, they contended that "the right of dower is no more nor less than a sort of vassalage, and a relic of that old common law of England."[77] To Mormon women, the dissolution of the right of dower showed Utah's and the Mormon Church's commitment to woman's equality. This perspective on the right of dower reflected their broader critique of coverture and the marriage system that sustained it.

From when Mormon women received the suffrage in 1870 until the end of the decade, they linked citizenship to the practice of plural marriage, expounding the advantages of both practices for the rest of the nation. In 1879, the Mormons lost a high profile Supreme Court case, *Reynolds v. United States*, that upheld the constitutionality of the Morrill Act criminalizing plural marriage. This ruling opened the door for Congress to pass the Edmunds Act in 1882, which put legal teeth into the Morrill Act and made plural marriage easier to prosecute. These two developments quickly altered the ways Mormon women formulated the relationship between woman suffrage and plural marriage.

Divorcing Woman Suffrage from Plural Marriage

While Mormon women continued to defend both plural marriage and woman suffrage, after 1879 they dissolved the ties between polygamy and suffrage that they had spent the previous decade forming. Mormon women increasingly espoused plural marriage and woman suffrage separately, connecting each to the preservation of the spirit of republicanism in America but not to each other. So complete was the separation of polygamy and woman suffrage that by 1883, Mormon women could declare, "Plural marriage does not enter into the question [of woman suffrage] at all."[78] They increasingly defended plural marriage less on the basis of its merits as a social system and its benefits for women and more in the name of religious freedom. At the same time, they increasingly defended woman suffrage less on the basis of what it could do for the state and for women and more on abstract republican principles of justice, equality, and civil rights. In the wake of increased anti-polygamy activism, this shift in emphasis tempered the radicalism of Mormonism's marital and communitarian ideas in an attempt to make Mormon women's suffrage claims more appealing to a hostile American public.

After 1879, Mormon women's defenses of both woman suffrage and polygamy increasingly relied on the symbolic value of the essential Americanness of the Mormon community. The ideas Mormon women mobilized after 1879 in support of suffrage were not entirely novel. Many of them had first been expounded in the Great Indignation Meeting of January 1870, a meeting held in opposition to anti-polygamy legislation. At that meeting, Mormon women linked themselves to American legacies, claiming, for example, as an impassioned Mrs. Miner did, that "my *chef-d'oeuvre* of womanly excellence has ever been those noble women of the Revolution who . . . laid their hearts, as it were, on the altar of their country by cheering and encouraging their fathers, brothers, husbands, and sons to battle, even to the death, for civil and religious liberty." Miner asked Congress, "Will you deny to us, the descendants of the Pilgrim fathers, the rights for which they forsook honors and wealth in their native land and endured the hardships of pioneer life?"[79] Linking anti-polygamy sentiment to the persecution that drove Puritans to settle the New World, Miner linked polygamy to the legacy of religious freedom that drove the settlement of America.

Between 1879 and 1890, Mormon women increasingly built on claims of this nature and established political credibility less by asserting the advantages of plural marriage to women's citizenship and more by linking both to two powerful American legacies: the Pilgrims who left England in the interest of religious freedom and the "patriots of 1776" who had fought and died to protect political equality and liberty of conscience. One woman pointed out, for example, that "Mormon women pioneers were most of them from the Eastern States. They were women of intelligence and endurance, with strong religious convictions like their foremothers and fathers, the pilgrims."[80]

In 1886, Mormon women held another mass meeting to protest the "indignities and insults heaped upon the wives and daughters of 'Mormons,' . . . and also against the proposed disenfranchisement of those of their sex who are innocent of breaking any law."[81] Nowhere was Mormon women's investment in the symbolic value of their own Americanness more evident than at this meeting. One speaker, Hannah Grover, presented her protest "as an American citizen, who count[s] my forefathers among the pilgrims who landed on Plymouth Rock."[82] Nearly every speaker at the meeting called upon an American family legacy to establish her credentials. Presendia L. Kimball established her credibility as a citizen by saying, "My grandfather fought in the revolutionary war to establish a free government on this continent, and my father fought in the war of 1812 to secure and perpetuate a free government and to protect the rights and liberties of the citizens of the republic."[83] Sarah D. Rich proclaimed herself "a descendent of men who imperiled their lives and fought in the revolutionary war. My ancestors helped to obtain those inestimable rights given by the Constitution—a God-given and God-inspired document."[84] For Mormon women, Mormonism continued the legacy of American forefathers seeking religious freedom. Under the Church's tutelage, one Mormon woman "learned to love the Stars and Stripes and honor the Constitution, which guaranteed to all 'life, liberty and the pursuit of happiness, and to every creed the right to worship God according to the dictates of conscience.' These ideas are indelibly stamped upon my soul."[85] After 1880, it was not as women made independent by plural marriage but as "members of that great commonwealth which our noble grandsires fought and bled to establish" that Mormon women asserted their political clout.[86]

Mormon women complemented this argument by imagining themselves recapitulating the drama of America's origins, with Mormons playing the part of the beleaguered settlers seeking freedom of religion and the U.S. government in the role of the tyrannical British. They pointed out that women had participated alongside men in the colonization of the West:

> Honest toil and preservation through every trial and difficulty has raised [Utah] to the position she now acquires as one of the most thriving territories in the Union. And is this the work of men alone? Not by any means. Women's courage, skill and labor have been here; woman's consolation and encouragement in the hours of sorrow and disappointment; woman's heroism and devotion in time of danger and death; her tenderness and love; her happiness and smiles when success crowned her labors. . . . Should she then not join with him in making and sustaining the laws of the country; of his country; of her country?[87]

It was as a new generation of American colonists that Mormon women resisted federal officials whose "business is to make laws that will disfranchise the very men and women who have spent their lives in building up the country and making an oasis in the desert."[88] For Mormon women, it was also as a new generation of American colonists that Mormons sought refuge from religious persecution. Like their leaders, Mormon women maintained that plural marriage was a religious issue.[89] Mormon women contended that while Mormons expanded America's legacy into the untamed West, the "spirit is prevailing in the hearts of some of the senators and representatives to destroy the original letter and meaning of the Constitution, which is more sacred and dear to every American citizen than life itself."[90] Anti-polygamy legislation violated the very legacy of republicanism that Mormons had carried into the American West. Mormon women protested "against the oppression of those who would take [f]rom us the rights and liberties which our fathers risked their lives to obtain."[91] One woman even went so far as to predict: "The names of those who voted for this infamous bill, [the Edmunds Act] will I believe yet be classed with such men as Benedict Arnold and those who have proved themselves traitors to their country."[92] Eliza R. Snow called anti-polygamy legislation "a disgrace to men in responsible stations" and accused their sponsors of "tear[ing] the Constitution to shreds" and "sapping the foundation of American freedom."[93] Mormon women asked in desperation, "[W]here is the spirit of 76? Where is the spirit of a Washington? where! oh where! is the spirit that animated the framers of the glorious Constitution of America?"[94] Anti-polygamy legislation had, in Mormon women's estimation, betrayed a central principle of American republicanism—freedom of religion.

As Mormon women saw it, the oppression of the Mormons was manifest not only in the repression of Mormons' religious liberties but also in the attempts to disenfranchise Mormon women. Mormon women pointed out that the "chains of tyranny were to be welded closer by taking from the women of Utah the ballot, which they had never used but in the promotion of honor, virtue, and good for all."[95] They insisted that the disenfranchisement of any American citizen, irrespective of that individual's marital practices, betrayed the principles of republicanism. Mormonism, on the other hand, preserved republicanism against an anti-American federal government by representing religious freedom and advocating women's civic equality. One Mormon woman alleged "that the Church of Jesus Christ of Latter-day Saints proclaims the greatest freedom and broadest charity for woman. She is regarded as man's equal."[96] Mormon women made these claims in the wake of an unprecedented legislative campaign against polygamy that repeatedly threatened to disenfranchise Mormon women.

In 1887, Congress made good on that threat; the Edmunds-Tucker Act disenfranchised all women in Utah—Mormon and non-Mormon, single, monogamous, and plurally married alike. In response, after seventeen years at the polls, Mormon women formalized and for the first time institutionalized their advocacy of woman suffrage. In January 1889, Utah women formed the Woman Suffrage Association of Utah, and within four months of its initial meeting, the WSAU had fourteen branches across the state. Over the next several years, Mormon women continued to extol the virtues of woman suffrage, divorced from plural marriage and rooted in the republican principles of equality and representative government. In 1896, six years after the Church officially discontinued plural marriage with the Woodruff Manifesto, Utah became a state with a state constitution that permanently enfranchised women.[97]

The relative ease with which Mormon women initially received the suffrage in 1870 bespeaks the ways that women in Mormondom enjoyed many civic and political equalities alongside their husbands. Despite their nearly total lack of ecclesiastical power, during the 1870s and 1880s Mormon women probably carried more economic and political clout in their community than most of their American sisters had in the rest of the nation. Ironically, through polygamy, women's ecclesiastical subordination gave rise to their political equality; Mormon women, second to receive the franchise, were the first American women to exercise it.

• • •

In the instance of woman suffrage, as in nearly every other instance, Mormons' self-conception and their conception of their millennial mission differed sharply from beliefs about Mormonism emerging from middle-class Americans. While Mormons saw themselves as quintessentially American, anti-Mormons found the practice of polygamy to be diametrically opposed to American citizenship. Where Mormons saw woman's equality in plural marriage, anti-Mormons saw only her slavery; where Mormons saw ordered cooperation and directed consensus, Americans saw polygamic theocracy; where Mormons saw divine purpose, Americans saw disloyalty and treason. These variances launched an enormous anti-Mormon movement that, over the course of the late nineteenth century, produced hundreds of volumes of discourse that communicated the meaning of the Mormon question for the nation at large. Mormon citizenship claims profoundly disturbed anti-polygamy activists, and the Mormon question evolved into both a strategy to assert dominance over national culture and a strategy to rid the nation of polygamy and its challenge to the crucially important categories of public and private.

"The Utter Destruction
of the Home Circle"

Polygamy and the Perversion
of the Private Sphere

The ways that Mormon marriage systems undermined the public/private divide were not lost on the rest of the nation. In response to the Mormon challenge, a phalanx of domestic novels, exposés, travel narratives, cartoons, magazine articles, political treatises, and other anti-Mormon writings assaulted the practice of polygamy in a campaign to safeguard that divide. This chapter examines how and in what ways anti-Mormon literature held in place their particular vision of the sanctity of the private sphere, an ideal anti-Mormons thought to be central to American national culture. White middle-class Americans mostly from the North produced volumes of anti-Mormon literature that asserted a middle-class identity rooted in a culture of private sentimentality separated from the public world.[1] Anti-Mormon literature worked to entrench the categories of public and private in the nineteenth-century imagination chiefly by depicting Mormon households as cautionary tales, showing the domestic chaos and political tyranny anti-Mormons believed ensued when Americans betrayed their most treasured ideals.

Projections of proper domestic life along with the configurations of gender and public and private that accompanied them were central to nineteenth-century expansionist nation building.[2] Especially in the mid-nineteenth century, in the wake of challenges from many directions, marriage became a kind of lightning rod that attracted debates about who exactly constituted "the people." This was particularly true in the contexts of westward expansion, Reconstruction, and immigration, as conflicts erupted over the citizenship status of former slave families as well as American Indian, Chicano/a, and Asian families.[3] In the late nineteenth century, the private family unit constituted by monogamous marriage became a central mechanism through which difference was to be either assimilated into the nation or barred from it. Lengthy debates about proper marriage and family configurations articulated the white middle-class assumption that only certain kinds of families could legitimately give rise to American citizens. Americans crafted an increasingly complex body of domestic law to establish their vision of the private sphere.[4] Deviation from a white, single-household, Christian, monogamous family model could variously and categorically disqualify the head of a deviant family from the rights and privileges of full citizenship.[5] Campaigns against Mormonism were an important piece of the attempt to homogenize family structure around heterosexual monogamy and the ideology of separate spheres and place it at the core of national identity.

A variety of white middle-class Americans produced anti-Mormon literature for a variety of reasons. The economics of the print industry motivated much nineteenth-century anti-Mormon literature. Novelists, pulp writers, and travelers to Utah sought to sell copy and cash in on the libidinous potential of plural marriage and sexuality in the West. Other more serious concerns generally accompanied economic motivations. Some producers of anti-Mormon literature, for instance, were active in campaigns for the federalization of marriage law. The Mormon question provided a case study to illustrate why an institution as important to the nation as marriage should be wrested from local control and placed under federal purview. Other writers were motivated by a desire to protect women's virtue from the deleterious effects of industrial and social upheaval.[6] For these constituents, campaigns against plural marriage served as a means by which to assert moral authority. Political concerns motivated still other anti-Mormons who saw Mormonism as a political theocracy upheld by polygamy that would open the door, beginning at the state level, to political despotism. Former Utah government officials led this campaign by publishing anti-Mormon tracts and exposés that linked polygamy with theocracy and urged political reform in Utah. No matter their specific cause, nearly all anti-Mormons identified plural marriage as central to the trouble with Mormonism, and nearly all rooted their criticisms of the Mormons in the inappropriate practice of private and public life.

The Origins of Anti-Polygamy

Anti-Mormonism did not begin with Orson Pratt's 1852 announcement of the practice of polygamy. Rather, it emerged almost coterminously with the

Church itself. From the 1830s until the mid-1850s, most anti-Mormon literature focused on four central issues: the validity of Joseph Smith as a prophet, the authenticity of the *Book of Mormon*, the practice of plural marriage, and the secrecy of Mormon temple ordinances. All four themes, as the titles of early anti-Mormon tracts indicate, served both to prove Mormonism as a fraud and to warn an American public of religious deceit and imposture. With titles and subtitles like *Delusions, Mormonism Unvailed [sic]; or A Faithful Account of that Singular Imposition and Delusion, Mormonism Dissected*, and *Knavery Exposed*, early anti-Mormon tracts claimed to be "Disclosing the Depths of Mormon Villainy Practiced in Nauvoo."[7] These early works established a long-standing trend in anti-Mormonism of which later anti-Mormons made much use: a fundamental conviction that among the Mormons all was not as it seemed.[8]

Before 1852, discussions of plural marriage in anti-Mormon literature were largely limited to apostate anti-Mormons such as John C. Bennett who had been privately aware of the practice before defecting from the Church. During the 1840s, anti-Mormon publications from former members censured polygamy first and foremost as an indication of Smith's and other Church officials' personal immorality, surely disqualifying them as agents of God.[9] Bennett, for instance, left the Church in 1842 and published *The History of the Saints; or, An Exposé of Joe Smith and Mormonism*. In it, he described a secret "Mormon Seraglio" of Mormon women whose sole purpose was to engage in intercourse with Mormon officials.[10] He charged that "these poor, deluded females, while incited by their very religion (if it deserves that name) to indulgence in the most degrading passions, have their consciences soothed, and their scruples appeased" by the sanction of the Prophet.[11] Bennett claimed that the central purpose of "spiritual wifery" was to appease the vast sexual depravity of Mormon officials.[12]

Among anti-Mormons with no Church affiliation, the few who accused the Mormons of practicing polygamy demonstrated special concern with the secrecy of the practice and its connection to other clandestine aspects of the Mormon faith. Early anti-Mormons reasoned that a religion shrouded so much in secrecy must be inherently deceitful and immoral. This literature focused particularly on Joseph Smith's doctrinal innovations in Nauvoo and the concurrent development of Mormon temple practices. Early Mormon temple practices centered around the "endowment" ceremony, which conferred upon its benefactors blessings and "keys" to the kingdom of Heaven in exchange for covenants of obedience, righteousness, and secrecy.[13]

Secrecy is tantalizing, and early anti-Mormons were quite taken with the prospect of uncovering the truth about goings on in the Nauvoo temple.[14] Disclosing the content and meaning of temple ordinances often signaled a person's departure from the fold. Catherine Lewis's 1848 exposé, *Narrative of Some of the Proceedings of the Mormons*, for example, offered an account of her conversion to Mormonism and subsequent disenchantment with the doctrine of plural marriage. After her conversion, Lewis had gone to Nauvoo, where she claimed Church authorities and their wives constantly pressured her to select a mate whose plural wife she would become. Upon entering the temple, Lewis claimed, she had agreed to participate in the endowment ceremony but not to marry. Yet when she reached the end of the ceremony, Mormon authorities told her that the endowment required Lewis's marriage to one of them. Church leaders apparently presented themselves to her and commanded her to select one of them. She refused, and, by her account, her departure from the temple marked her departure from Mormonism as well.[15]

Lewis's pamphlet was among the first to directly link temple practices to polygamy and condemn it within a larger paradigm: the problem of Mormon secrecy. Historian David Brion Davis succinctly outlined the logic of this aspect of early anti-Mormonism: "In a virtuous republic, why should anyone fear publicity or desire to conceal activities, unless those activities were somehow contrary to the public interest?"[16] Lewis's narrative claimed that the function of the secret endowment—indeed the purpose of the temple itself—was to support and extend the many clandestine practices of the Church, especially plural marriage.

Another factor animating the early anti-polygamy sentiment of the 1840s and 1850s was mid-century nativism, especially directed against Irish Catholics.[17] Increasing numbers of immigrants flowing into the nation gave rise to nativist campaigns which defined the nation as a white and Protestant entity and demanded assimilation to white, Anglo-Saxon Protestant norms. Nativists perceived in both Catholicism and Mormonism not only religious heresy but a troubling centralization of religious authority. Moreover, as literary historian Terryl Givens shows, linking Mormons to an already-existing anti-Catholic tradition enabled anti-Mormons to utilize stock themes familiar to American readers.[18] Early anti-Catholic literature represented nunneries as houses of prostitution that kept the sexual services of their inmates available for the pleasure of Irish Catholic priests.[19] These images easily translated into Mormon terms, since Mormons were also rumored to keep secret stashes of women available for Joseph Smith's, and later Brigham Young's, consumption.

Equally powerful were similarities between Catholic and Mormon structures of religious authority. Anti-Catholics suggested that Catholic loyalty to the Pope precluded any loyalty Irish Catholics might have to the United States. Early anti-Mormons argued that, like Catholics to the Pope, Mormons proclaimed undying loyalty to Joseph Smith, compromising their allegiance as American citizens.[20] (It did not help, of course, that early Mormon temple ceremonies following Smith's death were rumored to contain an oath swearing vengeance on the United States for the prophet's murder.[21]) References to Joseph Smith as a "Mormon pope" abounded during those decades, and the image persisted into later nineteenth-century characterizations of Brigham Young.

After Pratt's 1852 public announcement, the market for anti-Mormon publications exploded. Anti-Mormon literature became increasingly sophisticated and its tone fundamentally changed. Visitors to Utah recorded lengthy observations on the implications of polygamy for Mormon women and society, simultaneously formulating and deploring the ways the practice of polygamy flew in the face of American republicanism. Trends and themes established in earlier anti-Mormonism—the duplicity and imposture of Church leaders, the inaccuracy of the *Book of Mormon*, and Mormonism's penchant for secrecy— all remained part and parcel of anti-Mormonism but were brought under and into the service of larger rubrics that placed plural marriage at the hub of the Mormon question, the problem from which all others flowed.[22]

Terryl Givens points out that anti-polygamy domestic fiction emerged alongside a mushrooming of print industries in the nineteenth century. He argues that "the proliferation of the printed word meant a corresponding proliferation of types, categories, and genres."[23] Buoyed by the abundance of genres and print outlets, anti-Mormon discourse spread across virtually all of print culture and genres, and texts borrowed heavily from each other. The resulting "anarchy of discursive forms" encouraged the spread of anti-Mormonism across print culture."[24]

While the coupling of anti-Mormonism with anti-polygamy began in domestic fiction, it quickly spread to other genres of print and oral culture so rapidly as to become a familiar topic to most, if not all Americans. From 1855 through the 1870s, travel narratives increasingly accompanied anti-polygamy domestic literature on booksellers' shelves. These writings built upon the degradations of women that anti-polygamy novels depicted, drawing even more expansive conclusions about the implications of plural marriage for romantic love and for Mormon home and family life. Anti-Mormon literature of all sorts increased in volume as it populated the conceptual landscape with objection after objection to show an American public that Mormonism betrayed the female sex and subverted the domestic sphere.

Mormon Polygamy in Domestic Fiction

It is no surprise that the new surge of anti-Mormon sentiment specifically targeting polygamy began in domestic literature. As several scholars have contended, the nineteenth-century tales of sentiment in the domestic realm offered the reading public instructive glimpses into the private sphere, so that they could see how to properly conduct their gender and domestic relations.[25] According to Nancy Armstrong, domestic fiction played a generative role in defining contemporary gender roles among the white middle class. She notes that "the essential self was commonly understood in terms of gender."[26] From Armstrong's perspective, domestic fiction writers persuasively separated masculine authority in the public sphere from feminine authority in the private, and they deployed prescriptive norms of gender identity to shore up women's moral authority in the home.

During the antebellum era, the rise of what Mary Ryan called "the empire of the mother" sanctified women's authority in the domestic sphere. Because women were the imagined "keepers of the intimate and trusting realm of domesticity," their mandate was to govern the domestic sphere and make it a haven of peace and comfort, free from the politics and power that occurred outside it.[27] Of course, women's authority in the home was never total; men exercised authority as head of the household. Historian Colleen McDannell describes the differences between men's and women's authority in the home with biblical metaphors. Fathers' authority functioned like that of an Old Testament God, guiding and ensuring the spiritual direction of his household through "authority, obedience, and fear."[28] In keeping with this biblical formula, the popular Victorian advice writer Catharine E. Beecher referred to a father's authority as "absent," but "ever-present."[29]

In representing the home, domestic fiction upheld the notion that sentiment, the realm of private feeling, could and should be separated from public politics, that femininity could and should be set apart from masculinity, and that a feminine private could and should be disentangled from a masculine public. This is not to say that separate spheres were always inhabited only by a single gender, for men circulated through the private sphere as often as women did the public. Rather, the manufacturers of white middle-class culture believed that the natural proclivities of each gender made woman and man more "at home" in their respective spheres. Victorians understood women to be naturally more sentimental and private, and they imagined men to be naturally more rational, competitive, and public. By divine design, according to an 1869 primer of domestic science coauthored by sisters Catharine E. Beecher and

Harriet Beecher Stowe, women presided as the "chief minister" of the home, "the aptest earthly illustration of the heavenly kingdom."[30] Though historians Armstrong and Ryan perhaps overestimate women's influence, middle-class women did, through print culture, successfully manage to "disentangle the language of sexual relations from the language of power and, in so doing, to introduce a new form of political power" that rested on the rise of nineteenth-century domestic ideology.[31] By articulating how domestic life *should* be, domestic novelists enhanced both their own authority as writers and women's authority over the domestic sphere.

Domestic fiction writers imagined that the private family, with woman as its moral guidepost, established the moral order from which the public state and its citizens emanated. The state, they imagined, rested upon the home, and the home rested on proper relations between the sexes. The true woman was drawn to her opposite, bound by love for him, and found her best and happiest self as a wife and mother. Victorian supporters of domestic ideology believed that good government was built upon the restraint of the chaotic forces of male sexual desire. Only man's pure love for and loyalty to a true woman enabled him to rein in his sexual desire and produce order in the public sphere. Hence, domestic writers regarded men's authority in the public sphere to be dependent on women's complementary authority in the private. Part of the cultural work of nineteenth-century domestic literature was precisely to script in fiction the division between public and private as a social goal, if not norm, and to constitute the private sphere as uniquely feminine. The ways writers showed women characters enacting true womanhood in the private sphere shaped the gendered meaning of the concept in popular culture and attached women more firmly to the private sphere. With the rise of literacy and the availability of cheap print media, through reading, men and women of the middle class came to understand new models of how to love, how to marry, and how to perform the obligations of husband- and wifehood.[32]

In this context, it makes sense that anti-polygamy discourse first emerged within and drew heavily upon the genre of domestic literature. A series of anti-polygamy domestic novels published in the mid-1850s formulated the initial anti-Mormon response to Pratt's 1852 announcement. Totally inaccurate in its representation of Mormonism and the practice of plural marriage, anti-polygamy domestic fiction imagined a Mormonism widely divergent not only from how Mormonism imagined itself, but also from how polygamy was actually practiced. In large part, anti-polygamy novelists based their portrayals more on their own creative projections than any actual observation of or experience with Mormons. Written mainly for white middle-class readers, this early anti-

Mormon literature could press beyond the mere scripting of public and private to vividly demonstrate the dangers of dismantling the divide.

Over the past several years, scholars have pointed to the centrality of four early texts that established the core themes and narrative structures of anti-Mormon domestic literature: Maria Ward's *Female Life Among the Mormons*; Metta Victoria Fuller's *Mormon Wives: A Narrative of Facts Stranger Than Fiction*; Orvilla Belisle's *Mormonism Unveiled* (also printed under the title, *The Prophets; or, Mormonism Unveiled*); and Alfreda Eva Bell's *Boadicea*. Rooted in domestic ideology, each of these books exposed through domestic fiction a similar perspective on the problem with plural marriage.[33] These novels demonstrated to all Americans the degradations that writers imagined polygamy perpetrated upon Mormon women and the "consequent vices which extend through all the ramifications of the society."[34]

Givens points out that the truth claims of anti-Mormon literature must be understood in the context of the "perceived rules governing those particular literary forms in which statements are made."[35] In the nineteenth century, the proliferation of publishing, of newly invented genres, and of audiences all loosened standards of discursive authority. As a result, fiction was almost indistinguishable from autobiography and biography; the novel closely resembled the testimonial; and "religious propaganda, political polemics, and prurient sensationalism mingle[d] freely."[36] Anti-Mormon authors lacked "a sense of themselves *as* a novelist or of their task as being novel writing," and voices of author and character frequently merged. In anti-Mormon literature, truth claims were often "simply confessional," positing a "true confession" of events often of a fictional character who frequently had the same name as and was not easily distinguished from the author.[37]

Such was likely the case, for example, in Maria Ward's *Female Life Among the Mormons*, first published anonymously. The book claimed to be written by "the wife of a Mormon elder, recently from Utah," and an account of the author's actual life later published under the pseudonym "Maria Ward."[38] More likely, the book was a "memoir" of a fictional character that Ward cleverly named after her pseudonym. In either case, the novel illustrates Givens's claim that the anti-Mormon narratives of the 1850s relied heavily on "confessional authority" that could never be taken at its word. Constant errors of fact and theological misapprehensions show that novelists were more interested in what Sarah Barringer Gordon has called "emotional fact" than actual.[39] The emotional truths these novels first articulated would be, over the next forty years, integrated into broad claims about the absence among Mormons of the private sphere.

LIZZIE MONROE IN HER PRISON.—BRIGHAM YOUNG MAKING INSULTING PROPOSALS.

"Lizzie Monroe in Her Prison," first published in Orvilla Belisle, *The Prophets; or, Mormonism Unveiled* (1855), frontispiece. Courtesy of L. Tom Perry Special Collections, Harold B. Lee Library, Brigham Young University, Provo, Utah.

While domestic novels emphasized the domestic realm, all of these narratives placed polygamy at the center of Mormon community and political life. Maria Ward took for granted that polygamy "became the nucleus around which society formed itself, and thus entered at once into all the organizations of domestic and political affairs."[40] Anti-polygamy fiction generally argued that the multiple perceived troubles with Mormons "all relate, more or less, to that abominable system [of plural marriage], which makes the domestic altar a shrine of legal prostitution."[41] The frontispiece of Orvilla Belisle's *The Prophets* shows the heroine, Lizzie Monroe, "in her prison.—Brigham Young making insulting proposals."[42]

Though the characters and subplots varied, all four novels shared central plot lines. Ward's *Female Life* follows the Wards on their journey across the plains to Utah. Along the way, Maria, a non-Mormon married to a convert, meets several Mormon women who confide in her the betrayals of polygamy. Their geographic distance from the East corresponds with their discovery of the "truth" about Mormonism, and Maria, dissuaded by the many stories of betrayal and debauchery she encounters, escapes the grasp of Mormonism only after her husband takes his second wife. Similarly, in Fuller's *Mormon Wives*, readers follow Richard and Margaret, who immigrate to Utah. There Richard takes to wife Margaret's childhood friend, and Margaret consequently dies of a broken heart.

Orvilla Belisle's *Mormonism Unveiled* parallels the many early Mormon migrations with the intrigues of Church authorities. In it, as the Mormons move further west, debauchery increases, until it is finally complete with the murder of one Mormon woman, the abduction of another, and the dashing escape of a few others. Bell's novel, *Boadicea*, was a less complicated story of the betrayal of one woman in plural marriage that placed a special emphasis on the violence that putatively resulted from polygamy. The heroine Boadicea's husband, Bernard Yale (a thin disguise for Brigham Young, according to Sarah Barringer Gordon[43]) takes a second wife, Cephysia. After some time he sees through Mormonism, comes to himself, and plans to escape with his true love, Boadicea. Cephysia murders him in rage, and Boadicea falls ill as a result. She is then kidnapped by another Mormon elder who wishes to marry her, but she escapes by faking her own death.

All four books introduce readers to many heroines who were once "true women" of the most American sort. Belisle's main heroine was the "daughter of one of Massachusetts' most favored sons, one whose ancestors had fled from oppression in the old world . . . and [had] borne with him to the new world all the love of virtue which caused him to forsake a fatherland for a wilderness." Belisle's heroine "had passed to womanhood in an uncontaminated atmosphere, whose every breeze whispered to her ear liberty—freedom—purity."[44] In a similar vein, a heroine in Fuller's *Mormon Wives* is described as formerly "one of the most beautiful of those fair New England maidens who grew up amid the hills and chilly breezes as sweetly and delicately as Alpine roses."[45] True and virtuous women indeed, each heroine took great care in the maintenance of her small piece of the American domestic environment.[46] The heroine of each novel maintained her home as a refuge in which "no trouble could really perplex her, unless it intruded itself within those walls, upon the hearthstone of her home."[47] At the beginning of her marriage, each heroine was a portrait of Victorian wifehood, ensuring the happiness and restfulness of her husband and home.

Initially, husbands in the novels solemnly vow to love only their wives. (Bell's and Ward's central male characters had already converted at the time of marriage but swore never to enter polygamy, while Belisle's and Fuller's characters converted to the faith only after marriage.) Each appeared to be a true and virtuous representative of Victorian manliness, worthy of his wife's devotion. The manly virtue of these husbands at the outset acts as a foil to the depravity of Mormon men, and the husbands' gradual fall into corruption highlights the formidable and inescapable power of Mormon duplicity and licentiousness: a "Mormon, if he acted out the principles of his church, must be hypocritical, sensual, devoid of all conscience, and devilish."[48]

Still, bound by true love and ever faithful to her man, in each of these, each heroine endures the trials and tribulations of frontier life for the happiness of her husband. Content in her faith and trust in her husband, each heroine remains certain that her husband is different from other Mormons in that he "could not so suddenly abandon the holiest and sweetest institution of Christianity and civilization, and all that there is pure and saving in the midst of the selfishness of man: one abiding love, one hearth, one home."[49] However, in Missouri, in Nauvoo, on the journey west, or in Utah, each heroine befriends Mormon wives who had been violated and degraded by polygamy. Heroines watch in vain as Mormon plural wives are emotionally and morally destroyed, fall ill and die, or are murdered.[50] The unfortunate lives of these Mormon women consistently remind heroines—and readers—of the dangers of polygamy to women.

Lest readers believe the Mormon threat innocuous, the narrative of each novel demonstrates the ultimate error of the heroine's dedication to her husband. According to these novelists, the power of Mormonism to convert and corrupt otherwise respectable men lay in both the duplicity of its leaders and the illusory attractiveness of its message. In many cases, as seen in the novels of Belisle and Fuller, the avenue through which non-Mormon husbands converted to Mormonism was the prophet's promise of money and power. In Ward's novel, Joseph Smith promises potential converts, "Let those who are considered fools by their neighbors and relatives come to us—we will make them kings and priests."[51] Belisle's novel suggests that many a conversion of man, particularly overseas, turned upon the promise of power. In Wales, one Mormon tells his duped listeners that "the reign of the aristocrats is passing away.... A prophet among the lowly has arisen who will lead us to possess the high places of our oppressors, who, in turn, shall be brought down to earth, where they have so many ages held us in chains."[52] Belisle's heroine reflects on one husband that "The unhallowed tenets he had espoused had marred the purity of his soul, and tainted the atmosphere around him, while it lulled him with its mystic vapours, made him oblivious to the downward path in which he was fast hastening." Be it by vision, prophetic direction, or lust, each of the novels' husbands succumbs to "the poison that had been working in his heart [which] had blunted the finer sensibilities of his nature."[53] Each took another wife.

The devastation of plural marriage for the many heroines of domestic fiction cannot be overestimated. One of Belisle's heroines goes mad, and another is slain in a domestic quarrel.[54] The heartbreak of polygamy drives Bell's main character into a deep coma.[55] In perhaps the most melodramatic example, driven mad by polygamy, one of Fuller's heroines, Margaret, dies tragically of a broken heart, in essence murdered by her husband's polygamous betrayals.[56] Margaret's death, however, brings about the physical and spiritual rescue of her once dear friend and now sister-wife, Sarah Irving. Sarah declares to herself at Margaret's grave: "You are no true woman, Sarah Irving; you have debased yourself below the level of your sex; you are ashamed to face your own soul—ashamed to go back to the people from whence you came, and you find it impossible to go forward with those you have chosen. Oh, *what can you do*?"[57] Each novel ends with the restoration of true womanhood, either by merciful death or daring escape from Utah. One heroine sneaks off in the dead of night to join passersby, another dresses as an Indian and runs off, and a third hides in a cave. In each novel, true womanhood vindicates itself by rejecting polygamy.

The more popular of these novels were reprinted several times. Perhaps most frequently reissued were Ward's *Female Life Among the Mormons* and Fuller's *Mormon Wives*. Ward's novel sold forty thousand copies in the first year, to be reissued one year later and reissued in English at least nineteen times (sometimes under the title *The Mormon Wife: A Life Story of the Sacrifices, Sorrows and Sufferings of a Woman: A Narrative of Many Years' Personal Experience*), the last edition appearing in 1913.[58] Her book was also translated into at least four other languages. With the exception of Fuller, these novelists left the broader social and political implications of their narratives to their readers. While Fuller's introduction included an impassioned attack on Utah's early campaign for statehood, she stated that her primary agenda was, like her sister novelists,' to show the ways that polygamy enslaved and degraded American women, hoping that her "moral [would] sink deeply in the hearts of the people."[59]

As a whole, writers of anti-polygamy novels designed their narratives to evoke both empathy and outrage at the injustices plural marriage perpetrated on the weaker sex. In the interest of protecting American women from polygamy, novels like these four presented outlandish, dystopic constructions of Mormon women's lives. While many Mormon women in diaries and private writings expressed personal reservations and heartbreaks in connection with plural marriage (and some declared its virtues), Mormon women hardly experienced polygamy as the litany of oppression, violence, enslavement, and degradation that anti-polygamy novelists imagined it to be.[60] Neither were Mormon women the oppressed dupes of their husbands and seducers, nor the lusty prostitutes of Mormon harems, nor the silenced slaves of men's domestic tyranny. Whether or not novelists intended their books to be accurate representations of women's lives, they did intend to uncover, again in Gordon's terms, the "emotional facts" of polygamy and produce shock and indignation at the marital goings-on in Utah.

While these early novelists clearly misrepresented much about Mormon life, their work resonated with an American public because, from the perspective of their readers, the novels exposed a set of larger truths about Mormonism and its danger to the nation's women. Because their purpose was largely sentimental these early novelists left, in many senses, an interpretive void around the broader social and political meaning of the wrongs the Mormons perpetrated upon their women. Over the next twenty-five years, increasing numbers of narratives combined with other forms of anti-Mormonism to erect the discursive structures that buttressed these early sentimental stories with cultural and political meaning.

"The Whole Question of the Family is Wrapped Up in It"[61]

From 1852 to 1890, almost one hundred novels, dozens of book-length memoirs and exposés, and hundreds of magazine and newspaper articles flooded the country.[62] Various magazines reprinted articles broadly, and publishers often collected and reprinted article series in book form. To the reading public, this abundant literature confirmed that the tales early novelists told were not so outlandish as they might have seemed and that affairs in Utah were indeed facts stranger than fiction. At the same time, anti-Mormon literature of other sorts explicated the cultural and political implications of Mormonism in ways that sentimental storytelling could only suggest. While early novels focused on the degradation polygamy perpetrated on the weaker sex, after 1855 anti-Mormon literature broadened its analysis to examine Mormonism's impact more generally on the marriage relationship itself and especially its effect on the private sphere. It was in this literature that anti-Mormon writers clarified why the rest of the nation should care that a relatively isolated outpost of western settlers should engage in iconoclastic marriage practices. "The whole question of the family is wrapped up in it," one alarmed reformer stated. "Polygamy as against the Christian family is the issue presented at the center of American civilization in the near future."[63] Observers of polygamy came increasingly to believe that the offenses polygamy committed against women manifested a broader problem, the complete dissolution of the domestic sphere in Utah.

Anti-Mormons understood the parallel sociopolitical function plural marriage played for Mormons in ensuring loyalty to the polity of God. For Mormons, "the use and foundation of matrimony is to raise up a particular, holy people for the Kingdom of God."[64] The governor of Idaho noted polygamy's role in producing social cohesion and loyalty among the Mormons: "Polygamy is ... urged and made obligatory upon the members of the church for the purpose of binding them more fully to the organization."[65] Even observers who were not necessarily anti-Mormon viewed plural marriage as a kind of proto-nationalist project on the part of Mormons. Richard Burton, for example, commented that "Politically considered, the Mormons deem it [polygamy] necessary to their existence as a people." He further observed that Mormons understood their numbers—as opposed to morality, wealth, learning, civilization, or virtue—to be the strength of their community.[66] In addition to progeny, polygamy produced social cohesion. Mormons and non-Mormons alike agreed that plural marriage bound the community together even as it ensured loyalty to the Church. Anti-Mormons, however, found the cohesive functions of plural marriage in Mormon life disturbing rather than sanctifying.

Also disturbing to anti-Mormons was Mormonism's disregard for romantic love. Anti-Mormons argued that "the soul and mind, the mentality of woman points unerringly to monogamy as her only possible state for domestic happiness."[67] Furthermore, according to one anti-Mormon journalist, "The love of one man for the one woman is the only high and pure type of sexual relations."[68] Polygamy, by contrast, reduced the richness of love in the marital relation to the brute expression of sexuality. In polygamous marriages, women "are the companions of his [the husband's] passions, not his life; panderers of his lusts, instead of being partners of his affections; ... crushing out every dream of girlhood, every wish and every necessity of their deep woman hearts."[69] Under Mormonism, the sexual intimacy intended as an expression of true love "becomes a matter of mechanical employment; and no matter how often the workmen are changed, so long as the article is properly manufactured. The chaste union of two minds in the conjugal relationship becomes thus a thing entirely unknown."[70]

Anti-Mormons understood the implications of Mormon marriage not in terms of devotion to God and His people, a spiritual matter, but in terms of romantic love, a highly charged emotional and sexual matter. Legal historian Sarah Barringer Gordon has pointed out the threat polygamy posed to cherished Victorian beliefs: a "husband's union with another woman in precisely the same relationship [as marriage] would explode the fiction of perfect unity, replacing it with multiplicity and tumbling the intricate structure built on the fantasy."[71] In Ward's novel, one fictional Mormon wife declared that she "ought to have foreseen how all the sweet and familiar confidence of that most endearing relation . . . must be necessarily wanting, where the affections were divided on so many objects."[72] The multiplicity of polygamy rendered impossible the Victorian ideal of a romantic union within marriage of complementary opposites. Anti-Mormons argued that the reciprocity, equality, and love between man and woman in the marriage relation simply could not occur in plurality.[73]

Anti-Mormons also contended that the absence of the union of minds in Mormon marriages prevented Mormons from being part of the confederation of feeling that constituted national belonging. Nineteenth-century Americans deployed what Nancy Bentley calls "sentimental constitutionalism," the notion that attachment to the family not only paralleled but constituted attachment to the nation.[74] According to Bentley, "the struggle over polygamy offers one of the most vivid demonstrations of a reformulation of national identity as an imagined state of feeling."[75] She argues that in anti-polygamy novels, "The truest measure of American-ness . . . proved internal: Whether you belong depends on how you feel."[76] In this formulation, attachment to family constituted national belonging. Anti-Mormons felt that without romantic love, Mormons could in no way engage in the sentimentality and attachment to family that is central to private life, and without attachment, Mormons could not be part of a national culture. "States are made up of families, and can not [*sic*] be strongly compacted where the family is not a unit," anti-Mormons argued, and states "are the most united, enterprising, and efficient for the common good where [the family] is harmonious."[77]

In other words, most middle-class Americans believed that only in a peaceful home could Americans build the affective ties that held them together as a nation. If Mormon households were as consistently beset with violence and disorder as anti-Mormons believed, that failure to produce harmonious households effectively divorced Mormons from national belonging. As one commentator explained, "Polygamy introduces an element of disorder into families, and saps the foundations of social order according to the extent to which it prevails."[78] That a proper home "can ever enter into the disorganizing and heterogeneous dogmas of Mormonism, is too absurd even for contemplation, much less for argument," remarked another.[79] As a result, "the mass of the Mormons will be alike purged of American feelings."[80] According to J. H. Beadle, marriage made of man a member of the national community, "a citizen and a debtor to the public weal."[81] For Beadle, marriage performed a threefold function: it ordered male sexual desire, provided man with companionship, and embedded man in the commonwealth. Polygamy performed only the first of these functions, so Beadle argued that Mormon men were "only 1/3 married."[82] Anti-Mormons worried that without romantic love, Mormons could in no way perform the sentimentality central to private life and in turn could not perform its function in making Mormons part of a national culture. Anti-Mormons such as Beadle claimed that in its plurality, Mormon marriage undermined the sentimental unity of the home and, by extension, the nation.

To anti-Mormons, plural marriage by definition lacked any private sphere that might constitute an appropriate home in which an individual citizen and his civic virtue might be fashioned. This dissolution of the private sphere meant that the creation of the virtuous citizen could in no way proceed. That is, anti-Mormons disqualified Mormons for American citizenship because polygamy adulterated the birthplace of republican virtue. They agreed with the ideologues of domesticity that only under the domestic influence of the fairer sex could men become the virtuous citizens republicanism required. The absence of the harmonious private home under plural marriage divested women of this crucial function.

Some anti-Mormons found clear-cut proof of the problems with polygamous households in the architecture of some Mormon houses. As Colleen McDannell and others have shown, the shape and form of middle-class Victorian houses reflected the values of their inhabitants. Historian Gwendolyn Wright points out that broadly speaking, "detached dwellings in the countryside were taken as the symbol of certain key national virtues. On an individual level, they represented personal independence. On a social level, they showed family pride and self-sufficiency. Politically, the architecture seemed an expression of democratic freedom of choice. And economically, it mirrored the pattern of private enterprise, rather than planning for the overall public good, which characterized American society."[83] Others have pointed out that domestic architecture also scripted the function of the home in establishing private domestic space.[84] For the Victorian middle-class, privacy was essential on a number of levels. Within the household private rooms designated specialized gendered space, as kitchens and studies were increasingly segregated from living areas.[85] More importantly, Victorian houses reflected domestic space *itself* as private, "distinct from the public sphere of life."[86] Thus, as McDannell notes, porches, verandas, and lawns "created a spatial transition which separated the private family world from the public world of the street."[87] Atop a chapter heading titled "A Christian Home,"

First published in Catharine E. Beecher and Harriet Beecher Stowe,
The American Woman's Home; Or, Principles of Domestic Science (1869), 23.

Catharine E. Beecher and Harriet Beecher Stowe printed an image of what this
idealized private home might look like.[88]

Not only did men's private selves, consciences, and property qualify them for
public citizenship, but the domestic private also became a central location "in
which individuals [could] exercise their choices freely and create a subjective
moral vocabulary." Nineteenth-century houses increasingly featured individual
bedrooms in which family members could find the solace and privacy to de-

velop the individuated subjectivities that American citizenship required.[89] Hendrick Hartog explains that marital unity often stood as a synonym for privacy that "identified a private household, a bounded sphere within which husband and wife could work out their collective life and their relationship."[90] That is, the private home created a space in which couples could develop the exclusivity of romantic love and the uniqueness of their own special bond.

None of these essential characteristics seemed to anti-Mormons to be in evidence in Mormon homes, leaving them therefore vulnerable to the divisions, conflicts, and power plays of the public sphere. In 1854, Benjamin Ferris, for example, commented that "polygamy is introducing a new style of building at Salt Lake City. A man with half a dozen wives builds, if he can, a long, low dwelling, having six entrances from the outside."[91] Another visitor to Utah commented with obvious disdain, "Some have their wives lotted off by pairs in small disconnected houses, like a row of out-houses. Some have long low houses, and on taking a new wife, build a new room on to them, so that their rooms look like rows of stalls in a cow barn!"[92] As if to illustrate this same point, Mrs. C. V. Waite reprinted a floor plan of Brigham Young's domicile (called the Lion House after the statue of a lion resting at its entrance) in her book, *The Mormon Prophet and His Harem; or, An Authentic History of Brigham Young, His Numerous Wives and Children*. The second and third floors lotted off wives by number, each with her own room, while the size of the rooms implied hierarchy among wives.[93] Benjamin Ferris's *Utah and the Mormons* also reprinted images of Mormon "rowhouses," each room with its own entrance, presumably one for each wife.[94]

The object of Mormon architecture seemed obvious to anti-Mormon observers like Ferris: "to keep the women and babies, as much as possible, apart, and prevent those terrible cat-fights which sometimes occur."[95] For Victorian observers, the physical appearance of Mormon homes bespoke the systematic undermining of the unity of the home and showed the ways plural marriage introduced jealousy, competitiveness, and disdain into the single place they did not belong: the sentimental world of the home circle. "The jealousies between the wives make inevitable discords in the polygamous family."[96] This theme is illustrated in an image from Alfred Trumble's *The Mysteries of Mormonism*, which depicts two wives fighting with each other while other wives look on in amusement.[97] As images like these showed, polygamous life provided no true home: "These miserable creatures have houses where they stay, and a discordant and disunited association of women and children, but no *families*—there are none of the comforts and delights of home with the polygamist."[98] Anti-Mormons contended that the Mormon home could never be the self-enclosed realm of peace and intimacy that white middle-class Americans imagined to

PLANS OF THE LION HOUSE.

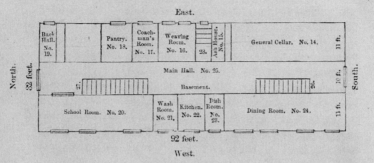

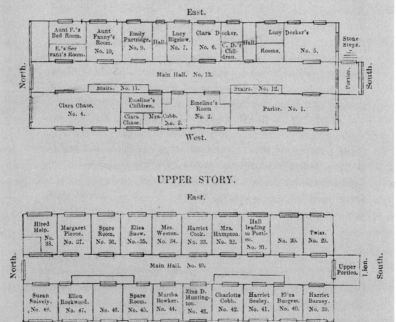

"Plans of the Lion House," first published in Mrs. C. V. Waite, *The Mormon Prophet and His Harem* (1868), 199. Courtesy of L. Tom Perry Special Collections, Harold B. Lee Library, Brigham Young University, Provo, Utah.

DR. CLINTON'S HAREM.

"Dr. Clinton's Harem," first published in Benjamin G. Ferris, *Utah and the Mormons* (1854), 309. Courtesy of L. Tom Perry Special Collections, Harold B. Lee Library, Brigham Young University, Provo, Utah.

be so central to national life.[99] One illustration from John D. Lee's *Mormonism Unveiled* exemplifies this concern, printing an image of "The Bishop's family at 2 a.m." In this sketch, wives and children fight among themselves while the harried husband hides atop a wardrobe.[100]

This absence of the private sphere threatened American middle-class visions of private life in several ways. Anti-Mormon W. F. Rae, for example, asserted the vital importance of domestic privacy: "If there be one point on which Americans and Englishmen are thoroughly agreed, and about which they are justly entitled to boast, it is that their homes are sanctuaries, and their houses castles; sanctuaries into which no stranger can enter unbidden; castles into which no stranger can demand admission."[101] As the Victorian middle class imagined it, according to scholar June Howard, "A man's home was his castle not because he was the king in miniature but because it was private."[102] Moreover, as Kenneth T. Jackson observes, "The violation of the house is almost as serious as the violation of the self."[103] The lack of architectural and sentimental integrity in Mormon homes evidenced for anti-Mormons the lack of that key protection

"The Jealous Wives," first published in An Apostle's Wife [Alfred Trumble], *The Mysteries of Mormonism* (1881), between pages 19 and 20. Courtesy of L. Tom Perry Special Collections, Harold B. Lee Library, Brigham Young University, Provo, Utah.

"The Bishop's Family at 2 a.m.," first published in John D. Lee, *Mormonism Unveiled* (1882), 185. Courtesy of L. Tom Perry Special Collections, Harold B. Lee Library, Brigham Young University, Provo, Utah.

of the private sphere from external invasion and violation. "[A] home, in the English and American sense of the word, has no existence among the Saints of the Great Salt Lake. For example, should a Bishop or other person in authority knock at the door of a Mormon house in his diocese, he must be admitted without question, and his orders must be obeyed without hesitation, under a heavy penalty. Should he think that the floor ought to be scrubbed, or the kettle polished, or any alteration made in househould [sic] arrangements, he has but to give the order, and the command is obeyed."[104] According to anti-Mormons, the institution of polygamy dissolved the boundaries of the home by subjecting it to the domination of Church elders. In so doing, it thrust the public government of the Church into the private sphere, disrupting the privacy upon which domestic unity rested.

The only conclusion anti-Mormon observers could make was that Mormon households were not homes at all in any viable sense.[105] This conclusion was ubiquitous in anti-Mormon literature: One concerned Christian reflected that in Utah households "there is no privacy—no oneness of sentiment—*no home;*"[106] another observer concluded that "the Mormon polygamist has NO HOME;"[107] and a third declared that "Polygamy... has separated the people from American homes."[108] Everyone seemed to agree with Fred E. Bennett that "The supremacy of the Mormon church means... the utter destruction of the home circle."[109]

• • •

Anti-Mormons objected to polygamy not only because they believed it promoted licentiousness and degraded its participants but, perhaps of deeper social consequence, because it also undercut the distinctions between public and private that middle-class white Americans so highly prized. Plural marriage upset the private intimacy of romantic love and introduced outside influence into the home circle. Under polygamy, anti-Mormons claimed, public and private merged together, such that neither the home nor the polity could exist in a viable form. Moreover, if monogamous private life created and maintained the good citizen, then the perversions of Mormon polygamy did the opposite; it turned privacy into religious despotism, private property into socialism, and citizens into blind followers incapable of independent thought. That is to say, plural marriage undermined the rights Americans placed at the center of republican government. Under polygamy, Mormons could not uphold the rights perhaps most fundamental to nineteenth-century republican ideology: the right of men to consent to their government, and of women to consent to the institution meant to govern them, marriage. For all of these reasons, according to anti-Mormons, Mormonism "can not [sic] exist in contact with republican institutions."[110]

CHAPTER 5

"They Can Not Exist in Contact with Republican Institutions"

Consent, Contract, and Citizenship under "Polygamic Theocracy"

In the imaginations of anti-Mormons and many of their contemporaries, the importance of the private sphere to public life could not be overestimated: the virtue, liberty, and very existence of America depended on proper American homes. Early on, anti-Mormon literature trumpeted the threat of Mormonism to the American home. However, in later decades connecting plural marriage to the destruction of the American home and the practice of plural marriage to theocratic government in Utah was a major tour de force for anti-Mormon literature. Over the 1870s and 1880s, anti-Mormons began concentrating their attentions on showing how the practice of polygamy undermined American citizenship and civic life among the Mormons. In an era historians have called the "age of contract," anti-Mormons argued that Mormonism rendered its subjects incapable of free conscience and of participating as free agents in marital or social contracts. Anti-Mormons asserted that Mormons therefore could not attain the independence, political virtue, and freedom of contract that good republican citizenship required, and without good citizens, public government would give way to political despotism. Put simply, polygamy led to both marital and political despotism.

Political ethicist Nancy Rosenblum provides a useful conceptual window through which to view how anti-Mormons understood the ways plural marriage undermined republican government. She argues that for many democratic theorists, "appropriately ordered intimate relations reinforce democracy." In some veins of American political theory, to which anti-Mormons ascribed, democracy required that the practice of sexuality be in "congruence with democratic principles."[1] Nineteenth-century anti-Mormons argued that monogamy gave rise to democratic impulses, while polygamy, in the words of Supreme Court Chief Justice Morrison R. Waite, "fetters the people in stationary despotism."[2] Polygamy, the logic followed, was not "democratic sex." This chapter traces the complex logics through which polygamy came to be understood as fundamentally opposed to the institutions of American government. Anti-Mormons drew heavily on the legal principles of contract and consent to spell out the dire consequences of polygamic marriage to American institutions and to show that Mormonism was incompatible with Americanness.

Women and Men in the Age of Contract

Legal historians have called the latter half of the nineteenth century the age of contract; the concepts of contract and consent were "so closely identified at mid-century with freedom and civic responsibility that lack of consent proved the lack of freedom."[3] Americans conceptualized freedom as the liberty of self-government identified by the right of consent to social, property, and marriage contracts. An individual's degree of autonomy was marked by his self-ownership, that is, his freedom to contract without outside influence or coercion.[4]

The social contract theory that grounded American government conceived subjects of the modern state as a creation of consent and contract between individuals. As formulated in classical political theory, "the 'individual' is a universal category that (in principle) includes everyone," a category marked by liberty, independence, and equality.[5] Several scholars have pointed out that the legal concept of the individual was not actually all-inclusive. Carole Pateman, Linda K. Kerber, and Carroll Smith-Rosenberg, among others, have shown that the category and its liberating potential was limited to propertied white men and remained so well into the nineteenth century.[6] By the end of the Civil War, however, the property restrictions had all but disappeared, and in their place was the ownership of the self and the ability to sell one's labor. Self-ownership replaced property ownership in constituting a citizen's public interest.

At the same time, the idea of separate spheres prescribed that individual autonomy, as expressed in the right to contract and in the nature of consent, was still a gendered concept. Men's liberty rested in consent to labor and social contracts, and women's liberty lay in consent to the marital contract. A woman (in theory) consented to contract with a husband who (theoretically) developed his individual autonomy in the private sphere and expressed it in the political and economic contracts that upheld life outside the home. Women's marital consent constituted her political consent to her husband's participation (not her own) in social and economic contracts.[7]

In the eighteenth and nineteenth centuries, ideas about the state and the family often functioned symbiotically, the one always shaping the other. In classical social contract theory, the family most often functioned in three ways: in partnership with the state, as a metaphor for the state, and as a kind of state in miniature. If the state was like a family, the family should be like the state, that is, a social contract between equals. As such, the broad eighteenth-century shifts from patriarchy to republicanism were accompanied by a shift in family models from patriarchal to what some historians have called the democratic or contractual family.[8] This new companionate model of family bolstered the connections nineteenth-century Americans made between social and marital contracts. The model constituted the family as a unity of shared, common interest and recast women's consent to marriage as her consent to government through her husband. By extension, in social contract theory, a husband entered the social contract as husband and father in relationship to his own family but as a brother in relationship to his fellow contractors.[9] Theoretically, equality and not patriarchy governed domestic and political relations in democratic families and governments. Moreover, future citizens learned the values and principles of republican government through experience and instruction in a democratic family setting or domestic sphere. A properly arranged domestic sphere ensured the liberty and civic morality of family members. Ideally, then, the voluntary participation and equality of each family member ordered the family more than the patriarchal authority of the father. The task of a companionate family was to facilitate and protect the moral development of each family member's unique individuality, and women, as wives and mothers, played a pivotal role.[10] The family established by the marital contract prepared citizens for participation in the social contract.

Mormonism, however, operated within a system of polygamic theocracy that was, according to anti-Mormons, in "direct opposition to the genius of true republicanism."[11] Benjamin Ferris proclaimed that Mormonism "must necessarily interfere with the rights of the citizen, and come into collision with the laws of the land."[12] Anti-Mormons believed that polygamy degraded the autonomy of the citizen, who then consented to the theocratic rule of the church. Absent the consent of a free citizenry, free government in Utah disappeared behind Church domination.

In seeking to understand anti-Mormon reasoning, two schools of thought have locked scholars into a debate over which contract—marital or social—

anti-Mormons considered to be more significant. That is, was it polygamy or theocracy that most troubled anti-Mormons? Much of this debate has been trapped in an artificial binary pitting polygamy against theocracy as the central obstacle to Utah statehood. Early historians like Klaus Hansen contend that polygamy "was largely a convenient excuse to strike at the political influence of the Mormon hierarchy."[13] Gustive Larson agrees, arguing that the polygamy controversy was mainly a local affair, and that legislators capitalized on anti-polygamy as a guise under which to suppress the political power of the Mormon Church. Both historians believe that polygamy was a relatively insignificant issue compared to the Church's domination of political affairs in Utah. They contend that federal officials worried that Mormon allegiance rested with the Church more than the federal state, and took measures in the form of anti-polygamy legislation to secure the capture of Mormon allegiance.[14] More recent scholarship, however, has argued that "the practice of plural marriage among the Latter-day Saints was the foremost obstacle to admission of Utah as a state." Edward Leo Lyman contends that Church interference in political affairs far outlasted the Woodruff Manifesto, but that after the 1890 declaration against new plural marriages, "other obstacles to statehood were removed with considerable dispatch."[15] Even more recent scholarship proposes a tie—that both polygamy and theocracy inflamed anti-Mormonism equally, though certain anti-Mormon factions were more concerned with one than the other. Jana K. Riess, for instance, argues that historians like Hansen and Larson who identify theocracy as a more central anti-Mormon complaint tend to look only at sources written by men. Women anti-Mormons, Riess claims, were far more concerned with plural marriage.[16] The most recent work to take up this question explicitly, however, returns to the views of earlier scholarship, contending that it was not plural marriage but conflicts over legitimate political authority that led to Mormons' confrontation with the federal government.[17]

To place polygamy and theocracy opposite each other, as these discussions have done, is to create a false debate.[18] Even to place them alongside each other neglects the complex interconnections between polygamy and theocracy in many anti-Mormon minds. Most anti-Mormons who privileged one of the two evils over the other were focused on tactical issues, debating the prohibition of which of the twin evils would most likely also dispense with the other. In this respect, historians have mistaken tactical debates for essential ones. Attention to change over time in anti-Mormon literature can help make sense of the ways that anti-Mormons connected polygamy and theocracy as two sides of the same coin.

In the anti-Mormon imagination, polygamy and theocracy were inextricably tied to one another in ways historians have asserted but have had trouble sorting out. Nancy Cott, for example, recognizes that "the thematic equivalency between polygamy, despotism, and coercion on the one side, and between monogamy, political liberty, and consent on the other resonated through the political culture of the U.S. all during the [nineteenth] century." But the network of intersections, convergences, and parallels among polygamy, despotism, and coercion remain largely unexplored in her work.[19] Acutely aware of the symbiotic relationship between family and government, anti-Mormons consistently argued that polygamy and theocracy upheld and bled into each other, corrupting free republican government in both home and polity. While polygamy deprived woman of her most important right, the right of marital consent, theocracy deprived men of political consent. In anti-Mormon thought, polygamy held in place the patriarchal structures of both filial and political authority that negated marital and social contracts between equals. Mormonism was a Church, a government, a society, a religion, and a family all rolled into one, making impossible the separations—of public from private, of church from state—that good government required.[20]

The logic that connected polygamy to theocracy developed over time. In anti-Mormon literature of the 1850s and 1860s discussion of the evils of plural marriage, especially for women, tended to outweigh concern over theocracy. Earlier anti-Mormons articulated the dangers plural marriage posed to individual morality and women's marital consent. However, in the wake of the failure of the 1862 Morrill Act outlawing polygamy, anti-Mormons over the 1870s and 1880s began to more clearly see and articulate the troubling interrelationship of plural marriage and Mormon theocracy.[21] Anti-Mormons began where contract theory began—with consent.

Religious Voluntarism and Mormon Coercion

The religious revivalism of the Second Great Awakening asserted the moral agency of the individual, emphasizing individual religious conscience over and above Calvinist doctrines of predestination. The Constitution had left it to the states to separate church and state, and several states retained established churches into the nineteenth century; the last state to disestablish religion was Massachusetts in 1820.[22] By that time, Americans had come to believe that the disestablishment of religion meant that religion was an expression of the private individual and protected him from religious coercion.[23] American Protestants increasingly came to view religion as a matter of liberty of conscience properly kept apart from the institutions of political life.

Noting with great irony that Mormons defended their faith, domestic practices, and Church rule under the guise of religious freedom, anti-Mormon literature was rife with descriptions of the absence of religious liberty in Utah. Anti-Mormons declared, "Nobody joins the Latter Day Saints from his or her uninfluenced judgment."[24] In anti-Mormon discourse, individual moral choice was shown to be limited to religions that a person could freely choose. For them Mormonism was no such religion. Mormons "present a combination of the elements of popular superstition and fanaticism, which, in its constitution and government, must necessarily interfere with the rights of the citizen, and come into collision with the laws of the land."[25] Refusing to believe that anyone could freely consent to Mormon leadership, anti-Mormons contended that the faith, "from first to last, is a system of delusion and imposition," and any conversion must be the result of mesmerism, deceit, delusion, or seduction; faith in such a hoax could only be maintained by fear and/or force.[26] In anti-Mormon literature Mormon leaders were portrayed as possessing great powers of "animal magnetism, mesmerism, or . . . hypnotism."[27] By anti-Mormon accounts, a Mormon abdicated possession of his or her liberty of conscience to the deceptions and machinations of Church leaders simply by converting.

Anti-Mormons reported that when mesmerism or deceit failed, Mormon leaders resorted to outright force. The literature abounded with tales of intimidation, coercion, and even murder to compel continued allegiance to the faith once the deceit or mesmerism had run its course. Anti-Mormons accused Brigham Young of sending a private army called the Danites to harass, intimidate, and coerce apostates into returning to the faith and to murder those who refused.[28] Much controversy has surrounded the role of the Danites in Mormon history and much about the band is still unknown. Most likely, the Danite band was a short-term experiment in vigilante justice in Missouri that disbanded within a few years of its organization.[29] Public outcry against the Danites emerged in 1839 for their role in the 1838 Mormon war in Missouri, and again shortly before Joseph Smith's assassination. The prophet disbanded the organization and denounced its leader, Sampson Avard, eventually excommunicating him from the Church. Many anti-Mormons, however, believed that the Danites carried out the controversial Mormon doctrine of blood atonement. The doctrine of blood atonement held that some sins extended beyond the power of Jesus's atonement to redeem. Murder, for example, could only be atoned for by the blood of the sinner.

Publicly, nineteenth-century Mormons interpreted the doctrine of blood atonement conservatively; blood atonement was only the death penalty in the ordinary American justice system.[30] Most anti-Mormons, however, took the doctrine at its word: "If a Mormon apostatizes his throat shall be cut and his blood poured out upon the ground for the remission of his sin," testified one anti-Mormon witness.[31] For anti-Mormons the doctrine of blood atonement motivated and set in motion the willful murder of gentiles and apostates in Utah. Probably most often in error, Mormons were accused of murdering disobedient members and unruly gentiles simply upon Brigham Young's request. These tales were propped up by the testimonies of excommunicated Mormons John D. Lee and Bill Hickman who confessed in well-read memoirs to murder at the beck and call of Church leadership.[32] Narratives such as these were also corroborated by the Mountain Meadows Massacre, one of the most controversial events in Mormon history. In 1857 Mormons, with the assistance of Piute Indians, massacred about 120 men, women, and children belonging to an emigrant party making their way west from Arkansas.[33] While not necessarily factual, thrilling tales of the Danites lent credence to Utah Judge John Cradlebaugh's claim that "the vengeance of Brigham, though silent, is swift, and fearful as the horrors of death can make it."[34] Another anti-Mormon charged that polygamy "calls in murder without hesitation, and no man's life is safe in Utah, who is not himself a polygamist, unless he is sheltered by a United States Fort."[35] No surprise, then, that anti-Mormons believed Mormonism of necessity coerced conversion and that free will and individual religious conscience had no place among the Saints.

Anti-Mormons also believed that the lack of consent Mormonism allegedly embodied had particular consequences for women. The contradictory reasoning of anti-Mormonism deduced that by consenting to plural marriage a Mormon woman demonstrated that she lacked self-ownership and freedom of conscience. No "woman of the republic" would "barter her rich inheritance of honor and female purity for the ambiguous and unsatisfactory position assigned to the frail Sapphos and Lesbias [sic] of a Mormon harem."[36] As such, Mormon marriages could only mark the loss of a woman's self-possession to her husband's mysterious Mormon powers; free, unconstrained consent to plural marriage was a logical impossibility. Justin McCarthy described the workings of Mormon seduction as one convert was enslaved by "a power which worked upon her senses and her superstitions."[37] Another woman in Maria Ward's *Female Life Among the Mormons*, alleged that in obtaining her hand in marriage a Mormon leader "exerted a mystical magical influence over me—a sort of sorcery that deprived me of the unrestricted exercise of free will."[38]

In some anti-Mormon accounts, women converted to Mormonism and consented to plural marriage because they knew not to what they had consented. Anti-Mormons reasoned that Mormon men must perpetrate great deceptions to obtain wives. Increase Van Deusen, for example, concluded that "the introduction and existence of these evils [polygamy]" could "alone be accomplished by the artifice and deception successfully practiced upon the yielding susceptibilities and the pliant nature of the female sex."[39] In anti-Mormon literature, women from foreign countries and the eastern United States were seduced by Mormon elders and brought to Utah only to find the new husbands already married. Hence, anti-Mormons believed that from the beginning Mormon husbands introduced deceit into the very relationship and situation that should be the most trusting—marriage. Mormon wives were procured and kept through seduction, mesmerism, entrapment, or deception, but never by consent. Myths of violence against women also highlighted Mormon women's supposed lack of marital consent. In some cases anti-Mormons accused Mormons of kidnapping adolescent girls and enslaving them in plural marriage.[40] Anti-Mormons also accused Mormons of murdering women who refused to practice polygamy or fled polygamous relations.[41] By some anti-Mormon accounts, women complaining about polygamy were sometimes mysteriously and secretly kidnapped, tied up, and drowned.[42]

For anti-Mormons, religious coercion was merely emblematic of the absence of all freedoms in Utah. Mormonism "absorbs not only the religious, but all the civil and political liberty of the individual member."[43] Thus Mormonism, according to anti-Mormons, denied its citizens the freedom of contract in both marital and social terms. Mormonism removed from women the power of marital consent and thus stripped her of all equality in the marriage relation and, by extension, of her most basic civil right and the foundation of her equality: the right to choose with whom she united her political, economic, and personal fortunes.

Polygamy, Woman's Agency, and the Marriage Contract

To anti-Mormons, Mormon mothers were the antithesis of true womanhood, and their degradation brought terrible consequences upon the individual members of the companionate family that women themselves were responsible for molding and shaping. The women of Mormondom, bereft of agency, could not fulfill that role. For one thing, anti-Mormons argued, the plurality of polygamy reduced women to "the fractional part of an individual . . . [T]he innate nobleness of self-respect is impaired, and a feeling of servile dependence usurps its place."[44] That servile state "renders her careless of intellectual and moral progress, and insensible to many of the highest and noblest duties of her sex."[45]

For another thing, according to anti-Mormons, polygamy robbed woman of uniqueness; she became merely one interchangeable wife of many. Indeed, one anti-Mormon concluded, "The observer is almost compelled to think that they must have ceased to be women altogether, in heart, in soul and in mind."[46] To witness the degradations of polygamy, observers proclaimed, one need only to glance at Mormon women: "Such faces, so dispirited, depressed, shapeless, hopeless, soulless faces! No trace of woman's graceful pride and neatness in these slatternly, shabby, slouching, listless figures; no purple light of youth over these cheeks; no sparkle in these half-extinguished eyes."[47]

By anti-Mormon observations, the damaging effects of plural marriage could be seen not only in a woman's appearance but in her poor health as well. One plural wife had become "a wretched specimen of a woman, poorly dressed, poorly fed, and exhibits a sense of degradation,"[48] while another became a "wasted and sallow wreck" and displayed "all the withering aspects of an anguished heart, wounded in its keenest susceptibility and sinking unloved, unpitied, and with griefs untold."[49] The consequences of polygamy were manifold and mortal: "A *wife*, in Utah, can not [*sic*] live out half her days ... In most cases, it is producing premature old age, and some have already sunk into an early grave under an intolerable weight of affliction."[50] Jealousies ensuing from plural marriage were also alleged to affect women physiologically. At least one woman supposedly died from her heart having turned to stone because her husband took another wife.[51]

To illustrate the status of women under Mormon polygamy, anti-Mormons made use of two interrelated nineteenth-century icons of female servitude, both imbued with the specter of sexual bondage: the slave woman and the prostitute. One of the first instances of paralleling polygamy with slavery surfaced in mid-century Republican Party politics. Anti-polygamy novelist Metta Victoria Fuller identified the evils of local government as a bastion for two sorts of bondage: slavery in the South and polygamy in the West.[52] The 1856 Republican Party platform echoed her concern, declaring slavery and plural marriage the "twin relics of barbarism."[53] Under the law, a link between polygamy and slavery actually did exist in the legal category of "domestic relations." In the early Republic, American common law traditions maintained that the states retained jurisdiction over the legal category of domestic relations, those laws regulating relations between "parent and child, husband and wife, guardian and ward, master and servant, or master and slave."[54] Republican reformers deployed the "twin relics" rhetoric to promote a strong federal government that could mitigate against the dangers that slavery and polygamy represented inherent in local and state control over domestic relations.[55] Nancy Cott observes, "When Mormon polygamy was discussed, slavery was never far from politicians' minds, and the reverse was also true."[56] Over the next forty years, Republican reformers hoped to use the power of the federal government to create a national culture based on individual liberty, freedom of contract, and the sanctity of the monogamous family.[57] Linking polygamy and slavery fused the legal questions of slavery, polygamy, and local control together under the solitary, pitiable figure of woman in bondage.

During and after the Civil War, the federal government asserted sovereignty over domestic relations like never before.[58] In part, this was in response to pressures from marriage reformers who wanted to federalize marriage law. The federal regulation of marriage, reformers contended, would bring Americans not conforming to national expectations into line with American norms. Marriage advocates encouraged various campaigns to institutionalize American monogamy among those people not conforming to Victorian marriage ideals, especially Mormons. Because Utah was a territory, not a state, it was an especially fruitful place to show the merits of a federalized marriage law. Centralists contended that in Utah, local control instituted and protected a system of marriage, namely polygamy, surely as immoral as slavery. In 1856, Representative Justin Morrill of Vermont introduced legislation that became the Morrill Act of 1862.

This legislation put Democratic defenders of slavery in an uncomfortable position. No American congressman debated the social, spiritual, and moral harm of polygamy. However, a few southern congressmen opposed the Morrill Act in the name of states' rights over domestic relations law. Representatives like L. M. Keitt of South Carolina and Miles Taylor of Louisiana feared that giving license to interfere in one sort of domestic relation, even in the territories, would enable Congressional interference in the matter of slavery.[59] More often, southern congressmen were able to support the Morrill Act by conceptually distancing the polygamy question from slavery and federal power in the territories from the issue of states' rights. For example, Congressman Simms from Kentucky justified federal power in the territories because they were the property of the federal government while states were not. In a second, less compelling attempt to dissociate polygamy from slavery, Simms supported the Morrill Act with the curious contention that polygamy was not a domestic relation. Simms agreed with northern congressmen that the marital relation "lies at the very foundation of our whole social system." Polygamy, he argued, besides failing to be a domestic relation, was worse, namely "an offense against the domestic relation of husband and wife," and the Morrill Act supported "domestic rights . . . by punishing crimes against them." Simms went on to claim that the protection of the husband/wife relationship under the law also protected the domestic institution of slavery. The Constitution, Simms maintained, upheld slavery as it did the husband-wife relation. He aimed "to repel the charge that the institution of American slavery stands upon no higher basis of right, under the Constitution of the United States, than polygamy does; that the power which could punish the last could destroy the first. One is upheld by the Constitution, has existed as a part of the civilization of every State, and has been protected and guaranteed by the laws of both continents; the other has been spurned by every Christian State, denounced by the common law as a crime—yea, by all law, human and divine—for near two thousand years." For Simms, slavery, an honorable part of the white man's burden, was a domestic relation liberated from federal regulation, while polygamy was not. Only when domestic relations failed to constitute the private individual's private interests did they require federal discipline. Appropriate, time-honored domestic relations like slavery and monogamy needed no federal intervention.[60]

Simm's logic failed to stem the tide of anti-slavery agitation, and the assertion of federal power to regulate one domestic relation, slavery, encouraged campaigns to reform another, marriage. Marriage reformers wanted a national marriage law, arguing that a matter of such national importance should not be left to the states. In part in response to pressure from those reformers, Congress passed the Morrill Act in 1862, which declared bigamy a crime, punishable by a fine of five hundred dollars and a five-year prison term. It also annulled all territorial legislation designed to "establish, support, maintain, shield, or countenance polygamy."[61] However, the law contained no funding for enforcement, and the court system in Utah remained largely under the control of the Church. Moreover, because Mormon marriages were not regulated by territorial or federal supervision, convictions under the Morrill Act were hard to come by.[62]

Anti-Mormons were convinced that Mormon marriage was "not only one of the most ingenious, but is one of the most perfect [practices] that was ever devised to corrupt and degrade the holy ordinance of matrimony."[63] They used Mormonism as a foil to demonstrate the political dangers of a domestic sphere not correctly ordered. As such, the controversy over polygamy became a central locus for discussions of the relationship between marriage and home and American citizenship and government. In the wake of the Civil War, describing polygamous wives as slaves provided a useful trope through which to argue that Mormonism undermined women's freedom in Utah.

Early in the controversy over Utah, anti-Mormons bypassed the Republican condemnation of local sovereignty to focus on polygamy and slavery. The impulse to equate polygamy with slavery followed quickly. Alfreda Eva

Bell in 1855 declared that women in Utah "are in fact white slaves; are required to do all the most servile drudgery."[64] One anti-Mormon apostate went so far as to call herself the "nigger" of a polygamous marriage. Her husband's first wife declared that "she wanted him to marry me because I would make a good *'nigger,'* for she meant the second wife to be nothing but a 'nigger' who would know her place and keep it, too."[65] One illustration appearing in Alfred Trumble's *The Mysteries of Mormonism* exemplifies anti-Mormon concern over the enslavement of Mormon women. It displays a Mormon husband sitting on a fence with a whip while his wives work in the fields. Beneath the sketch is the caption, "Wives as Slaves."[66]

Literary historian Nancy Bentley shows that a side effect of anti-polygamy sentimental fiction was to prop up the Victorian era social fiction of marital consent. She contends that the nineteenth-century claim that women's freedom lay in consent to marriage overlooked that the sentiments of the female heart were, in many respects, already scripted. Marriage was, she argues, a process by which "sexual subordination is, through the alchemy of contract, ratified as free consent." In truth, Bentley contends, consent was far from being free and unfettered. "The pressures of family, faith, and economic need constitute an x-factor that make their choice so opaque as to render the idea of consent all but meaningless—meaningless until, that is, it is juxtaposed with the forced abjection of the slave." The figure of the polygamous wife, beaten into submission by a tyrannical husband, echoed the "scourged body of the bondswoman." Early anti-Mormon fiction, Bentley points out, described "states of sexual bondage in scenes that replicate the stylized abjection of black women's bodies only to replace them with the bodies of white wives."[67] She cites as an example one narrative from Maria Ward's *Female Life Among the Mormons*, in which an errant wife "was taken one night, . . . gagged, carried a mile in the woods, stripped nude, tied to a tree, and scourged until the blood ran from her wounds to the ground."[68] In narratives like this one, the "familiar choreography of bondage" was well rehearsed in anti-polygamy fiction throughout the rest of the century, repeating the "pantomime of displaced scenes of plantation slavery."[69] By contrast, monogamous marriage appeared to grant women agency and choice. In Bentley's estimation, by mobilizing the tropes of polygamy as slavery anti-Mormon rhetoric defined monogamy as the only contract of marital consent.[70]

Ironically, the rhetorical power of equating polygamy to slavery increased as the federal triumph over slavery pushed polygamy and its evils into the foreground of national attention. According to anti-Mormons, the slavery of polygamy actually exceeded the evils of African-American slavery because

"Wives as Slaves," first published in An Apostle's Wife [Alfred Trumble], *The Mysteries of Mormonism* (1881), between pages 20 and 21. Courtesy of L. Tom Perry Special Collections, Harold B. Lee Library, Brigham Young University, Provo, Utah.

Mormon wives "suffer as the slave women of the South never did. Slave women were torn from their homes by masters while their husbands mourned; the Mormon women are slaves to their husbands, concubines to their religion, and martyrs to a despotism as immoral as the cursed Sodom of old."[71] In her preface to Fanny Stenhouse's *"Tell it All": The Story of a Life's Experience in Mormonism*, Harriett Beecher Stowe applauded the outcome of the Civil War: "Our day has seen the glorious breaking of fetters. The slave-pens of the south have become a nightmare of the past." Yet, she asks, "Shall we not then hope that the hour is come to loose the bonds of a cruel slavery whose chains have cut into the very hearts of thousands of our sisters—a slavery which debases and degrades womanhood, motherhood, and the family?"[72] Many anti-Mormons joined Stowe in wondering, "Why did this nation shed the life-blood of half a million citizens in the crushing of slavery, if it shall continue to encourage the enslaving of women, the mothers of the race?"[73] Even after the manumission of African-American slaves, did not white American women remain enslaved body and soul by their husbands in Utah?

Over the 1860s and 1870s, anti-polygamy campaigns bundled the complex issues of plural marriage and slavery untidily together with prostitution.[74] This was partly due to a large-scale shift in perceptions regarding women's nature and the causes of prostitution. By the 1850s, reform-minded Americans were more likely to perceive prostitutes as victims of male seduction and crime than sexual deviants themselves.[75] By the 1860s, anti-prostitution campaigns had familiarized American readers with the proposition that prostitutes were, in essence, slaves.[76] Anti-prostitution reformers paralleled the buying and selling of white women's sexuality to the buying and selling of African-American labor. So, too, did anti-polygamy reformers: "Slavery rests on a denial of the rights of labour; Mormonism on a denial of the rights of woman; the one treats the black race as things not persons; the other treats the weaker sex as the ministers of man's pleasure, not as the heirs with him of the grace of life."[77] In the age of contract, opponents of polygamy reasoned that prostitution and polygamy—both forms of slavery—were intolerable because they were not consensual, contractual exchanges.

The links among slavery, prostitution, and polygamy hinged upon ownership of property in the self and upon consent. Anti-polygamy reformers imagined that, like the slave and the nineteenth-century prostitute, women under polygamy became the property of men, available for men's sexual consumption. In a sense, wives became, literally, "public women" (a Victorian euphemism for prostitutes because of their visibility in public space). According to Benjamin Ferris, "A dozen women, the common property of one man, some of them divorced from other men, lodged under the same roof, and often more than one in the same room, soon begin to feel that they might as well be the common property each of a dozen men."[78] Polygamy, that is, made women *feel* like prostitutes. Many contended that polygamy was sexual slavery worse than prostitution because it brought prostitution into the privacy of the marriage covenant, making the "domestic altar a shrine to prostitution."[79] Cornelia Ferris reported a particularly disturbing sight in Utah: upon the announcement of the plural marriage of one Mormon woman, "a father danc[ed] a merry jig over the prostitution of his own daughter."[80]

From the viewpoint of anti-Mormons, plural wives became virtually the public property of Mormon men. Hence, Mormon marriage introduced into the private sphere the slavery of prostitution, a particularly vile notion in Victorian America where the marriage contract and the home it created were the centerpiece of woman's equality to man and the location of her rights and freedom.[81] Woman's equality rested in her power of marital consent and her domestic influence. Polygamy, in making the home the locus of woman's enslavement, was "a sin against God's law of equality in marriage, and therefore an outrage on the inalienable rights of humanity, which outrage would, if allowed, infallibly destroy the freedom of women."[82] Indeed, according to anti-Mormons, plural marriage "destroy[ed] the civil rights of woman."[83] By anti-Mormon accounts, the domestic slavery of women under polygamy stripped women of their rights, freedom, and equality under the guise of religion.

No aspect of anti-Mormonism was as puzzling to Mormons as the way anti-Mormons linked prostitution, slavery, and polygamy. For Mormons, monogamy was the source of social ills: "This law of monogamy, or the monogamic system, laid the foundation for prostitution and the evils and diseases of the most revolting nature."[84] Mormons contended that no prostitution existed in Utah until "gentile" settlement introduced brothels and saloons.[85] Far from being equivalent to prostitution, Mormons argued, plural marriage served as a prophylaxis against the social evils attending unrestrained licentiousness: prostitution, social disease, seduction, desertion, and infanticide.[86] It sheltered women's virtue against the wrongs of evil men and elevated women by sealing them only to men worthy of their loyalties.[87] In fact, according to Mormon women, polygamy promoted the kind of social order to which the rest of the Republic should aspire.[88]

Mormons equally resented the equation of polygamy with slavery. Rather than feeling or being enslaved, Mormons, women especially, consistently maintained publicly that Mormon women freely consented to plural marriage and were quite happy in plural relationships.[89] In addition, as chapter 3 discussed at length, women in polygamy attested that they were freer and more equal with their husbands under polygamy than women in monogamous relations. Especially after the granting of woman suffrage in 1870, Mormons found women's relative financial and political independence emblematic of greater freedom and individuality than women possessed anywhere else.

After 1871, woman suffrage became a focal point for discussions of women's liberty in Utah. Anti-Mormons disputed Mormon women's claims that suffrage afforded them considerable freedom. To anti-Mormons, it seemed self-evident that the patriarchal Church controlled women's lives and their votes.[90] Mormon women were incapable of exercising suffrage freely because they were "too throughly [sic] paralyzed by years of submission to avail themselves of power."[91] According to this view, Mormon woman suffrage only "bestow[ed] upon her the ballot in a way that makes it a nullity if contested, and compels her to use it to perpetuate her own degradation."[92] Under polygamic theocracy, woman suffrage was a cruel joke that "rivet[ed women's] bonds still tighter."[93] Moreover, according to anti-Mormons, a woman's lack of marital consent mirrored her lack of political consent. The individual and political constraints the Church placed on the man to whom her fortunes were bound merely multiplied the ways a Mormon woman lacked agency. Woman, under Mormonism, was thus doubly bound: free to choose neither her husband nor her government.

Over the late 1870s and 1880s, demands to disenfranchise Mormon women increased as part of a larger agenda against un-American politics in Utah. As anti-Mormons saw it, the women of Mormondom were merely puppets. "The franchise conferred by a theocracy, exercised under its dominance, made to conserve its power, to perpetuate polygamous life, and to clothe lawlessness with authority, is not the franchise of a Christian republic."[94] In 1879, Utah Governor George Emery's Annual Message to Congress petitioned for the disenfranchisement of Utah women.[95] A few years later, former U.S. Vice President Shuyler Colfax concurred with Emery's request, declaring it unacceptable "to allow a polygamist half a dozen extra votes of his household to fortify his illegal conduct and to magnify his importance and power at elections for Congressmen."[96] Here, Colfax replicated the logic of coverture, indicating that votes represented households, not individuals. For Colfax, the problem with Mormon woman suffrage was that it allowed a Mormon head-of-household more votes than he rightly deserved.

Despite anti-suffrage activism on the national level, local anti-polygamists in Utah had avoided the issue of woman suffrage until they no longer could. To oppose polygamy on grounds that it enslaved women and then to object to woman suffrage seemed to them a contradiction in terms. Moreover, in possession of the vote themselves, the women of the Anti-Polygamy Society, a local organization founded in 1878, held out hope that the monogamous women of Utah could defeat plural marriage at the polls. The Anti-Polygamy Society held to the policy that it "has no direct interest in the matter of female suffrage."[97] For the most part, the Society advocated the disenfranchisement of both polygamist men and women, more than the disenfranchisement of women per se.[98] In the election of 1883, after the Edmunds Act had disenfranchised all polygamists, Mormon leaders still swept local elections. That made it clear to the Anti-Polygamy Society that the monogamous women of the Church voted much like their polygamist sisters. In response most, though not all, members of the Society joined national anti-polygamists in the campaign against woman suffrage in Utah.[99]

As anti-polygamy reformer Cornelia Paddock explained, gentile women in Utah were willing to sacrifice their own suffrage to rid the territory of plural marriage.[100] In 1887, when Congress passed the Edmunds-Tucker Act, designed in part "to relieve the Mormon women of Utah from the slavehood of being obliged to exercise a political function which is to keep her in a state of degradation," Utah's gentiles did not object.[101] Anti-Mormons concluded that so damaging was polygamous woman suffrage both to Mormon women and to free and public government that Mormon women's political voices must be silenced in order to free them. The Edmunds-Tucker Act disenfranchised all Utah women until 1896, when the Utah Constitution enfranchised them once again.

Anti-Mormons maintained that the ignominy of women under polygamy also incapacitated them to produce future citizens of nations, arguing, "childhood can have the right training, and youth can attain true manhood and true womanhood only in the monogamic family."[102] "The private happiness of family associations, the preservation of moral and religious sentiments, exerting, as they unquestionably do, a powerful influence on civilized life," a proper domestic sphere was crucial to the development of American civilization.[103] To anti-Mormons, it seemed obvious that the polygamous household simply could not provide the requisite moral environment. They also believed that Mormon women neglected their most sacred duties toward their children. Travelers through Utah often remarked that children were unsupervised, dirty, and unkempt. Benjamin Ferris observed, "Nowhere out of the 'Five Points' in New York city [*sic*] can a more filthy, miserable, neglected-looking, and disorderly rabble of children be found than in the streets of Great Salt Lake City."[104] Anti-Mormons often imagined children the victims of neglectful parents. Robert G. McNiece, a writer for the *Presbyterian Review*, wrote, "No pen can describe the demoralizing effect of polygamy upon the young, nor adequately set forth the lack of morality on the part of the vast majority of young men and women who are brought up in connection with it. In fact, they don't seem to know what the term *morality* means."[105] Anti-Mormons reasoned that the degraded environment of Mormon home life could not help but affect the children of polygamous marriages. Surely children raised in such a situation could not grow up to be the virtuous adults on which the nation depended. It was clear to anti-Mormons that the training for public virtue necessary for good citizenship could not occur under polygamy.

Theocracy, the (Male) Citizen, and the Social Contract: Can a Mormon be an Individual?[106]

By the 1870s, anti-Mormons increasingly concluded that the negative consequences of plural marriage for women were rivaled only by the consequences for male citizenship and public government. By anti-Mormon accounts, plural marriage undermined not only the marriage contract but the social contract as well. J. H. Beadle claimed that "something peculiar to Mormonism takes it

out of the sphere of religion and necessarily brings it into conflict with a republican people and their institutions."[107] Anti-Mormons imagined that, while
republicanism began in the democratic contractual monogamous family, the
despotism of Mormonism began in the plural family; theocracy began at home.
As anti-Mormons saw it, plural marriage embedded the citizen not in republican institutions that facilitated individual liberty, but in corporate structures
of Mormonism that facilitated Church theocracy. Anti-Mormons also argued
that the despotic household of plural marriage naturally created citizens fitted
to political despotism. Under polygamy "the passions and lusts harmonize
with the love of power and dominion," and the domestic tyranny of polygamy
spilled out of the home into political affairs in Utah.[108] Men driven by passion
and power, men who exercised tyranny in the home, were unfit to participate
in the fraternity of the American social contract.

According to anti-Mormons, in foregrounding male authority in the home,
polygamy undermined equality in marriage: "The husband loses respect for
her who sits at his feet, rather than by his side."[109] With a note of sarcastic admiration, Samuel Bowles agreed: "The Mormon religion is an excellent institution for maintaining masculine authority in the family."[110] Another image in
Trumble's *The Mysteries of Mormonism* illustrates this point. A husband brings
home a new wife in her wedding dress and points to a banner reading, "I rule
the ranch."[111] On a slightly different tack, Mrs. C. V. Waite argued that plurality
necessitated subordination and inferiority in the home because all wives could
not be equal with one husband and with each other.[112] She further noted that,
as a result, "this necessary assumption of superiority and power, on the part of
the man, at once mars, if it does not destroy, all the finer and holier of the marriage relations."[113] Thus, in the words of anti-polygamy congressman Justin Morrill, plural marriage "ma[d]e woman no longer an equal and man the tyrant,"
promoting despotism in the home where ironfisted men ruled over subservi-
ent women.[114] Another image of "Mormon household discipline," again from
Trumble's *The Mysteries of Mormonism*, showed a Mormon husband wielding
a club over his wife as she ate her supper.[115]

Plural marriage, anti-Mormons argued, trained citizens for political despotism, an outcome only to be expected since polygamy "brutalizes man, teaching
him to despise and domineer over his wives, over all women."[116] In anti-Mormon
imaginations, tyranny in the home bled outward into the polity. Representative Ferris Jacobs of New York, for instance, predicted that under polygamy
"society at large thus becomes a combination, not of fathers of families, but of
household tyrants, who by the practice of tyranny have been fitted to endure
it."[117] Mormon men's tyranny over their wives and children, the logic went,

First published in An Apostle's Wife [Alfred Trumble], *The Mysteries of Mormonism* (1881), between pages 42 and 43. Courtesy of L. Tom Perry Special Collections, Harold B. Lee Library, Brigham Young University, Provo, Utah.

MORMON HOUSEHOLD DISCIPLINE.

"Mormon Household Discipline," first published in An Apostle's Wife [Alfred Trumble], *The Mysteries of Mormonism* (1881), between pages 33 and 34. Courtesy of L. Tom Perry Special Collections, Harold B. Lee Library, Brigham Young University, Provo, Utah.

prepared them to tolerate the political despotism of Church rule, in a sense simply exchanging male rule in the home for subjection to Church authority.

As anti-Mormons saw it, the reign of household tyrants was upheld by a peculiarly Mormon perversion of the social contract: a partnership in crime and credulity. Or, as Cornelia Ferris more fully details it, Mormonism "is just one unvarying picture of rascality, folly, imposition, credulity, and crime."[118] Her husband, Benjamin Ferris, agreed, reporting that Mormon men committed all manner of murder, theft, deception, laziness, and evil. He satirized, "The [Mormon] legislator, wise enough to legalize bigamy, burglary, forgery, perjury, theft, and murder, would do away with the necessity of penitentiaries and criminal codes."[119] Another perhaps not so tongue-in-cheek commentator on Mormon society observed, "The Mormon leaders have shrewdly calculated that by making of the society a large community of interest in crime, its members can be the more easily persuaded and influenced to aid in carrying into execution the political schemes of the priesthood."[120] The perverted social contract of Mormonism, according to these anti-Mormons, was made not between a brotherhood of equals but between the father-king figure of Brigham Young and his gang of criminals.

Anti-Mormons also argued that by making Mormon men partners in crime, the plural marriage system held in place a political authority that was "temporal as well as spiritual. Nothing is left to the free will of the people."[121] One apostate also claimed that the secret Mormon temple rituals of celestial marriage bound members to Young's despotism: "From the first to the last, the intention of the mystery [of the temple] is to teach unlimited obedience to Brigham."[122] Plural marriage lent itself to the "strictest obedience to the will of one person, and that person [is] the head of the church."[123] That is to say, Mormons could possess neither freedom of religious conscience, nor independent political will. John M. Coyner, founder of the Salt Lake Collegiate Institute, a Presbyterian mission school in Salt Lake City, maintained, "He, and he only, is fitted to become a citizen of our commonwealth who strives to be an independent thinker, and who follows no guide but his own conscientious sense of right and wrong; while he, and he only, is regarded as a Mormon who obeys counsel without question or gainsaying." For Coyner, while republicanism "opposes the centralization of power, and makes the individual the king," Mormonism "has for its chief corner-stone the dogma of central power, and blind submission to that power."[124] As a result, according to yet another incensed anti-Mormon, "To Mormons, freedom of thought or of action is as impossible as to idiots or slaves."[125] In anti-Mormon imaginations, Mormonism subjected its members to a tyranny so complete that it penetrated even into an individual's private mind, leaving no room for individual conscience.

German sociologist Jürgen Habermas has argued that one of the most important innovations of early modern bourgeois culture was what he calls the "public sphere," by which he refers to the public forum where the citizenry debated matters of public concern.[126] The absence of any such forum for political discussion in Utah alarmed anti-Mormons. They charged that Mormonism "disintegrates the political, and robs it of identity."[127] C. C. Goodwin noted that the Mormon polity seemed characterized by its "*oneness*, this utter death of free thought, this slavish obedience to the masters, and this entire prostitution of free and popular government."[128] Eli H. Murray, as well, singled out for censure this same troubling trait in Utah politics: "The 'oneness' of the Mormons," among other things, "is the fruitful source of all their trouble."[129]

For anti-Mormons, in part because there simply was no public sphere for political discussion in Utah, the equality so central to the social contract seemed to have evaporated. Nearly all anti-Mormons felt that polygamy was at the root of this problem. One proof that plural marriage was incompatible with republican equality was that "no nation of freemen ever allowed or tolerated polygamy. The institution is death to civil liberty." According to this same source, polygamy destroyed "the republican equality of men."[130] In anti-Mormon thought, companionate marriage was a defining marker of equality among citizens, as well as a fundamental right of citizenship. "In every republic men certainly have an equal right to the one woman for each man which the Creator persistently sees fit to provide."[131] By extension, "for any man to take more than his one woman *is a robbery inflicted on the rest of mankind*."[132] Mormon men clearly violated this principle of equality by taking more than their fair share of women.

In Mormondom, polygamy also translated into social hierarchy, according to at least one anti-Mormon. Polygamy, he censured, "gives direction to the social currents, and measures their velocity. While invading man's natural rights, it likewise curtails his social privileges, marking out channels of trade and shaping the movements of public industry."[133] Anti-Mormons also noted with disdain that the numerical tally of wives placed some men above others in the social hierarchy: "the greatness of a true Mormon is measured, indeed, by the number of wives he can keep in sweet and loving and especially obedient subjugation."[134] Anti-Mormons argued that, given the economic determinants of this hierarchy, "if polygamy were generally practiced it would be one of the worst monopolies in the world, for it would take away from the poor man all chance of having a home of his own."[135]

In addition, Mormonism also abrogated the contractual standard of individual property rights at the heart of American politics. Instead, for Mormons, the law of consecration placed the property of Church members in the cooperative possession of the privatized Church family. The political convictions of most Americans did not lend themselves well to approving or even understanding an economy conducted on these terms. Anti-Mormons noted the interrelation of polygamy and consecration and launched pointed critiques of Mormon systems of property management in polygamous contexts. For anti-Mormons, the overlap of polygamy with consecration combined Church rule over the private home and private property. It was a double assault on the notion of private property. On the one hand, polygamy undermined the individual as representative of the private sphere, while on the other, the practice of consecration undercut the notion of private property.

Anti-Mormons were right about this feature of the principle of consecration. Under consecration, the labor of an individual benefited not only him and his family but the entire community. One observer commented on property ownership in Brigham Young's United Order community, Orderville: "With the proceeds of his labor . . . he saw new buildings going up, new acres coming under cultivation. But none of them belonged to him. He never became a proprietor, an owner, a master. . . . [H]e was deprived of [life's] noblest ambitions." In establishing the authority of the Church over the private individual and his property, consecration undercut foundational American notions of private property and also of individuality. The same observer continued: "Tastes, therefore, could not be cultivated for the want of means, and any special faculties which members might individually possess were of necessity kept in abeyance."[136] According to anti-Mormons, subjects of the United Order, because they lacked private property, could not become their own self-directed private persons.

Travel narratives also reported that Mormon property ideals, besides undermining individuality, left families impoverished and living in squalor, while husbands deeded family funds over to Church officials. The marriage contract provided that in exchange for a wife's domestic and sexual service, husbands maintain the economic well-being of their wives.[137] However, anti-Mormons asserted that when plural marriage multiplied the economic demands on husbands beyond their abilities to provide, they neglected wives and left children "nearly naked and indescribably filthy."[138] Moreover, as one indignant government official noted, "the wealth of the father speedily finds its way into the coffers of the church, and the daughters are, in due time distributed among the high-priests."[139] As this comment indicates, most anti-Mormons were more than ready to believe the worst: the lack of private ownership of material and filial property among Mormons could only mean that the leaders of a Church-ruled monopoly were getting both much married and wealthy through their theocratic authority over property and family relations.

For anti-Mormons, there was nothing and nowhere—not the private self, the private home, nor private property—that Church government could not penetrate, no location in which a Mormon individual might exercise his liberty. Polygamy structured social, marital, religious, and economic hierarchy, obliterating any possible self-ownership and equality upon which free and public government in Utah might rest. As such, Mormonism sustained no individuals capable of making the kind of unfettered political choices upon which republicanism depended. A community with no qualified citizenry could not maintain free republican government, and on that basis anti-Mormons believed that the accoutrements of republicanism in Utah were a sham, emptied of all political meaning. One anti-Mormon claimed, "The republican *form* of government in Utah is a dead letter, existing only *pro forma*, and only so much of the tattern [*sic*] remnants are exhibited as will secure the largesses of the National Government; while the real *bona fide* government is that of the Mormon priesthood."[140] Anti-Mormons charged that Mormonism merged church, state, and family under the theocratic rule of Brigham Young. As Utah Judge John Cradlebaugh told Congress in 1863, "Brigham's house is at once tabernacle, capitol, and harem; and Brigham himself is king, priest, lawgiver, and chief polygamist."[141] In anti-Mormon imaginations, Mormons divested citizens of the power of consent, "casting from them, as so much waste, the things which all other white men have learned to regard as the most precious conquests of time and thought—personal freedom, family life, change of rulers, right of speech, concurrence in laws, equality before the judge, liberty of writing and voting. They [the Mormons] cast aside these conquests of time and thought in favor of Asiatic obedience to a man without birth, without education, whom they have chosen to regard as God's own vicar on the earth."[142]

Yet throughout the late nineteenth century, Mormons argued that the mixture of family, religion, economics, and government that constituted the privatized kingdom of God grew out of the republican principle of local rule and insisted that Church political authority could exist alongside and in harmony with secular American civil government. Anti-Mormons, however, saw in Utah not a privatized Church family separate from the American state, but rather a political despotism that replaced republican government with theocracy. In replacing marital and political consent with polygamic theocracy, anti-Mormons argued, Mormonism dispensed with the institutional protections of the social contract. Anti-Mormons observed that Mormons "put private relation to a high priest above moral instinct and public law." In doing so, they "subvert[ed] all principles of social duty."[143] Mormonism, anti-Mormons argued, simply "can not exist in contact with republican institutions."[144]

• • •

Over the 1870s and 1880s, anti-Mormons gradually convinced themselves that Mormon polygamic theocracy was a grave threat to republican government and threatened the very essence of Americanness. The trouble for anti-Mormons, however, was that many Mormons were already American citizens and removing them from the polity proved constitutionally difficult. In response to this roadblock, anti-Mormons, in the wake of westward expansion, Reconstruction, and unprecedented immigration rates, turned to perhaps the most powerful tropes in late-nineteenth-century America to rid the nation of the Mormon menace: race and social class. The next chapter will show that in the late nineteenth century, as ideologies of social Darwinism and tropes of racial degeneration became increasingly salient discourses, racial and class tropes had particular power to frame anti-Mormon demonstrations of the un-Americanness of Mormons. Race and class became central mechanisms by which a religion born on American soil and which located its origins in American ideals came to be regarded as an alien growth that must be excised from the body politic.

CHAPTER 6

"The Foulest Ulcer on the Body of Our Nation"

Race, Class, and Contagion in Anti-Mormon Literature

In 1866, a writer for *Frank Leslie's Illustrated Newspaper* called Mormonism "a great anomaly in American history."[1] Plural marriage, this writer contended, made Mormonism an anomaly in national culture that Americans simply could not tolerate. In their unrelenting attempts to cast the Mormon anomaly out of the American body politic, anti-Mormons most often turned to some of the most powerfully charged sources of fear and prejudice in the nineteenth century, race and class. Nativist attitudes along with prejudice toward immigrant poorer classes came with a ready-made set of tropes, images, analogies, and allusions to apply to Mormonism and manufacture deeply repelling differences between Mormons and "true" Americans. In the course of this decades-long literary and political campaign, anti-Mormon discourse articulated for all Americans the boundaries beyond which they could not go and remain truly American.

Painting Mormonism with the stripes of race and class difference, however, had built-in limitations. The origins of Mormonism were inextricably bound up with American institutions, and the Church's early membership shared similar ideological legacies and European gene pools of the nation at large. As Terryl Givens states, "Mormons *were* Americans, and in a most vexing way at that."[2] What was truly offensive to national sensibilities was the emergence of Mormon difference from an original sameness. In an attempt to distance themselves from plural marriage, anti-Mormons invested the practice with negative racial and class meanings.

"Turkey is In Our Midst"[3]:
Orientalist Anti-Mormonism

Orientalism was perhaps the most popular and widespread technique of ra-
cializing Mormons. The mindset that Edward Said has labeled Orientalism
emerged in the context of European imperialism that framed the Orient as
backward, underdeveloped, and in need of the civilizing influence of European
rule. Said's influential treatise, *Orientalism*, argues that beginning in the late
eighteenth century, Orientalism emerged "as a Western style for dominating,
restructuring, and having authority over the Orient."[4] Broadly speaking, Orientalism "was ultimately a political vision of reality whose structure promoted
the difference between the familiar (Europe, the West, 'us') and the strange
(the Orient, the East, 'them')."[5] Since before the American Revolution, American Protestants have "used the knowledge of Islam that they produced both
to reinforce their brand of Protestantism over its challengers such as Deism or
Catholicism, and to delegitimize Islam and Muslims religiously, morally, and
racially."[6] In the decades following the Revolution, American presses flooded
the nation with books about the Muslim world. According to Robert J. Allison,
those captivity narratives, histories, novels, and poems "conveyed a consistent
picture of the Muslim world, an inverted image of the world the Americans were
trying to create anew." For Americans in the early Republic, "the Muslim world
was a lesson . . . in what not to do, in how not to construct a state, encourage
commerce, or form families."[7] In this early literature, "a wicked religion [Islam]
had fostered bad government, and bad government thwarted social progress."[8]
Moreover, Muslim rulers were reported to have kept harems full of beautiful
women, "slaves to the tyrant's lust."[9]

Anti-Mormons no doubt drew on this early literature as they cast Mormons as Oriental, and one does not have to look far to find Orientalist binary
reasoning in anti-Mormon thought.[10] To anti-Mormons, Mormonism looked
suspiciously like the religious, domestic, and political despotism transplanted
onto American soil that Orientalists believed characterized the cultures of
the Orient. Orientalist metaphors could account for the Mormon marital, religious, and political structures that anti-Mormons found so heinously anti-
democratic. Although Orientalism was not a dominant trope for understanding Mormonism until the 1850s, the comparison between Joseph Smith and
the prophet of Islam had been made as early as 1831, and Smith himself made
the comparison in 1838.[11] In his 1842 *The History of the Saints*, John C. Bennett
rehearsed connections anti-Mormons made between Mormon polygamy and
Islam. Bennett claimed that Joseph Smith "closely resembles his master and

model, Mahomet, [*sic*] [in] the secret regulations he has formed for directing the relations of the sexes." For anti-Mormons, Mormon polygamy was worse than "Muhammedan" polygamy and would appear incredible even in "those licentious Oriental courts" of the "modern Turkish and Moorish sultans."[12]

After Pratt's 1852 announcement of plural marriage, comparing Mormonism to Catholicism (see chapter 4) became a much less useful analogy because, as anti-Mormon Utah Judge John Cradlebaugh would point out eleven years later, "Mormonism repudiates the celibacy imposed by the catholic religion upon its priesthood, and takes in its stead the voluptuous impositions of the Mohammedan church."[13] The practice of polygamy offered anti-Mormonism a unique opportunity to transfer many of its early anti-Catholic claims into a much more comprehensive set of accusations attached to ideologies of race and racial progress. Orientalism proved particularly useful to anti-Mormon strategies because it allowed more of Mormonism under its tent than did associations with Catholicism—it could account for both polygamy and theocracy and connect those practices to the more "backward" races of the East. During the 1850s, polygamy, not popery, became the defining characteristic of Mormonism's un-Americanness. Islam, not Catholicism, became the primary signifier by which Americans understood Mormonism. Former territorial Court Justice John Cradlebaugh outlined the theological similarities he saw between Mormonism and Islam—that each "preaches openly that the more wives and children its men have in this world, the purer, more influential and conspicuous will they be in the next; that wives, children, and property will not be restored, but doubled in the resurrection."[14]

Descriptions of the "customs of Constantinople" practiced in the harems or seraglios of "the Orient of the American West" and references to the "Muhammedan" prophets Joseph Smith and Brigham Young abounded throughout anti-Mormon literature.[15] To anti-Mormons the practice of plural marriage obviously identified Mormons with "those oriental and tropical races practicing polygamy."[16] Anti-Mormons also linked plural marriage variously to Indians, Native Americans, Africans and African-American slaves, Asians and Asian immigrants, and the "Oriental" cultures of the Near East.[17] Polygamy, anti-Mormons argued, "belongs now to the indolent and opium-eating Turks and Asiatics, the miserable Africans, the North American savages, and the latter-day saints."[18] One image, part of a composite of illustrations from *Puck* magazine, showed a Mormon polygamist and several wives dressed in "Oriental" clothing while wives waited on and entertained their husband (see bottom left image).[19]

Anti-Mormons genuinely alarmed by the presence of Orientalism in the American West worried that the Mormons were more like the backward

"A Desperate Attempt to Solve the Mormon Question," first published in *Puck*, 13 February 1884, *376–77*. Courtesy of Library of Congress Prints and Photographs Online Catalogue.

cultures of the "Orient" than the forward-looking civilization of the United States. Anti-Mormon writer Fanny Stenhouse concurred, for example, that in Utah "the teachings of Christianity had been supplanted by an attempt to imitate the barbarism of Oriental nations in a long past age."[20] What was at stake if Mormonism spread? In an early article written against Utah's 1855 campaign for statehood, then renowned political ethicist Francis Lieber declared, "Wedlock, or monogamic marriage, . . . is one of the elementary distinctions—historical and actual—between European and Asiatic humanity. . . . Strike it out and you destroy our very being; and when we say *our*, we mean our race—a race which has its great and broad destiny, a solemn aim in the great career of civilization, with which no one of us has any right to trifle."[21] Yet another writer asserted, "Where polygamy has superseded monogamy, as in cases of conversion to Mohammedanism, there has been a decline in national character. Where monogamy has superseded polygamy, there has been a corresponding rise."[22]

Anti-Mormons puzzled over development of polygamy in the United States. "[Mormonism's] doctrines and its formulas are so foreign to our dispositions and habits of thought that we should never have supposed that it would have gained a thousand proselytes among men of Anglo-Saxon blood." This writer professed "astonishment at the progress of this wonderful people. Transplanting the institutions of the mystic East into the practical and active West, . . . uniting the voluptuous sensuality of the Oriental harem with the stern virtue and far-seeing shrewdness of the American republican, these, we confess, are anomalies of which we cannot determine the result."[23] This writer and others like him mobilized the language and mythos of racial progress to stigmatize Mormons as unevolved barbarians. From this vantage point, monogamous marriage became freighted with the entire weight of civilized progress.

Not only did anti-Mormons understand plural marriage to be an anachronism, holding back racial progress of the West, but polygamy seemed to them a climatological oddity as well. "The Asiatic institution was never meant to flourish on American soil," one commented. It "is tenfold more unnatural to such a climate and race than in southern Asia or Africa." Anti-Mormons found it baffling that "[w]ith snow in sight the year round, [the Mormons] pattern their domestic life after that of inter-tropical barbarians, and vainly hope to produce the vigor of hardy North-men from the worst practices of effeminate Asiatics."[24] Some Orientalist characterizations of Mormons bordered on the ridiculous. For example, one anti-Mormon contended that Salt Lake City "wears a distinctly Oriental appearance. So we of the Far West who have only dreamed of the East, imagine how Damascus may look. . . . A dome, a tower, a spire that may answer for a minaret, . . . a sky of more than Oriental softness overhead."[25]

Another observed that "the Mormon's handkerchief, straggling from under his hat, reminds one of the Bedouin *kefiyeh* [*sic*]."[26] The absurdity of descriptions like these indicates that they were not merely observations, but rather served a productive function—they *made* Mormons Oriental, hence un-American.

In anti-Mormon imaginations, part of what united the backward cultures of the Orient with Mormonism was a shared belief in the inferiority of women. Only those nations which viewed women as inferior to men would practice polygamy, and thus nothing showed the Orientalism of Mormons as thoroughly as the practice of plural marriage. Anti-Mormons truly believed that women under polygamy were bought and sold like cattle. Francis Willard expressed the views of many anti-Mormons when she declared, "Modern Mohammedanism has its Mecca at Salt Lake, where Prophet Heber C. Kimball speaks of his wives as 'cows.'" In a community where women were debased as mere animals, she declared, "Turkey is in our midst," and then added that Turkey "is doubtless the most debased country on earth."[27] By anti-Mormon accounts, under plural marriage hundreds of years of the progress of civilization degenerated into a society where men, "Oriental in their views," treated women like property.[28]

The Orientalization of Mormonism went beyond marriage practices, climate, and the status of women to racialize the connections between polygamy and theocracy. In conceptualizing the Mormon as an Occidental Oriental, anti-Mormons embraced wholeheartedly the Orientalist reasoning that wed polygamy to political despotism. Comparing Utah to the Orient, anti-Mormons argued that polygamy gave rise to theocracy, and theocracy protected polygamy. One anti-Mormon claimed, for example, that "polygamy is one of the most odious relics of Asiatic despotism."[29] "Arabian" idolatry and the "voluptuous paradise" of the harems of the modern sultan were, in anti-Mormon imaginations, "the results of that despotic sway of a government which, acting upon ignorance and superstition, have so greatly contributed to the political and moral degradation of a powerful yet deluded portion of the posterity of Adam."[30] One apostate even claimed, "Imitating Mohammed in polity of government, the Mormons obtain some of the results of Moslem rule"—polygamy, fanaticism, and stagnation.[31]

Perhaps the most damning statement connecting polygamy and theocracy to the Orient came in the Supreme Court decision in the *Reynolds* case of 1879 that upheld the constitutionality of anti-polygamy legislation. Chief Justice Morrison R. Waite stated: "Polygamy has always been odious among the northern and western nations of Europe, and, until the establishment of the Mormon Church, was almost exclusively a feature of the life of Asiatic and of African people . . . and from the earliest history of England, polygamy has been treated as an offence against society." In addition, Waite advanced his opinion that "according as monogamous or polygamous marriages are allowed do we find the principles on which the government of the people, to a greater or lesser extent, rests." In this, Waite echoed the prevailing views of Orientalist anti-Mormonism which linked the practice of polygamy to political despotism. He compared polygamy to the Indian practice of Suttee, in which a widow allows herself to be cremated on her husband's funeral pyre to show her devotion to him, implying under Mormonism polygamy required the self-immolation of women. The court agreed with decades of Orientalist anti-Mormonism that polygamy, theocracy, and the oppression of women were inextricably linked and simply could not be tolerated on American soil.[32]

Despite the rhetorical force and pervasiveness of Orientalist anti-Mormonism, scholars must approach it with great caution. To think of the Mormon question only in Orientalist terms is to risk misconstruing anti-Mormonism as a colonialist discourse and Mormons as colonized subjects. On the contrary, Mormons were at least as much agents of the colonization of the American West as they were subjects colonized by a repressive federal government. To think of them otherwise is to fail to companion the religious and ideological difference of Mormonism with its participation in the colonization of the American West. Precisely where Orientalism helps us understand the nature of anti-Mormonism is where it fails as a paradigm for understanding the more complex set of historical relations within which anti-Mormonism occurred. Nonetheless, after acknowledging limitations, Orientalist anti-Mormonism can only make sense within the binary legacy of colonialism that established the "us" and "them" of West and East and informed American political ideas into the nineteenth century. America inherited and adopted many of the legacies of European Orientalism and translated them into particularly American contexts, setting Occidental America apart from the "Orient" it believed it encountered in Utah.[33]

In Bruce Burgett's terms, the Orientalization of Mormonism went beyond a simple process of racial "othering" to participate in "the imperial consolidation of the nation-state."[34] In other words, by making Mormons Oriental, anti-Mormons clarified what it meant to be American. To be an American meant to possess liberty of conscience; to be monogamous and democratic; and perhaps most importantly, to participate in the nation's racial progress.[35] Orientalist anti-Mormonism produced a means of understanding Mormonism which, while far different from Mormons' understanding of themselves, at least made the Mormon anomaly intelligible to Americans and held in place the meanings of national culture that anti-Mormons found most compelling. By showing that

Mormons were "really" Orientals in American clothing, Orientalism made sense of the oxymoron of polygamous Americans. By claiming that Mormons were not truly American, Orientalist anti-Mormons helped make Mormons into targets of federal discipline.

However, the Orientalization of Mormonism was inherently limited by the fact that it was largely an American faith peopled almost entirely from the populations of the Occident. As Dr. I. S. Briggs wrote in 1849, the Mormons "are bone of our bone and flesh of our flesh."[36] Thus, Orientalism could never quite move past the level of simile, showing the many ways Mormons were like the cultures of the Orient. This left anti-Mormons with a few paradoxes: Utah was not the Orient but the American West, and Mormon skin was overwhelmingly as white as that of their eastern antagonists. Though Orientalist metaphors persisted in anti-Mormon literature throughout the latter half of the nineteenth century, from the 1860s through the 1880s they were accompanied by the ultimately more convincing discourse of nativism. Nativist anti-Mormonism more successfully reckoned with Mormon whiteness while also more successfully distancing Mormons from the racial body politic.

"Not to America, But to Zion"[37]: The Class and Racial Politics of Mormon Immigration

In 1881, popular anti-Mormon writer C. C. Goodwin declared, "The Mormon church is a foreign kingdom, hostile in all its features to a republican form of government; it is guided and controlled by foreigners, and depends on foreigners and children of foreigners for future expansion and power."[38] Scholars have found that in 1870, 67.9 percent of Utah residents over twenty-five years old were foreign-born.[39] Of even more interest, though, is how anti-Mormons ingeniously deployed the concept of foreignness to reckon with the faith's successes among Anglo-Europeans and still maintain that Mormons were maritally, racially, and politically backward.

Nativist anti-Mormonism must be distinguished from the general nativism that animated the late nineteenth-century "America for Americans" movement in its campaign against immigration.[40] Most nativism directed its attacks at immigrants from Central and Eastern Europe, Asia, and Mexico, whose racial characteristics were broadly understood to be undesirable.[41] Anti-Mormon nativism, on the other hand, was a response to large numbers of Mormon immigrants from Western Europe, mainly from the British Isles and Scandinavia, but also from the Netherlands, Germany, Switzerland, Italy, and France, and, to a lesser extent, colonies in the South Pacific and South Africa. Mormons came from the world's "better" racial stock.[42] Mormon immigrants, like Mormons native to the United States, were from largely the same genetic sources and political legacies as most Americans. To cast Mormons as anomalous, nativist anti-Mormons had to make a distinction between the sorts of Europeans who had become American not so many generations ago and the sorts of Europeans then converting to Mormonism. They did so through the vehicle of social class.

As anti-Mormons deployed it, social class separated desirable Anglo-Europeans from undesirable ones and established that Mormonism attracted the latter. Anti-Mormons used the rhetoric of social Darwinism, often interpreted loosely, to distinguish desirable from undesirable Anglo-Europeans and credit the socio-economic structure of Western society to genetic meritocracy. Social Darwinists claimed that the natural law British philosopher Herbert Spencer termed "survival of the fittest" was a social and economic law as well.[43] For social Darwinists, the socio-economic status of groups within Western nations also bespoke their natural order. The successes of wealthier and more powerful people indicated their natural superiority, while the failures of the working classes denoted their natural shortcomings.

Anti-Mormons believed that the supposed poor genetic quality of European converts to Mormonism was no coincidence. Well versed in social Darwinist logic, anti-Mormons noted that immigrant Mormon converts were a class of "ignorant, almost pauper emigrants of the old world."[44] Anti-Mormons were deeply concerned with the new hereditary element the influx of working-class European immigrants introduced into the United States through Utah, claiming that the backward nature of Mormonism corresponded with the quality of immigrants coming to the New World under Mormonism's aegis. They argued that Mormon immigrants "are all of the peasantry, the lower classes of working people at home [in Europe]; and so the congregations of the Mormons do not exhibit the marks of high acuteness and intelligence.... [T]he great mass, both in size, looks and dress, was below the poorest, hardest-working and most ignorant classes of our eastern large towns."[45] A writer for *The Home Missionary* concurred, claiming that Mormon converts "are poor creatures, for the most part, gathered up in the ignorant back-country districts of Europe by shrewd missionaries."[46] For these anti-Mormons, Mormonism attracted to America the evolutionary dregs of Western Europe.

Some anti-Mormons believed that Mormonism was only kept alive by immigration. One writer for *Harper's New Monthly Magazine*, for instance, contended: "But for the steady influx of foreigners—low, base-born foreigners, hereditary bondsmen—the two dreadful features of the Mormon Church, polygamy and the exalting of the church over the state, would die out in America in two generations."[47] In explanation, the same writer shared his conviction that Mormonism "is an institution so absolutely un-American in its requirements that it would die of its own infamies within twenty years, except for the yearly infusion of fresh serf blood from abroad."[48]

As conduits of heredity, women played a special role in anti-Mormon concerns. Anti-Mormons often claimed that Mormon women converts in particular were foreigners of the "lower-classes."[49] One anti-Mormon was certain that immigrant women "are not intelligent enough to have learned much about the practices of the 'Saints,' save what is told them by the missionaries."[50] Some anti-Mormons described how the women were procured. Mormon elders exploited the ignorance of working-class European women, seducing and shipping them to the United States in droves. One illustration of the arrival of Mormon women immigrants highlighted "Pure White 'Mormon Immigration' On the Atlantic Coast. More *cheap* 'help-mates' for Mr. Polygamist." In this image, dilapidated dregs of Europe wore signs around their necks that read, "seamstress," "laundress," "nurse," "waitress," "chambermaid," and "cook."[51] The implication of images like these was clear: immigrant women of dubious reproductive stock arrived in Zion prepared for polygamous enslavement. Mormon elders attracted women converts whose degeneracy matched their own, then used the dregs of Europe to sustain the Mormon community.

While widespread, the censure of Mormon immigrants was not universal. A few anti-Mormons were encouraged by the influx of European converts into Utah. One writer for the *Phrenological Journal*, for example, took hope in the fact that English converts and American Mormons, "of the American type proper—republican and not theocratic," had begun the Godbeite New Movement in Utah. (The Godbeite movement, as mentioned earlier, was a reform movement that began in 1869 in opposition to Brigham Young's economic policies that forbade trade with non-Mormons and grew to oppose both theocratic Church leadership and plural marriage.) Anti-Mormons optimistic about European immigration argued that a majority of Mormon converts "have the capacity and weight of the Anglo-Saxon head, and are wonderfully adapted for the formation of the body of a new society of a hardy, industrious, conservative people."[52] These anti-Mormons hoped that European immigration would improve the hereditary character of the Mormon polity.[53]

These exceptions notwithstanding, the anti-Mormon nativism of the 1870s and 1880s sustained the connections early Orientalist anti-Mormonism made between the undertow of polygamy, theocracy, and evolutionary regression

PURE WHITE "MORMON IMMIGRATION" ON THE ATLANTIC COAST.
More *cheap* "help-mates" for Mr. Polygamist.

"Pure White 'Mormon Immigration' on the Atlantic Coast," first published in
Harper's Weekly, 25 March 1882, 191. Courtesy of the Church History Library,
The Church of Jesus Christ of Latter-day Saints, Salt Lake City, Utah.

on one hand, and the higher ground of monogamy, republicanism, and evolutionary superiority on the other. In the wake of European immigration, anti-
Mormons increasingly deployed Orientalist and nativist connections in another
racial binary that opposed Americans of better evolutionary stock to Mormons
and their converts in order to account for the whiteness of Mormons and the
influx of Western Europeans into Utah. Noting the supposed quality of Mormon European immigrants, anti-Mormon nativism set a young and vigorous
American race against an aging, spent, aristocratic, and despotic European

Old World. Anti-Mormons situated Mormonism as a vestige of the decadent aristocratic structure of the Old World of an earlier evolutionary age.[54] They argued that Mormonism took the racial development of Anglo-Europeans back in time to an early age, an age of political despotism and aristocracy. For the immigrants of this sort who came to Utah, living in America marked not progress, but a return to an earlier age of monarchy. In this anti-Mormon schematic, polygamy played a central role not only in marking and perpetuating racial degeneration, but also in re-establishing the aristocratic social structure of the Old World in the American West. One observer noted, for example, that Brigham Young, the chief polygamist, dressed like an English aristocrat.[55] Another remarked, "It is enough to say, in summary, that polygamy never could exist except as the privilege of a despotic aristocracy."[56] In nativist anti-Mormon imaginations, Brigham Young governed his subjects like a monarch, while his priesthood regenerated the detested aristocratic structure of Old Europe.

Some anti-Mormons contended that Mormon immigrants came to Utah in search of aristocratic power. According to at least one anti-Mormon "visitor to Utah," Mormonism promised the "indigent and hopelessly ignorant" classes of Europe the power and prestige of Mormon priesthood authority. In addition, this writer claimed that Mormon converts also immigrated to Utah under the promise of wealth and free land.[57] According to anti-Mormons, the power and wealth Mormonism promised was a tantalizing possibility for Europe's powerless lower classes, caught as they were in an older political age. One anti-Mormon characterized the "foreign kingdom" of Mormonism as "a theocracy managed by a plebian aristocracy."[58] In these visions, European immigrants arrived hoping to duplicate in Utah the aristocracy of the Old World, only with themselves as the aristocrats.

Other anti-Mormons contended that Mormon immigrants came to the New World with no aspirations to better themselves in ways that might be properly termed "American." Instead, they joined forces with "The only form of religion in this country which refuses to conform either to the spirit of progress and improvement and enlightened humanity which characterizes the age in which we live, or to our laws and the genius of our free institutions."[59] In this version, the nature of the immigrants arriving from Europe showed anti-Mormons that "[t]he effect of the Mormon creed is, evidently, to gather together a low class of villains, and still a lower class of dupes; and it follows that the latter are easily governed."[60] It was clear to anti-Mormons that whether to become the Mormon aristocracy or to be ruled by its despotism, European immigrants came to the New World not to escape the aristocracy of Old Europe, but to reinstate it. Mormon immigrants "did not come here in the love of republicanism; . . . they came . . . 'not to America but to Zion;' not in the admiration of American institutions, but in the confident expectation of assisting to subvert them."[61] In anti-Mormon minds, the very un-Americanness of Mormonism accounted for the success of Mormon missionary efforts abroad. The recruitment of the foreign lower classes was, one anti-Mormon contended, "a necessity for perfecting the new scheme, the so-called 'Kingdom of God,' for such a despotism could not have been organized with an American laity."[62] Rather, to perpetuate its absolute rule, Mormonism had to attract a class of Europeans "impelled hither not by a love of republicanism, but rather by a desire to change a political for a religious monarchy."[63]

Anti-Mormons saw the participation of the Mormon polity in a theocratic system as a resounding rejection of the American principles of self-determination, liberty, and individual sovereignty in favor of the same kind of political structures from which the American Revolution had liberated the nation. Mormonism reduced republicanism to theocratic rule, and paradoxically, "this, the only American church, has lost every trace of Americanness and become an essentially foreign theocracy—drawing its entire strength from the peasantry of the old world."[64] However, though theocracy could not dupe true Americans, it still posed a danger. In reconstituting the aristocracy of the old world, Mormonism threatened not only to undo the marital and political achievements of republican progress, but also to subject the rest of the nation to Mormonism's polygamic theocracy. Thus, by construing the Mormons as Oriental, with all the negative qualities that signified, and emphasizing the foreignness and degenerate quality of Mormon immigrants, anti-Mormons characterized Mormonism as a disease threatening to infect the national body politic.

Foreign Influence, Mormon Contagion, and the "Dream of Polygamic Empire"[65]

Over the 1870s, as the membership of the Church increased and federal legislation proved impotent against Mormon polygamy, anti-Mormons increasingly turned to metaphors of contagion to convey the magnitude of the Mormon problem. Mormonism, they argued, threatened to spread its foreign influence into the national body politic. Anti-Mormons characterized the Mormon community itself as a foreign nation menacing the sovereign body of America with cultural and political infection. By the mid-1870s, no metaphor was as ubiquitous in anti-Mormon literature as that of contagion. No characteristic of Mormonism attracted metaphors of contagion more than plural marriage; hardly a discussion of polygamy passed without comparing it to a blight, disease, cancer, ulcer, fever, scourge, miasma, or poison.

Contagion was a particularly powerful trope by which to illustrate the dangers Mormonism and plural marriage posed to the body politic. Contagion metaphors evoked an element of biological malevolence in ways no other set of metaphors could. In one of the earliest references to Mormonism as contagion, early anti-polygamy novelist Metta Victoria Fuller likened polygamy to a "slow march of disease which threatens to desolate all households."[66] She called upon the nation to declare to Utah, "'Away with thee, and cleanse thyself.'"[67] In other anti-Mormons' words, polygamy was "more destructive in its effects upon the public and private relations of life than the direful inflictions of the most dreaded pestilence or national scourge."[68] In yet another's, polygamy "is like a wasting fever—a withering miasma on the moral purpose and mental energy of the individual man; it consumes the vitality of soul . . . and thus effectively hinders the material progress and intellectual greatness of a people."[69] Far from being safely quarantined in the western deserts of Utah, the "Asiatic cancer"[70] of plural marriage, "the foulest ulcer on the body of our nation,"[71] was on the move. "The shameful, deep, devouring, sloughing spot of corruption . . . from its stronghold in Utah, is eating its way beyond the borders into the neighboring communities."[72] These were not isolated examples. Statements like these abounded in anti-Mormon literature.

One attempt to reckon with the Mormon threat came in the form of calls to limit Mormon political influence. For anti-Mormons, the Mormon vote contaminated the purity of an American electorate with foreign un-American influence that jeopardized the survival of the Republic. Anti-Mormons believed that the "Mohammedan" nature of Utah's marital and political institutions and the influx of "Old World" immigrants had made Mormondom more like a foreign nation unto itself than a community of American citizens. One anti-Mormon writer stated that the Mormons certainly affected the "manners and morals of a nation."[73] Moreover, anti-Mormons noted over the 1870s and 1880s that Mormonism was also becoming more literally foreign, "drawing constantly from foreign countries hosts of votaries."[74] By extension, a Mormon could not be truly American.

Anxiety over the influence of Old World immigrants became particularly evident in discussions of woman suffrage in the 1870s. Lenient territorial suffrage acts allowed immigrants, both women and men, who had lived in Utah only six months the right to vote. Anti-Mormons predicted disaster. "[A]lien women with the odor of the immigrant ship still upon their clothes, without ever having taken an oath of allegiance to the United States, without the slightest idea of the meaning of the act they are performing, or what is intended by it, cast their votes as they are instructed to do, in some tongue unknown to ordinary Americans, and go away dazed."[75] Since women did not possess the suffrage in most of the rest of the nation, Utah women made easy targets for disenfranchisement. Calls to disenfranchise Utah women began almost immediately after their enfranchisement in 1870. By depriving Mormon women of the vote, anti-Mormons hoped to decrease the potential Mormon pollution of American politics.

The indignation voiced over Mormon woman suffrage in many ways stood in for anti-Mormons' mistrust and indignation with all aspects of Mormon political life. Mormons demonstrated an unnatural political unity that, anti-Mormons contended, could not exist except by despotic rule. To Mormons, on the other hand, Mormon bloc voting represented the political unity of the kingdom of God. In 1879, Church official Orson Pratt declared, "Thank God that in this Territory we have supported a republican form of government without being under the necessity of impressing upon the people that they should be divided. We do not impress any such thing upon their minds. It is not part of the Republican government to be divided."[76] To anti-Mormons, Mormon voting patterns showed that Mormons voted not the individual consciences of good Americans, but the demands of polygamic theocracy. In this sense, anti-Mormons concurred with suffrage advocate Susan B. Anthony that "suffrage is as much of a success for the Mormon women as for the men," which, for anti-Mormons, was no success at all because both were dominated by priesthood hierarchy.[77]

One powerful image of the Mormon threat repeated in at least three places, one of which is reprinted here, was the image of the Mormon cephalopod. One especially powerful iteration of this image appeared in *Puck* magazine in 1881 (see figure earlier in this chapter) and showed an octopus-like monster bearing the head of then-prophet John Taylor and the label "Mormonism." The monster's tentacles grasped such American icons as the capitol building, the lady justice, Uncle Sam, a figure representing public opinion, the YMCA, the public school system, and others. The image bore the caption, "How long will this destructive monster be allowed to live?"[78] Another incarnation of the cephalopod was an image that placed the body of an octopus over the Utah Territory, with its tentacles grasping at Wyoming, Colorado, New Mexico, Arizona, Nevada, and Idaho.[79] The image of Mormonism spreading out from Utah across the nation intermeshed with anti-Mormon concerns about what one former Utah official called the "dream of polygamic empire that dazzles the leaders of these

First published in R. G. McNiece, *Present Aspects of the Mormon Question* (1898), frontispiece. Courtesy of L. Tom Perry Special Collections, Harold B. Lee Library, Brigham Young University, Provo, Utah.

people."[80] Many anti-Mormons were sincerely worried that Mormons intended treason against the United States, taught it in their temples, and schemed to overtake the U.S. government with polygamic theocracy. One anti-Mormon declared, for example, that Mormons "mean to destroy free government in the United States, and reproduce in this country such a state of affairs as rules in Mohammedan countries."[81] America, in the minds of not a few anti-Mormons, was under attack by Mormons.

The work of anthropologist Mary Douglas offers a useful interpretive framework for understanding one of the most important outcomes of the prevailing anti-Mormon anxieties about Mormon contagion. Over the late nineteenth century, anti-Mormons came to view Mormonism as, in the words of Douglas, an "offen[se] against order"—an anomaly.[82] She defines an anomaly as "an element which does not fit a given set or series," and "When something is firmly classed as anomalous," she claims, "the outline of the set in which it is not a member is clarified."[83] By casting Mormons as anomalous, anti-Mormons clarified the nature of America itself, the identity and characteristics of an American imagined community.[84] Douglas also argues that "some pollutions are used as analogies for expressing a general view of the social order."[85] Anti-Mormons viewed Mormonism as such a pollutant and their anxieties about possible contagion reflected the hierarchical relations that in the minds of most Americans set monogamy above polygamy, demarcated the relationship between Mormons and the rest of the nation, and symbolized the dangers Mormonism reportedly posed.

For Douglas, as for anti-Mormons, the identification of contagion has a productive function: "Eliminating [contaminants] is not a negative movement, but a positive effort to organize the environment" in order to "create unity of experience."[86] In this instance, identifying Mormons as pollutants of the nation served to clarify the outline of the monogamous set at the center of an American identity to which Mormons did not belong. Similarly, classifying some people as un-American identified others as more authentically American. In Douglas's terms, "separating, purifying, demarcating, and punishing transgressions" help to "exaggerat[e] the difference between within and without, about and below, male and female, with and against," constituting social order.[87] Thus the separation, demarcation, and eventual punishment of Mormon polygamists served to clarify distinctions and seal off monogamous Americans from the influence of polygamist Mormons.

As anti-Mormons viewed it, not to do so—to leave the anomaly of Mormonism in place—would eat away at the very moorings of the Republic. Convinced that anomalies could not exist in a state of abeyance, anti-Mormons argued that either Mormons had to conform to national norms or the nation would become like the Mormons.[88] Mrs. C. V. Waite declared, "no community can happily exist with an institution so important as that of marriage wanting in all those qualities that make it homogeneal [*sic*] with institutions and laws of neighboring civilized communities having the same object."[89] Another writer proclaimed, "Either the Mormon theory of government is true in all particulars, in which case the federal officials are usurpers and the gentiles intruders and rebels against the 'Kingdom of God;' or it is false in every particular and must be totally subverted."[90] Anti-Mormons thus placed Mormonism and Americanness in a binary relation and argued that only one—Mormonism or Americanness—could survive. Coexistence was impossible; with Mormonism within it, there could be no true America.

• • •

The tropes of race, class, and contagion proved successful in laying the groundwork for legislative campaigns against Mormons. Through the language of race and class, anti-Mormons demonstrated that Mormonism was indeed a foreign influence on American soil that threatened to infect the rest of the nation with its polygamic theocracy. The next chapter discusses the congressional debates over the legal anti-polygamy campaigns of the 1880s that, ultimately, ended the practice of plural marriage in the LDS Church. Decades of anti-Mormon rhetoric informed these discussions, shaping the ways legislators understood the problem with Mormons and the solutions they proposed. Legislators, anti-Mormons claimed, could only respond to the contagion of Mormonism with the strong medicine of legal expulsion.

CHAPTER 7

"Suffer a Surrender . . . ?
No, Never!"

The End of Plural Marriage

The anti-polygamy reform "crusade" that emerged in the late 1870s and 1880s
was stimulated, in part, by a grassroots women's anti-polygamy movement
launched in Utah that quickly became a national movement.[1] In the early 1880s,
a local Utah organization turned national, the Ladies Anti-Polygamy Society,
was part of a successful campaign to prevent polygamist George Q. Cannon
from assuming office as Utah's territorial representative to Congress. That campaign brought broad prominence to anti-polygamy reform campaigns in a nation already prepared for anti-polygamy activism by decades of anti-Mormon
discourse. Women's reform associations like the Women's Christian Temperance Union jumped on the anti-polygamy bandwagon. Public lectures from
the likes of Kate Field, Anna Dickenson, and the prophet Brigham Young's
former wife, Ann Eliza Young, abounded, and mass meetings, organized by a
variety of women's reform organizations, collected signatures for the hundreds
of anti-polygamy petitions that flooded the U.S. Congress. These petitions
were often presented to Congress along with speeches from reformers like
Jennie Froiseth, Angie Newman, and again Kate Field entreating federal officials to use what Field called the "dynamite of law" to put teeth into federal
anti-polygamy legislation.[2]

Bringing Utah "Into Its Republican Relations with the Great Republic that Surrounds It"[3]

By the time reform campaigns against polygamy emerged in the late 1870s, legislation against polygamy had proved a dismal failure. In 1874, Congress passed the Poland Act, which asserted more federal power over the Utah court system.[4] This act shifted jurisdiction over polygamy cases from territorial to federal courts and put in place new procedures for selecting jurors that Congress hoped would result in more convictions. While the Poland Act ensured that juries serving in polygamy cases would not be stacked with Mormons, it failed to address the difficulties already encountered under the Morrill Act in identifying the practitioners of plural marriage with sufficient evidence to prosecute them. Utah did not require marriages to be registered with the state, so proof of more than one marriage was often difficult to come by. Moreover, Mormons had managed to successfully protect themselves against prosecution for the crime of plural marriage; very few men had been convicted.[5] In October 1875, prominent Mormon George Reynolds was indicted for polygamy and convicted under the Morrill Act. The Utah Supreme Court upheld his conviction, so Reynolds, with the support of Church officials hoping to prove the unconstitutionality of anti-polygamy legislation, appealed his case to the United States Supreme Court.

The landmark decision in *Reynolds v. United States*, handed down in 1879, upheld the constitutionality of federal anti-polygamy legislation. With a burgeoning anti-polygamy reform movement behind it, the case wrote into the canon of American law the conclusions anti-Mormon literature had been forwarding for decades.[6] The legal issues in the trial related to jury selection and witness testimony in the lower courts, but for Mormons the larger agenda of the case was to establish the unconstitutionality of the Morrill Act on grounds of religious freedom. Upholding the constitutionality of anti-polygamy legislation, Chief Justice Morrison Waite argued the majority opinion. He contended that while Congress could not legislate religious belief, according to a Virginia law "Congress was left free to reach actions which were in violation of social duties or subversive of good order."[7] To permit a citizen to "excuse his practices ... because of his religious belief" would be "to permit every citizen to become a law unto himself."[8]

The challenge for Waite was to articulate how plural marriage constituted an act against public order. Waite rested his opinion on decades of anti-Mormon literature that had produced a vision of the implications of polygamy for public life and governmental principles. Like anti-Mormons before him, Waite argued the primal significance of marriage: "Upon [marriage] society may be said to be built, and out of its fruits spring social relations and social obligations and duties, with which government is necessarily required to deal." Marriage was, "in most civilized nations," within the purview of the state, "a civil contract, and usually regulated by law." But for Waite, as for the anti-Mormons before him, marriage was a compelling state interest not just as the basis of social relationships but as the foundation of government principles as well: "[A]ccording as monogamous or polygamous marriages are allowed, do we find the principles on which the government of the people, to a greater or less extent, rests." Polygamy leads to patriarchy in the home and to patriarchal rule in communities which, according to the Chief Justice, "fetters the people in stationary despotism, while that principle cannot long exist in connection with monogamy."[9] Following the logic of decades of anti-Mormon rhetoric, the court tied polygamy inextricably to Mormon theocracy, identifying political despotism as the most significant of the "evil consequences that were supposed to flow from plural marriage."[10] Maintaining a proper private sphere that safeguarded the individual and the family was a social duty that Mormons failed to perform, and plural marriage constituted an act against public order because it trapped Mormons in a despotic theocracy. In this court ruling, it was evident that despite previous legislative failures, the logic and urgency of anti-Mormonism had finally penetrated the federal government.

In December 1879, President Rutherford B. Hayes's Third Annual Message to Congress clarified what would be the implications of anti-polygamy legislation for Mormon citizenship. The *Reynolds* decision released lawmakers from the premise that anti-polygamy legislation violated religious freedom, and in its wake Hayes called for "more comprehensive and more searching methods for preventing as well as punishing this crime [polygamy]." He declared, "If necessary to secure obedience to the law, the enjoyment and exercise of the rights and privileges of citizenship in the Territories of the United States may be withheld or withdrawn from those who violate or oppose the enforcement of the law on this subject."[11]

The *Reynolds* decision energized Congress to respond to the anti-polygamy reform campaigns that flooded both houses with petition after petition. Campaigns for stronger legal action against polygamy reached such a fervor by 1880 that they could no longer go unnoticed. One Senator in particular, Republican George Edmunds from Vermont, jumped at the opportunity to reform marriage in Utah. In the decade following the *Reynolds* decision, Congress commenced unprecedented legislative campaigns against plural marriage that, along with strengthening the criminal provisions of the Morrill Act, began to erode Mormon citizenship rights, attempting to seal off the body politic from the political contagion Mormonism engendered.

Buoyed by the *Reynolds* decision and hoping to protect the nation from what one congressman called the "festering sore on the body politic" that was Mormonism, the anti-polygamy legislation of the 1880s attempted to do three things: to punish polygamists, to undercut the political power of the Church, and to excise Mormons from national political influence.[12] Debates over the first two agendas have been well analyzed in other places.[13] Overlooked, however, have been the ways debates over anti-polygamy legislation of the 1880s also revealed congressional ideas about Mormon citizenship rights, political participation, and national belonging. Many congressmen became convinced that Mormons, many of whom were U.S. citizens, did not and could not enact good citizenship. The Edmunds and Edmunds-Tucker Acts of 1882 and 1887 attempted to rectify that problem. These acts not only punished Mormon polygamists but also disciplined all American citizens in the practice of private and public life and shaped the conception of citizenship itself.

The provisions of the first of these acts, the Edmunds Act of 1882, were many. The act restated the criminality of bigamy under the Morrill Act and also made "unlawful cohabitation" a misdemeanor punishable by a fine of three hundred dollars and a six-month prison term. In an attempt to secure criminal convictions in Utah, it also provided that polygamists and believers in polygamy could be barred from jury service, effectively excluding all Mormons. The bill also disenfranchised and barred from public office "any person cohabiting with more than one woman, and [any] woman cohabiting with any of the persons described as aforesaid."[14] The practice of plural marriage, in effect, barred Mormons from exercising some of the most fundamental rights of citizenship.

Almost all senators agreed that Mormons should not be citizens. Debates focused around issues of constitutionality, particularly local sovereignty, and with this particular principle at stake, opposition to anti-polygamy legislation emanated from the South.[15] As with the Morrill Act, some southern congressmen opposed the Edmunds Act on the grounds of local sovereignty. No doubt in the interest of protecting Jim Crow legislation in the South, in the minds of some southern congressmen the right of self-government outweighed the evils of polygamy.[16] Southern opponents of Edmunds also contended that the act would be both an ex post facto law, punishing polygamists for marriages contracted before the 1862 Morrill Act, and a bill of attainder, disenfranchising polygamists without benefit of a trial.[17]

Supporters of the Edmunds Act contended, however, that voting belonged to "that class of rights which affect the public as distinct from those which appertain to the individual"—voting was a privilege of citizenship, not a right.[18] They claimed that voting affected national politics at large, not just individual citizens, and so the nation could legislate the voting qualifications it wished. Congressmen contended that since Utah was a territory under federal control, and not a state, it was up to the federal government as representatives of the national body to decide who possessed that right. Finally, Edmunds Act supporters claimed, polygamous theocracy in Utah justified the use of unusual congressional power to foster monogamous republicanism.[19] Utah, they argued, was an exceptional situation that required the exceptional exercise of federal sovereignty.

Congressmen supporting the Edmunds Act were quite deliberate in claiming that the legislation was disciplinary not only in the punitive sense, but also in the normative sense. For instance, Representative Cassidy of Nevada argued, "This bill is a premium to non-polygamous Mormons to behave themselves in the future; to continue to obey the laws of the land and bring order out of disorder."[20] As the act's sponsor claimed, the point of the Edmunds Act was to "bring the political community that exists within the boundaries of that Territory into its republican relations with the great Republic that surrounds it. That is all."[21]

Convinced that polygamous Mormons—believers as well as practitioners—could not enact good American citizenship, Congress attempted to force Mormons into more American marital and political institutions. For Congress, as for the producers of much anti-Mormon literature, "republican relations" depended on proper order in the private sphere. Representative Ferris Jacobs of New York argued, the "domestic virtues [are] the chief sources of all patriotism," and "there is no custom more averse to [those virtues] than that of polygamy."[22] Supporters of the Edmunds Act claimed that polygamists must be disenfranchised because, as decades of anti-Mormon rhetoric had established, absent a suitable private life, a polygamist could be neither a patriot nor a citizen but only a blind follower of the theocratic authority of the Mormon prophet. Under the Edmunds Act, proper participation in public politics depended on the proper arrangement of the private sphere, and Americans whose private lives were inconsistent with normative family structures should not be endowed with the vote.

The familiar tropes of Orientalism also bolstered the rationale behind congressional anti-Mormon legislation. They appeared in debates over the Edmunds Act when Jacobs claimed that "all along down the ages the human race has been marshaled in these two grand divisions. Asia, with polygamy on the one hand, after all its struggles and convulsions, to-day the same rigid, unchangeable, hopeless empire of force as in the dawn of the world. Europe and

America, with monogamy on the other, and the irresistible devotion to coun-try it engenders, mounting through centuries . . . to the possession of personal liberty and constitutional government."[23] By the 1880s, legislators agreed with anti-Mormons and the Supreme Court that polygamy inherently gave rise to theocracy, and a community dominated by polygamists, in the words of Sena-tor George Edmunds, "ought not to be allowed to carry on a government."[24]

The Edmunds Act left the definition of "unlawful cohabitation" a bit unclear, so in 1884, at the trial of Rudger Clawson, territorial judge Charles Zane advised the jury that "cohabitation . . . means the living together of a man and woman as husband and wife, or under such circumstances as induces a reasonable belief of the practice of intercourse."[25] However, in 1886 the Supreme Court upheld the conviction of Angus Cannon for "holding out" a woman as his plural wife, disregarding as irrelevant evidence that Cannon had not engaged in intercourse with her since the Edmunds Act was passed.[26] In this judicial context, as legal historian Edwin Brown Firmage points out, "proving cohabitation became ridiculously easy for federal prosecutors."[27]

While Mormons were outraged at the prosecution of a law they considered to be unconstitutional and un-American, most distressing to them was the systemic disenfranchisement of polygamists in Utah that resulted, indirectly, from the Edmunds Act. The act created the Utah Commission, five federally-appointed officials, to oversee all elections in Utah. The Utah Commission required all voters to submit to a test oath to register to vote, requiring them to swear

> that I am not a bigamist nor a polygamist; that I am not a violator of the laws of the United States prohibiting bigamy or polygamy; that I do not live or cohabit with more than one woman in the marriage relation, nor does any relation exist between me and any woman which has been entered into or continued in violation of the said laws of the United States prohibiting bigamy or polygamy, (and if a woman) that I am not the wife of a polygamist nor have I entered into any relation with any man in violation of the laws of the United States concerning polygamy or bigamy.[28]

As though to add insult to injury, an addition to the act known as the Hoar Amendment enabled Utah's anti-Mormon Governor, Eli H. Murray, to ap-point territorial officials to serve until the commission could supervise the next election.[29] As enforced by the Utah Commission, Mormons affirmed that the Edmunds Act was indeed a bill of attainder, punishing citizens with disenfran-chisement without trial, and an ex post facto law, punishing polygamists who contracted their marriages before polygamy was declared illegal.[30] Mormon outrage also rested on the inclusion of the language "in the marriage relation" in the test oath. That phrase, Mormons argued, allowed men to vote who kept mistresses, patronized prostitutes, and engaged in other licentious behaviors, while polygamous Mormons could not.[31]

Mormons also understood that the Edmunds Act was an attack "not upon us as individuals but . . . upon the church as a body."[32] The test oath "and other laws, notably the Edmunds Act, . . . inflict disabilities upon those of our people who are not in any way associated by their acts, with polygamy. Thus, probably about nine-tenths of our community are punished for alleged offenses for which they are in no way responsible, and in which they have taken no part." Mormons accused the Utah Commission of applying the test oath unevenly, deciding on a whim when a Mormon was or was not sincere in his oath.[33] The *Latter-day Saints' Millennial Star* reported that in the 1882 election, the first under the Utah Commission, voter registration for Mormons had come in significantly lower than it should, indicating what B. H. Roberts later called "an unfairness towards the majority of the people of Utah."[34]

Mormon leaders asserted that Mormons must defend the Constitution against the encroachments of federal officials. Shortly after the Edmunds Act became law, Mormon prophet John Taylor addressed his followers to clarify how they should respond to the Utah Commission. He advised those who could truthfully take the test oath to do so in order to "do all in your power to maintain religious liberty and free, republican government in these mountains, and to preserve every constitutional right intact."[35] Thus, it was the responsibility of Mormons who did not practice polygamy to vote in protection of the rights of their polygamous coreligionists and in protection of religious freedom and free government.

Taylor also recommended that polygamists plead innocent of unlawful cohabitation and that every polygamy prosecution be brought to trial: "We do not think it advisable for the brethren to go to the court and plead guilty. . . . Every case should be defended with all the zeal and energy possible."[36] Not every polygamist took Taylor's advice. In 1885, Orson P. Arnold, who was a respected businessman, Bishop John Sharp, and S. W. Sears all pleaded guilty and promised to obey the law if they were not incarcerated.[37] A nebulous definition of unlawful cohabitation and loose standards of evidence in prosecutions—prosecutors found evidence for cohabitation, for example, in taking provisions to a wife's house, watering horses on a wife's property, and attending family birthday celebrations at which a wife was also present—led to high conviction rates.[38] Territorial court records reveal that in 1885 and 1886, prosecutors secured convictions in more than 92 per cent of unlawful cohabitation cases. Nonetheless, by contesting the act in the courts, Taylor claimed, Mormons exercised their remaining citizenship rights, "to legitimately and legally test in the courts . . . the legality and constitutionality of the law and the Commissioners' rulings."[39] Church officials continually urged those who could do so to avail themselves of any and all political rights, at the polls and in the courtroom, in defense of the Church and American principles as Mormons understood them.

While Mormons resented Congress's incursion on their constitutional liberties they maintained faith that God would deliver them. In the wake of anti-polygamy prosecutions, Taylor maintained that "you can safely trust in the Lord. . . . He has promised to fight your battles. His word has never failed."[40] Mormons imagined themselves to be carrying out the work of the Lord in preserving religious freedom for themselves and their posterity, and they campaigned against the Edmunds Act both legally, in the courtroom and at the polls, and culturally, in speeches and in the press. Some Church leaders even went so far as to claim the 1880s as the time when Joseph Smith had predicted that it would fall to the Latter-day Saints to protect the Constitution. John Taylor and George Q. Cannon claimed, for example, that events surrounding the Edmunds Act "[seem] to be forcing us into the exact position so plainly described by the Prophet through the spirit of prophecy." In their opinion, "Attempts are now being made to destroy our rights under the Constitution, and to effect this, that instrument . . . is being trampled upon by those who should be its administrators and guardians."[41] In a statement of grievances addressed to the federal government and the nation at large, Church leaders protested "against the tyranny of federal officials and contrivance in office of men who disgrace their position and use their official powers as a means of oppression."[42] In 1884, Church apostle Erastus Snow accused federal officials of a "continual desire for aggression upon the liberties of the people."[43] Denying the anti-Mormon claim that Mormons were un-American, Mormons accused federal officials themselves of being anti-republican.

These declarations were to no avail, though, and the demand to give up plural marriage took a heavy toll on the Mormon polity. The legal campaigns of the 1880s had their most tragic consequences during the government instituted "raids" of the mid-1880s.[44] In a zealous effort to enforce the Edmunds Act, federal officials burst into Mormon homes under the cover of darkness, often without warrant, hoping to find unlawful cohabitation occurring.[45] Curiously, in resisting the encroachments of federal law, Mormons invoked the language of the private sphere on behalf of the plural family. To them, the enforcement of the criminal provisions of the Edmunds Act pointed to the ironies of anti-polygamy campaigns: the invasion of the private sphere on behalf of its protec-

"The Mormon Question," first published in *Daily Graphic*,
22 October 1883, 815. Courtesy of the Church History Library,
The Church of Jesus Christ of Latter-day Saints, Salt Lake City, Utah.

tion and the destruction of the family in the name of its preservation. Mormons found a certain absurdity in the rationale of anti-Mormon legislation. "Families are dissevered and broken up, the most sacred ties are rent asunder, [and] homes made desolate" in the name of protecting the family.[46] A Mormon man's home, under the Edmunds Act, was no longer his castle.[47] Moreover, in the courtroom the trust and tender relations of domestic life also came under assault "when little children are set in array against their fathers and mothers, and women and children are badgered before courts, and made to submit, unprotected, to the gibes of libertines and corrupt men; when wives and husbands are pitted against each other and threatened with pains, penalties, and imprisonment, if they will not disclose that which among all decent people is considered sacred, and which no man of delicacy, whose sensibilities had not been blunted by low associations, would ever ask."[48] It seemed Mormons had caught anti-polygamy prosecution in its own logical inconsistencies.

While the Edmunds Act was successful in securing convictions for unlawful cohabitation, it was not successful in bringing about the demise of plural marriage.[49] Indeed, one image from the *Daily Graphic*, printed the year after the Edmunds Act was passed, demonstrated its weakness against Mormon polygamy. In this image, a police officer with his arm in a sling labeled "Edmunds law," appears in the doorway of a polygamist household. The husband, a strong fellow with his wives chained to his belt, prepares to fight. The caption reads, "The Mormon Question: What is Uncle Sam going to do about it?" This illustration demonstrates anti-Mormon anxieties about the failure of the Edmunds Act to stop polygamy.[50]

Moreover, Mormon men and women proved willing to perjure themselves in the courtroom, spend time in prison, and sacrifice their livelihood on behalf of plural marriage. Church leaders, too, continued boldly to defend the practice. After the Edmunds Act, in an official conference of the Church, John Taylor asked, "are we going to suffer a surrender of this point? No, never! No, Never!"[51] In 1884, Taylor instructed all Church officials serving in bishoprics or stake presidencies to prepare to take plural wives or be released from their callings.[52] At the same time, several Church leaders, Taylor and other polygamists, went into hiding or, as Mormons called it, went on the "underground."

"To Refrain from Contracting Any Marriage Forbidden by the Laws of the Land"[53]: The End of Plural Marriage

Determined to bring Utah to heel, Congress passed an even stricter anti-polygamy law in 1887, the Edmunds-Tucker Act, which marked the beginning of the end of polygamy. By that year, fewer cases went to trial because more than 75 percent of those charged pleaded guilty, most likely discouraged by high conviction rates.[54] The Edmunds-Tucker Act extended the Edmunds Act, strengthening the juridical force of the anti-polygamy statues by formally requiring plural wives to testify against husbands in court (though before Edmunds-Tucker territorial courts had at times required them to testify). The act also bolstered adultery and incest clauses, and it required the legal registration of all marriages in the territories. Edmunds-Tucker disincorporated the Church, disbanded the Perpetual Emigrating Fund, which was the money the Church had used to support immigration from Europe, and attacked the economic structure of the Church, escheating all Church property in excess of fifty thousand dollars.[55]

Most troubling to Mormons, the Edmunds-Tucker Act continued to chip away at Mormon citizenship. It wrote into federal law a test oath even more restrictive than the one the Utah Commission had put in place. It required all Utah voters to swear that they would not only obey anti-polygamy laws but "will not, directly or indirectly, aid or abet, counsel or advise, any other person to commit any of said crimes."[56] As Mormons understood it, they were being accused of wrongdoing without cause, for "by this law it is presumed that the citizens of this territory are disposed to violate the law and they must therefore rebut the presumption by taking the oath!" No longer innocent until proven guilty, this violation of the rights of citizenship, Mormons argued, "is without a parallel even among despotic governments."[57] While the status of the first test oath under the Utah Commission had been constitutionally ambiguous, the Edmunds-Tucker Act wrote the test oath into federal law, disenfranchising not only those Mormons who practiced plural marriage, but those unwilling to swear their disbelief in the practice as well. The act also disenfranchised all Utah women, many of whom had never engaged in plural marriage.[58] These aspects of Edmunds-Tucker attempted to break the electoral power of the Mormon polity. Under the law, many Mormons found themselves disenfranchised not only without trial but without crime. The act showed Mormons and all Americans that not only could an unsuitable private life result in disenfranchisement, but that government might revoke citizenship rights for even supporting the improper practice of domestic life.

Polygamy prosecutions escalated in the wake of the Edmunds-Tucker Act. By 1888, the Church's response to polygamy prosecutions had also changed. Rather than resisting prosecution in court, First Presidency Counselor George Q. Cannon surrendered, pleaded guilty, went to trial, and served a six-month prison term.[59] Over the next few years the Mormon Church struggled to maintain its institutional integrity. Three additional developments laid the more immediate ground for the surrender of polygamy in 1890. First, the difficulty of running a large organization while in hiding or jail took its toll, and Mormon Church officials became increasingly concerned that the Church as an institution would collapse. The very existence of Mormonism, it seemed, depended on sacrificing polygamy.[60] The two more immediate triggers of the Woodruff Manifesto were congressional debate over the Cullom-Strubble bill, followed by two Supreme Court decisions handed down in 1890. Introduced in 1889, the Cullom-Strubble bill would have disenfranchised all Mormons, disbanded the current territorial government, and appointed a congressional commission to govern Utah. In the spring of 1890, it appeared likely that the bill would pass. That same year, the Supreme Court ruled against the Church in two cases testing the constitutionality of anti-polygamy legislation. In the mid-1880s, Idaho had passed a law that required every voter to swear that he or she was not a "member of any ... organization ... which teaches ... its members ... to commit the crime of bigamy or polygamy ... as a duty arising or resulting from membership in such ... organization ... or which practices bigamy or polygamy or plural or celestial marriage as a doctrinal rite of such organization."[61] In February, *Davis v. Beason* upheld the constitutionality of this test oath as the Cullum-Strubble bill threatened to enact a similar test oath nationwide.[62] In April the court handed down the *Late Corporation of the Church of Jesus Christ of Latter-day Saints v. United States* decision, upholding the constitutionality of the escheatment of Church property under the Edmunds-Tucker Act.[63]

In the wake of these court decisions and under the threat of the Cullom-Strubble bill, Mormons decided that the dissolution of the Church proved too high a price to pay for plural marriage. The night before Church President Wilford Woodruff released the document that would forbid any new plural marriages, he recorded in his journal that "I have arrived at a point in the history of my life as president of the Church of Jesus Christ of Latter-day Saints where I am under the necessity of acting for the temporal salvation of the church."[64] On September 24, 1890, the Woodruff Manifesto capitulated to federal demands. The Mormon prophet declared that the Church would no longer sanction new plural marriages but did not require the dissolution of existing plural marriages. Read carefully, the Woodruff Manifesto concedes little. It did not undo the doctrinal status of polygamy, but rather declared the prophet's "advice to the Latter-day Saints ... to refrain from contracting any marriage forbidden by the law of the land."[65] Some scholars argue that in 1890 Church authorities never intended the Manifesto as a permanent document, but believed instead in the eventual restoration of plural marriage as part of the institution of the kingdom of God that would come to pass in the future.[66]

Some anti-Mormons charged that the Manifesto was a ruse and that Mormons were still conducting plural marriages in secret.[67] Nonetheless, for the most part, the Woodruff Manifesto took the wind out of the sails of anti-polygamy campaigns. By and large, in 1890 the Mormon Church sacrificed the majority of their nontraditional marital practices upon the altar of Americanness, capitulating to federal demands for filial uniformity in exchange for access to citizenship and statehood. In an effort to seem less theocratic, the Church also made deliberate attempts to assimilate to American political behaviors.[68] By the 1892 election, for example, the Church had disbanded its political party, the People's Party, and instructed the faithful to join Democratic or Republican parties.

In December 1891, Church officials petitioned U. S. President Benjamin Harrison, requesting "that full amnesty may be extended to all who are under disabilities because of the operation of the so-called Edmunds and Edmunds-Tucker laws." Mormons argued that after the Civil War the government had restored political rights in the South "along the old lines of citizenship," intimating that the same should be done for Mormons who had, since 1890, ceased their polygamous practices.[69] In 1892, the Utah Commission reported that polygamy had indeed ended in Utah, and the next year President Harrison granted limited amnesty to ex-polygamists.[70] In 1894, President Grover Cleveland granted general amnesty, restoring the citizenship rights of all Mormons not currently practicing polygamy.[71] Within six years of the manifesto, Congress concluded that its attempt to bring the political community of Utah "into its republican relations with" the nation had been successful and granted the Territory statehood with a Constitution that banned polygamy. In part due to Mormon women's struggle to include a woman suffrage clause in the Utah Constitution, Utah women regained the vote they had lost in 1887.[72] Once Utahns surrendered their peculiar domestic institution, the nation, by and large, welcomed them in.

The incorporation of Utah into the Republic was much more rapid than was the broad, difficult transformation that the Manifesto heralded. Initially, the Mormon surrender was more a practical shift than an ideological one. The Manifesto was not the end of the Church's move away from plural marriage but the beginning. Whether the Manifesto marked a doctrinal shift or, in the words of one historian, a "tactical maneuver" intended to be temporary, over the twenty years that followed, the Church leaders seemed to make deliberate choices to exchange Mormon peculiarities for a more American identity.[73] That is to say, the Manifesto was only the beginning of a much longer process of transition that only began with the official end of plural marriage. Scholarship has shown that the practice of plural marriage died a slow death despite the Manifesto.[74] Church officials solemnized plural marriages in Mexico, Canada, and the United States from 1890 at least until 1904, when Joseph F. Smith issued what has been termed the "Second Manifesto."[75] In 1909 the Church began excommunicating practitioners of polygamy, and no known plural marriage has been contracted within the mainstream Church since 1910. However, the discontinuation of plural marriage was too much for some Mormons to take, and splinter groups branched off from the mainstream Church, many of which continue to practice plural marriage.[76]

The capitulation of polygamy was accompanied by the gradual shift in a whole set of theological, political, and communitarian ideas.[77] Over the 1890s Mormons somewhat reluctantly came to abandon the immediacy of the Millennium. Forsaking the claim that the kingdom of God was at hand, they began preparing for the second coming of Jesus in a more distant future.[78] This theological turn profoundly affected the ways Mormons viewed the American Republic and their place within it. Marking one's citizenship in the kingdom of God through the acceptance of polygamy became a less fundamental precept of Mormon religious practice, freeing up political and conceptual space for Mormon membership in the Republic.

Economic accommodations accompanied political and theological shifts. The Church adjusted to modern American capitalism by de-emphasizing the practice of consecration. The economic cooperatives that characterized United Order experiments became joint stock corporations modeled after other American businesses. At individual and family levels, the Church began to speak of the law of consecration in more limited ways, embodied by the payment of tithing, individual contributions of a portion of one's income (usually 10 percent) to the Church, as well as other financial offerings.[79] In the twentieth century, consecration came to look more like church offerings than communal living.

• • •

These broad cultural, political, and economic shifts accomplished what one scholar has called the "Americanization" of Utah in preparation for statehood.[80] Only six years after the Woodruff Manifesto, Utah was admitted to the Union with "polygamous or plural marriages forever prohibited" by the state constitution. Anti-Mormonism had accomplished its cultural work by constituting Mormons as an un-American threat to the nation and its legal work by taking aim at the citizenship rights of Mormons. The Mormon Church, in the end, capitulated, ending a nearly forty-year campaign of resistance to national marital norms.

Conclusion

Polygamy continues to fascinate and repel Americans. From the HBO television series *Big Love* and TLC's reality show *Sister Wives* to the numerous appearances of polygamists on *Oprah, Dr. Phil, Anderson Cooper 360, Good Morning America, Larry King Live*, and other television talk and news programs, millions of Americans have become acquainted with the practice of plural marriage in contemporary America.[1] The 2008 raid of a fundamentalist Mormon Yearning for Zion (YFZ) Ranch in Texas, when Texas officials seized over four hundred children, received widespread news coverage and amplified public interest in polygamy. This fascination is not new; it has its roots in the Mormon question of the nineteenth century.

In the nineteenth century, debates about plural marriage were central to national discussions of citizenship, especially as those discussions were framed around the public/private divide. The categories of public and private were central to nineteenth-century middle-class constructions of American citizenship, framing American political culture around male political and economic participation in the public sphere and around female domesticity in the private sphere. The practice of plural marriage upset the distinction between public and private in a number of ways, and the Mormons' alternative family practices denaturalized middle-class constructions of family and citizenship. This, I have argued, was at the root of the Mormon question.

Plural marriage was central to a cluster of doctrines—celestial marriage; the plan of salvation; priesthood and the powers of sealing, adoption, and ordinance work for the dead; and eternal increase—that Joseph Smith articulated in Nauvoo. Moreover, plural marriage continued to be preached as essential to the highest degree of exaltation until the Woodruff Manifesto of 1890. By the same token, Joseph Smith established early on the centrality of the United States in Mormon theology. The *Book of Mormon* suggested that the principle of religious freedom facilitated the restoration of the true church of Christ in America. American religious freedom prepared the way "that these things might come forth."[2]

Ideally, plural marriage knit the Mormon community together as though it were one great family. Mormons considered the entire Mormon community as God's family, governed by the privatized kingdom of God, thereby casting Mormon marital and political affairs as private. Mormons juxtaposed this broad communal private family to both the American public and to the public institutions of American government, at the same time maintaining that they were quintessentially American. They did so by formulating a political dualism which held that Mormons could be private citizens in God's kingdom while public citizens in the American state. The American traditions of religious liberty and local sovereignty, Mormons argued, protected their unique domestic and political arrangements.

One controversial outgrowth of the ways plural marriage undercut the public/private divide was Mormon woman suffrage. In 1870, Utah granted women the vote, and from that point forward, Mormon women articulated their vision of a polygamous republicanism. Until the 1880s, they critiqued the Victorian model of female domesticity and male citizenship rooted in the public/private divide, arguing that polygamy actually better prepared women for citizenship than did monogamy. In the 1880s, public pressure forced them to divorce polygamy from the cause of woman suffrage. Although they lost the vote in 1887, as a result of anti-Mormon legislation, Mormon women remained ardent suffragists and secured the vote in the Utah State Constitution of 1896. The Mormon challenge to the public/private dichotomy had prepared the way for Mormon women to receive the vote with very little resistance from a patriarchal and supposedly despotic Church hierarchy.

Between 1852 and 1890, when polygamy was openly practiced in Utah, anti-Mormons responded virulently to the ways plural marriage undercut the public/private divide. They wrote prolifically about the multiple ways Mormonism threatened "the utter destruction of the home circle" which they imagined was at the center of American political culture.[3] Anti-Mormon texts demonstrated to a curious American public that plural marriage destroyed the family by destroying the sentiment and exclusivity of romantic love and the harmony of the domestic sphere. For anti-Mormons, in a context in which monogamous private life was imagined to create good American citizens, the consequences of polygamy were grave. Destroying the natural order and harmony of the domestic sphere destroyed the affective ties that held the nation together.

Many also believed that polygamy threatened the nineteenth-century American political values of consent and contract, undermining the rights of American citizenship. In an era historians have called the "age of contract," consent was of paramount importance to conceptions of American citizenship. As anti-Mormons understood it, however, Mormonism rendered its subjects incapable of consent—to religion, to marriage, or to government. Polygamy, as portrayed in anti-Mormon literature, denied Mormon women the power of marital consent through manipulation or outright force. Moreover, by creating despotic rule at home, polygamy fitted male citizens in turn to be acquiescent subjects to the despotic rule of Mormon Church leaders. By undermining marital and political consent, polygamy made Mormons simply un-American. A polygamist, therefore, could not be a good citizen of the American Republic and, furthermore, posed a threat to that form of government. According to anti-Mormons, Mormons "can not [sic] exist in contact with republican institutions."[4]

The problem with these critiques, of course, was that in many respects Mormons were American. Most early converts had been born in the United States, and Mormonism was a faith founded on American soil that touted American values and asserted its compatibility with American republicanism. Anti-Mormons thus faced the task of making Mormons foreign; they did so through the tropes of race and class. Linking Mormons to Middle Eastern "Orientals" enabled anti-Mormons to illustrate not only the un-Americanness of plural marriage but its links to political despotism as well. Anti-Mormons argued that in Mormondom, as in the Orient, plural marriage gave rise to despotic government. Over the 1870s and 1880s, anti-Mormon discourse turned increasingly to the language of social class, claiming that new Mormon converts—the evolutionary dregs of Europe—came to America not to be Americans, but to join the Mormons in their un-American project. Anti-Mormons, feeling deeply threatened by these foreign influences, mobilized metaphors of contagion to demonstrate Mormonism's potential to infect the nation. Mormonism became "the foulest ulcer on the body of our nation."[5]

Roused by anti-Mormon rhetoric and activism, in the 1880s the federal government embarked on an unprecedented campaign against Mormons. The Edmunds and Edmunds-Tucker Acts, aimed directly at Mormon marriage practices, stripped Mormons of fundamental rights of American citizenship. In 1890 the Church, imperiled from every side, finally capitulated, publicly stating it would no longer support plural marriage. Mormons sacrificed plural marriage in exchange for full American citizenship.

Ultimately, the resolution of the controversy over plural marriage was a story of Mormon defeat and federal victory in consolidating the relationship of monogamy and the public/private divide to conceptions of American citizenship. The legal campaigns against polygamy in the 1880s effectively suppressed one of the most significant challenges to nineteenth-century connections between family and the meaning of citizenship, reifying the public/private divide and the sanctity of marriage. That Mormons capitulated to national demands does not, however, make their challenge to nineteenth-century American political culture any less significant. For nearly forty years, from 1852 to 1890, Mormons maintained their distinctive marital and political practices, showing at every turn that there was nothing natural or especially American about the public/private divide. For those forty years, Mormonism was a refiner's fire, forcing anti-Mormons to endlessly rehearse and rearticulate the separation of public and private at the center of nineteenth-century American political culture. Mormonism's forty-year refusal to accommodate to American visions of family and government provoked an unprecedented campaign against the Mormons, capsizing perhaps the most powerful nineteenth-century alternative to normative American marital ideals.

Ironically, the LDS church has become one of the staunchest defenders of normative, monogamous marriage between a man and a woman. The Church's official statement, "The Family: A Proclamation to the World," one of the most influential pronouncements of the twentieth-century Church, states that "marriage between man and woman is ordained of God and that the traditional family is the foundation of society." It also upholds traditional gendered notions of public and private, declaring, "By divine design, fathers are . . . responsible to provide the necessities of life and protection for their families. Mothers are primarily responsible for the nurture of their children."[6] In many ways, the Proclamation documents Mormonism's attempts to fully assimilate with American family ideals. Nonetheless, troubled by its polygamous past, Mormonism is a religion in process whose Americanization is doomed to be incomplete. Contemporary Mormonism still bears the legacy of the nineteenth-century conflict over plural marriage in ways that have proved difficult to escape, despite the fact that the mainstream Church has not practiced plural marriage for over one hundred years.

Other sects, however, have continued the practice in earnest. Between 30,000 and 50,000 fundamentalist Mormon individuals practice plural marriage in the American West largely unencumbered by legal deterrents.[7] This is particularly troubling for the mainstream Church since these fundamentalist groups share with the mainstream LDS Church an origin in the 1830 church established by Joseph Smith and at least a sixty-year historical legacy through the 1890 Woodruff Manifesto. The mainstream Church struggles to distinguish itself from the many fundamentalist LDS sects, communities, and families still practicing plural marriage. Many of the Church's attempts to distance itself from contemporary fundamentalists have centered around the use of the term "Mormon." On September 8, 1998, LDS Church President Gordon B. Hinckley appeared on the television talk show *Larry King Live* stating that since practicing polygamists do not belong to the mainstream Church, "there are actually no Mormon fundamentalists."[8] The implication was that the term "Mormon" should not be used to describe polygamists because they do not belong to the mainstream Church. However, as contemporary polygamy scholar Janet Bennion points out, "polygamists have a great deal in common with mainstream Mormons.... [B]oth types of Mormons share many of the same early doctrines and values, they share ancestors who crossed the plains with Brigham Young, and they eat the same foods, read the same scriptures, and live in much the same way."[9] Moreover, fundamentalist Mormons "have more cultural traits in common with Mormons than with members of any other religion."[10] These similarities trouble the mainstream Church, which struggles to control the use of the term "Mormon" to refer exclusively to itself.

As popular press and television attention to plural marriage has increased over the past few years, the LDS Church has continued to struggle to define its relationship to contemporary polygamists. In April 2008, after a local domestic violence shelter received a phone call from someone claiming to be a victim of sexual abuse at the YFZ Ranch (the call later turned out to be a hoax), Texas officials raided the YFZ Ranch and removed over four hundred children. The children were later released into the care of their parents, but several convictions for sexual assault and bigamy resulted from the raid.[11] In the wake of this much-publicized action, the mainstream Mormon Church launched a public relations campaign distinguishing itself from those still practicing plural marriage. In the words of a Church news release, "The polygamists and polygamist organizations in parts of the western United States and Canada have no affiliation whatsoever with The Church of Jesus Christ of Latter-day Saints, despite the fact that the term 'Mormon'—widely understood to be a nickname for

Latter-day Saints—is sometimes misleadingly applied to them."[12] Again, the implication was that because they practice polygamy, fundamentalists should not be called "Mormons." Nonetheless, despite the contemporary Church's many attempts to distinguish itself from fundamentalist Mormons, contemporary mainstream Mormons are still widely associated with plural marriage, and the Church continues to struggle to move past the historical legacy of nineteenth-century polygamy. The historical conflicts over plural marriage continue to affect the Church's public image, especially as the sanctity of marriage continues to be debated in contemporary America.

The Church's 2008 support of Proposition 8 in California, which declared that "only marriage between a man and a woman is valid or recognized in California," also raised the historical specter of plural marriage that continues to vex the contemporary church. In a controversial and much publicized campaign, Church members donated over twenty million dollars to organizations campaigning on behalf of the proposition.[13] Mormonism's opposition to same-sex marriage was and continues to be, among other things, a continuation of the Americanization process begun in 1890, as Mormonism strives to be accepted as a mainstream form of conservative Christianity despite its polygamous history. In the words of one reporter, the Church's enthusiastic support for Proposition 8 "oozes irony."[14] This irony was not missed by protesters, bloggers, newspaper reporters, and writers of letters to the editor. One commentator in the *New Yorker* quipped, "You might think that an organization that for most of the first of its not yet two centuries of existence was the world's most notorious proponent of startlingly unconventional forms of wedded bliss would be a little reticent about issuing orders to the rest of humanity specifying exactly who should be legally entitled to marry whom."[15]

One forthright and insightful "insider" noted the irony inherent in the Church's support of Proposition 8. Mormon women's historian Lola Van Wagenen, in an astute opinion piece for the *L.A. Times*, declares that "there is no religious group in our country that should be more tolerant of 'nontraditional' forms of marriage than those of us whose ancestors were polygamist Mormons, who were persecuted because of their 'nontraditional' marriages."[16] She points out that nineteenth-century polygamists were derided, much as homosexuals are now, for the dangers plural marriage posed to the children of those marriages and for the dangers such marriage posed to the groundings of American civilization and social order. At least some of the controversy surrounding the Church's support of Proposition 8 referenced these connections. Protesters, for example, held signs saying, "Brigham Young had 55 wives, I want just 1."[17] and "One Man One Woman?! . . . Not According to Joseph Smith."[18] The connections made between same-sex marriage and plural marriage once again raised, in ways uncomfortable for the contemporary Church, the specter of plural marriage.

The Church chose to offer no official response to the connections made between same-sex and plural marriage, but for many members, comparing same-sex marriage to polygamy is, in the words of Sarah Barringer Gordon, "like comparing apples and oranges."[19] Admittedly, the comparison of same-sex marriage to plural marriage has its limitations. Same-sex couples are demanding legal recognition for their unions, while polygamists, for the most part, want to be left alone. For Church members, monogamous marriage maintains Mormonism's theological commitment to the reproductive family as the institution through which exaltation is achieved. Nonetheless, that the comparisons were made at all is significant in terms of the continuing legacy of plural marriage for the contemporary mainstream Mormon Church. As the Church continues to promote normative heterosexual and gendered marital norms, continuing in the twenty-first century to reify the public/private divide, it is still haunted by its nineteenth-century past. The Mormon question is still alive and well.

Notes

Introduction

1. The technically correct term for Mormon plural marriage is "polygyny," the practice of having more than one wife. Although the term "polygamy" refers to having plural spouses of either sex, I use the term because it was the term most often used in the nineteenth century and has been commonly associated with Mormonism well into the present. Mormons generally used the term "plural marriage" and for historical and stylistic reasons I sometimes do the same. Also, in the nineteenth century, as today, members of The Church of Jesus Christ of Latter-day Saints, or the LDS Church, were commonly known as "Mormons," named after their grounding spiritual text, the *Book of Mormon*. Contemporary Mormons resist the term, preferring instead to be called "Latter-day Saints," but the term did not seem to trouble nineteenth-century Latter-day Saints in the same way. I use it, here, to describe members of the nineteenth-century Church, and occasionally the twentieth-century Church, but intend no affront in either case.

2. For an analysis of marriage and family structures among Oneidans, Shakers, and Mormons, see Lawrence Foster, *Religion and Sexuality: Three American Communal Experiments of the Nineteenth Century* (New York: Oxford University Press, 1981); Lawrence Foster, *Women, Family, and Utopia: Communal Experiments of the Shakers, the Oneida Community, and the Mormons* (Syracuse: Syracuse University Press, 1991). See also Paul E. Johnson and Sean Wilentz, *The Kingdom of Matthias: A Story of Sex and Salvation in Nineteenth-Century America* (New York: Oxford University Press, 1994).

3. See Ellen DuBois and Linda Gordon, "Seeking Ecstasy on the Battlefield: Danger and Pleasure in Nineteenth-Century Feminist Sexual Thought," *Feminist Studies* 9, no. 1 (Spring 1983): 7–25.

4. Howard Roberts Lamar, *The Far Southwest 1846–1912: A Territorial History* rev. ed., (Albuquerque: University of New Mexico Press, 2000).

5. See James H. Kettner, *The Development of American Citizenship, 1608–1870* (Chapel Hill: University of North Carolina Press, 1978); and Catherine A. Holland, *The Body Politic: Foundings, Citizenship, and Difference in the American Political Imagination* (New York: Routledge, 2001), 96–162.

6. Kettner, 334–51, quoted material on 351.

7. See Richard D. Poll, "The Political Reconstruction of Utah Territory, 1866–1890," *Pacific Historical Review* 27, no. 2 (May 1958): 111–26; and Sarah Barringer Gordon, *The Mormon Question: Polygamy and Constitutional Conflict in Nineteenth-Century America* (Chapel Hill: University of North Carolina Press, 2002), 119–20.

8. Carroll Smith-Rosenberg, "Dis-Covering the Subject of the 'Great Constitutional Discussion,' 1786–1789," *Journal of American History* 79, no. 3 (December 1992), 843.

9. Gurpreet Mahajan, "Introduction: The Public and the Private: Two Modes of Enhancing Democratization," in *The Public and the Private: Issues of Democratic Citizenship*, ed. Gurpreet Mahajan (New Delhi: Sage Publications, 2003), 11. See also T. N. Madan, "Of the Social Categories 'Private' and 'Public': Considerations of Cultural Context," in Mahajan, *The Public and the Private*, 88–89.

10. June Howard, *Publishing the Family* (Durham: Duke University Press, 2001), 239.

11. Linda K. Kerber, "Separate Spheres, Female Worlds, Woman's Place: The Rhetoric of Women's History," *Journal of American History* 75, no. 1 (June 1988), 30.

12. Patricia Uberoi, "Feminism and the Public-Private Distinction," in Mahajan, *The Public and the Private*, 206. On the public/private distinction in American republican thought, see Ruth Bloch, "The American Revolution, Wife Beating, and the Emergent Value of Privacy," *Early American Studies* 5, no. 2 (Fall 2007): 223–51; Mary Dietz, "Context Is All: Feminism and Theories of Citizenship," *Daedalus* 116, no. 4 (Fall 1987): 1–24; Mahajan, "Introduction," 9–33; and Anne Phillips, *Engendering Democracy* (University Park: Pennsylvania State University Press, 1991). On the gendering of citizenship, see Linda K. Kerber, "Can a Woman Be an Individual?: The Discourse of Self-Reliance," in *Toward an Intellectual History of Women: Essays* (Chapel Hill: University of North Carolina Press, 1997): 200–223.

13. Gordon S. Wood, *The Radicalism of the American Revolution* (New York: Alfred A. Knopf, 1992), 44.

14. Ibid., 82.

15. Ibid., 83.

16. Ibid., 148.

17. Jay Fliegelman, *Prodigals and Pilgrims: The American Revolution against Patriarchal Authority, 1750–1800* (Cambridge: Cambridge University Press, 1985), 126.

18. Wood, *The Radicalism of the American Revolution*, 149.

19. For an examination of contractual families in the mid- to late-nineteenth century, see Amy Dru Stanley, *From Bondage to Contract: Wage Labor, Marriage, and the Market in the Age of Slave Emancipation* (Cambridge: Cambridge University Press, 1998).

20. Gordon, *The Mormon Question*, 77–78, quoted material on 77. See also Arlin M. Adams and Charles J. Emmerich, *A Nation Dedicated to Religious Liberty: The Constitutional Heritage of the Religion Clauses* (Philadelphia: University of Pennsylvania Press, 1990); Frank Lambert, *The Founding Fathers and the Place of Religion in America* (Princeton: Princeton University Press, 2003); and Kent Greenawalt, *Religion and the Constitution, Volume 1: Free Exercise and Fairness* (Princeton: Princeton University Press, 2006), 11–25.

21. Gordon, *The Mormon Question*, 75–78, quoted material on 75.

22. Ibid., 77.

23. Bloch, "The American Revolution, Wife Beating, and the Emergent Value of Privacy."

24. Ibid., 226.

25. Nancy F. Cott, *Public Vows: A History of Marriage and the Nation* (Cambridge, Mass.: Harvard University Press, 2000), 5.

26. Cott, *Public Vows*, 23. See also Carole Pateman, *The Sexual Contract* (Stanford: Stanford University Press, 1986); Nancy F. Cott, "'Giving Character to Our Whole Civil Polity': Marriage and the Public Order in the Late Nineteenth Century," in *U.S. History as Women's History: New Feminist Essays*, eds. Linda K. Kerber, Alice Kessler-Harris, and Kathryn Kish Sklar (Chapel Hill: University of North Carolina Press, 1995): 107–24; Nancy F. Cott, "Marriage and Women's Citizenship in the United States, 1830–1934," *The American Historical Review* 103, no. 5 (December 1998): 1440–74; Linda K. Kerber, "A Constitutional Right to be Treated Like American Ladies: Women and the Obligations of Citizenship," in Kerber, Kessler-Harris, and Sklar, 17–35; and Linda K. Kerber, *No Constitutional Right to Be Ladies: Women and the Obligations of Citizenship* (New York: Hill and Wang, 1998).

27. Contemporary discussions of coverture abound, but some of the more influential are Pateman, *The Sexual Contract*; Linda K. Kerber, *Women of the Republic: Intellect and Ideology in Revolutionary America* (Chapel Hill: University of North Carolina Press, 1980), especially 137–56; Kerber, *No Constitutional Right to be Ladies*; Dietz, "Context Is All"; Jean Bethke Elshtain, *Public Man, Private Woman: Women in Social and Political Thought* (Princeton: Princeton University Press, 1981); and Hendrik Hartog, *Man and Wife in America: A History* (Cambridge, Mass.: Harvard University Press, 2000).

28. Perhaps the most well-known iteration of this claim is Mary P. Ryan, *Cradle of the Middle Class: The Family in Oneida County, New York, 1790–1865* (Cambridge: Cambridge University Press, 1981). See also Charles Sellers, *The Market Revolution: Jacksonian America, 1815–1846* (New York: Oxford University Press, 1991); and Nancy Armstrong, *Desire and Domestic Fiction: A Political History of the Novel* (New York: Oxford University Press, 1987).

29. Ryan, *Cradle of the Middle-Class*; Mary P. Ryan, *The Empire of the Mother: American Writing about Domesticity, 1830–1860* (New York: Institute for Research in History and the Haworth Press, 1982); Nancy F. Cott, *The Bonds of Womanhood: "Woman's Sphere" in New England, 1780–1835* (New Haven: Yale University Press, 1977), especially 98. See also Barbara Welter, "The Cult of True Womanhood," *American Quarterly* 18 (Spring 1966): 151–74; Kerber, *Women of the Republic*; and Armstrong, especially 14.

30. Although this phrase was first used in 1977 by Christopher Lasch, historians have since incorporated it as an identifying feature of the idealized nineteenth-century home. Christopher Lasch, *Haven in a Heartless World: The Family Besieged* (New York: Norton, 1977).

31. Welter, "The Cult of True Womanhood." See also Cott, *The Bonds of Womanhood*; Kerber, "Separate Spheres, Female Worlds, Woman's Place," 11–13; Mary P. Ryan, "Gender and Public Access: Women's Politics in Nineteenth-Century America," in *Feminism, the Public and the Private*, ed. Joan B. Landes (New York: Oxford University Press, 1998), 195–96; Leonore Davidoff, "Regarding Some 'Old Husbands' Tales: Public and Private in Feminist History," in Landes, *Feminism, the Public, and the Private*, 164–65; Carroll Smith-Rosenberg, "Female Worlds of Love and Ritual," in *Disorderly Conduct: Visions of Gender in Victorian America* (New York: Alfred A. Knopf, 1985), 53–76; Blanche Wiesen Cook, "Female Support Networks and Political Activism: Lillian Wald, Crystal Eastman, and Emma Goldman," in *A Heritage of Her Own: Toward a New Social History of American Women*, eds. Nancy F. Cott and Elizabeth Hafkin Pleck (New York: Simon and Schuster, 1979), 412–44; Cott, *The Bonds of Womanhood*. See also, Mary P. Ryan, "The Power of Women's Networks: A Case Study of Female Moral Reform in Antebellum America," *Feminist Studies* 5 (Spring 1979): 66–85; and Estelle Freedman, "Separatism as Strategy: Female Institution Building and American Feminism, 1870–1930," *Feminist Studies* 5 (Fall 1979): 512–29.

32. Cott, "Giving Character to Our Whole Civil Polity," 111.

33. Cott, *Public Vows*, 32. See also Cott, "Giving Character to Our Whole Civic Polity"; Kerber, "A Constitutional Right to be Treated Like American Ladies"; Kerber, *No Constitutional Right to Be Ladies*; and Laura F. Edwards, "'The Marriage Covenant Is at the Foundation of All Our Rights': The Politics of Slave Marriages in North Carolina after Emancipation," *Law and History Review* 14 (Spring 1996): 81–124.

34. Catharine E. Beecher, *Treatise on Domestic Economy* (Boston: T. H. Webb, & Co., 1842), 29.

35. Howard, *Publishing the Family*, 236.

36. Kathleen Flake, "The Emotional and Priestly Logic of Plural Marriage," *Leonard J. Arrington Mormon History Lecture Series*, paper 15, 2009, http://digitalcommons.usu .edu/arrington_lecture/15 (accessed September 25, 2010).

37. Mahajan, "Introduction," 13–16, quoted material on 16. See also Gwendolyn Wright, *Building the Dream: A Social History of Housing in America* (New York: Pantheon Books, 1981), 112; and Steven Mintz and Susan Kellogg, *Domestic Revolutions: A Social History of American Family Life* (New York: The Free Press, 1988), 44.

38. On women's domestic influence, see Paula Baker, "The Domestication of Politics: Women and American Political Society, 1780–1920," *American Historical Review* 89 (June 1984): 620–47; Jan Lewis, "The Republican Wife: Virtue and Seduction in the Early Republic," *The William and Mary Quarterly* 44, no. 4 (October, 1987): 689–721; and Kerber, *Women of the Republic*, 185–294.

39. An ideological configuration, to be sure, the true woman was imagined as pious, pure, submissive, and domestic. Barbara Welter, "The Cult of True Womanhood."

40. Mary Chapman and Glenn Hendler, *Sentimental Men: Masculinity and the Politics of Affect in American Culture* (Berkeley: University of California Press, 1999). For a late nineteenth-century example, see Margaret Marsh, "Suburban Men and Masculine Domesticity, 1870–1915," in Marc C. Carnes and Clyde Griffin, eds., *Meanings for Manhood: Constructions of Masculinity in Victorian America* (Chicago: University of Chicago Press, 1990): 111–27.

41. Freedman, "Separatism as Strategy." See also Anne M. Boylan, *The Origins of Women's Activism: New York and Boston, 1797–1840* (Chapel Hill: University of North Carolina Press, 2002); Ryan, "The Power of Women's Networks"; Barbara Leslie Epstein, *The Politics of Domesticity: Women, Evangelism, and Temperance in Nineteenth-Century America* (Middletown, Conn.: Wesleyan University Press, 1981); Nancy Hewett, *Women's Activism and Social Change: Rochester, New York, 1822–1872* (Ithaca: Cornell University Press, 1984); Barbara Meil Hobson, *Uneasy Virtue: The Politics of Prostitution and the American Reform Tradition* (New York: Basic Books, 1987); and Lori D. Ginzberg, *Women and the Work of Benevolence: Morality, Politics, and Class in the Nineteenth-Century United States* (New Haven: Yale University Press, 1990).

42. See Davidoff, "Regarding Some 'Old Husbands' Tales,'" 178.

43. For the most recent and complete historiographical essay on plural marriage, see Martha Sonntag Bradley, "Out of the Closet and Into the Fire: The New Mormon Historians' Take on Polygamy," in *Excavating Mormon Pasts: The New Historiography of the Last Half Century*, ed. Newell G. Bringhurst and Lavina Fielding Anderson (Salt Lake City: Greg Kofford Books, 2004), 303–22.

44. See Martha Sonntag Bradley and Mary Firmage Woodward, "Plurality, Patriarchy, and the Priestess: Zina D. H. Young's Nauvoo Marriage," *Journal of Mormon History* 20 (Spring 1994): 84–118; and B. Carmon Hardy, "Lords of Creation: Polygamy, the Abrahamic Household, and Mormon Patriarchy," *Journal of Mormon History* 20 (Spring 1994): 119–52.

45. See Maureen Ursenbach Beecher, "A Feminist among the Mormons: Charlotte Ives Cobb Godbe Kirby," *Utah Historical Quarterly* 59 (Winter 1991): 22–31; Maureen Ursenbach Beecher, "Inadvertent Disclosure: Autobiography in the Poetry of Eliza R. Snow," *Dialogue: A Journal of Mormon Thought* 23 (Spring 1990): 54–107; Jill Mulvay Derr, "Woman's Place in Brigham Young's World," *BYU Studies* 18, no. 3 (Spring 1978): 377–95; Kenneth W. Godfrey, Audrey M. Godfrey, and Jill Mulvay Derr, eds., *Women's Voices: An Untold History of the Latter-day Saints, 1830–1900* (Salt Lake City: Deseret Book Co., 1982); and Carol Cornwall Madsen, "Emmeline B. Wells: A Voice for Mormon Women," *John Whitmer Historical Association Journal* 2 (1982): 11–21.

46. Kathryn M. Daynes, *More Wives Than One: Transformation of the Mormon Marriage System, 1840–1910* (Urbana: University of Illinois Press, 2001), 2–3.

47. Ibid., 131.

48. Gordon, *The Mormon Question*, xiv.

49. Mark W. Cannon, "The Crusades Against the Masons, Catholics and Mormons: Separate Waves of a Common Current," *BYU Studies* 3 (Winter 1961): 23–40; and David Brion Davis, "Some Themes of Counter-Subversion: An Analysis of Anti-Masonic, Anti-Catholic, and Anti-Mormon Literature," *Mississippi Valley Historical Review* 47, no. 2 (September 1960): 205–44. For a more contemporary study of anti-Mormon and anti-Catholic sentiment that focuses on how Mormons and Catholics perceived each other, see Matthew J. Grow, "The Whore of Babylon and the Abomination of Abominations: Nineteenth-Century Catholic and Mormon Mutual Perceptions and Religious Identity," *Church History* 73, no. 1 (March 2004): 139–67.

50. Charles A. Cannon, "The Awesome Power of Sex: The Polemical Campaign against Mormon Polygamy," *Pacific Historical Review* 43, no. 1 (February 1974): 62.

51. Richard H. Cracroft, "Distorting Polygamy for Fun and Profit: Artemis Ward and Mark Twain Among the Mormons," *BYU Studies* 14, no. 2 (Winter 1974): 272.

52. Davis Bitton and Gary L. Bunker, *The Mormon Graphic Image, 1834–1914* (Salt Lake City: University of Utah Press, 1983).

53. Craig L. Foster, "Victorian Pornographic Imagery in Anti-Mormon Literature," *Journal of Mormon History* 19, no. 1 (Spring 1993): 115–32.

54. Terryl Givens, *The Viper on the Hearth: Mormons, Myths, and the Construction of Heresy* (New York: Oxford University Press, 1997).

55. Ibid., 13.

56. Sarah Barringer Gordon, "'Our National Hearthstone': Anti-Polygamy Fiction and the Sentimental Campaign Against Moral Diversity in Antebellum America," *Yale Journal of Law and the Humanities* 8, no. 2 (Summer 1996): 298. See also, Gordon, *The Mormon Question*, 1–54.

57. Gordon, "'Our National Hearthstone,'" 301.

58. Patrick Q. Mason, *The Mormon Menace: Violence and Anti-Mormonism in the Postbellum South* (New York: Oxford University Press, 2011), 62.

59. J. Spencer Fluhman, *"A Peculiar People": Anti-Mormonism and the Making of Religion in Nineteenth-Century America* (Chapel Hill: University of North Carolina Press, 2012), 21–102.

60. Ibid., 103.

61. Ibid., 103–25.

62. Under theological mandate, the early church not only preserved almost all of the documents they themselves produced, but also most of many volumes of anti-Mormonism produced over the late nineteenth century. See *The Doctrine and Covenants of The Church of Jesus Christ of Latter-day Saints*, printed with *The Book of Mormon: Another Testament of Jesus Christ* (Salt Lake City: The Church of Jesus Christ of Latter-day Saints, 1986), 123:1–6. This edition, like most others, includes three Mormon books of scripture: *The Book of Mormon, The Doctrine and Covenants*, and *The Pearl of Great Price*. References to these three books will list section and verse numbers but not page numbers. Section and verse numbers are included in every twentieth-century reprint and give more precise locations that can be found in a broad variety of editions.

63. Benedict Anderson, *Imagined Communities: Reflections on the Origin and Spread of Nationalism*, rev. ed., (London: Verso, 1991), 4–7.

64. Brigham Young, January 12, 1868, in Brigham Young, President of The Church of Jesus Christ of Latter-day Saints, His Two Counsellors [*sic*], the Twelve Apostles, and Others, *Journal of Discourses* 26 vols. (1855–1886; reprint [Salt Lake City: Deseret Book Co.], 1966), 12:153. I rely on the *Journal of Discourses* because it represents not only the largest collection of nineteenth-century Mormon public addresses but also because it was deliberately selected by Brigham Young and other church officials to represent a canon of Mormon doctrine and theology. While many other written and oral Mormon sources exist, the *Journal of Discourses* forms the bulwark of early Mormon thought, and most (though not all) of the sermons published in it were given at the semiannual general conference when Mormons gathered to hear the revelations they believed God had revealed to his prophet and officials. Those sermons were widely reprinted in newspapers and as pamphlets and papers in Utah and abroad. While nineteenth-century Mormons likely saw the sermons included in the journal as doctrinal treatises, the contemporary church has posted on its official website that members should understand the *Journal of Discourses* as "a compilation of sermons and other materials from the early years of the church, which were transcribed and then published. It includes practical advice as well as doctrinal discussion, some of which is speculative in nature and some of which is only of historical interest." http://lds.org/study/topics/the-journal-of-discourses?lang=eng# (accessed May 16, 2011).

65. Blanche Beechwood [Emmeline B. Wells], "A Mormon Woman's View of Marriage," *Woman's Exponent*, 1 September 1877, 54.

66. Fred E. Bennett, *A Detective's Experience Among the Mormons; or, Polygamist Mormons: How They Live and the Land They Live In* (Chicago: Laird and Lee Publishers, 1887), 18.

67. Veronique Petit, *Plural Marriage the Heart-History of Adele Hersch*, 4th ed. (Ithaca: E. D. Norton, Printer, 1885), preface.

Chapter 1.
Early Mormonism and the American Republic

"That these things might come forth": *Book of Mormon* (Salt Lake City: The Church of Jesus Christ of Latter-day Saints, 1986), 3 Nephi, 21:4.

1. Joseph Fielding Smith, *History of The Church of Jesus Christ of Latter-day Saints*, 7 vols. 13th ed. (1951; reprint, Salt Lake City: Deseret Book Co., 1959), 1:4–6. On the burned-over district, see Whitney R. Cross, *The Burned-Over District: The Social and Intellectual History of Enthusiastic Religion in Western New York, 1800–1850*, 2nd ed. (New York: Harper & Row, 1965); Michael Barkun, *Crucible of the Millennium: The Burned-Over District of New York in the 1840s* (Syracuse: Syracuse University Press, 1986); and Paul E. Johnson, *A Shopkeeper's Millennium: Society and Revivals in Rochester, New York, 1815–1837* (New York: Hill and Wang, 2004).

2. *Doctrine and Covenants*, 13.

3. *Doctrine and Covenants*, 20, italics added.

4. The history of the church's many migrations has been well traced elsewhere and need not be repeated here. See James B. Allen and Glen M. Leonard, *The Story of the Latter-day Saints* (Salt Lake City: Deseret Book Co., 1992); Leonard J. Arrington and Davis Bitton, *The Mormon Experience: A History of the Latter-day Saints*, 2nd ed. (Urbana: University of Illinois Press, 1992); Milton V. Backman, Jr., *The Heavens Resound: A History of the Latter-day Saints in Ohio, 1830–1838* (Salt Lake City: Deseret Book Co., 1983); Claudia Bushman and Richard L. Bushman, *Building the Kingdom: A History of Mormons in America* (New York: Oxford University Press, 2001); Jan Shipps, *Mormonism: The Story of a New Religious Tradition* (Urbana: University of Illinois Press, 1985); Marvin S. Hill, *Quest for Refuge: The Mormon Flight from American Pluralism* (Salt Lake City: Signature Books, 1989); and Kenneth H. Winn, *Exiles in a Land of Liberty: Mormons in America, 1830–1846* (Chapel Hill: University of North Carolina Press, 1989).

5. James L. Kimball, Jr. "A Wall to Defend Zion: The Nauvoo Charter," *BYU Studies* 15, no. 4 (Summer 1975): 496.

6. Larry C. Porter and Milton V. Backman, Jr., "Doctrine and the Temple in Nauvoo," *BYU Studies* 32 (Winter 1992): 50–51.

7. For more thorough discussions of these doctrines, see B. Carmon Hardy, *Solemn Covenant: The Mormon Polygamous Passage* (Urbana: University of Illinois Press, 1992), 1–126, and Porter and Backman, "Doctrine and the Temple in Nauvoo," 41–54.

8. See Joseph Smith, Jr., *Teachings of the Prophet Joseph Smith: Taken from His Sermons and Writings as They are Found in the Documentary History and Other Publications of the Church and Written or Published in the Days of the Prophet's Ministry*, comp. Joseph Fielding Smith (Salt Lake City: Deseret Book Co., 1976), 301. See also *Doctrine and Covenants*, 93:29.

9. *Doctrine and Covenants*, 76:24.

10. Orson Hyde, October 4, 1857, in *Journal of Discourses*, 5:283.

11. On the development of Mormon priesthood, see Gregory A. Prince, *Power from on High: The Development of Mormon Priesthood* (Salt Lake City: Signature Books, 1995).

12. On the development of Mormon temple worship, see David John Buerger, *The Mysteries of Godliness: A History of Mormon Temple Worship* (Salt Lake City: Signature Books, 2002).

13. Brigham Young, November 2, 1856, in *Journal of Discourses*, 4:58–59.

14. See Andrew F. Ehat and Lyndon W. Cook, comps. and eds., *The Words of Joseph Smith: The Contemporary Accounts of the Nauvoo Discourses of the Prophet Joseph* (Provo, Utah: Religious Studies Center, Brigham Young University, 1980), 298.

15. Brigham Young, November 2, 1856, in *Journal of Discourses*, 4:58–59, quoted material on 58.

16. Jonathan A. Stapley, "Adoptive Sealing Ritual in Mormonism," *Journal of Mormon History* 37 (Summer 2011): 53–117.

17. Ephesians 2:19. AV. On the shift from belonging to a group or household of God to the Mormon notion of individual family relationships, see Samuel M. Brown, "Early

Mormon Adoption Theology and the Mechanics of Salvation," *Journal of Mormon History* 37 (Summer 2011): 3–52.

18. Gordon Irving, "The Law of Adoption: One Phase of the Development of the Mormon Concept of Salvation, 1830–1900," *BYU Studies* 14, no. 3 (Spring 1974): 294. See also Brigham Young, September 4, 1873, in *Journal of Discourses*, 16:186–87.

19. Stapley, "Adoptive Sealing Ritual in Mormonism," 74–90.

20. Ibid., 99–117.

21. Irving, "The Law of Adoption," 310–13.

22. See Smith, *Teachings of the Prophet Joseph Smith*, 181.

23. Ibid., 345.

24. Ehat and Cook, *The Words of Joseph Smith*, 83–84 n. 9.

25. See *Book of Mormon*, 2 Nephi, 9:13 and Alma, 11:42–44.

26. John Taylor, *The Gospel Kingdom: Selections from the Writings and Discourses of John Taylor*, selected, arranged, and annotated by G. Homer Durham (Salt Lake City: Bookcraft, Inc., 1987), 14. See also John Taylor, April 9, 1882, in *Journal of Discourses*, 23:65.

27. For a reprint of Smith's words, see Smith, *Teachings of the Prophet Joseph Smith*, 369–75. On the King Follett Discourse, see Van Hale, "The Doctrinal Impact of the King Follett Discourse," *BYU Studies* 18, no. 2 (Winter 1978): 209–25; Donald Q. Cannon, "The King Follett Discourse: Joseph Smith's Greatest Sermon in Historical Perspective," *BYU Studies* 18, no. 2 (Winter 1978): 179–92; Stanley Larson, "The King Follett Discourse: A Newly Amalgamated Text," *BYU Studies* 18, no. 2 (Winter 1978): 193–208; and Donald Q. Cannon and Larry E. Dahl, *The Prophet Joseph Smith's King Follett Discourse: A Six Column Comparison of Original Notes and Amalgamations* (Provo, Utah: BYU Printing Service, 1983).

28. See Smith, *Teachings of the Prophet Joseph Smith*, 372. This notion corresponded with Paul's affirmation that "to us [there is but] one God, the Father." I Corinthians 8:6. AV.

29. See Robert J. Matthews, "The 'New Translation' of the Bible, 1830–1833: Doctrinal Development During the Kirtland Era," *BYU Studies* 11, no. 4 (Summer 1971): 416–17.

30. That year, Smith apparently told one of his confidants, Lyman Smith, that "plural marriage was a correct principle." Smith, *History of the Church*, 5:537. See also Daniel W. Bachman, "New Light on an Old Hypothesis: The Ohio Origins of the Revelation on Eternal Marriage," *Journal of Mormon History* 5 (1978): 19–31.

31. Richard L. Bushman, *Joseph Smith: Rough Stone Rolling* (New York: Alfred A. Knopf, 2005), 323–27; Todd Compton, *In Sacred Loneliness: The Plural Wives of Joseph Smith* (Salt Lake City: Signature Books, 1997), 25–36; and Don Bradley, "Mormon Polygamy Before Nauvoo? The Relationship of Joseph Smith and Fanny Alger," in *The Persistence of Polygamy: Joseph Smith and the Origins of Nauvoo Polygamy*, eds. Newell G. Bringhurst and Craig L. Foster (Independence, Mo.: John Whitmer Books, 2010), 14–58.

32. An analysis of this early history of polygamy is found in Richard S. Van Wagoner, *Mormon Polygamy: A History*, 2nd ed. (Salt Lake City: Signature Books, 1989), 1–35. See also Daniel W. Bachman, "A Study of the Mormon Practice of Plural Marriage before the

Death of Joseph Smith." (Master's thesis, Purdue University, 1975); Bachman, "New Light on an Old Hypothesis," 19–32; and Bushman, *Rough Stone Rolling*, 437.

33. For accounts of plural marriage during the Nauvoo period, see Compton, *In Sacred Loneliness*; George D. Smith, *Nauvoo Polygamy: "But We Called It Plural Marriage"* (Salt Lake City: Signature Books, 2008); and Daynes, *More Wives Than One*, 25–32.

34. Hardy, *Solemn Covenant*, 52. See also, Steven C. Taysom, "A Uniform and Common Recollection: Joseph Smith's Legacy, Polygamy, and Public Memory, 1852–2002," in *Dimensions of Faith: A Mormon Studies Reader*, ed. Stephen C. Taysom (Salt Lake City: Signature Books, 2011): 187–91.

35. Daynes, *More Wives Than One*, 225–6n; Craig L. Foster, "Doctrine and Covenants Section 132 and Joseph Smith's Expanding Concept of Family," in Bringhurst and Foster, *The Persistence of Polygamy*, 96–98.

36. George Q. Cannon, October 31, 1880, in *Journal of Discourses*, 22:124–25.

37. George Q. Cannon's 1869 discussion of celestial marriage, for example, made clear its meaning in his theological analysis of the parallel Old Testament practice of plural marriage. George Q. Cannon, October 9, 1869, in *Journal of Discourses*, 13:197–98. That same year, Wilford Woodruff's discussion of patriarchal marriage references American laws against it, suggesting that patriarchal marriage was necessarily plural marriage. Wilford Woodruff, December 12, 1869, in *Journal of Discourses*, 13:166–67. These examples, like those in the notes to follow, are illustrative, not exhaustive, for an exhaustive list of references to this effect would be longer than most academic bibliographies.

38. Nearly all remaining records are collected in Ehat and Cook's book, *The Words of Joseph Smith*, and Smith's early positions not only on polygamy but on a host of other topics remain unclear.

39. Porter and Backman, "Doctrine and the Temple in Nauvoo," 51.

40. Porter and Backman, "Doctrine and the Temple in Nauvoo," 41–54.

41. Orson Pratt, August 29, 1852, in *Journal of Discourses*, 1:54.

42. Brigham Young, February 20, 1870, in *Journal of Discourses*, 13:239.

43. *Nauvoo Expositor*, 7 June 1844, 2.

44. Ibid., 1.

45. Ibid., 2.

46. Ibid., 3.

47. Kenneth Winn argues that persecution in Illinois, indeed the entire history of Mormon persecution from 1830 to 1846, resulted from divergent interpretations of republican ideology. See Winn, *Exiles in a Land of Liberty*, especially 162–238. Marvin S. Hill offers a different interpretation, arguing that persecutions of Mormons in their early history were motivated by a powerful strain of Mormon antipluralism that rejected the religious diversity of Jacksonian America. See Hill, *Quest for Refuge*.

48. See "Who Shall Be Our Next President?" *Times and Seasons*, 15 February 1844, 439–41; Joseph Fielding Smith, *Church History and Modern Revelation*, 4 vols. (Salt Lake City: Council of the Twelve Apostles of The Church of Jesus Christ of Latter-day Saints, 1946–1949), 4:172; Smith, *Essentials in Church History*, 353–60; Newell G. Bringhurst and

Craig L. Foster, *Mormon Quest for the Presidency* (Independence, Mo.: John Whitmer Books, 2008), 7–49; and D. Michael Quinn, *The Mormon Hierarchy: Origins of Power* (Salt Lake City: Signature Books, 1994), 120.

49. See Arnold K. Garr, "Joseph Smith: Candidate for President of the United States," in *Regional Studies in Latter-day Saint Church History, Illinois,* ed. H. Dean Garrett (Provo, Utah: Department of Church History and Doctrine, Brigham Young University, 1995): 151–65, specifically 162.

50. Bushman, *Rough Stone Rolling,* 546; Richard Ostling and Joan K. Ostling, *Mormon America: The Power and the Promise* (San Francisco: HarperSanFrancisco, 1999), 17. For a more detailed account of the events leading to and flowing from Smith's assassination, see Allen and Leonard, *The Story of the Latter-day Saints,* 190–98.

51. For a detailed description of men's and women's roles on the Overland trail that focuses on Midwestern emigrants migrating to Oregon and California, see John Mack Faragher, *Women and Men on the Overland Trail,* 2nd ed. (New Haven: Yale University Press, 2001).

52. Utahns celebrate July 24, the date of Young's arrival, as a state holiday with nearly as much festivity, celebration, and public ritual as the nation celebrates the Fourth of July.

53. Smith, *Essentials in Church History,* 473.

54. Bushman, *Joseph Smith and the Beginnings of Mormonism,* 188.

55. Jan Shipps, *Mormonism.*

56. The Mormon recapitulation of Old Testament narrative was not conscious, Shipps argues, but rather experiential. See Shipps, *Mormonism,* 50–63.

57. Ibid., 67–85.

58. *Book of Mormon,* Moroni, 10:2.

59. *Doctrine and Covenants,* 101:78.

60. *Book of Mormon,* 3 Nephi, 21:4. See also, *Doctrine and Covenants,* 101:77, 80.

61. Smith, *Teachings of the Prophet Joseph Smith,* 147. Smith called himself "the greatest advocate of the Constitution of the United States there is on the earth." Smith, *Teachings of the Prophet Joseph Smith,* 326.

62. *Doctrine and Covenants,* 101:80.

63. "Who Shall Be Our Next President?" Reprinted in Smith, *History of the Church,* 6:214.

64. Ehat and Cook, *The Words of Joseph Smith,* 279 n. 1. See also Brigham Young, *Discourses of Brigham Young,* selected and arranged by John A. Widtsoe (Salt Lake City: Deseret Book Co., 1978), 469; and Joseph F. Smith, *Gospel Doctrine: Selections from the Sermons and Writings of Joseph F. Smith,* selected and arranged by John A. Widtsoe (Salt Lake City: Deseret Book Co., 1961), 403.

65. This editorial is reprinted in Smith, *History of the Church,* 5:382.

66. See Smith, *History of the Church,* 5:490.

67. See *Doctrine and Covenants,* 97:21 and 101:18; and "Articles of Faith," reprinted in James Reuben Clark, comp., *Messages of the First Presidency of The Church of Jesus Christ of Latter-day Saints 1833–1964,* 6 vols. (Salt Lake City: Bookcraft, Inc., 1966), 3:210. This

article of faith has been printed in various permutations, the most recent of which reads, "Zion (the New Jerusalem) will be built upon the American continent." See also Ehat and Cook, *The Words of Joseph Smith*, 362–65, wherein church officials report that Joseph Smith said "the whole America is Zion itself."

68. Klaus J. Hansen, *Quest for Empire: the Political Kingdom of God and the Council of Fifty in Mormon History* (Lincoln: University of Nebraska Press, 1967), 5.

69. For a little-known analysis of Joseph Smith's political thoughts on world government from inside the LDS faith, see Hyrum L. Andrus, *Joseph Smith and World Government* (Salt Lake City: Deseret Book Co., 1958).

70. See D. Michael Quinn, "The Council of Fifty and Its Members, 1844–1945," *BYU Studies* 20, no. 2 (Winter 1980); Hansen, *Quest for Empire*; Hyrum L. Andrus, *Doctrines of the Kingdom—Foundations of the Millennial Kingdom of Christ*, vol. 3 (Salt Lake City: Bookcraft, Inc., 1973); John Taylor, *The Government of God* (Liverpool: S. W. Richards, 1852); and Taylor, *The Gospel Kingdom*.

71. Quinn, "Council of Fifty," 1.

72. Ibid., 21.

73. Brigham Young, August 9, 1874, in *Journal of Discourses*, 17:156.

74. Parley P. Pratt, *Proclamation of the Twelve Apostles of The Church of Jesus Christ of Latter-day Saints* ([New York: Prophet Office, 1845?]), his emphasis.

75. See Erastus Snow, April 4, 1881, in *Journal of Discourses*, 22:150–51, and George Q. Cannon, April 6, 1878, in *Journal of Discourses*, 20:86–87. Joseph Smith and later John Taylor called God's government a "theo-democracy," a term Taylor popularized in his treatise, *The Government of God*; Joseph Smith, Jr., "The Globe," *Times and Seasons*, 15 April 1844, 510.

76. Smith, *History of the Church*, 6:365.

Chapter 2.
Mormonism and the Public/Private Divide

"We shall then live together as one great family": Brigham Young, January 12, 1868, in *Journal of Discourses*, 12:153.

1. Orson Pratt, August 29, 1852, in *Journal of Discourses*, 1:53–66.

2. Bennett, *A Detective's Experience Among the Mormons*, 18.

3. Benjamin G. Ferris, *Utah and the Mormons: The History, Government, Doctrines, Customs, and Prospects of the Latter-day Saints. From Personal Observations During a Six Months' Residence at Great Salt Lake City* (New York: Harper and Brothers, 1854), 146.

4. The most recent and reliable study, written by historian Kathryn Daynes, estimates that during the peak of the practice in 1860 between 30 and 40 percent of Mormon adults practiced plural marriage. Statistics varied by location, reaching their highest rate at 66 percent in Orderville, Utah. Polygamy was least practiced in the town of Panaca, bottoming out at 4.6 percent. Moreover, the practice of polygamy waxed and waned over time in response to internal and external pressures. At its lowest point in the 1880s, Daynes

estimates that about 20–25 percent of Mormon adults practiced plural marriage. See Daynes, *More Wives Than One*, 100–115.

5. Ibid., 75. Daynes, however, disagrees with my interpretation of this data, claiming that polygamy was peripheral to Mormon doctrine. Her reading is that plural marriage was allowed under Mormon doctrine, but not required. See 225–26n.

6. See John Taylor, March 14, 1869, in *Journal of Discourses*, 13:18 and Wilford Woodruff, December 12, 1869, in *Journal of Discourses*, 13:166–67.

7. Lorenzo Snow, October 11, 1857, in *Journal of Discourses*, 5:315–16.

8. Brigham Young, April 6, 1868, in *Journal of Discourses*, 12:194.

9. Brigham Young, August 19, 1866, in *Journal of Discourses*, 11:268.

10. Jedediah M. Grant, October 26, 1856, in *Journal of Discourses*, 4:128.

11. On nineteenth-century sex ratios in Utah, see Daynes, 110–15.

12. Brigham Young, April 6, 1868, in *Journal of Discourses*, 12:194.

13. George Q. Cannon, November 16, 1884, in *Journal of Discourses*, 25:366–69. Church historians have for some time misread these statements to argue that a numerical gender imbalance required men to take more than one wife if all the community's women were to receive the benefits of marriage. However, historical statistics no longer support such an imbalance. Rather, as Daynes points out, polygamy tightened competition among Mormon men for available women, resulting in a surplus of single men. See Daynes, *More Wives Than One*, 91–115.

14. See George Q. Cannon, November 16, 1884, in *Journal of Discourses*, 25:366–69, quoted material on 366.

15. George Q. Cannon, October 9, 1869, in *Journal of Discourses*, 13:204. See Daynes, 133–34.

16. John Taylor, October 21, 1887, in *Journal of Discourses*, 19:149–50.

17. Orson Pratt, "Celestial Marriage," *The Seer*, June 1853, 91. See also Lorenzo Snow, January 4, 1857, in *Journal of Discourses*, 4:155.

18. John Taylor, October 10, 1875, in *Journal of Discourses*, 18:138.

19. "Monogamy, Polygamy, and Christianity," *Latter-day Saints' Millennial Star*, 6 August 1853, 515.

20. Brigham Young, November 29, 1868, in *Journal of Discourses*, 12:312.

21. Joseph F. Smith, July 7, 1878, in *Journal of Discourses*, 20:30–31.

22. Brigham Young, August 31, 1873, in *Journal of Discourses*, 16:166–67.

23. See Erastus Snow, October 7, 1882, in *Journal of Discourses*, 123:297–300.

24. See Daynes, *More Wives Than One*, 128.

25. John Taylor, 14 October 1882, as quoted in Wilford Woodruff, *Wilford Woodruff's Journals, 1833–1898*, Scott Kearney ed., 9 vols. (Midvale, Utah: Signature Books, 1983–1984), 8:126.

26. For an analysis of Mormon elites, see Quinn, *The Mormon Hierarchy: Origins of Power*; and D. Michael Quinn, *The Mormon Hierarchy: Extensions of Power* (Salt Lake City: Signature Books in association with Smith Research Associates, 1997).

27. Daynes, *More Wives Than One*, 128.

28. Ibid., 128–37.

29. George Q. Cannon, October 9, 1869, in *Journal of Discourses*, 13: 204.

30. Daynes, *More Wives Than One*, 127.

31. For an exposition of the connections between priesthood, plural marriage, and political and social organization in the kingdom of God, see John Taylor, October 10, 1875, in *Journal of Discourses*, 18:138.

32. Brigham Young, January 12, 1868, in *Journal of Discourses*, 12:153.

33. *Doctrine and Covenants*, 105:4. Injunctions to unity are multiple in Mormon scripture. For a few additional examples, see *Doctrine and Covenants* 38:27, which reads "Be One; and if ye are not one, ye are not mine"; and *Book of Mormon*, Mosiah, 18:21, where God commands His ancient kingdom "that they should look forward with one eye, having one faith and one baptism, having their hearts knit together in unity and in love towards one another."

34. Givens, *Viper on the Hearth*, 82.

35. *Doctrine and Covenants*, 29:34.

36. See, for example, Brigham Young, April 8, 1879, in *Journal of Discourses*, 20:172–73.

37. Heber C. Kimball, October 8, 1852, in *Journal of Discourses*, 1:207.

38. Wilford Woodruff, July 4, 1880, in *Journal of Discourses*, 21:281.

39. Godfrey, Godfrey, and Derr, *Women's Voices*, 8.

40. Quoted in Edward W. Tullidge, *The Life of Brigham Young; or, Utah and her Founders* (New York: n. pub., 1876), 221–22.

41. See Daynes, *More Wives Than One*, 77–83; and Quinn, *The Mormon Hierarchy: Extensions of Power*, 163.

42. Karen Lystra, *Searching the Heart: Women, Men, and Romantic Love in Nineteenth-Century America* (New York: Oxford University Press, 1989), 7. For an alternative vision of the place of romantic love in nineteenth-century marriages, especially in the American West, that argues that the sexual division of labor, not romance, was the central feature of most marriages in the Midwest and the West, see Faragher, *Women and Men on the Overland Trail*, 147–55.

43. Lystra, *Searching the Heart*, 18.

44. Ibid., 17.

45. Ibid., 54.

46. Ibid., 31.

47. Ibid., 8.

48. Ibid., 77–80, quoted material on 80.

49. Letter from Emmeline B. Woodward Whitney to Newel K. Whitney, October 16, 1847, Newel K. Whitney Papers, 1825–1906, L. Tom Perry Special Collections, Brigham Young University, Provo, Utah.

50. Letter from Martha Hughes Cannon to Angus M. Cannon, July 9, 1886, reprinted in Constance L. Lieber and John Sillito, eds., *Letters from Exile: The Correspondence of Martha Hughes Cannon and Angus M. Cannon, 1886–1888* (Salt Lake City: Signature Books in association with Smith Research Associates, 1989), 30.

51. Letter from Martha Hughes Cannon to Angus M. Cannon, August 16, 1886, reprinted in ibid., 36.

52. See Julie Dunfey, "'Living the Principle' of Plural Marriage: Mormon Women, Utopia, and Female Sexuality in the Nineteenth Century," *Feminist Studies* 10, no. 3 (Fall 1984): 523–36.

53. See Flake, "The Emotional and Priestly Logic of Plural Marriage," 10–16.

54. Karen Lynn, "Courtship and Romance in Utah Territory: Doing Away with 'The Gentile Custom of Sparkification,'" in *A Sesquicentennial Look at Church History: Sidney B. Sperry Symposium, January 26, 1980, Brigham Young University Campus, Provo, Utah* (Provo, Utah: Brigham Young University Church Educational System, 1980), 211–23.

55. Mrs. Joseph [Isabella] Horne, "Migration and Settlement of the Latter-day Saints, Salt Lake City, 1884," original on file in Bancroft library, University of California, Berkeley, Banc mss. P-F 24, as quoted in Lawrence Foster, *Women, Family, and Utopia: Communal Experiments of the Shakers, the Oneida Community, and the Mormons* (Syracuse: Syracuse University Press, 1991), 193.

56. Quoted in Jean Bickmore White, "Martha H. Cannon," in Vicky Burgess-Olson, ed., *Sister Saints* (Provo, Utah.: Brigham Young University Press, 1978), 391.

57. Zina D. H. Young, "Utah Unveiled," *New York World*, 19 November 1869.

58. Flake, "The Emotional and Priestly Logic of Plural Marriage," 10–16. See also Carrie A. Miles, "'What's Love Got to Do With It?': Earthly Experience of Celestial Marriage, Past and Present," in *Modern Polygamy in the United States: Historical, Cultural, and Legal Issues*, ed. Cardell K. Jacobson and Lara Burton (New York: Oxford University Press, 2011): 185–207.

59. Quoted in Godfrey, Godfrey, and Derr, *Women's Voices*, 360.

60. Ellis Reynolds Shipp, *While Others Slept: Autobiography and Journal of Ellis Reynolds Shipp, M.D.* (Salt Lake City: Bookcraft, Inc., 1962), 84.

61. Flake, "The Emotional and Priestly Logic of Plural Marriage," 15.

62. See Paula Kelly Harline, "Polygamous Yet Monogamous: Cultural Conflict in the Writings of Mormon Polygamous Wives," in *Old West—New West: Centennial Essays*, ed. Barbara Howard Meldrum (Moscow: University of Idaho Press, 1993): 115–32.

63. Quoted in Godfrey, Godfrey, and Derr, *Women's Voices*, 278–79.

64. Mary Lois Walker Morris, *Before the Manifesto: The Life Writings of Mary Lois Walker Morris*, ed. Melissa Lambert Milewski (Logan, Utah: Utah State University Press, 2007), 121.

65. Marie Cornwall and Laga Van Beek, "The Mormon Practice of Plural Marriage: The Social Construction of Religious Identity and Commitment," in *Religion and the Social Order*, Marion S. Goldman and Mary Jo Neitz, eds. (Greenwood, Conn.: JAI Press, 1995), 24–25.

66. Orson Pratt, October 7, 1869, in *Journal of Discourses*, 13:185.

67. [Belinda Marden Pratt], "Defense of Polygamy, by a Lady of Utah, in a Letter to Her Sister in New Hampshire," *Latter-day Saints' Millennial Star*, 29 July 1854, 470.

68. Brigham Young, *Discourses of Brigham Young*, selected and arranged by John A. Widtsoe (Salt Lake City: Deseret Book Co., 1978), 179.

69. Jessie L. Embry, *Mormons and Polygamy (Setting the Record Straight)* (Orem, Utah: Millennial Press, 2007), 8.

70. Shipp, *While Others Slept*, especially 55–56.

71. Ibid., 80–81.

72. Mary Jane Mount Tanner, *A Fragment: The Autobiography of Mary Jane Mount Tanner*, ed. Margery W. Ward (Salt Lake City: Tanner Trust Fund, 1980), 6, 181.

73. Ibid., 6.

74. Romania B. Pratt Penrose, "Memoir of Romania B. Pratt, M.D." (1881), accessed June 27, 2011, http://jared.pratt-family.org/parley_family_histories/romania_bunnell_memoirs .html. For a more complete analysis of women's feelings about plural marriage, see Embry, *Mormons and Polygamy*, 97–101.

75. Emmeline B. Wells, "Woman Against Woman," *Woman's Exponent*, 1 May 1879, 234.

76. Louisa Barnes Pratt, *The History of Louisa Barnes Pratt: Being the Autobiography of a Mormon Missionary, Widow, and Pioneer*, ed. S. George Ellsworth (Logan, Utah: Utah State University Press, 1998), 323.

77. Brigham Young, July 18, 1869, in *Journal of Discourses*, 6:1.

78. Susa Young Gates, "Family Life among the Mormons," *The North American Review*, 150, no. 400 (March 1890): 349.

79. Quoted in Gail Farr Casterline, "'In the Toils' or 'Onward for Zion': Images of the Mormon Woman, 1852–1890" (M.A. thesis, Utah State University, 1974), 76–77.

80. Elizabeth Wood Kane, *Twelve Mormon Homes Visited in Succession on a Journey through Utah to Arizona* (Philadelphia: s.n., 1874), 5.

81. *Doctrine and Covenants*, 51:3.

82. Brigham Young, June 6, 1867, in *Journal of Discourses*, 12: 56–57.

83. *Doctrine and Covenants*, 42:32.

84. In post–World War II America, the Church has largely contended that the United Order maintained the concept of private property. However, I contend that this claim can only be understood as a consequence of the World War II and cold-war era in which it was produced, as Mormons worked diligently to distinguish the United Order from communism. For an example typical of the church's mid-century perspectives, see "Message of the First Presidency to the Church," April 6, 1942, in Clark, *Messages of the First Presidency*, 6:151–52.

85. Orson Pratt, August 6, 1873, in *Journal of Discourses*, 16:153–54.

86. Orson Pratt, "The Equality and Oneness of the Saints," *The Seer*, July 1854, 294.

87. See *Doctrine and Covenants* 38:4; and *Pearl of Great Price*, Moses 6–8.

88. See Orson Pratt, September 10, 1854, in *Journal of Discourses*, 2:98–100, and Orson Pratt, March 9, 1873, in *Journal of Discourses*, 16:153–55.

89. Orson Pratt, August 16, 1873, in *Journal of Discourses* 16: 153–54.

90. "Zion's Cooperative Mercantile Institution, July 10, 1875," in Clark, *Messages of the First Presidency*, 2:268.

91. *Doctrine and Covenants*, 70:14. See also *Doctrine and Covenants*, 78:6, which reads "For if ye [the saints] are not equal in earthly things, ye cannot be equal in obtaining heavenly things."

92. See *Doctrine and Covenants*, 104. For a detailed account of the Mormons' various attempts to live the law of consecration in various guises, see Leonard J. Arrington, Feramorz Y. Fox, and Dean L. May, *Building the City of God: Community and Cooperation among the Mormons*, 2nd ed. (Urbana: University of Illinois Press, 1992).

93. Ibid., 61.

94. Quoted in Godfrey, Godfrey, and Derr, *Women's Voices*, 286.

95. Brigham Young, April 7, 1873, in *Journal of Discourses*, 16:8–9.

96. Brigham Young, George Albert Smith, and Daniel H. Wells, "To the President, Vice Presidents and Board of Directors of the United Order at St. George," in Clark, *Messages of the First Presidency*, 2:252.

97. Brigham Young, August 31, 1873, in *Journal of Discourses*, 16:170.

98. Arrington, Fox, and May, *Building the City of God*, 254, 203.

99. E. M. Webb, in the Orderville Ward Manuscript History, 1878, MS, Church History Library, The Church of Jesus Christ of Latter-day Saints, Salt Lake City, Utah, as quoted in ibid., 269.

100. Arrington, Fox, and May, *Building the City of God*, 203.

101. Brigham Young, October 9, 1872, in *Journal of Discourses*, 15:221.

102. Thomas Carter, "Living the Principle: Mormon Polygamous Housing in Nineteenth-Century Utah," *Winterthur Portfolio* 35, no. 4 (Winter 2000): 223–24. See also C. Mark Hamilton, *Nineteenth-Century Mormon Architecture and City Planning* (New York: Oxford University Press, 1995), 109–10.

103. Dolores Hayden's book, *The Grand Domestic Revolution*, describes a number of architectural experiments sex radicals, utopians, and feminists designed in the mid-nineteenth century, many of which were similar to Young's communal household under the Order. While it seems doubtful that Young actually studied any of the architecture Hayden describes, he was undoubtedly influenced by the collective living designs of his contemporaries. Dolores Hayden, *The Grand Domestic Revolution: A History of Feminist Designs for American Homes, Neighborhoods, and Cities* (Cambridge, Mass.: MIT Press, 1981), especially 1–133.

104. Utah, *Acts, Resolutions and Memorials Passed at the Several Annual Sessions of the Legislative Assembly of the Territory of Utah* (Salt Lake City: Joseph Cain, 1855), chap. 17, sec. 3, 104.

105. See Daynes, *More Wives Than One*, 65–66.

106. See Erastus Snow, April 4, 1881, in *Journal of Discourses*, 22:151–52, and Brigham Young, April 8, 1879, in *Journal of Discourses*, 20:172–73.

107. For an extensive discussion of parallel court systems in Utah, see Edwin Brown Firmage and Richard Collin Mangrum, *Zion in the Courts: A Legal History of The Church of Jesus Christ of Latter-day Saints, 1830–1900* (Urbana: University of Illinois Press, 1988).

108. Brigham Young, February 18, 1855, in *Journal of Discourses* 2:188. See also John

Taylor, August 23, 1857, in *Journal of Discourses*, 5:153–57; John Taylor, January 10, 1858, in *Journal of Discourses*, 7:122–23; Orson Pratt, July 4, 1860, in *Journal of Discourses*, 8:112–13; and Brigham Young, March 9, 1862, in *Journal of Discourses*, 10:39–40.

109. James McKean, quoted in Van Wagoner, *Mormon Polygamy*, 110.

110. Heber C. Kimball, August 2, 1857, in *Journal of Discourses*, 5:131.

111. John Taylor, November 1, 1857, in *Journal of Discourses*, 6:19–23.

112. Orson Pratt, August 14, 1859, in *Journal of Discourses*, 7:224–25.

113. *Doctrine and Covenants*, 20:65.

114. Brigham Young, August 9, 1874, in *Journal of Discourses*, 17:156. See also Orson Pratt, April 10, 1870, in *Journal of Discourses*, 13:125–26.

115. Brigham Young, July 31, 1859, in *Journal of Discourses*, 6:342.

116. Orson Pratt, August 14, 1859, in *Journal of Discourses*, 7:215.

117. Parley P. Pratt, January 3, 1853, in *Journal of Discourses*, 1:173–74.

118. Perhaps nothing illustrates this concept better than Mormonism's own history. Among several church leaders to be excommunicated were Oliver Cowdery and Orson Pratt. Both, upon concession, returned to the church later in their lives. Joseph Fielding Smith records merely that Oliver Cowdery was excommunicated in 1838 for "disobedience and rebellion." See Smith, *Church History and Modern Revelation*, 4:69. Richard S. Van Wagoner illustrates that tensions between Cowdery and Smith probably had more to do with polygamy than anything else. Cowdery charged Smith with adultery with Fanny Alger, and tensions between Smith and Cowdery escalated until his excommunication. See Van Wagoner, *Mormon Polygamy*, 10–14. In the late 1840s, when Cowdery became convinced of the divinity of Smith's leadership, he was rebaptised. Orson Pratt initially resisted the doctrine of plural marriage in 1841. He, too, was excommunicated and removed from church leadership. Months later, however, Pratt became convinced of the divine inspiration of plural marriage, and his membership was restored. Upon the public pronouncement of polygamy, Pratt became and remained one of its staunchest defenders. On Oliver Cowdery's excommunication, see Smith, *History of the Church*, 3:13–22; and B. H. Roberts, *Comprehensive History of The Church of Jesus Christ of Latter-day Saints, Century I*, 6 vols. (New York: National Americana Society, 1909–1915), 1:145–46. On Orson Pratt's excommunication, David J. Whittaker, "Pratt, Orson," *Encyclopedia of Mormonism: The History, Scripture, Doctrine, and Procedure of The Church of Jesus Christ of Latter-day Saints*, ed. Daniel H. Ludlow, 4 vols. (New York: Macmillan Publishing, 1992), 3:1114–15.

119. See Charles Penrose, September 23, 1883, in *Journal of Discourses*, 24:310–15.

120. See Jedediah Grant, March 2, 1856, in *Journal of Discourses*, 3:234; Brigham Young, June 7, 1857, in *Journal of Discourses*, 5:35; and John Taylor, November 1, 1857, in *Journal of Discourses*, 6:19–23.

121. Wilford Woodruff, July 20, 1883, in *Journal of Discourses*, 24:239–40.

122. Young, *Discourses of Brigham Young*, 361–62.

123. Brigham Young, February 18, 1855, in *Journal of Discourses*, 2:170–71, quoted material on 171.

124. Joseph Young, July 26, 1857, in *Journal of Discourses*, 6:228–29. See also John Taylor, March 31, 1867, in *Journal of Discourses*, 11:343–45; George Albert Smith, August 13, 1871, in *Journal of Discourses*, 14:217; and Orson Pratt, October 6, 1879, in *Journal of Discourses*, 20:327.

125. See Kettner, *The Development of American Citizenship*, especially 137–333.

126. Gordon, *The Mormon Question*, 224.

127. Ibid., 110–11.

128. Newell G. Bringhurst, *Saints, Slaves, and Blacks: The Changing Place of Black People Within Mormonism* (Westport, Conn.: Greenwood Press, 1981), 109–22.

129. Ibid., 68–70. See also Dennis L. Lythgoe, "Negro Slavery in Utah," *Utah Historical Quarterly* 39 (1971): 40–54.

130. Bringhurst, *Saints, Slaves, and Blacks*, 111.

131. Kirk H. Porter, comp., *National Party Platforms* (New York: The MacMillan Company, 1924), 48.

132. For a more lengthy discussion of the Morrill Act, see chapter 7. For an analysis of the conflict over states' rights in the context of Mormonism in the 1850s, see Fluhman, *"A Peculiar People,"* 107–10. Here, Fluhman frames the conflict in terms of the U.S. empire coming into conflict with the Mormon kingdom of God.

133. See Daniel H. Wells, July 24, 1854, in *Journal of Discourses*, 2:28; and Daniel H. Wells, April 6, 1861, in *Journal of Discourses*, 8:373.

134. Orson Pratt, October 6, 1879, in *Journal of Discourses*, 20:324–25.

135. Wilford Woodruff, *The Discourses of Wilford Woodruff: Fourth President of The Church of Jesus Christ of Latter-day Saints*, ed. G. Homer Durham (Salt Lake City: Bookcraft, Inc.,[1998]), 195.

136. Pratt, "Celestial Marriage," 128.

137. John Taylor, *The Gospel Kingdom: Selections from the Writings and Discourses of John Taylor*, selected, arranged, and annotated by G. Homer Durham (Salt Lake City: Bookcraft, Inc., 1987), 307–8.

138. George Q. Cannon, July 21, 1878, in *Journal of Discourses*, 25:254–55.

Chapter 3.
Polygamy and Mormon Woman's Citizenship

"More the companion and much less the subordinate": Blanche Beechwood [Emmeline B. Wells], "A Mormon Woman's View of Marriage," 54.

1. *Phrenological Journal*, November 1871, as quoted in Beverly Beeton, *Women Vote in the West: The Woman Suffrage Movement, 1869–1896* (New York: Garland Publishing, Inc., 1986), 23.

2. Lola Van Wagenen, "In Their Own Behalf: The Politicization of Mormon Women and the 1870 Franchise," *Dialogue: A Journal of Mormon Thought* 24, no. 4 (Winter 1991), 41.

3. Eliza R. Snow address, "Great Indignation Meeting of the Ladies of Salt Lake City, to Protest against the Passage of Cullom's Bill," *Deseret News Weekly*, 19 January 1870, 555.

4. See Young, *Discourses of Brigham Young*, 367. See also Brigham Young, October 9, 1852, in *Journal of Discourses*, 1:217–18.

5. Eliza R. Snow address, "Great Indignation Meeting," 555.

6. See Leonard J. Arrington, *Brigham Young: American Moses* (New York: Alfred A. Knopf, 1985), 364–65.

7. See Roberts, *Comprehensive History of The Church*, 5: 324.

8. The reasons women's suffrage was granted in Wyoming remain unclear and under-studied. For a brief summary of the debates surrounding woman suffrage in Wyoming, see Beeton, *Women Vote in the West*, 1–22; and Michael Massie, "Reform is Where You Find It: The Roots of Woman Suffrage in Wyoming," *Annals of Wyoming* 62, no. 1 (Spring 1990): 2–22.

9. "Stray Notes," *Woman's Exponent*, 15 July 1879, 28.

10. Sarah M. Kimball, *Woman Suffrage Leaflet* (Salt Lake City: n.p., 1892).

11. "Stray Notes," 28.

12. George Albert Smith, May 10, 1874, in *Journal of Discourses*, 17:87. For a discussion of Mormon women's civic education in the Relief Society, see Thomas G. Alexander, "An Experiment in Progressive Legislation: The Granting of Woman Suffrage in Utah in 1870," in Carol Cornwall Madsen, ed., *Battle for the Ballot: Essays on Woman Suffrage in Utah, 1870–1896* (Logan, Utah: Utah State University Press, 1997), 111.

13. For a more detailed account of the dilemmas national suffragists encountered in Utah, see Joan Smyth Iversen, "The Mormon-Suffrage Relationship: Personal and Political Quandaries," in Madsen, *Battle for the Ballot*, 150–72.

14. As cited in Louise Michele Newman, *White Women's Rights: The Racial Origins of Feminism in the United States* (New York: Oxford University Press, 1999), 62.

15. Eleanor Flexner, *Century of Struggle: The Woman's Rights Movement in the United States* (New York: Atheneum, 1970), 152.

16. Joan Smyth Iversen, "A Debate on the American Home: The Anti-Polygamy Controversy, 1880–1890," *Journal of the History of Sexuality* 1, no. 4 (April 1991): 598.

17. *Woman's Journal*, 22 October 1881, quoted in "Woman Suffrage in Utah," *Woman's Exponent*, 15 November 1881, 92.

18. Iversen, "The Mormon-Suffrage Relationship," 156.

19. For more detailed accounts of these visits, see Iversen, "The Mormon-Suffrage Relationship"; Lola Van Wagenen, "Sister Wives and Suffragists: Polygamy and the Politics of Woman Suffrage, 1870–1896" (Ph.D. diss., New York University, 1994) 1–2 and 25–28, quoted language on 11. For accounts of the Godbeite movement, see Grant H. Palmer, "The Godbeite Movement: A Dissent against Temporal Control" (Master's thesis, Brigham Young University, 1968); and Ronald W. Walker, "The Godbeite Protests in the Making of Modern Utah" (Ph.D. diss., University of Utah, 1977).

20. See Ida Husted Harper, *The Life and Work of Susan B. Anthony*, 2 vols. (Indianapolis: The Hollenbeck Press, 1898), 1: 389.

21. For a detailed account of this visit, see Van Wagenen, "Sister-Wives and Suffragists," 74–80; and Iversen, "The Mormon-Suffrage Relationship."

22. Beeton, *Women Vote in the West*, 27.

23. See Roberts, *Comprehensive History of The Church*, 5: 437. In 1873, the *Woman's Exponent* reported that Frederick Frelinghuysen of New Jersey, longtime opponent of plural marriage, introduced similar legislation in the Senate. See Lillie Devereux Blake, "The Proposition to Disfranchise the Women of Utah," *Woman's Exponent*, 15 June 1873, 15.

24. "Women of To-day," *Woman's Exponent*, 1 August 1878, 36.

25. Ibid., 36.

26. "Why Women Should Vote," *Woman's Exponent*, 1 August 1876, 36.

27. Isabella Pratt Walton, "The Right of Franchise," *Woman's Exponent*, 1 August 1878, 38.

28. "Women in Politics," *Woman's Exponent*, 1 August 1874, 40.

29. "Failings in Men and Women," *Woman's Exponent*, 15 October 1873, 76.

30. Mary Ann Pratt, "Give those Rights to Whom Rights Belong," *Woman's Exponent*, 1 April 1880, 165.

31. Quoted in Jill Mulvay Derr, "Eliza R. Snow and the Woman Question," in Madsen, *Battle for the Ballot*, 83.

32. "Woman on Woman's Needs," *Woman's Exponent*, 1 May 1873, 180.

33. Clara Nicolson, "A Statistical View of the Woman Question," *Woman's Exponent*, 15 March 1875, 155.

34. Ibid., 155.

35. For an analysis of women's power in the Mormon marital economy, see Daynes, *More Wives Than One*, 91–115.

36. Mary, "Woman—Woman's Worst Enemy," *Woman's Exponent*, 1 January 1879, 117.

37. E., "Woman's Rights and Wrongs," *Woman's Exponent*, 1 June 1872, 6.

38. Mary, "Woman—Woman's Worst Enemy," 117.

39. Helen Mar Whitney, "Answer to Woman and Sin," *Woman's Exponent*, 1 March 1884, 146.

40. On the role of coverture in constituting male property ownership and citizenship, see Pateman, *The Sexual Contract*; Hartog, *Man and Wife in America*; Cott, "Marriage and Women's Citizenship"; and Kerber, *Women of the Republic*, especially 115–56.

41. Norma Basch, "Invisible Women: The Legal Fiction of Marital Unity in Nineteenth-Century America," *Feminist Studies* 5, no. 2 (Summer 1979): 346–66.

42. Ibid., 346. See also Richard H. Chused, "Married Women's Property Law: 1800–1850," *Georgetown Law Journal* 71 (June 1983): 1359–425; Hartog, *Man and Wife in America*, 112–15 and 187–92.

43. Norma Basch, "The Emerging Legal History of Women in the United States: Property, Divorce, and the Constitution," *Signs* 12, no. 1 (Autumn 1986): 111.

44. *Minor v. Happersett*, 88 U.S. 162 (1875).

45. Basch, "Invisible Women," 354.

46. Blanche Beechwood [Emmeline B. Wells], "Woman's Work," *Woman's Exponent*, 15 November 1875, 94.

47. For a more complete analysis of church and federal marriage law and practice in Utah, see Daynes, *More Wives Than One*, 55–87. As Firmage and Mangrum point out,

church authorities subjected more than a few men to church discipline for "going to the gentile law" with marital matters. See Firmage and Mangrum, *Zion in the Courts*, 326.

48. "The 'Woman Question,'" *Woman's Exponent*, 1 June 1873, 5.

49. G., "Working Men and Working Women," *Woman's Exponent*, 15 May 1873, 187.

50. "Woman on Woman's Needs," 180.

51. L. E. H., "Woman In Politics," *Woman's Exponent*, 1 July 1882, 18.

52. Eliza R. Snow address, "Celebration of the Twenty-fourth at Ogden," *Deseret News Weekly*, 26 July 1871.

53. Fifteenth Ward Relief Society Minutes, February 19, 1870, Church History Library, The Church of Jesus Christ of Latter-day Saints, Salt Lake City, Utah.

54. Hannah T. King, "Thoughts on the Woman Question," *Woman's Exponent*, 1 September 1878, 56. The next month, King asked somewhat rhetorically, "Is woman aware that it is God who has enfranchised her?" Hannah T. King, "Woman," *Woman's Exponent*, 1 October 1878, 72.

55. G., "Working Men and Working Women," 187.

56. "Woman's Suffrage," *Woman's Exponent*, 1 February 1884, 132.

57. For a summary of these positions, see Cott, *Public Vows*, 56–76.

58. Blanche Beechwood [Emmeline B. Wells], "Real Women," *Woman's Exponent*, 1 January 1874, 118.

59. "The Women of Utah," *Woman's Exponent*, 1 July 1878, 20.

60. Blanche Beechwood [Emmeline B. Wells], "Why, Ah! Why," *Woman's Exponent*, 1 October 1874, 67.

61. "Woman's Expectations," *Woman's Exponent*, 1 July 1877, 20.

62. Beechwood [Wells], "A Mormon Woman's View of Marriage," 54.

63. "The Women of Utah," 20.

64. Helen Mar Whitney, *Why We Practice Plural Marriage* (Salt Lake City: Published at the Juvenile Instructor Office, 1884), 24.

65. "Patriarchal Marriage," *Woman's Exponent*, 15 August 1877, 44.

66. "R.S., Y.L.M.I.A. and Primary Reports," *Woman's Exponent*, 1 July 1882, 24.

67. "An Address by Eliza R. Snow . . . August 14, 1873," *Latter-day Saints' Millennial Star*, 13 January 1874, 21.

68. "Women Talkers and Women Writers," *Woman's Exponent*, 15 August 1876, 44.

69. Wells, "Woman Against Woman," 234.

70. An Act Concerning the Property Rights of Married Persons, 16 February 1872, 1876 *Compiled Laws of Utah* (Salt Lake City: Herbert Pembroke, 1888), 342.

71. "Woman's Right of Dower," *Woman's Exponent*, 1 December 1882, 100.

72. "Woman on Woman's Needs," 180.

73. Ibid., 180.

74. Quoted in "Anti-Mormon Petitions," *Woman's Exponent*, 1 August 1884, 36.

75. Shuyler Colfax, "The Mormon Defiance to the Nation. Suggestions as to How It Should be Met." *Chicago Advance*, 22 December 1881. Colfax's article was reprinted as

chapter 23 of Jennie Anderson Froiseth, *The Women of Mormonism; or The Story of Polygamy As Told by the Victims Themselves* (Detroit, Mich.: C. G. G. Paine, 1887), 357–64.

76. "Woman Suffrage in Utah," 92.

77. "Woman's Right of Dower," 100.

78. "One Woman's Opinion," *Woman's Exponent*, 1 February 1883, 132.

79. *Proceedings in Mass Meeting of the Ladies of Salt Lake City, to Protest Against the Passage of Cullom's Bill, January 14, 1870* ([Salt Lake City?]: n.p., 1870), 8.

80. "Suffrage In Utah," *Woman's Exponent*, 15 January 1884, 124.

81. *"Mormon" Women's Protest: An Appeal for Freedom, Justice and Equal Rights. The Ladies of The Church of Jesus Christ of Latter-day Saints Protest Against the Tyranny and Indecency of Federal Officials in Utah, and Against Their Own Disenfranchisement Without Cause. Full Account of Proceedings at the Great Mass Meeting Held in the Theatre, Salt Lake City, Utah, Saturday, March 6, 1886* ([Salt Lake City]: Deseret News, Printers, [1886?]), iii.

82. *"Mormon" Women's Protest*, 69.

83. Presendia L. Kimball, "The Ladies' Mass Meeting," *Woman's Exponent*, 1 March 1886, 148.

84. *"Mormon" Women's Protest*, 55.

85. "Prejudice Blind To Facts," *Woman's Exponent*, 1 September 1886, 50.

86. H.C. Brown, "The Ladies' Mass Meeting," *Woman's Exponent*, 1 March 1886, 148.

87. "A Mass Meeting," *Woman's Exponent*, 1 December 1889, 103.

88. "The Topic of the Day," *Woman's Exponent*, 1 June 1885, 4.

89. They maintained, "Our covenants belong not to the world, but are inseparable from our religion, and on these grounds are not subject to the control of the civil law." *"Mormon"Women's Protest*, 16.

90. "Women In Politics," *Woman's Exponent*, 15 January 1884, 121.

91. Kimball, "The Ladies' Mass Meeting," 148.

92. "That Wonderful Bill," *Woman's Exponent*, 15 April 1881, 171.

93. *Proceedings in Mass Meeting*, 4–5.

94. "Is This a Land Of Liberty?" *Woman's Exponent*, 1 July 1883, 15.

95. Ellen B. Ferguson, "The Ladies' Mass Meeting," *Woman's Exponent*, 1 March 1886, 149.

96. "Prejudice Blind To Facts," 50.

97. A complete reprint of the Woodruff Manifesto can be found in any standard issue of the *Doctrine and Covenants* printed since the 1890s, immediately after the last section under the title, "Official Declaration."

Chapter 4.
Polygamy and the Perversion of the Private Sphere

"The utter destruction of the home circle": Bennett, *A Detective's Experience Among the Mormons*, 18.

1. See Howard, *Publishing the Family*, 231–41.

2. See Amy Kaplan, "Manifest Domesticity," *American Literature* 70, no. 3 (September 1998): 581–606.

3. On the illegitimacy of Black, American Indian, Asian, and Mormon families, see Cott, *Public Vows*, 114–21.

4. On domestic law in the nineteenth century, see Michael Grossberg, *Governing the Hearth: Law and the Family in Nineteenth-Century America* (Chapel Hill: University of North Carolina Press, 1985).

5. On Reconstruction-era conflicts, see Katherine Franke, "Becoming a Citizen: Reconstruction-Era Regulation of African-American Marriages," *Yale Journal of Law and the Humanities*, 11, no. 2 (Summer 1999): 251–309; Nancy Bercaw, *Gendered Freedoms: Race, Rights, and the Politics of Household in the Delta, 1861–1875* (Gainesville: University Press of Florida, 2003); and Elizabeth Regosin, *Freedom's Promise: Ex-Slave Families and Citizenship in the Age of Emancipation* (Charlottesville: University Press of Virginia, 2002).

6. See Joan Smyth Iversen, *The Antipolygamy Controversy in U.S. Women's Movements, 1880–1925: A Debate on the American Home* (New York: Garland, 1997); Peggy Pascoe, *Relations of Rescue: The Search for Female Moral Authority in the West* (New York: Oxford University Press, 1990); Jana Kathryn Riess, "Heathen in Our Fair Land: Anti-Polygamy and Protestant Women's Missions to Utah, 1869–1910" (Ph.D. diss., Columbia University, 2000); and Barbara Hayward, "Utah's Anti-Polygamy Society, 1878–1884" (Master's thesis, Brigham Young University, 1980).

7. Alexander Campbell, *Delusions: An Analysis of the Book of Mormon; With an Examination of Its Internal and External Evidences, and a Refutation of Its Pretences to Divine Authority* (Boston: Benjamin H. Greene, 1832); Eber D. Howe, *Mormonism Unvailed [sic]; or, A Faithful Account of That Singular Imposition and Delusion, From Its Rise to the Present Time* (Painesville, Ohio: Printed and Published by the Author, 1834); One Who Hates Imposture, *Mormonism Dissected; or, Knavery "On Two Sticks," Exposed: Composed Principally From Notes Which Were Taken From the Arguments of Dr. Orr, in the Recent Debate on the Athenticity [sic] of the "Book of Mormon," Between Him and E. H. Davis, Mormon Preacher, the Whole Being Designed As a Check to the Further Progress of Imposition, by Placing in the Hands of Every One the Means of Unmasking This "Latter Day" Humbug* (Bethania, Pa.: Printed by R. Chambers, 1841).

8. For an analysis of early anti-Mormon claims that Joseph Smith was a religious imposter who duped and deluded early Mormon believers, see Fluhman, *"A Peculiar People,"* 21–77.

9. John Cook Bennett, *The History of the Saints; or, An Exposé of Joe Smith and Mormonism* (Boston: Leland and Whiting, 1842), 217–25.

10. Ibid., 220.

11. Ibid., 222.

12. Ibid., 223–25.

13. Mormons then and since have maintained strict secrecy about the precise nature of temple ritual. Then and since, Mormons have always regarded temple ceremonies too sacred, in the words of a modern Mormon authority, to be "bandied about by brutish

persons." Bruce R. McConkie, *The Mortal Messiah: From Bethlehem to Calvary*, 4 vols. (Salt Lake City: Deseret Book Co., 1981), 1: 104.

14. See, for example, Increase McGee Van Deusen, *The Sublime and Ridiculous Blended: Called, the Endowment: As Was Acted, by Upwards of Twelve Thousand, in Secret, in the Nauvoo Temple, Said to be Revealed From God as Reward for Building That Splendid Edifice, and the Express Object for Which It Was Built* (New York: The Author, 1848); and Increase McGee Van Deusen, *Startling Disclosures of the Wonderful Ceremonies of the Mormon Spiritual Wife System: Being the Celebrated "Endowment," as it was Acted by Upwards of Twelve Thousand Men and Women in Secret, in the Nauvoo Temple, in 1846, and Said to Have Been Revealed From God* (New York: [s.n.], 1852).

15. Catharine Lewis, *Narrative of Some of the Proceedings of the Mormons; Giving an Account of Their Iniquities, With Particulars Concerning the Training of the Indians by Them, Description of the Mode of Endowment, Plurality of Wives, & C., & C.* (Lynn [Mass.]: The author, 1848).

16. Davis, "Some Themes of Counter-Subversion," 211.

17. Givens, *Viper on the Hearth*, 104–30; Cannon, "The Crusades Against the Masons, Catholics, and Mormons," 23–40.

18. Givens, *Viper on the Hearth*, 104–6.

19. See Marie Anne Pagliarini, "The Pure American Woman and the Wicked Catholic Priest: An Analysis of Anti-Catholic Literature in Antebellum America," *Religion and American Culture: A Journal of Interpretation* 9, no. 1 (Winter 1999): 97–128.

20. See, for example, Maria Ward [pseud.], *Female Life among the Mormons: A Narrative of Many Years' Personal Experience* (New York: J. C. Derby, 1855), 99–100; William Hepworth Dixon, *New America* (Philadelphia: J.B. Lippincott and Co., 1867), 173; "Mormons and Mormonism," *The North American Review*, July 1862. See also Cannon, "The Crusades against the Masons, Catholics, and Mormons."

21. See Samuel Bowles, *Across the Continent: A Summer's Journey to the Rocky Mountains, The Mormons, and the Pacific States, With Speaker Colfax* (Springfield, Mass.: Samuel Bowles & Company, 1865), 19–21; and Increase McGee Van Deusen and Maria Van Deusen, *Startling Disclosures of the Great Mormon Conspiracy Against the Liberties of This Country: Being the Celebrated "Endowment," As It Was Acted by Upwards of Twelve Thousand Men and Women in Secret in the Nauvoo Temple in 1846 and Said to Have Been Revealed From God* (New York: Blake and Jackson, 1849).

22. See Fluhman, *"A Peculiar People,"* 13.

23. Givens, *Viper on the Hearth*, 97–120, quoted language on 98.

24. Ibid., 113–14.

25. See Jane Tompkins, *Sensational Designs: The Cultural Work of American Fiction, 1790–1860* (New York: Oxford University Press, 1985); Armstrong, *Desire and Domestic Fiction*; Ryan, *The Empire of the Mother*; Mary Kelley, *Private Woman, Public Stage: Literary Domesticity in Nineteenth-Century America* (New York: Oxford University Press, 1984); Shirley Samuels, *The Culture of Sentiment* (New York: Oxford University Press, 1992); and Howard, *Publishing the Family*.

26. Armstrong, *Desire and Domestic Fiction*, 14.

27. Howard, *Publishing the Family*, 235.

28. Colleen McDannell, *The Christian Home in Victorian America* (Bloomington: Indiana University Press, 1986), 108–13, quoted language on 109.

29. Catharine E. Beecher, *Religious Training of Children in the School, the Family and the Church* (New York: Harper and Bros., 1864), 33.

30. Catharine E. Beecher and Harriet Beecher Stowe, *The American Woman's Home; or, Principles of Domestic Science* (New York: J. B. Ford, 1869), 19.

31. Armstrong, *Desire and Domestic Fiction*, 3.

32. Lystra, *Searching the Heart*, 192.

33. Ward, *Female Life Among the Mormons*; Metta Victoria Fuller, *Mormon Wives: A Narrative of Facts Stranger Than Fiction* (New York: Derby and Jackson, 1856); Alfreda Eva Bell, *Boadicea; The Mormon Wife: Life Scenes in Utah* (Baltimore: Arthur R. Orton, 1855); Orvilla S. Belisle, *Mormonism Unveiled; or, A History of Mormonism From Its Rise to the Present Time* (London: Charles H. Clarke, 1855). A few years later, Ward's novel was accompanied by a companion volume apparently written by her nephew. Austin N. Ward, *The Husband in Utah; or, Sights and Scenes Among the Mormons: With Remarks on their Moral and Social Economy*, ed. Maria Ward (New York: Derby and Jackson, 1859). On the centrality of these four texts, see Leonard J. Arrington and Jon Haupt, "Intolerable Zion: The Image of Mormonism in Nineteenth-Century American Literature," *Western Humanities Review* 22 (Summer 1968): 243–60; and Gordon, *The Mormon Question*, 29.

34. Ward, *Female Life Among the Mormons*, iv.

35. Givens, *Viper on the Hearth*, 108.

36. Ibid., 108–19. Quoted language on 113.

37. Ibid., 114–15, his emphasis.

38. Sarah Barringer Gordon points out that in the 1930s, bibliographer Joseph Sabin contended that the book was actually written by Cornelia Ferris, the spouse of Territorial Secretary Benjamin Ferris and author of the early travel narrative, *The Mormons at Home*, and a serial article in *Putnam's Monthly*, "Life Among the Mormons." See Gordon, "'Our National Hearthstone,'" 331 n. 116.

39. Gordon, "'Our National Hearthstone,'" 305–6.

40. Ward, *Female Life Among the Mormons*, 207.

41. Ibid., 221.

42. Orvilla S. Belisle, *The Prophets; or, Mormonism Unveiled* (Philadelphia: Wm. White Smith, 1855), frontispiece.

43. Gordon, "'Our National Hearthstone,'" 322.

44. Belisle, *Mormonism Unveiled*, 60.

45. Fuller, *Mormon Wives*, 27.

46. See Belisle, *Mormonism Unveiled*, 59–61; and Fuller, *Mormon Wives*, 40–43.

47. Fuller, *Mormon Wives*, 197.

48. Ward, *Female Life Among the Mormons*, 291.

49. Fuller, *Mormon Wives*, 199.

50. See Bell, *Boadicea*, 31–32; and Belisle, *Mormonism Unveiled*, 121–27.

51. Ward, *Female Life Among the Mormons*, 101. See also Fuller, *Mormon Wives*, 78–79, and Belisle, *Mormonism Unveiled*, 72–73.

52. Belisle, *Mormonism Unveiled*, 75.

53. Ibid., 105.

54. Ibid., 114 and 214–15.

55. Bell, *Boadicea*, 74–75.

56. Fuller, *Mormon Wives*, 213–308.

57. Ibid., 312–13, her emphasis.

58. See *The National Union Catalog: Pre-1956 Imprints* (London: Mansell Publishing, 1979), 648: 287–88, as quoted in Gordon, "Our National Hearthstone" 308 n. 44. Victor's novel was also reprinted four times from 1856 to 1860. See Chad J. Flake, *A Mormon Bibliography, 1830–1930: Books, Pamphlets, Periodicals, and Broadsides Relating to the First Century of Mormonism*, ed. Chad J. Flake and Larry W. Draper, 2nd revision, revised and enlarged (Provo, Utah: Religious Studies Center, Brigham Young University, 2004).

59. Fuller, *Mormon Wives*, iii.

60. For analyses of Mormon women's experiences in plural marriage, see Claudia Bushman, ed., *Mormon Sisters: Women in Early Utah* (Cambridge, Mass.: Emmeline Press, 1976); Dunfey, "'Living the Principle'"; Cornwall and Van Beek, "The Mormon Practice of Plural Marriage"; Marie Cornwall, Camela Courtright, and Laga Van Beek, "How Common the Principle? Women As Plural Wives in 1860," *Dialogue: A Journal of Mormon Thought* 26 (Summer 1993): 139–53; Jessie L. Embry, *Mormon Polygamous Families: Life in the Principle* (Salt Lake City: University of Utah Press, 1987); Kathleen Marquis, "Diamond Cut Diamond: Mormon Women and the Cult of Domesticity" (Ph.D. diss., University of Michigan, 1976).

61. George Whitfield Philips, *The Mormon Menace: A Discourse Before the New West Education Commission on Its Fifth Anniversary at Chicago November 15, 1885* (Worcester, Mass.: [s. n.], 1885), 11. For an exploration of similar themes emanating from southern anti-Mormonism, see Mason, *The Mormon Menace*, 62–78.

62. Gordon, *The Mormon Question*, 29.

63. Philips, *The Mormon Menace*, 11.

64. John Williams Gunnison, *The Mormons, or Latter-day Saints, in the Valley of the Great Salt Lake: A History of their Rise and Progress, Peculiar Doctrines, Present Condition, and Prospects, Derived from Personal Observation During a Residence Among Them* (Philadelphia: J. B. Lippincott and Co., 1856), 68.

65. Quoted in Dudley Chase Haskell, *Mormonism and Polygamy: An Address Delivered by D. C. Haskell, of Kansas, at Central Music Hall, Chicago, June 8, 1881, Before the National Convention of the American Home Missionary Society* (Lawrence, Kansas: Republican Journal Steam Printing Establishment, 1881), 36.

66. Richard Burton, *The City of the Saints, and Across the Rocky Mountains to California* (London: Longman, Green, Longman and Roberts, 1861), 383.

67. J. H. Beadle, *Life in Utah; or, The Mysteries and Crimes of Mormonism. Being an Exposé of the Secret Rites and Ceremonies of the Latter-Day Saints, With a Full and Authentic History of Polygamy and the Mormon Sect from Its Origin to the Present Time* (Philadelphia: National Publishing Company, 1870), 355.

68. R. E. Thompson, "Mormon Solution of the Mormon Problem," *American: A National Journal*, 1882, 68.

69. "The Mormons at Home," *Frank Leslie's New Family Magazine*, 1871, 227.

70. Ferris, *Utah and the Mormons*, 254–55.

71. Gordon, *The Mormon Question*, 67.

72. Ward, *Female Life Among the Mormons*, 219.

73. Mrs. C. V. Waite, *The Mormon Prophet and His Harem; or, An Authentic History of Brigham Young, His Numerous Wives and Children*, 5th ed. (Chicago: J. S. Goodman and Company, 1868), 192.

74. Nancy Bentley, "Marriage as Treason: Polygamy, Nation, and the Novel," in *The Futures of American Studies*, eds. Donald E. Pease and Robyn Wiegman (Durham: Duke University Press, 2002), 353–56.

75. Ibid., 352.

76. Ibid., 354.

77. Ferris, *Utah and the Mormons*, 257–58.

78. Ibid., 257–58.

79. Increase McGee Van Deusen and Maria Van Deusen, *Spiritual Delusions: Being A Key to the Mysteries of Mormonism, Exposing the Particulars of That Astounding Heresy, the Spiritual Wife System, As Practiced by Brigham Young, of Utah* (New York: I. and M. Van Deusen, 1854), 36.

80. Ferris, *Utah and the Mormons*, 142.

81. Beadle, *Life in Utah*, 356.

82. Ibid., 156–57.

83. Wright, *Building the Dream*, 89.

84. See McDannell, *The Christian Home in Victorian America*; Kenneth T. Jackson, *Crabgrass Frontier: The Suburbanization of the United States* (New York: Oxford University Press, 1985); Wright, *Building the Dream*.

85. Wright, *Building the Dream*, 96–113; and Howard, *Publishing the Family*, 123–26.

86. Mintz and Kellogg, *Domestic Revolutions*, 44.

87. McDannell, *The Christian Home in Victorian America*, 26.

88. Beecher and Stowe, *The American Woman's Home*, 23.

89. Mahajan, "Introduction," 13–16, quoted material on 16. See also Wright, *Building the Dream*, 112; and Mintz and Kellogg, *Domestic Revolutions*, 44.

90. Hartog, *Man and Wife in America*, 108.

91. Ferris, *Utah and the Mormons*, 307–8. See also 249–50.

92. "The Mormons at Home," 280.

93. Waite, *The Mormon Prophet and His Harem*, 199.

94. Ferris, *Utah and the Mormons*, 307–9. This image appears on 309.

95. Ibid., 308.

96. Haskell, *Mormonism and Polygamy*, 25.

97. An Apostle's Wife [Alfred Trumble], *The Mysteries of Mormonism. A Full Exposure of Its Secret Practices and Hidden Crimes* (New York: Richard K. Fox, 1881), image appears between pages 19 and 20.

98. Ferris, *The Mormons at Home*, 129.

99. See Waite, *The Mormon Prophet and His Harem*, 244.

100. John D. Lee, *Mormonism Unveiled: Including the Remarkable Life and Confessions of the Late Mormon Bishop, John D. Lee (Written by Himself): and Complete Life of Brigham Young, Embracing a History of Mormonism from its Inception Down to the Present Time, with an Exposition of the Secret History, Signs, Symbols, and Crimes of the Mormon Church: also the True History of the Horrible Butchery Known as the Mountain Meadows Massacre*, 10th ed. (St. Louis: Sun Pub. Co., 1882), 185.

101. W. F. Rae, *Westward by Rail: The New Route to the East* (New York: D. Appleton and Company, 1871), 120–21.

102. Howard, *Publishing the Family*, 111.

103. Jackson, *Crabgrass Frontier*, 52.

104. Rae, *Westward by Rail*, 122.

105. Beadle, *Life in Utah*, 358.

106. Haskell, *Mormonism and Polygamy*, 25, emphasis in original.

107. "The Mormons at Home," 280, emphasis in original.

108. A. S. Bailey, "Anti-American Influences in Utah," in *The Situation in Utah. The Discussions of the Christian Convention, Held in Salt Lake City, Utah. April 1888* (Salt Lake City: Parsons, Kendall and Co., 1888), 21.

109. Bennett, *A Detective's Experience Among the Mormons*, 18.

110. Ferris, *Utah and the Mormons*, 146.

Chapter 5.
Consent, Contract, and Citizenship under "Polygamic Theocracy"

"They can not exist in contact with republican institutions": Ferris, *Utah and the Mormons*, 146.

1. Nancy L. Rosenblum, "Democratic Sex: *Reynolds v. U.S.*, Sexual Relations, and Community," in *Sex, Preference, and Family: Essays on Law and Nature*, ed. David M. Estlund and Martha C. Nussbaum (New York: Oxford University Press, 1997), 63.

2. *Reynolds v. United States*, 98 U.S. 145 (1879), 165–66.

3. Sarah Barringer Gordon, "'The Liberty of Self-Degradation': Polygamy, Woman Suffrage, and Consent in Nineteenth-Century America," *Journal of American History* 83, no. 3 (December 1996): 833.

4. For a discussion of the gendered nature of property in the self, see Pateman, *The Sexual Contract*, 13–14 and 55–59; and Stanley, *From Bondage to Contract*, 10–11 and 16–17.

5. Pateman, *The Sexual Contract*, 77.

6. Ibid.; Kerber, *Women of the Republic*; and Smith-Rosenberg, "Dis-Covering the Subject of the 'Great Constitutional Discussion.'"

7. For a discussion of the importance of consent to nineteenth-century ideas of freedom, see Stanley, *From Bondage to Contract*, 2–16. For a discussion of legal doctrines of consent in relationship to Mormon polygamy, see Gordon, "'The Liberty of Self-Degradation,'" 815–48.

8. See Mintz and Kellogg, *Domestic Revolutions*, 43–65; Carl N. Degler, *At Odds: Women and the Family in America From the Revolution to the Present* (Oxford: Oxford University Press, 1980) 8–25; and Stephanie Coontz, *The Social Origins of Private Life: A History of American Families, 1600–1900* (London: Verso, 1988).

9. Pateman, *The Sexual Contract*, 77–78.

10. See Gillian Brown, *Domestic Individualism: Imagining Self in Nineteenth-Century America* (Berkeley: University of California Press, 1990); Mintz and Kellogg, *Domestic Revolutions*, 43–66; Johnson, *A Shopkeeper's Millennium*, 6–8; and Hartog, *Man and Wife in America*, 234.

11. J. M. Coyner, *Letters on Mormonism* (Salt Lake City: Tribune Printing and Publishing Co., 1879), 8.

12. Ferris, *Utah and the Mormons*, 146.

13. Hansen, *Quest for Empire*, 170–72, quoted material on 171.

14. See Gustive O. Larson, *The "Americanization" of Utah for Statehood* (San Marino, Calif.: The Huntington Library, 1971). Howard Roberts Lamar makes a similar argument in Part Three of *The Far Southwest, 1846–1912: A Territorial History*. Lamar, *The Far Southwest*, 265–357.

15. Edward Leo Lyman, *Political Deliverance: The Mormon Quest for Utah Statehood* (Urbana: University of Illinois Press, 1986), 2. See also Firmage and Mangrum, *Zion in the Courts*; and Gordon, *The Mormon Question*, 260–61 n. 6.

16. Riess, "Heathen in Our Fair Land"; Gordon, "'Our National Hearthstone'"; and Bentley, "Marriage as Treason."

17. Eric Michael Mazur, *The Americanization of Religious Minorities: Confronting the Constitutional Order* (Baltimore: The Johns Hopkins University Press, 2004), 62–93.

18. See Fluhman, *"A Peculiar People,"* 119.

19. Cott, *Public Vows*, 9–23, quoted material on 23.

20. James William Marshall, "The Mormon Problem," *The Ladies Repository*, April 1875, 307–8.

21. On the history of legislative campaigns against polygamy, see Orma Linford, "The Mormons and the Law: The Polygamy Cases," parts 1 and 2, *Utah Law Review* 9, no. 2 (Winter 1964): 308–70; 9, no. 3 (Summer 1965): 543–91; Poll, "The Political Reconstruction of Utah Territory;" and Gordon, *The Mormon Question*.

22. See Gordon, *The Mormon Question*, 6–8.

23. Ibid., 75.

24. "Mormonism from a Secular Standpoint." *The Home Missionary*, October 1881, 160.

25. Ferris, *Utah and the Mormons*, 146.

26. Austin N. Ward, *Male Life Among the Mormons; or, The Husband in Utah: Detailing Sights and Scenes Among the Mormons; With Remarks on Their Moral and Social Economy* (Philadelphia: John E. Potter and Company, 1863), 272. For a cogent analysis of themes of seduction and bondage in anti-Mormon fiction, see Givens, *Viper on the Hearth*, 126–42.

27. Davis Bitton and Gary L. Bunker, "Mesmerism and Mormonism," *BYU Studies* 15, no. 2 (Winter 1975): 146.

28. See Ann Eliza Young, *Life in Mormon Bondage: A Complete Exposé of Its False Prophets, Murderous Danites, Despotic Rulers and Hypnotized, Deluded Subjects* (Philadelphia: Aldine Press, 1908); Rebecca Foster Cornwall and Leonard J. Arrington, "Perpetuation of a Myth: Mormon Danites in Five Western Novels, 1840–90," *BYU Studies* 23, no. 2 (Spring 1983): 147–65; and Leland H. Gentry, "The Danite Band of 1838," *BYU Studies* 14 (Summer 1974): 421–50.

29. See Stephen C. LeSueur, *The 1838 Mormon War in Missouri* (Columbia: University of Missouri Press, 1987); and Hansen, *Quest for Empire*, 57–58.

30. See Charles W. Penrose, *Blood Atonement, As Taught by Leading Elders of the Church of Jesus Christ of Latter-day Saints. An Address Delivered in the Twelfth Ward Assembly Hall, Salt Lake City, October 12, 1884, by Elder Charles W. Penrose* (Salt Lake City: Printed at Juvenile Instructor Office, 1884).

31. John Cradlebaugh, *Mormonism: A Doctrine That Embraces Polygamy, Adultery, Incest, Perjury, Robbery and Murder: Speech . . . in the House of Representatives in 1863* ([Salt Lake City: n.p., 1877?]), 5.

32. John D. Lee, *Mormonism Unveiled; or The Life and Confessions of the Late Mormon Bishop, John D. Lee (Written By Himself) Embracing a History of Mormonism From Its Inception Down to the Present Time, with an Exposition of the Secret History, Signs, Symbols and Crimes of the Mormon Church; Also the True History of the Horrible Butchery Known as the Mountain Meadows Massacre* (St Louis: Bryan, Brand and Co., 1877); and William Adams Hickman, *Brigham's Destroying Angel: Being the Life, Confessions, and Startling Disclosures of the Notorious Bill Hickman, the Danite Chief of Utah* (New York: G. A. Crofutt, Publishers, 1872).

33. On the Mountain Meadows Massacre, see Juanita Brooks, *The Mountain Meadows Massacre* (Norman: University of Oklahoma Press, 1966); Juanita Brooks, *John Doyle Lee: Zealot, Pioneer Builder, Scapegoat* (Logan, Utah: Utah State University Press, 1992); Will Bagley, *Blood of the Prophets: Brigham Young and the Massacre at Mountain Meadows* (Norman: University of Oklahoma Press, 2002); Sally Denton, *American Massacre: The Tragedy at Mountain Meadows, September 1857* (New York: Alfred A. Knopf, 2003); and Ronald W. Walker, Richard E. Turley, and Glen M. Leonard, *Massacre at Mountain Meadows* (New York: Oxford University Press, 2008).

34. Cradlebaugh, *Mormonism*, 10.

35. Hamilton Child, *Gazetteer and Business Directory of Wayne County, New York for 1867–1868* (Syracuse: Printed at the Journal Office, 1867), 55.

36. Van Deusen and Van Deusen, *Spiritual Delusions*, 30. See also Ward, *Female Life Among the Mormons*, 215.

37. Justin McCarthy, "Brigham Young," *The Galaxy*, February 1870, 180.

38. Maria Ward, *Female Life Among the Mormons*, 38. See also Givens, *Viper on the Hearth*, 151; and Bunker and Bitton, "Mesmerism and Mormonism."

39. Van Deusen and Van Deusen, *Spiritual Delusions*, 39–40.

40. Belisle, *Mormonism Unveiled*, 160–61; and Ward, *The Husband in Utah*, 209–12.

41. [Trumble], *The Mysteries of Mormonism*, 39–55.

42. A Mormon of 1831, *The Crimes of the Latter-Day Saints in Utah: A Demand for a Legislative Commission, a Book of Horrors* (San Francisco: A. J. Leary, 1884).

43. Pomeroy Tucker, *The Origin, Rise, and Progress of Mormonism: Biography of Its Founders and History of Its Church: Personal Remembrances and Historical Collections Hitherto Unwritten* (New York: D. Appleton and Company, 1867), 264–65.

44. "Plurality of Wives," *Overland Monthly*, December 1871, 554.

45. Waite, *The Mormon Prophet and His Harem*, 244.

46. "The Mormons at Home," 227.

47. McCarthy, "Brigham Young," 181. Benjamin Ferris observed a "sad, complaining, suffering look, obvious to the most ordinary observer, which tells the story, if there were no other evidence on the subject." See Ferris, *Utah and the Mormons*, 259.

48. Cornelia Ferris, "Life Among the Mormons," *Putnam's Monthly*, August 1855, 147.

49. John Hyde, Jun., *Mormonism: Its Leaders and Designs*, 2nd ed. (New York: W. P. Fetridge and Company, 1857), 59.

50. Ferris, *Utah and the Mormons*, 259.

51. John Hanson Beadle, "The Mormon Theocracy" (editorial), *Scribner's Monthly*, July 1877, 359–60; Rose Cooke, "The Mormon's Wife. A Tale," *Putnam's Monthly*, June 1855, 641–49.

52. See Fuller, *Mormon Wives*, iv–v.

53. Porter, *National Party Platforms*, 48.

54. Representative William Simms of Kentucky, *Appendix to the Congressional Globe*, 36 Cong. 1 sess., 198 (4 April 1860).

55. See Gordon, *The Mormon Question*, 51–116.

56. Cott, *Public Vows*, 73.

57. See Iversen, *The Anti-Polygamy Controversy in U. S. Women's Movements*, especially 103–7.

58. Stanley, *From Bondage to Contract*, 55–59.

59. See Representative Miles Taylor of Louisiana, *Appendix to the Congressional Globe*, 36 Cong. 1 sess., 187–90 (2 April 1860); and Representative Laurence Keitt of South Carolina, *Congressional Globe*, 36 Cong., 1 sess., 195–98 (4 April 1860).

60. *Appendix to the Congressional Globe*, 36 Cong., 1 sess., 198, 199, and 201 (4 April 1860).

61. *Stat.* 501 [1862].

62. See Daynes, *More Wives Than One*, 55–87.

63. "The Mormons at Home," 229.

64. Bell, *Boadicea*, 54.

65. Froiseth, *The Women of Mormonism*, 99, emphasis in original. See also 26; Ward, *The Husband in Utah*, 53; and Belisle, *Mormonism Unveiled*, 148.

66. [Trumble], *Mysteries of Mormonism*, image appears between pages 20 and 21.

67. Bentley, "Marriage as Treason," 346. See also Stanley, *From Bondage to Contract*, 27.

68. Maria Ward, *The Mormon Wife: A Story of the Sacrifices, Sorrows, and Sufferings of Women* (Hartford, Conn.: Hartford Press, 1872), 429. According to Alfreda Eva Bell, this story was not unique. Mormon women everywhere "are painfully impressed with their utter inferiority, in divers [sic] ways and at all seasons; and are frequently subjected to personal violence and . . . corporeal punishment." Bell, *Boadicea*, 54.

69. Bentley, "Marriage as Treason," 346.

70. Ibid., 347. See also 361–66.

71. Mary Hudson, *Esther the Gentile* (Topeka: Crane, 1880), 132, as quoted in Bentley, "Marriage as Treason," 347. See also Walter M. Barrows, "How Shall the Mormon Question be Settled?" *The Home Missionary*, September 1879, 161–88; and C. C. Goodwin, "The Mormon Situation," *Harper's New Monthly Magazine*, October 1881, 762–63.

72. Harriet Beecher Stowe, preface to Fanny Stenhouse, *"Tell it All": The Story of a Life's Experience in Mormonism. An Autobiography . . . Including a Full Account of the Mountain Meadows Massacre, and the Life, Confession, and Execution of Bishop John D. Lee* (Hartford, Conn.: A. D. Worthington and Co., 1874), vi.

73. A Mormon of 1831, *Crimes of the Latter Day Saints*, 78.

74. As Stanley demonstrates, anti-prostitution campaigns also linked slavery and prostitution. See Stanley, *From Bondage to Contract*, 218–63.

75. See Hobson, *Uneasy Virtue*, 11–84.

76. See ibid., 61–66; and Gordon, *The Mormon Question*, 174.

77. "The Twin Curses in American Society," *University Magazine*, October 1861, 418.

78. Ferris, *Utah and the Mormons*, 306–7.

79. Ward, *Female Life*, 221.

80. Ferris, *The Mormons at Home*, 182–83.

81. For an analysis of how domestic hierarchies that gave husbands the right to wives' labor traveled alongside ideas about women's freedom, see Stanley, *From Bondage to Contract*, 138–74.

82. One of the People [William Dallin], *Opinions Concerning the Bible Law of Marriage* (Philadelphia: Claxton, Remsen and Haffelfinger, 1871), x.

83. [Dallin], *Opinions Concerning the Bible Law of Marriage*, 233. See also Ward, *Female Life*, 290; and Belisle, 210–15.

84. Orson Pratt, October 7, 1869, in *Journal of Discourses*, 13:194.

85. For selected examples, see Orson Pratt, August 29, 1852, in *Journal of Discourses*, 1:61, (this sermon was also the sermon that publicly proclaimed the practice of plural marriage); Amasa Lyman, April 5, 1866, in *Journal of Discourses*, 11:202–3; and John Taylor, October 6 and 7, 1884, in *Journal of Discourses*, 25:310–13. See also Jeffrey Nichols, *Prostitution, Polygamy, and Power: Salt Lake City, 1847–1918* (Urbana: University of Illinois Press, 2002), 9–44.

86. Franklin D. Richards, October 6, 1879, in *Journal of Discourses*, 20:312–13; George Q. Cannon, April 6, 1869, in *Journal of Discourses*, 13:102; Erastus Snow, October 8, 1879, in *Journal of Discourses*, 20:374; and John Taylor, February 11, 1883, in *Journal of Discourses*, 24:5–6.

87. Charles W. Hemenway, *Memoirs of My Day In and Out of Mormondom. Written in Prison, Undergoing Sentence for Alleged Libel* (Salt Lake City: Deseret News Company, 1887), 193.

88. John Taylor, November 30, 1879, in *Journal of Discourses*, 20:355–56.

89. See, for example, *The Cullom Bill! Remonstrance and Resolutions Adopted by a Mass Meeting of the Citizens of Utah, Held in the Tabernacle, Salt Lake City, March 31st, 1870* (Salt Lake City: Printed at the Deseret News Office, [1870]); The Church of Jesus Christ of Latter-day Saints. Women's Committee, *Memorial of the Mormon Women of Utah to the President and Congress of the United States, April 6, 1886* (Washington, D. C.: [s.n.], 1886); and Whitney, *Why We Practice Plural Marriage*.

90. See John Codman, *A Solution of the Mormon Problem* (New York: G. P. Putnam's Sons, 1885), 13.

91. Victoria Reed, "The Mormon Church," *The Bay State Monthly*, October 1885, 353.

92. John McBride, "Utah and Mormonism," *International Review*, February 1882, 195.

93. "The Present Phase of the Mormon Problem," *National Quarterly Review*, July 1879, 91.

94. Angie F. Newman, "Woman Suffrage in Utah," *Woman's Exponent*, 15 July 1886, 32. This is a reprint of portions of a petition Newman presented to the U.S. Senate. See U.S. Senate, *Woman Suffrage in Utah*, 49 Cong., 1 sess., 1–9 (8 June 1886), S. Mis. Doc. 122 (Congressional Edition 2346).

95. See "The Utah Question Once More," *Woman's Exponent*, 15 January 1879, 126.

96. "Colfax's Speech," *Salt Lake Tribune*, 29 January 1882.

97. "Reorganization of the Liberal Party of Utah," *Anti-Polygamy Standard*, September 1880, 44.

98. Hayward, "Utah's Anti-Polygamy Society," 71–72.

99. For discussions of Froiseth's convictions on woman suffrage, see ibid., 74; and Kathryn L. MacKay, comp., "Chronology of Woman Suffrage in Utah," in Madsen, *Battle for the Ballot*, 315.

100. "Petition to Disenfranchise Women," *Woman's Exponent*, 15 June 1884, 11.

101. Senator George Edmunds of Vermont, *Congressional Record*, 49 Cong., 1 sess., 405 (5 January 1887).

102. Eli H. Murray, "The Crisis in Utah," *North American Review*, April 1882, 22.

103. Van Deusen, *Spiritual Delusions*, 33.

104. Ferris, *Utah and the Mormons*, 249. In the nineteenth century, the "Five Points" was an immigrant neighborhood in New York City.

105. Robert G. McNiece, "Mormonism" *The Presbyterian Review*, April 1881, 334–35, emphasis in original. See also Hyde, *Mormonism*, 77.

106. Here, I allude to Kerber, "Can a Woman Be an Individual?"

107. Beadle, "The Mormon Theocracy," 391. See also Child, *Gazeteer and Business Directory of Wayne County*, 54; Hyde, *Mormonism*, 310; "The Mormons at Home," 282; Goodwin, "The Mormon Situation," 762; and Givens, *Viper on the Hearth*, 18–21.

108. Waite, *The Mormon Prophet and His Harem*, 192.

109. Ibid., 244.

110. Bowles, *Across the Continent*, 124.

111. [Trumble], *Mysteries of Mormonism*, image appears between pages 42 and 43.

112. Waite, *The Mormon Prophet and His Harem*, 243.

113. Ibid., 244.

114. *Speech of Hon. Justin S. Morrill of Vermont, on Utah Territory and Its Law—Polygamy and Its License; Delivered in the House of Representatives, February 23, 1857* (Washington, D.C., 1857), 10.

115. [Trumble], *The Mysteries of Mormonism*, image appears between pages 33 and 34.

116. Bowles, *Across the Continent*, 115.

117. Representative Jacobs of New York, *Congressional Record*, 47 Cong., 1 sess., 3057 (19 April 1882).

118. Cornelia Ferris, *The Mormons at Home; With Some Incidents of Travel From Missouri to California, 1852–3. In a Series of Letters* (New York: Dix and Edwards, 1856), 187. See also Child, *Gazeteer and Business Directory of Wayne County*, 55.

119. Ferris, *Utah and the Mormons*, 252.

120. Haskell, *Mormonism and Polygamy*, 6. Haskell attributes his original source to the Governor of Idaho.

121. Rae, *Westward by Rail*, 122.

122. Hyde, *Mormonism*, 101.

123. "The Mormons at Home," 281.

124. Coyner, *Letters on Mormonism*, 9.

125. Rae, *Westward by Rail*, 118. Mormonism was "designed to rob men of their freedom" and create a Kingdom "to be ruled over by one man." *The Mormon Conspiracy to Establish an Independent Empire to Be Called the Kingdom of God on Earth. The Conspiracy Exposed by the Writings, Sermons, and Legislative Acts of the Prophets and Apostles of the Church* (Salt Lake City: The Tribune Co., 1886), 4.

126. Jürgen Habermas, *The Structural Transformation of the Public Sphere: An Inquiry into a Category of Bourgeois Society,* trans. Thomas Burger, (Cambridge, Mass.: MIT Press, 1989). It is important to note that Habermas's public sphere is not the same "public" that nineteenth-century Americans juxtaposed to the private home.

127. Marshall, "The Mormon Problem," 307.

128. Goodwin, "The Mormon Situation," 762.

129. Murray, "The Crisis in Utah," 330.

130. [Dallin], *Opinions Concerning the Bible Law of Marriage*, 229, x.

131. George W. Samson, "The False Claim of Mormonism," *Scribner's Monthly*, March 1872, 574–78. See also [Dallin], *Opinions Concerning the Bible Law of Marriage*, 239.

132. Hyde, *Mormonism*, 295, his emphasis.

133. Marshall, "The Mormon Problem," 309.

134. Bowles, *Across the Continent*, 124.

135. Barrows, "How Shall the Mormon Question be Settled?" 163.

136. Phil Robinson, *Sinners and Saints: A Tour Across the States and Around Them, with Three Months Among the Mormons* (Boston: Roberts Brothers, 1883), 228.

137. Hartog, *Man and Wife in America*, 136–66.

138. Ward, *The Husband in Utah*, 45.

139. Ferris, *Utah and the Mormons*, 285. See also 142.

140. Charles L. Woodward, coll. and arr., *The First Half Century of Mormonism. Papers, Engravings, Photographs, and Autograph Letters* vol. 1 (New York: n.p., 1880), 11, his emphasis. This is a reprint of an article that appeared in the *New York Daily Tribune*, 25 April 1857.

141. Cradlebaugh, *Mormonism*, 8.

142. Dixon, *New America*, 172.

143. Thompson, "Mormon Solution of the Mormon Problem," 69.

144. Ferris, *Utah and the Mormons*, 146.

Chapter 6.
Race, Class, and Contagion in Anti-Mormon Literature

"The foulest ulcer on the body of our nation": [Trumble], *The Mysteries of Mormonism*, 7.

1. "Brigham Young," *Frank Leslie's Illustrated Newspaper*, 28 July 1866, n.p.

2. Givens, *Viper on the Hearth*, 123.

3. Frances E. Willard, Introduction to Froiseth, *The Women of Mormonism*, xvi .

4. Edward Said, *Orientalism* (New York: Pantheon Books, 1978), 3.

5. Ibid., 43.

6. Thomas S. Kidd, "'Is It Worse to Follow Mahomet than the Devil?' Early American Uses of Islam," *Church History* 72, no. 4 (December 2003): 767.

7. Robert J. Allison, *The Crescent Obscured: The United States and the Muslim World, 1776–1815* (Chicago: University of Chicago Press, 2000), xvii. See also Thomas S. Kidd, *American Christians and Islam: Evangelical Culture and Muslims from the Colonial Period to the Age of Terrorism* (Princeton: Princeton University Press, 2009), 1–36.

8. Ibid., 53.

9. Ibid., 61.

10. See Cott, *Public Vows*, 9–23.

11. J. Spencer Fluhman, "An 'American Mahomet': Joseph Smith, Muhammad, and the Problem of Prophets in Antebellum America," *Journal of Mormon History* 34, no. 2 (Summer 2008): 23–45. See also Fluhman, *"A Peculiar People,"* 29–36.

12. Bennett, *The History of the Saints*, 218.

13. Cradlebaugh, *Mormonism*, 2.

14. Ibid., 6.

15. William John Conybeare, *Mormonism: Reprinted from the "Edinburgh Review," No.*

202. For April, 1854. Printed by Subscription. (Cuttack [Indiana]: The Orissa Mission Press, W. Brooks, 1855), 361. A multitude of references to Smith and Young as "Mohammedan" prophets are much too numerous to list here.

16. C. G. Forshey, as quoted in Samuel A. Cartwright, "Hereditary Descent; or, Depravity of the Offspring of Polygamy Among the Mormons," *DeBow's Review*, February 1861, 211.

17. For a typology of these racial linkages, see Bitton and Bunker, *The Mormon Graphic Image*, 75–122. On comparisons of Mormons to American Indians, see Louis J. Kern, *An Ordered Love: Sex Roles and Sexuality in Victorian Utopias: The Shakers, the Mormons, and the Oneida Community* (Chapel Hill: University of North Carolina Press, 1981), 67. On links between Mormons and Chinese immigrants, see Gordon, *The Mormon Question*, 192–94.

18. Ferris, *Utah and the Mormons*, 247. See also Forshey, as quoted in Cartwright, "Hereditary Descent," 211.

19. "A Desperate Attempt to Solve the Mormon Question," *Puck*, 13 February 1884, 376–77.

20. Stenhouse, *"Tell It All:" The Story of a Life's Experience in Mormonism*, ix.

21. Francis Lieber, *A Manual of Political Ethics: Designed Chiefly for the Use of Colleges and Students at Law*, 2 vols. (Boston: C. C. Little and J. Brown, 1839–1847), 234. Lieber's two major works, *Manual of Political Ethics* and *On Civil Liberty and Self-Government* had become college texts by the 1850s, and, according to Sarah Barringer Gordon, his *Political Ethics* had become "the standard work cited in legal treatises and lawyer's briefs on the proper respect for, and restriction of, women in politics and law." Gordon, *The Mormon Question*, 140. See also Cott, *Public Vows*, 114–15.

22. Thompson, "Mormon Solution of a Mormon Problem," 68.

23. F. C. Barber, "Mormonism in the United States," *DeBow's Review*, April 1854, 370 and 382.

24. Beadle, *Life in Utah*, 375, 376, and 380.

25. Charles Heber Clark [Max Adeler, pseud.], *The Tragedy of Thompson Dunbar: A Tale of Salt Lake City* (Philadelphia: Stoddart, 1879), 10.

26. "Mormons and Mormonism," 201.

27. Willard, Introduction to Froiseth, *The Women of Mormonism*, xvi. See also William Barrows, *An Appeal to the Christian Women in America. In Behalf of the Mormon and the Mexican Woman, and Their Children* (n.p.: 1879), 2–4, which states, "Mormon Country is Turkey in America—the harem of the United States."

28. Dixon, *New America*, 172.

29. "False Claim of Mormonism," *The Century*, March 1872, 573.

30. Van Deusen and Van Deusen, *Spiritual Delusions*, 8.

31. Hyde, *Mormonism*, 113.

32. *Reynolds v. United States*, 98 U.S. 145 (1879).

33. For analyses of the legacy of European colonialism in an American context, see Cott, *Public Vows*, 9–11 and 20–23; Holly Edwards, *Noble Dreams, Wicked Pleasures: Orientalism*

in America, 1870–1930 (Princeton: Princeton University Press, 2000); and Fuad Sha'ban, *Islam and Arabs in Early American Thought: The Roots of Orientalism in America* (Durham: The Acorn Press, 1991).

34. Bruce Burgett, "On the Mormon Question: Race, Sex, and Polygamy in the 1850s and 1990s," *American Quarterly* 57, no. 1 (March 2002): 77.

35. Burgett, "On the Mormon Question"; and Angela Willey, "'Christian Nations,' 'Polygamic Races' and Women's Rights: Toward a Genealogy of Non/Monogamy and Whiteness," *Sexualities* 9, no. 5 (2006), 530–46.

36. I. S. Briggs, "Medical History of a California Expedition," *Boston Medical and Surgical Journal* 41 (9 January 1850): 479–80.

37. Hyde, *Mormonism*, 315.

38. C. C. Goodwin, "The Political Attitude of the Mormons," *North American Review*, March 1881, 283.

39. Lee L. Bean, Geraldine P. Mineau, and Douglas L. Anderton, *Fertility Change on the American Frontier: Adaptation and Innovation* (Berkeley: University of California Press, 1990), 143–44. For a detailed analysis of Mormonism's missionary efforts abroad and the many migrations from foreign countries to Zion, see Conway B. Sonne, *Saints on the Seas: A Maritime History of Mormon Migration, 1830–1890* (Salt Lake City: University of Utah Press, 1983).

40. See Bitton and Bunker, *The Mormon Graphic Image*; and Givens, *Viper on the Hearth*, 47–49.

41. On late-nineteenth and early-twentieth-century nativism, see John Higham, *Strangers in the Land: Patterns of American Nativism, 1860–1925*, 2nd ed. (New Brunswick: Rutgers University Press, 1988); and Dale T. Knobel, *America for the Americans: The Nativist Movement in the United States* (New York: Twayne Publishers, 1996).

42. See Helen Z. Papanikolas, ed., *The Peoples of Utah* (Salt Lake City: Utah State Historical Society, 1976); William Mulder, *Homeward to Zion: The Mormon Migration From Scandinavia* (Minneapolis: University of Minnesota Press, [1957]); Sonne, *Saints on the Seas*; P. A. M. Taylor, *Expectations Westward: The Mormons and the Emigration of Their British Converts in the Nineteenth Century* (Ithaca: Cornell University Press, 1966); and Bean, Mineau, and Anderton, *Fertility Change on the American Frontier*.

43. See Richard Hofstader, *Social Darwinism in American Thought* (Philadelphia: University of Pennsylvania Press, 1945); Carl N. Degler, *In Search of Human Nature: The Decline and Revival of Darwinism in American Social Thought* (New York: Oxford University Press, 1991), 10–17; and Daniel J. Kevles, *In the Name of Eugenics: Genetics and the Uses of Human Heredity* (Cambridge, Mass.: Harvard University Press, 1995), 20–21.

44. Petit, *Plural Marriage*, preface.

45. Bowles, *Across the Continent*, 117.

46. "Mormonism from a Secular Standpoint," 160.

47. "The Mormon Situation," *Harper's New Monthly Magazine*, June-November 1881, 758.

48. Ibid., 759.

49. Beadle, *Life in Utah*, 365.

50. "Mormonism from a Secular Standpoint," 160.

51. Thomas Nast, *Harper's Weekly*, 25 March 1882, 191. This image is reprinted in Bitton and Bunker, *The Mormon Graphic Image*, 124.

52. "The Mormons: Who and What They Are," *Phrenological Journal* 52 (January 1871), 45.

53. See "Mormonism—Past and Present" [Edinburgh: Clark, 1863], 228–34.

54. Fuad, *Islam and Arabs in Early American Thought*, 15–26.

55. McCarthy, "Brigham Young," 181.

56. Samson, "The False Claim of Mormonism," 578.

57. Charles Marshall, "Characteristics of Mormonism. By a Recent Visitor to Utah," *Fraser's Magazine*, June 1871, 693–95.

58. Goodwin, "The Political Attitude of the Mormons," 283.

59. Waite, *The Mormon Prophet and His Harem*, 3.

60. Ferris, *The Mormons at Home*, 131.

61. Hyde, *Mormonism*, 315.

62. "The Mormon Theocracy," *The Century*, July 1877, 393.

63. Waite, *The Mormon Prophet and His Harem*, 3.

64. "The Mormon Theocracy," 392.

65. Murray, "Crisis in Utah," 345.

66. Fuller, *Mormon Wives*, iii.

67. Ibid., vii.

68. Van Deusen and Van Deusen, *Spiritual Delusions*, 38.

69. One of the People, *Opinions Concerning the Bible Law of Marriage*, 72.

70. William Barrows, *An Appeal to the Christian Women in America*, 2–4.

71. [Trumble], *The Mysteries of Mormonism*, 7.

72. [Trumble], *The Mysteries of Mormonism*, 8.

73. "The Mormons," *Harper's Weekly*, 24 April 1857, 257.

74. Waite, *The Mormon Prophet and His Harem*, 3.

75. "The Mormon Situation," 760. The unknown tongue to which the author referred was probably Brigham Young's ill-fated attempt to institute a "Deseret alphabet" among the Saints that substituted various signs for sounds in phonetic English.

76. Orson Pratt, October 6, 1879, in *Journal of Discourses*, 20:324. On anti-Mormon conclusions, see Gordon, "Liberty of Self-Degradation," 827–30. For discussions of political homogeneity among Mormons, see Hansen, *Quest for Empire*, 121–46; Lyman, *Political Deliverance*, 13.

77. U. S. Senate, *Proposing Amendment to Constitution of United States Extending Right of Suffrage to Women*, 49 Cong., 1 sess., 4 (2 Feb 1886), S. Rep. 70 (*Serial Set* 2355).

78. "A Desperate Attempt to Solve the Mormon Question," 376–77.

79. McNiece, *Present Aspects of the Mormon Question*, frontispiece.

80. Murray, "Crisis in Utah," 345.

81. Goodwin, "The Mormon Situation," 762.

82. Mary Douglas, *Purity and Danger: An Analysis of Concept of Pollution and Taboo,* Routledge Classics Edition (London: Routledge, 2002), 2.

83. Ibid., 47.

84. Anderson, *Imagined Communities.*

85. Douglas, 4.

86. Ibid., 2–3.

87. Ibid., 5.

88. Waite, *The Mormon Prophet and His Harem,* 89–90.

89. Ibid., 89.

90. "The Mormon Theocracy," 391–97; quote on 397.

Chapter 7.
The End of Plural Marriage

"Suffer a surrender . . . ? No, never!": John Taylor, August 20, 1882, in *Journal of Discourses,* 23:240–41.

1. See Iversen, *The Anti-Polygamy Controversy in U. S. Women's Movements,* 99; Hayward, "Utah's Anti-Polygamy Society 1878–1884"; and Gordon, *The Mormon Question,* 55–83 and 147–81.

2. Kate Field, *Chicago Tribune,* June 6, 1886, as cited in Gordon, "'Our National Hearth-stone,'" 295.

3. Senator Edmunds of Vermont, *Congressional Record,* 47 Cong., 1 sess., 1213 (16 February 1882).

4. *Stat.* 253. See Firmage and Mangrum, *Zion in the Courts,* 148–51.

5. Kathryn M. Daynes and Sarah Barringer Gordon, "In-Laws and Outlaws: Criminal Prosecution of Mormon Polygamists in Utah Territory" (Paper presented at the annual meeting of the American Historical Association, Philadelphia, Pennsylvania, January 2006), 2.

6. *Reynolds v. United States,* 98 U.S. 145 (1879).

7. Ibid., 164.

8. Ibid., 167.

9. Ibid., 166.

10. Ibid., 168.

11. Rutherford B. Hayes, "Third Annual Message," in United States President, *A Compilation of the Messages and Papers of the Presidents, 1789–1897,* comp. James D. Richardson (Washington, D.C.: United States Government Printing Office, 1896–1899), 7:559–60.

12. Representative Miller of Pennsylvania, *Appendix to the Congressional Globe,* 47 Cong. 1 sess., 28 (14 March 1882).

13. See Gordon, *The Mormon Question,* 151–57, and 185–87; Firmage and Mangrum, *Zion in the Courts,* 161–82 and 201–56; Richard D. Poll, "The Legislative Anti-Polygamy Campaign," *BYU Studies* 26, no. 4 (Fall 1986): 107–19; and Edwin Brown Firmage, "The Judicial Campaign against Polygamy and the Enduring Legal Questions," *BYU Studies* 25 (Summer 1987): 91–113.

14. *Stat.* 30.

15. For a more thorough discussion of southern congressmen's positions on anti-polygamy legislation during the 1880s, see Mason, *The Mormon Menace*, 89–92.

16. See David Buice, "A Stench in the Nostrils of Honest Men: Southern Democrats and the Edmunds Act of 1882," *Dialogue: A Journal of Mormon Thought* 21 (Autumn 1988): 100–113; and Gains M. Foster, *Moral Reconstruction: Christian Lobbyists and the Federal Legislation of Morality, 1865–1920* (Chapel Hill: University of North Carolina Press, 2007), 54–72.

17. Senator Vest of Missouri was particularly representative of this argument. See *Congressional Record*, 47 Cong. 1 sess., 1157–58 (15 February 1882).

18. Senator Jones of Florida, *Congressional Record*, 47 Cong. 1 sess., 1206 (16 February 1882).

19. See, for example, Senator Bayard of Delaware, *Congressional Globe*, 47 Cong. 1 sess., 1156–57 and 1159–61 (15 February 1882).

20. Representative Cassidy of Nevada, *Congressional Record*, 47 Cong. 1 sess., 1863 (13 March 1882).

21. Senator Edmunds of Vermont, *Congressional Record*, 47 Cong. 1 sess., 1213 (16 February 1882).

22. *Congressional Record*, 47 Cong. 1 sess., 3057 (19 April 1882).

23. Ibid.

24. *Congressional Record*, 47 Cong. 1 sess., 1212 (16 February 1882).

25. "Zane's Ruling," *Ogden Standard Examiner*, 30 April 1885, as cited in Daynes and Gordon, "In-Laws and Outlaws," 5.

26. *United States v. Cannon*, 118 U.S. 355 (1886).

27. Firmage, "The Judicial Campaign against Polygamy," 98.

28. See *Murphy v. Ramsey*, 114 U.S. 15 (1885), 19.

29. *Stat.* 30, section 9.

30. John Taylor, "Ecclesiastical Control in Utah," *North American Review*, January 1884, 1–8.

31. See, for example, John Taylor, "An Address to the Members of The Church of Jesus Christ of Latter-day Saints," in Clark, *Messages of the First Presidency*, 3:343.

32. George Q. Cannon, October 8, 1882, in *Journal of Discourses*, 23:272.

33. John Taylor and George Q. Cannon, "An Epistle from the First Presidency. To the Officers and Members of the Church of Jesus Christ of Latter-day Saints," in Clark, *Messages of the First Presidency*, 3: 30–31.

34. See Roberts, *Comprehensive History of The Church*, 6:59.

35. John Taylor, George Q. Cannon, and Joseph F. Smith, "An Address to the Members of The Church of Jesus Christ of Latter-day Saints," in Clark, *Messages of the First Presidency*, 2:343–46.

36. John Taylor and George Q. Cannon, "To the Presidents of Stakes and their Counselors, the Bishops and their Counselors, and the Latter-day Saints Generally," in *Messages of the First Presidency* 3:16.

37. Lyman, *Political Deliverance*, 28.

38. Firmage and Mangrum, *Zion in the Courts*, 187–90.

39. Taylor, "Ecclesiastical Control in Utah," 4.

40. Taylor, Cannon, and Smith, "An Address," in Clark, *Messages of the First Presidency*, 3:346.

41. Taylor and Cannon, "To the Presidents of Stakes and their Counselors," in Clark, *Messages of the First Presidency*, 3:13–14.

42. "An Address to The President and People Of The United States," reprinted in Roberts, *Comprehensive History of the Church*, 6: 151. See also *Deseret News Weekly*, 6 May 1885, 244–45.

43. Erastus Snow, March 9, 1884, in *Journal of Discourses*, 25:108.

44. For a more detailed account of the raids, see Leonard J. Arrington, *Great Basin Kingdom: An Economic History of the Latter-day Saints, 1830–1900* (Lincoln: University of Nebraska Press, 1966), 352–79.

45. Tracy E. Panek, "Search and Seizure in Utah: Recounting the Antipolygamy Raids," *Utah Historical Quarterly* 62, no. 4 (Fall 1994): 316–34; and Daynes and Gordon, "In-Laws and Outlaws," 11–12.

46. John Taylor and George Q. Cannon, "An Address to the Latter-day Saints in the Rocky Mountain Region and Throughout the World," in Clark, *Messages of the First Presidency*, 3:19.

47. John Taylor and George Q. Cannon, "Epistle of the First Presidency, President's Office, Salt Lake City, April 4, 1885," in Clark, *Messages of the First Presidency*, 3:7.

48. John Taylor, February 1, 1885, in *Journal of Discourses*, 26:156. See also John Taylor and George Q. Cannon, "An Epistle of the First Presidency to the Church of Jesus Christ of Latter-day Saints. Read at the Semi-Annual Conference, held at Coalville, Summit County, Utah, October, 1886," in Clark, *Messages of the First Presidency*, 3:78–79.

49. Daynes and Gordon, "In-Laws and Outlaws," 10–11.

50. "The Mormon Question," *Daily Graphic*, 22 October 1883, 83.

51. John Taylor, August 20, 1882, in *Journal of Discourses*, 23:240–41.

52. D. Michael Quinn, "LDS Church Authority and New Plural Marriages, 1890–1904," *Dialogue: A Journal of Mormon Thought* 18, no. 1 (Spring 1985): 27.

53. "Official Declaration," found at the end of any standard edition of the *Doctrine and Covenants*.

54. Gordon and Daynes, "In-Laws and Outlaws," 10–11.

55. *Stat.* 635.

56. *Stat.* 635, section 24.

57. "The Test Oath," in Clark, *Messages of the First Presidency*, 3:119

58. *Stat.* 635, section 20.

59. See Lyman, *Political Deliverance*, 100.

60. Firmage and Mangrum, *Zion in the Courts*, 204–5; Hansen, *Quest for Empire*, 175–79; and Thomas G. Alexander, *Mormonism in Transition: A History of the Latter-day Saints, 1890–1930* (Urbana: University of Illinois Press, 1986), 3–5.

61. "An Act to Provide for Holding Elections," Idaho, *13th Session Laws* (1884–1885), Sec. 16, p. 110, as cited in Joseph H. Groberg, "The Mormon Disfranchisements of 1882 to 1892," *BYU Studies* 16 (Spring 1976): 401.

62. *Davis v. Beason*, 133 U.S. 333 (1890).

63. *Late Corporation of The Church of Jesus Christ of Latter-day Saints v. United States*, 136 U.S. 1 (1890).

64. "Official Declaration," *Doctrine and Covenants*.

65. Woodruff, *Wilford Woodruff's Journal*, 112–13.

66. For some well-known examples, see Hansen, *Quest for Empire*, 177–79; and Larsen, *The "Americanization" of Utah for Statehood*, 136–43. Thomas G. Alexander contends that the continued practice of plural marriage after the Manifesto showed not duplicity on the part of church officials, but that "any practice once engrained so positively in the public sentiment is difficult to end." See Alexander, *Mormonism in Transition*, 12–13, quoted material on page 12.

67. For examples of anti-Mormons disbelieving the end of polygamy in 1890 see Kate Field, "Miss Kate Field on Mormon Statehood," *Our Day*, March-April 1894, 165; and *The Inside of Mormonism. A Judicial Examination of the Endowment Oaths Administered in All the Mormon Temples, by the United States District Court for the Third Judicial District of Utah, to Determine Whether Membership in the Church is Consistent with Citizenship in the United States* (Salt Lake City: Published by the Utah Americans, 1903); and Shelby M. Cullom, "The Menace of Mormonism," *North American Review*, September 1905, 379–85.

68. See Larson, *The "Americanization" of Utah for Statehood*.

69. Wilford Woodruff, George Q. Cannon, Joseph F. Smith, Lorenzo Snow, Franklin D. Richards, Moses Thatcher, Francis M. Lyman, H. J. Grant, John Henry Smith, John W. Taylor, M. W. Merrill, Anthony H. Lund, and Abraham H. Cannon, "Amnesty Petition to the President of the United States, December 19, 1891," in Clark, *Messages of the First Presidency*, 3:230–31.

70. United States, President, *A Compilation of the Messages and Papers of the Presidents, 1789–1897*, vol. 9, comp. James D. Richardson (Washington, D.C.: United States Government Printing Office, 1896–1899), 368–69.

71. Ibid., 510–11.

72. Jean Bickmore White, "Woman's Place Is in the Constitution: The Struggle for Equal Rights in Utah in 1895," *Utah Historical Quarterly* 42 (Fall 1974): 344–69.

73. Hansen, *Quest for Empire*, 177. See also Larson, *The "Americanization" of Utah*; and Quinn, "LDS Church Authority and New Plural Marriages."

74. Quinn, "LDS Church Authority and New Plural Marriages"; Kenneth L. Cannon, II, "Beyond the Manifesto: Polygamous Cohabitation among LDS General Authorities After 1890," *Utah Historical Quarterly* 46 (Winter 1978): 24–36; Hardy, *Solemn Covenant*, 167–243; and Jan Shipps, "The Principle Revoked: A Closer Look at the Demise of Plural Marriage," *Journal of Mormon History* 11 (1984): 65–78.

75. The Second Manifesto is reprinted as "Official Statement," in Clark, *Messages of the First Presidency*, 4:84.

76. See Jacobson and Burton, *Modern Polygamy in the United States*; and Irwin Altman and Joseph Ginat, *Polygamous Families in Contemporary Society* (Cambridge: Cambridge University Press, 1996).

77. See Larsen, *The "Americanization" of Utah for Statehood*; and Alexander, *Mormonism in Transition*.

78. See Hansen, *Quest for Empire*, 180–90.

79. On economic shifts in the church, see Alexander, *Mormonism in Transition*, 74–92 and 180–211. On cooperatives becoming joint stock corporations, see especially 182. For a detailed account of broad shifts from the United Order to the modern church welfare system, see Arrington, Fox, and May, *Building the City of God*, 311–58.

80. Larsen, *The "Americanization" of Utah for Statehood*.

Conclusion

1. For an analysis of media coverage of plural marriage, see Janet Bennion, *Polygamy in Primetime: Media, Gender, and Politics in Mormon Fundamentalism* (Waltham, Mass.: Brandeis University Press, 2012), especially part 2.

2. *Book of Mormon*, 3 Nephi, 21:4.

3. Bennett, *A Detective's Experience Among the Mormons*, 18.

4. Ferris, *Utah and the Mormons*, 146.

5. [Trumble], *The Mysteries of Mormonism*, 7.

6. The First Presidency and the Council of the Twelve Apostles of The Church of Jesus Christ of Latter-day Saints, "The Family: A Proclamation to the World," http://lds.org/library/display/0,4945,161-1-11–1,00.html, accessed March 30, 2013.

7. For statistics on fundamentalist polygamy, see D. Michael Quinn, "Plural Marriage and Mormon Fundamentalism," in *Fundamentalisms and Society: Reclaiming the Sciences, the Family, and Education*, eds. Martin E. Marty, R. Scott Appleby, Helen Hardacre, and Everett Mendelsohn (Chicago: University of Chicago Press, 1993), 240–51; Daynes, *More Wives Than One*, 210; and Martha Sonntag Bradley, "Polygamy-Practicing Mormons," in *Religions of the World: A Comprehensive Encyclopedia of Beliefs and Practices*, 4 vols., eds. J. Gordon Melton and Martin Baumann (Santa Barbara, Calif.; Denver, Colo.; and Oxford, England: ABC-CLIO, 2002), 3:1023–25. As of this writing, Utah's Attorney General Mark Shurtleff has declared that while plural marriage is illegal in both Utah and Arizona, "law enforcement agencies in both states have decided to focus on crimes within polygamous communities that involve child abuse, domestic violence, and fraud." "Polygamy," http://attorneygeneral.utah.gov/polygamy.html, accessed July 6, 2012.

8. Larry King and Gordon B. Hinckley, "Gordon B. Hinckley Interview," *Larry King Live*, CNN, September 8, 1998.

9. Bennion, 54–55. For another exploration of contemporary polygamy in the United States, see Jacobson and Burton, *Modern Polygamy in the United States*.

10. For these reasons, Bennion claims, contemporary scholars "feel justified in calling them 'Mormon fundamentalists.'" Bennion, 306, n.7.

11. For more on the raid in Texas, see Stuart A. Wright and James T. Richardson, eds., *Saints under Siege: The Texas Raid on the Fundamentalist Latter Day Saints* (New York: New York University Press, 2011).

12. "Polygamy: Latter-day Saints and the Practice of Plural Marriage," www.mormon newsroom.org/article/polygamy-latter-day-saints-and-the-practice-of-plural-marriage, accessed July 6, 2012. See also "Senior Church Leader Appeals to Media to Make Distinction," www.mormonnewsroom.org/ldsnewsroom/eng/news-releases-stories/senior-church-leader-appeals-to-media-to-make-distinction, accessed July 6, 2012; and "Reports of Polygamy Story Vary Across the World," www.mormonnewsroom.org/ldsnewsroom/eng/news-releases-stories/reports-of-polygamy-story-vary-across-the-world, accessed July 6, 2012.

13. *8: The Mormon Proposition*. Directed by Reed Cowan (United States: David v. Goliath Films, 2010).

14. Rebecca Walsh, "LDS Stand on Prop. 8 Oozes Irony," *Salt Lake Tribune*, November 2, 2008, http://saltlakecity.backpage.com/LegalServices/lds-mormon-stand-on-californias-proposition-8-oozes-irony/933155; http://www.sltrib.com/News/ci_10879061, accessed July 27, 2012.

15. Hendrick Hertzberg, "Eight is Enough," *The New Yorker*, December 1, 2008, http://www.newyorker.com/talk/comment/2008/12/01/081201taco_talk_hertzberg, accessed October 7, 2009.

16. Lola Van Wagenen, L.A. Times editorial, http://www.latimes.com/news/opinion/la-oe-fiveoneight1-2008nov01,0,3298830.story?page=2, accessed December 18, 2010.

17. See image at http://msinformedblog.com/2008/11/, accessed January 9, 2013. See also image at http://www.flickr.com/photos/whatupwilly/3057760037/, accessed January 9, 2013.

18. "Opponents of Prop 8 Demonstrate in Front of Church of the Latter Day Saints," accessed December 18, 2010. http://www.life.com/image/83609592, accessed October 7, 2009.

19. Quoted in Walsh.

Bibliography

Primary Sources

NEWSPAPERS AND MAGAZINES

American: A National Journal
Anti-Polygamy Standard
The Bay State Monthly
Boston Medical and Surgical Journal
The Century
Chicago Advance
Daily Graphic
DeBow's Review
Deseret News
Deseret News Weekly
Frank Leslie's Illustrated Newspaper
Frank Leslie's New Family Magazine
Fraser's Magazine
The Galaxy
Harper's New Monthly Magazine
Harper's Weekly
The Home Missionary
Hours at Home
International Review
Journal History

The Juvenile Instructor
L.A. Times
The Ladies Repository
Latter-day Saints' Millennial Star
The Nation
National Quarterly Review
Nauvoo Expositor
New America
New York Daily Tribune
New York Times
The New Yorker
North American Review
Northwestern Pulpit
Our Day
Overland Monthly
Phrenological Journal
The Presbyterian Review
Puck
Putnam's Monthly
The Revolution
Salt Lake Tribune
Scribner's Monthly
The Seer
Times and Seasons
University Magazine
Woman's Exponent
Woman's Journal

BOOKS AND PAMPHLETS

Anderson, Karl Ricks. *Joseph Smith's Kirtland: Eyewitness Accounts*. Salt Lake City, Utah: Deseret Book Co., 1996.

An Apostle's Wife [Alfred Trumble]. *The Mysteries of Mormonism. A Full Exposure of Its Secret Practices and Hidden Crimes*. New York: Richard K. Fox, 1881.

Appalling Disclosures! Mormon Revelations, Being the History of Fourteen Females, Emma Hale, Mrs. Hatfield, Lucy Murray, Alice Foster, Mrs. Williams, Lizzie Monroe, Marian Gage, Adeline Young, Mrs. Jones, Lady Bula, Marg. Guildford, Maud Hatfield, Rose Hatfield, Mrs. Richards, Victims of Mormon Spiritual Marriages! London: Printed and Published by H. Elliot, [1856?].

Barker, F. E. *Public Discussion of the Doctrines of the Gospel of Jesus Christ, Held in the Tabernacle, Ogden, Utah, May 8 and 9, 1884. Between the Rev. Richard Hartley, Pastor of the Baptist Church, Ogden City and Ben. E. Rich, an Elder of the Church of Jesus Christ of Latter-day Saints. Reported by F. E. Barker*. Salt Lake City: Juvenile Instructor Office, 1884.

Barrows, William. *An Appeal to the Christian Women in America. In Behalf of the Mormon and the Mexican Woman, and Their Children.* N.p.: 1879.

Bashore, Melvin L., comp. *Index to the Writings of Helen Mar Whitney in the Woman's Exponent.* [Salt Lake City]: The Church Library, The Church of Jesus Christ of Latter-day Saints, Historical Department, 1975.

Beadle, J. H. *Life in Utah; or, The Mysteries and Crimes of Mormonism. Being an Exposé of the Secret Rites and Ceremonies of the Latter-Day Saints, With a Full and Authentic History of Polygamy and the Mormon Sect From Its Origin to the Present Time.* Philadelphia: National Publishing Company, 1870.

Beecher, Catharine E. *Religious Training of Children in the School, the Family and the Church.* New York: Harper and Bros., 1864.

———. *A Treatise on Domestic Economy.* Boston: T. H. Webb & Co., 1842.

Beecher, Catharine E., Margaret Fuller, and M. Carey Thomas. *The Educated Woman in America; Selected Writings of Catharine Beecher, Margaret Fuller, and M. Carey Thomas,* edited by Barbara M. Cross. Classics in Education, 25. New York: Teacher's College Press, 1965.

Beecher, Catharine E., and Harriet Beecher Stowe. *The American Woman's Home; or, Principles of Domestic Science.* New York: J.B. Ford, 1869.

Beers, R. W. *The Mormon Puzzle and How to Solve It.* Chicago: Funk and Wagnalls, Publishers, 1887.

Belisle, Orvilla S. *Mormonism Unveiled; or, A History of Mormonism, From Its Rise to the Present Time.* London: Charles H. Clarke, 1855.

———. *The Prophets; or, Mormonism Unveiled.* Philadelphia: Wm. White Smith, 1855.

Bell, Alfreda Eva. *Boadicea; The Mormon Wife: Life Scenes in Utah.* Baltimore: Arthur R. Orton, 1855.

Bennett, Fred E. *A Detective's Experience Among the Mormons; or, Polygamist Mormons: How They Live and the Land They Live In.* Chicago: Laird and Lee Publishers, 1887.

Bennett, John Cook. *The History of the Saints; or, An Exposé of Joe Smith and Mormonism.* Boston: Leland and Whiting, 1842.

Bishop, Joel Prentiss. *Commentaries on the Law of Marriage and Divorce.* 4th ed. Boston: Little Brown, 1864.

A Book of Commandments, for the Government of the Church of Christ, Organized According to Law, on the 6th of April, 1830. Independence, Mo.: Reprinted by Herald House Publishing Division of the Reorganized Church of Jesus Christ of Latter Day Saints, 1972.

Bowes, John. *Mormonism Exposed, in Its Swindling and Licentious Abominations: Refuted in Its Principles and in the Claims of Its Head, the Modern Mohammed, Joseph Smith, Who Is Proved to Have Been a Deceiver and No Prophet of God.* London: E. Ward, [1850?].

Bowles, Samuel. *Across the Continent: A Summer's Journey to the Rocky Mountains, The Mormons, and the Pacific States, With Speaker Colfax.* Springfield, Mass.: Samuel Bowles and Company, 1865.

Bradshaw, Wesley. *Brigham Young's Daughter. A Most Thrilling Narrative of Her Escape From Utah, With Her Intended Husband, Their Pursuit by the Mormon Danites or Aveng-*

ing Angels. Together With an Account of the Adventures and Perils of the Fugitives on the Prairies and While Crossing the Rocky Mountains. To Which Is Added a Full Exposure of the Schemes of the Mormon Leaders to Defy and Defeat the U.S. Government in Its Attempts to Suppress the Horrible Practice of Polygamy in Utah.* Philadelphia: C.W. Alexander, 1876.

Briggs, Edmund C., and R. M. Atwood. *Address to the Saints in Utah and California. Polygamy Proven an Abomination by Holy Writ. Is Brigham Young President of the Church of Jesus Christ, or Is He Not?* Rev. Joseph Smith and William W. Blair. Plano, Ill.: Published by the Church of Jesus Christ of Latter Day Saints, 1869.

Briggs, I. S. "Medical History of a California Expedition." *The Boston Medical and Surgical Journal* 41 (9 January 1850): 479–80.

Briggs, Jason. *The Basis of Brighamite Polygamy: A Criticism Upon the (So Called) Revelation of July 12, 1843.* Lamoni, Iowa: Reorganized Church of Christ, [1875].

Burton, Richard. *The City of the Saints, and Across the Rocky Mountains to California.* London: Longman, Green, Longman and Roberts, 1861.

A Cambridge Clergyman. *Mormonism or the Bible? A Question for the Times.* Cambridge: T. Dixon, 1852.

Campbell, Alexander. *Delusions: An Analysis of the Book of Mormon; With an Examination of Its Internal and External Evidences, and a Refutation of Its Pretences to Divine Authority.* Boston: Benjamin H. Greene, 1832.

Campbell, James. *The History and Philosophy of Marriage; or, Polygamy and Monogamy Compared.* 3rd ed. Salt Lake City: Joseph Hyrum Parry and Co., 1885.

Carlier, Auguste. *Marriage in the United States.* Trans. Joy Jeffries. Boston: DeVries, Ibarra and Co., 1867.

Caswell, Henry. *The City of the Mormons; or, Three Days at Nauvoo.* London: Printed for J. G. F. and J. Rivington, 1843.

Chapman, R. D. *Freelove a Law of Nature: A Plea for the Liberation of the Sexes, An Essay Wherein Are Set Forth the Demerits of Prostitution, Polygamy, and Monogamy.* New York: The Author, 1881.

Child, Hamilton. *Gazetteer and Business Directory of Wayne County, New York for 1867–1868.* Syracuse: Printed at the Journal Office, 1867.

The Church of Jesus Christ of Latter-day Saints. Women's Committee. *Memorial of the Mormon Women of Utah to the President and Congress of the United States, April 6, 1886.* Washington, D.C.: [s.n.], 1886.

Clark, Charles Heber [Max Adeler, pseud.]. *The Tragedy of Thompson Dunbar: A Tale of Salt Lake City.* Philadelphia: Stoddart, 1879.

Clark, James Reuben, comp. *Messages of the First Presidency of The Church of Jesus Christ of Latter-day Saints 1833–1964.* 6 vols. Salt Lake City: Bookcraft, Inc., 1966.

Clark, John A. *Gleanings by the Way.* Philadelphia: W. J. and J. K. Simon, 1842.

Clegg, William. *A Plea for the Slighted Ones! An Original Poem.* Provo, Utah: Sleater and McEwan, Book and Job Printers, n.d.

Codman, John. *The Mormon Country. A Summer with the Latter-Day Saints.* New York: United States Publishing Company, 1874.

————. *A Solution of the Mormon Problem*. New York: G. P. Putnam's Sons, 1885.

Coffin, Charles. *Our New Way Round the World*. Boston: Fields, Osgood, and Co., 1869.

Colfax, Shuyler. *The Mormon Question Being a Speech of Vice-President Shuyler Colfax at Salt Lake City: A Reply Thereto by Elder John Taylor and a Letter of Vice-President Colfax Published in the New York Independent, With Elder Taylor's Reply*. [Utah?: s.n.], 1870.

Collier, Fred C., ed. *Unpublished Revelations of the Prophets and Presidents of The Church of Jesus Christ of Latter Day Saints*, vol. 1. Salt Lake City: Colliers, 1981.

Conybeare, William John. *Mormonism: Reprinted From the "Edinburgh Review," No. 202. For April, 1854. Printed by Subscription*. Cuttack [Indiana]: The Orissa Mission Press, W. Brooks, 1855.

Coyner, J. M. *Letters on Mormonism*. Salt Lake City: Tribune Printing and Publishing Co., 1879.

Cradlebaugh, John. *Mormonism: A Doctrine That Embraces Polygamy, Adultery, Incest, Perjury, Robbery and Murder: Speech . . . in the House of Representatives in 1863*. [Salt Lake City: n.p., 1877?].

Crocheron, Augusta Joyce. *Representative Women of Deseret, a Book of Biographical Sketches to Accompany the Picture Bearing the Same Title*. Salt Lake City: J. C. Graham and Co, 1884.

The Cullom Bill! Remonstrance and Resolutions Adopted by a Mass Meeting of the Citizens of Utah, Held in the Tabernacle, Salt Lake City, March 31st, 1870. Salt Lake City: Printed at the Deseret News Office, [1870].

Curtis, George Ticknor. *Letter to the Secretary of the Interior on the Affairs of Utah, Polygamy, "Cohabitation," & C*. Washington, D.C.: Gibson Bros., 1886.

————. *A Plea for Religious Liberty and the Rights of Conscience: An Argument Delivered in the Supreme Court of the United States, April 28, 1886, in Three Cases of Lorenzo Snow, Plaintiff in Error v. The United States, on Writs of Error to the Supreme Court of Utah Territory*. Washington, D.C.: Printed for the Author by Gibson Bros., 1886.

[Dallin, William]. *True Mormonism; or, The Horrors of Polygamy From the Pen of an Ex-Mormon Elder*. Chicago: W. P. Dunn and Co., Printers, 1885.

Dickenson, Ellen E. *New Light on Mormonism*. New York: Funk and Wagnalls, 1885.

Discourses on the Holy Ghost: Also Lectures on Faith as Delivered at the School of the Prophets at Kirtland, Ohio. Comp. N. B. Lundwall. Salt Lake City: Bookcraft, Inc., 1959.

Dixon, William Hepworth. *New America*. Philadelphia: J. B. Lippincott and Co., 1867.

Done, Ballard S. *How to Solve the Mormon Problem. Three Letters*. New York: American News Company Agents, 1877.

Doyle, Arthur Conan. *A Study in Scarlet*, edited by Owen Dudley Edwards. Oxford: Oxford University Press, 1993.

Dunn, Ballard S. *The Twin Monsters: And How National Legislation May Help to Solve the Mormon Problem, and Restore to Society Somewhat of the Sacramental Character of the Rite of Holy Matrimony*. New York: James Pott and Co., n.d.

Ehat, Andrew F., and Lyndon W. Cook, comps. and eds. *The Words of Joseph Smith: The Contemporary Accounts of the Nauvoo Discourses of the Prophet Joseph*. Provo, Utah: Religious Studies Center, Brigham Young University, 1980.

[Ellis, Charles]. *Mormons and Mormonism: Why They Have Been Opposed, Maligned, and Persecuted: Inside History of the Present Anti-Mormon Crusade, by a Non-Mormon, Ten Years in Utah.* Salt Lake City: Press of the Magazine Printing Company, 1899.

Emmons, S. B. *Philosophy of Popular Superstitions and the Effects of Credulity and Imagination Upon the Moral, Social, and Intellectual Condition of the Human Race.* Boston: L. P. Crown and Co., 1853.

An Epistle of the First Presidency to the Church of Jesus Christ of Latter-day Saints, in General Conference Assembled. Read April 6, 1886 at 56th General Conference, Provo Utah. Salt Lake City: The Deseret News Company, Printers, 1887.

Federal Jurisdiction in the Territories. Right of Local Self-Government. Judge Black's Argument for Utah, Before the Judiciary Committee of the House of Representatives, February 1, 1883. Washington, D.C.: Gibson Brothers, 1883.

Ferris, Benjamin G. *Utah and the Mormons: The History, Government, Doctrines, Customs, and Prospects of the Latter-day Saints. From Personal Observation During a Six Months' Residence at Great Salt Lake City.* New York: Harper and Brothers, 1854.

Ferris, Cornelia. *The Mormons at Home; With Some Incidents of Travel From Missouri to California, 1852–3. In a Series of Letters.* New York: Dix and Edwards, 1856.

Ferry, Jeannette. *The Industrial Christian Home Association of Utah.* Salt Lake City: The Salt Lake Lithographic Company, 1893.

The First Presidency and the Council of the Twelve Apostles of The Church of Jesus Christ of Latter-day Saints, "The Family: A Proclamation to the World." Accessed March 30, 2013. http://lds.org/library/display/0,4945,161–1-11–1,00.html.

Froiseth, Jennie Anderson. *The Women of Mormonism; or The Story of Polygamy As Told by the Victims Themselves.* Detroit: C. G. G. Paine, 1887.

Fuller, Metta Victoria. *Mormon Wives: A Narrative of Facts Stranger Than Fiction.* New York: Derby and Jackson, 1856.

Gates, Susa Young. *History of the Young Ladies Mutual Improvement Association of the Church.* Salt Lake City: Deseret News, 1911.

A Gentile. *Social Problems of Today; or, The Mormon Question in Its Economic Aspects. A Study of Co-Operation and Arbitration in Mormondom, From the Standpoint of a Wage-Worker.* New York: D. D. Lum and Co., 1886.

A Gentile [Dyer D. Lum]. *Utah and Its People. Facts and Statistics Bearing on the "Mormon Problem."* New York: R.O. Ferrier and Co., Publishers, 1882.

Giles, Alfred Ellingwood. *Marriage: Monogamy and Polygamy on the Basis of Divine Law, of Natural Law, and of Constitutional Law: An Open Letter to the Massachusetts Members of Congress, by One of Their Constituents, With Observations on the Opinion of the Supreme Court in Reynolds Vs. [sic] United States, 98 U.S. Supreme Court Reports.* Boston: James Campbell, 1882.

Goodrich, E. S. *Mormonism Unveiled. The Other Side. From An American Standpoint.* [Salt Lake City?: Deseret News?], 1884.

Governor West and the Polygamists. Report of His Interview with Apostle Lorenzo Snow, May 13, 1886, at the Utah Penitentiary. [Salt Lake City?: s.n., 1886].

Graham, Mrs. M. M. *The Polygamist's Victim: or, The Life Experiences of the Author During a Six Years' Residence Among the Mormon Saints, Being a Description of the Massacres, Struggles, Dangers, Toils and Vicissitudes of Border Life.* San Francisco: Women's Union Printing Office, 1872.

Grant, Jedediah M. *Three Letters to the New York Herald, From J.M. Grant, of Utah.* [New York: s.n., 1852].

Green, Nelson Winch. *Fifteen Years Among the Mormons: Being the Narrative of Mrs. Mary Ettie V. Smith, Late of Great Salt Lake City; A Sister of One of the Mormon High Priests, She Having Been Personally Acquainted With Most of the Mormon Leaders, and Long in the Confidence of the "Prophet," Brigham Young.* New York: H. Dayton, Publishers, 1860.

———. *Fifteen Years' Residence With the Mormons. With Startling Disclosures of the Mysteries of Polygamy by a Sister of One of the High Priests.* Chicago: Phoenix Publishing Company, 1876.

Gunnison, John Williams. *The Mormons, or Latter-day Saints, in the Valley of the Great Salt Lake: A History of Their Rise and Progress, Peculiar Doctrines, Present Condition, and Prospects, Derived From Personal Observation During a Residence Among Them.* Philadelphia: J. B. Lippincott and Co., 1856.

Gurley, Z. H. *The Polygamic Revelation. Fraud! Fraud! Fraud.* Lamoni, Iowa: The True Latter Day Saints Herald Office, [1852].

Haskell, Dudley Chase. *Mormonism and Polygamy: An Address Delivered by D. C. Haskell, of Kansas, at Central Music Hall, Chicago, June 8, 1881, Before the National Convention of the American Home Missionary Society.* Lawrence, Kans.: Republican Journal Steam Printing Establishment, 1881.

Hemenway, Charles W. *Memoirs of My Day In and Out of Mormonism. Written in Prison, Undergoing Sentence for Alleged Libel.* Salt Lake City: Deseret News Company, 1887.

Hickman, William Adams. *Brigham's Destroying Angel: Being the Life, Confessions, and Startling Disclosures of the Notorious Bill Hickman, the Danite Chief of Utah.* New York: G. A. Crofutt, Publishers, 1872.

Howe, Eber D. *Mormonism Unvailed [sic]; or, A Faithful Account of That Singular Imposition and Delusion, From Its Rise to the Present Time.* Painesville, Ohio: Printed and Published by the Author, 1834.

Hyde, John, Jun. *Mormonism: Its Leaders and Designs.* 2nd ed. New York: W. P. Fetridge and Company, 1857.

The Inside of Mormonism. A Judicial Examination of the Endowment Oaths Administered in All the Mormon Temples, by the United States District Court for the Third Judicial District of Utah, to Determine Whether Membership in the Church is Consistent with Citizenship in the United States. Salt Lake City: Published by the Utah Americans, 1903.

Jackson, Joseph H. *The Adventures and Experience of Joseph H. Jackson: Disclosing the Depths of Mormon Villainy Practiced in Nauvoo.* Warsaw: Printed for the Publisher, 1846.

Jaques, John. *Catechism for Children, Exhibiting the Prominent Doctrines of The Church of Jesus Christ of Latter-day Saints.* Salt Lake City: David O. Calder, 1877.

———. *The Church of Jesus Christ of Latter-day Saints. Its Priesthood, Organization, Doc-*

trines, Ordinances and History. Salt Lake City: Deseret News Company, Printers and Publishers, 1882.

Jarman, W. *U.S.A. Uncle Sam's Abscess, or Hell Upon Earth for U.S. Uncle Sam.* Exeter, England: s.n., 1884.

.Johnson, Joseph. *The Great Mormon Fraud; or, The Church of Jesus Christ of Latter-Day Saints Proved to Have Had a Falsehood for Its Origin, a Record of Crime for Its History, and for Doctrines: Cruelty, Absurdity, and Infamy.* Manchester: Butterworth and Nodal, Printers, 1885.

Jones, M. W. *Salt Lake Fruit: A Thrilling Latter-Day Romance.* New York: M.W. Jones, 1891.

Kane, Elizabeth Wood. *Twelve Mormon Homes Visited in Succession on a Journey through Utah to Arizona.* Philadelphia: s.n., 1874.

Kent, Austin. *Conjugal Love—The True and the False.* [Stockholm?, New York: s.n., 1872].

Kidder, Daniel P. *Mormonism and the Mormons: A Historical View of the Rise and Progress of the Sect Self-Styled Latter-Day Saints.* New York: Lane and Scott, 1852.

Kimball, Sarah M. *Woman Suffrage Leaflet.* Salt Lake City: n.p., 1892.

King, Larry, and Gordon B. Hinckley. "Gordon B. Hinckley Interview," *Larry King Live*, CNN, September 8, 1998.

Lea, Henry Charles. *Bible View of Polygamy.* Philadelphia?: s.n., 1863.

Lee, John D. *A Mormon Chronicle: The Diaries of John D. Lee.* 2 vols. Edited by Robert Glass Cleland, and Juanita Brooks. San Marino, Calif.: Huntington Library, 1955.

———. *Mormonism Unveiled; or, The Life and Confessions of the Late Mormon Bishop, John D. Lee (Written By Himself) Embracing a History of Mormonism From Its Inception Down to the Present Time, With an Exposition of the Secret History, Signs, Symbols and Crimes of the Mormon Church; Also the True History of the Horrible Butchery Known as the Mountain Meadows Massacre.* St. Louis: Bryan, Brand and Co., 1877.

———. *Mormonism Unveiled: Including the Remarkable Life and Confessions of the Late Mormon Bishop, John D. Lee (Written by Himself): and Complete Life of Brigham Young, Embracing a History of Mormonism from its Inception Down to the Present Time, with an Exposition of the Secret History, Signs, Symbols, and Crimes of the Mormon Church: also the True History of the Horrible Butchery Known as the Mountain Meadows Massacre.* 10th ed. St. Louis: Sun Pub. Co., 1882.

Legislative Assembly of the Territory of Utah. *Acts, Resolutions, and Memorials.* Salt Lake City: Joseph Bull, public printer, 1870.

Lewis, Catharine. *Narrative of Some of the Proceedings of the Mormons; Giving an Account of Their Iniquities, With Particulars Concerning the Training of the Indians by Them, Description of the Mode of Endowment, Plurality of Wives, & C., & C.* Lynn [Mass.]: The Author, 1848.

Lieber, Francis. *A Manual of Political Ethics: Designed Chiefly for the Use of Colleges and Students at Law.* 2 vols. Boston: C. C. Little and J. Brown, 1839–1847.

———. *On Civil Liberty and Self Government.* London: Richard Bentley, 1853.

Lyford, C. P. *Brigham Young's Record of Blood! Or, the Necessity for That Famous "Bible and*

Revolver." *A Lecture Delivered in the First M. E. Church, Salt Lake City, Jan. 23d, 1876.* Salt Lake City: Tribune Publishing Company, [1876].

[MacKay, Chas]. *History of the Mormons, or Latter-Day Saints. With Memoirs of the Life and Death of Joseph Smith, the "American Mohamet."* Auburn: Miller, Orton, and Mulligan, 1854.

[Marshall, Charles]. *By a Recent Visitor to Utah. Characteristics of Mormonism.* N.p.: s.n., 1871.

Mason, John. *Latter-Day Saints: The Dupes of a Foolish and Wicked Imposture.* New York: Tract Society, [1850?].

McNiece, R. G., *Present Aspects of the Mormon Question.* New York: League for Social Service, [1898].

The Mormon Conspiracy to Establish an Independent Empire to Be Called the Kingdom of God on Earth. The Conspiracy Exposed by the Writings, Sermons, and Legislative Acts of the Prophets and Apostles of the Church. Salt Lake City: The Tribune Co., 1886.

A Mormon of 1831. The Crimes of the Latter Day Saints in Utah: A Demand for a Legislative Commission, a Book of Horrors. San Francisco: A. J. Leary, 1884.

"Mormon" Protest Against Injustice: An Appeal for Constitutional and Religious Liberty. Salt Lake City: Jos. Hyrum Parry and Co., 1885.

"Mormon" Women's Protest: An Appeal for Freedom, Justice and Equal Rights. The Ladies of The Church of Jesus Christ of Latter-day Saints Protest Against the Tyranny and Indecency of Federal Officials in Utah, and Against Their Own Disenfranchisement Without Cause. Full Account of Proceedings at the Great Mass Meeting Held in the Theatre, Salt Lake City, Utah, Saturday, March 6, 1886 ([Salt Lake City]: Deseret News, Printers, [1886?])

Mormonism Exposed: In Which Is Shown the Monstrous Imposture, the Blasphemy, and the Wicked Tendency of That Enormous Delusion, Advocated by a Professedly Religious Sect Calling Themselves "Latter Day Saints." New York: New York Watchman, 1842.

Mormonism, or, Some of the False Doctrines and Lying Abominations of the So-Called Latter-Day Saints Confuted and Exploded by the Bible, the Word of God. Ormskirk: Leak and Hutton, [ca. 1860].

Morris, Mary Lois Walker. *Before the Manifesto: The Life Writings of Mary Lois Walker Morris,* edited by Melissa Lambert Milewski. Logan, Utah: Utah State University Press, 2007.

Mulder, William, and A. Russell Mortensen, eds. *Among the Mormons: Historic Accounts by Contemporary Observers.* New York: Alfred A. Knopf, 1858.

Musser, Amos Milton. *Malicious Slanders Refuted: A Few Plain Facts Plainly Spoken, in Regard to the Pretended "Crisis" in Utah.* [Manchester? England: Millennial Star Print, 1878?].

———. *The Fruits of Mormonism by Non-Mormon Witnesses.* Salt Lake City: Deseret News Steam Printing Establishment, 1878.

Newman, J. P., and Orson Pratt. *A Sermon by The Rev. Dr. Newman, Pastor of the Metropolitan Methodist Church, on Plural Marriage, to Which Is Added an Answer by Elder Orson*

Pratt, *One of the Twelve Apostles of the Church of Jesus Christ of Latter-day Saints.* Salt Lake City: Printed at the Deseret News Office, 1870.

Nimmo, Joseph Jr. *The Mormon Usurpation, an Open Letter Addressed to the Committee on the Judiciary of the House of Representatives.* New York: The Long Islander Print, n.d.

Noble, Reverend F. A. *The Mormon Iniquity. A Discourse Delivered Before the New West Education Commission, in the First Congregational Church, Sunday Evening, November 2, 1884.* Chicago: Jameson and Morse, Printers, 1884.

One of the People [William Dallin]. *Opinions Concerning the Bible Law of Marriage.* Philadelphia: Claxton, Remsen, and Haffelfinger, 1871.

One Who Hates Imposture. *Mormonism Dissected; or, Knavery "On Two Sticks," Exposed: Composed Principally From Notes Which Were Taken From the Arguments of Dr. Orr, in the Recent Debate on the Athenticity* [sic] *of the "Book of Mormon," Between Him and E. H. Davis, Mormon Preacher, the Whole Being Designed As a Check to the Further Progress of Imposition, by Placing in the Hands of Every One the Means of Unmasking This "Latter Day" Humbug.* Bethania, Pa.: Printed by R. Chambers, 1841.

"Opponents of Prop 8 Demonstrate in Front of Church of the Latter Day Saints." Accessed December 18, 2010. http://www.life.com/image/83609692.

Our Constitutional Rights and Congressional Privileges, Containing the Declaration of Independence, Constitution, Washington's Farewell Address, 1862 Law, Poland Law, Edmunds Law, Edmunds Tucker Law, and Instructions to Registrars and Test Oath, and Suggestions of Central Committee of the People's Party. Salt Lake City: J.H. Parry and Co, 1887.

Paddock, Cornelia. *The Fate of Madame LaTour: A Tale of Great Salt Lake.* New York: Fords, Howard, and Hubert, 1881.

———. *In the Toils; or, Martyrs of the Latter Days.* Chicago: Shepard, Tobias, and Co., 1879.

———. *Saved at Last From Among the Mormons.* Springfield, Ohio: n.p., 1881.

Park, Mrs. S. E. *The Mormons: Their Religion, and Identity With the Bible.* 3rd ed. San Francisco: Jos. Winterburn and Co., 1875.

Parsons, Tyler. *Mormon Fanaticism Exposed: A Compendium of the Book of Mormon, or Joseph Smith's Golden Bible: Also, the Examination of Its Internal and External Evidences With the Argument to Refute Its Pretences to a Revelation From God, Argued . . . Between Freeman Nickerson, a Mormon, and the Author, Tyler Parsons.* Boston: Printed for the Author, 1841.

Penrose, Charles W. *Blood Atonement, As Taught by Leading Elders of the Church of Jesus Christ of Latter-day Saints. An Address Delivered in the Twelfth Ward Assembly Hall, Salt Lake City, October 12, 1884, by Elder Charles W. Penrose.* Salt Lake City: Printed at Juvenile Instructor Office, 1884.

Penrose, Romania B. Pratt. "Memoir of Romania B. Pratt, M.D." (1881). Accessed June 27, 2011. http://jared.pratt-family.org/parley_family_histories/romania_bunnell_memoirs.html.

Petit, Veronique. *Plural Marriage the Heart-History of Adele Hersch.* 4th ed. Ithaca: New York: E. D. Norton, Printer, 1855.

Philips, George Whitfield. *The Mormon Menace: A Discourse Before the New West Education Commission on Its Fifth Anniversary at Chicago November 15, 1885*. Worcester, Mass.: [s.n.], 1885.

Pickard, Samuel. *Autobiography of a Pioneer, or, The Nativity, Experience, Travels, and Ministerial Labors of Rev. Samuel Pickard, the "Converted Quaker": Containing Stirring Incidents and Practical Thoughts; With Sermons by the Author, and Some Account of the Labors of Elder Jacob Knapp*, edited by O. T. Conger. Chicago: Church and Goodman, 1866.

"Polygamy." Accessed July 6, 2012. http://attorneygeneral.utah.gov/polygamy.html.

"Polygamy: Latter-day Saints and the Practice of Plural Marriage." Accessed July 6, 2012. www.mormonnewsroom.org/article/polygamy-latter-day-saints-and-the-practice-of-plural-marriage.

Porter, Kirk, comp. *National Party Platforms*. New York: The MacMillan Company, 1924.

Pratt, Belinda Marden. *Defence of Polygamy, by a Lady of Utah, in a Letter to Her Sister in New Hampshire*. Salt Lake City: n.p., 1854.

Pratt, Louisa Barnes. *The History of Louisa Barnes Pratt: Being the Autobiography of a Mormon Missionary, Widow, and Pioneer*, edited by S. George Ellsworth. Logan, Utah: Utah State University Press, 1998.

Pratt, Orson. *A Series of Pamphlets by Orson Pratt, One of the Twelve Apostles of the Church of Jesus Christ of Latter-day Saints, With Portrait*. Liverpool: Franklin D. Richards, 1851.

Pratt, Orson, and J. P. Newman. *The Bible and Polygamy. Does the Bible Sanction Polygamy? A Discussion Between Professor Orson Pratt, One of the Twelve Apostles of the Church of Jesus Christ of Latter-day Saints, and Rev. Doctor J. P. Newman, Chaplain of the United States Senate, in the New Tabernacle, Salt Lake City, August 12, 13, and 14, 1870. To Which Is Added Three Sermons on the Same Subject, by Prest. George A. Smith and Orson Pratt and George Q. Cannon*. Salt Lake City: The Deseret News Steam Printing Establishment, 1874.

Pratt, Parley P. *Mormonism Unveiled: Zion's Watchman Unmasked, and Its Editor, Mr. L. R. Sunderland, Exposed: Truth Vindicated: The Devil Mad, and Priestcraft in Danger*. New York: Published by O. Pratt and E. Fordham, 1838.

Proclamation of the Twelve Apostles of The Church of Jesus Christ of Latter-day Saints. [New York: Prophet Office, 1845?].

Proceedings in Mass Meeting of the Ladies of Salt Lake City, to Protest Against the Passage of Cullom's Bill, January 14, 1870. [Salt Lake City?]: n.p., 1870.

Proclamation of the Twelve Apostles of the Church of Jesus Christ of Latter-day Saints. [New York: Prophet Office, 1845?].

Rae, W. F. *Westward by Rail: The New Route to the East*. New York: D. Appleton and Company, 1871.

"Reports of Polygamy Story Vary Across the World." Accessed July 6, 2012. www.mormonnewsroom.org/ldsnewsroom/eng/news-releases-stories/reports-of-polygamy-story-vary-across-the-world.

Rigdon, Sidney. *Oration Delivered by Mr. S. Rigdon on the 4th of July, 1838*. Far West, Mo.: Journal Office, 1838.

Roberts, B. H. *Comprehensive History of The Church of Jesus Christ of Latter-day Saints. Century I.* 6 vols. New York: National Americana Society, 1909–1915.

———. *Mormonism. The Relations of the Church to Christian Sects.* Salt Lake City: the Church, Deseret News Print, n.d.

Robinson, Phil. *Sinners and Saints: A Tour Across the States and Around Them, With Three Months Among the Mormons.* Boston: Roberts Brothers, 1883.

Russell, John. *Claudine Lavalle; or, the First Convict; The Mormoness, or, The Trials of Mary Maverick.* Alton: Courier Steam Press Print, 1853.

Schroeder, Theodore Albert. *Polygamy and the Constitution.* [New York?: s.n.], 1906.

———. *Some Facts Concerning Polygamy.* [Salt Lake City: s.n.], c1898.

Seneca Falls Convention of 1848. "Declaration of Sentiments and Resolutions." In *Issues in Feminism: An Introduction to Women's Studies.* 4th ed., edited by Sheila Ruth. Mountain View, Calif.: Mayfield Publishing Company, 1998.

"Senior Church Leader Appeals to Media to Make Distinction." Accessed July 6, 2012. www.mormonnewsroom.org/ldsnewsroom/eng/news-releases-stories/senior -church-leader-appeals-to-media-to-make-distinction.

Sheldon, William. *Mormonism Examined: or, Was Joseph Smith a Divinely Inspired Prophet?* Broadhead, Wis.: William Sheldon, n.d.

Shipp, Ellis Reynolds. *While Others Slept: Autobiography and Journal of Ellis Reynolds Shipp, M.D.* Salt Lake City: Bookcraft, Inc., 1962.

Simms, Joseph. *Physiognomy Illustrated, or, Nature's Revelations of Character. A Description of the Mental, Moral, and Volitive Dispositions of Mankind, As Manifested in the Human Form and Countenance.* 8th ed. New York: Murray Hill, 1887.

Sincere Friend and Well-Wisher. *Mormonism Examined: A Few Kind Words to a Mormon.* [Birmingham: J. Groom, 1855?].

The Situation in Utah. The Discussions of the Christian Convention, Held in Salt Lake City, Utah. April 1888. Salt Lake City: Parsons, Kendall and Co., 1888.

Smalling, Cyrus. *The Mormons; or, Knavery Exposed.* Frankford, Pa.: E. G. Lee, 1841.

Smith, Elbert A. *All Brighamite Roads Lead to Polygamy.* Lamoni, Iowa: Herald House, [n.d.].

Smith, George Albert. *The Rise, Progress, and Travels of the Church of Jesus Christ of Latter-day Saints, Being a Series of Answers to Questions, Including the Revelation on Celestial Marriage and a Brief Account of the Settlement of Salt Lake Valley With Interesting Statistics, by President George A. Smith.* Liverpool: Published by Albert Carrington, 1873.

Smith, Joseph, III. *Reply to Orson Pratt, by Joseph Smith, President of the Reorganized Church of Jesus Christ of Latter Day Saints.* Plano, Ill.: Published by the Reorganized Church of Jesus Christ of Latter Day Saints, [1870?].

Smith, Joseph, Jr. *The Book of Mormon.* Nauvoo, Illinois: Printed by Robinson and Smith, Stereotyped by Shepard and Steams, 1840.

———. *The Book of Mormon.* Salt Lake City: The Church of Jesus Christ of Latter-day Saints, 1986.

———. *The Doctrine and Covenants of The Church of Jesus Christ of Latter-day Saints.* Salt Lake City: The Church of Jesus Christ of Latter-day Saints, 1986.

———. *The Essential Joseph Smith.* Salt Lake City: Signature Books, 1995.

———. *General Smith's Views of the Powers and Policy of the Government of the United States.* Nauvoo, Ill.: John Taylor, Printer, 1884.

———. *The Holy Scriptures, Containing the Old and New Testaments: An Inspired Version of the Authorized Version.* Independence, Mo.: Herald Publishing House, 1844.

———. *Joseph Smith: Selected Sermons and Writings,* edited by Robert L. Millet. New York: Paulist Press, 1990.

———. *The Pearl of Great Price.* Salt Lake City: The Church of Jesus Christ of Latter-day Saints, 1977.

———. *Teachings of the Prophet Joseph Smith: Taken From His Sermons and Writings As They Are Found in the Documentary History and Other Publications of the Church and Written or Published in the Days of the Prophet's Ministry.* Comp. Joseph Fielding Smith. Salt Lake City: Deseret Book Co., 1976.

Smith, Joseph, Jr., and Brigham Young. *Discourses Delivered by Presidents Joseph Smith and Brigham Young, on the Relation of "Mormons" to the Government of the United States.* Salt Lake City: Printed at the Office of the Deseret News, 1855.

Smith, Joseph, Jr., Oliver Cowdery, Sidney Rigdon, and Frederick G. Williams, comps. *Doctrine and Covenants of The Church of The Latter Day Saints: Carefully Selected From the Revelations of God.* Independence, Mo.: Reprinted by the Herald House Publishing Division of the Reorganized Church of Jesus Christ of Latter Day Saints, 1971.

Smith, Joseph, Jr., and John Taylor. *Items of Church History, The Government of God, and The Gift of the Holy Ghost.* Salt Lake City: Jos. Hyrum Parry and Co., 1886.

Smith, Joseph F. *Gospel Doctrine: Selections from the Sermons and Writings of Joseph F. Smith,* selected and arranged by John A. Widtsoe. Salt Lake City: Deseret Book Co., 1961.

Smith, William. *Mormonism—A True Account of the Origin of the Book of Mormon.* Lamoni, Iowa: Herald Steam Book and Job Office, 1883.

Social Problems of Today; or, The Mormon Question in Its Economic Aspects. A Study of Co-Operation and Arbitration in Mormondom, From the Standpoint of a Wage-Worker. Port Jervis, N.Y.: D. D. Lum and Co., 1886.

Speech of Hon. Justin S. Merrill of Vermont, on Utah Territory and Its Law—Polygamy and Its License; Delivered in the House of Representatives, February 23, 1857. Washington, D.C., 1857.

Spencer, Orson. *Patriarchal Order, or Plurality of Wives!* Liverpool: S. W. Richards, [1853].

Stanton, Elizabeth Cady. *Eighty Years and More (1815–1897): Reminiscences of Elizabeth Cady Stanton.* New York: European Publishing Company, 1898.

Stanton, Mary O. *Encyclopedia of Face and Form Reading.* Philadelphia: F. A. Davis Company, 1895.

Stenhouse, Fanny. *"Tell It All": The Story of a Life's Experience in Mormonism. An Autobiography . . . Including a Full Account of the Mountain Meadows Massacre, and the Life, Confession, and Execution of Bishop John D. Lee.* Hartford, Conn.: A. D. Worthington and Co., 1874.

Stenhouse, T. B. H. *An Englishwoman in Utah: The Story of a Life's Experience in Mormonism: An Autobiography*. London: Sampson Low, Marston, Searle, and Rivington, 1882.

Stillman, James Wells. *The Constitutional and Legal Aspects of the Mormon Question: Speech of James W. Stillman, in Science Hall, Boston, Mass., April 2d, 1882*. Boston: Stillman, 1882.

Sunderland, LaRoy. *Mormonism Exposed: In Which Is Shown the Monstrous Imposture, the Blasphemy, and the Wicked Tendency, of That Enormous Delusion, Advocated by a Professedly Religious Sect, Calling Themselves "Latter Day Saints."* New York: Printed and Published at the Office of the New York Watchman, 1842.

Swartzell, William. *Mormonism Exposed: Being a Journal of Residence in Missouri From the 28th Day of May to the 20th of August, 1838, Together With an Appendix Containing the Revelation Concerning the Golden Bible, With Numerous Extracts From the "Book of Covenants" & C. & C.* Pittsburgh: A. Ingram, Jr., Printer, 1840.

Tanner, Mary Jane Mount. *A Fragment: The Autobiography of Mary Jane Mount Tanner*, edited by Margery W. Ward. Salt Lake City: Tanner Trust Fund, 1980.

Taylder, T. W. P. *Twenty Reasons for Rejecting Mormonism*. London: Partridge and Co, 1857.

Taylor, John. *The Gospel Kingdom: Selections From the Writings and Discourses of John Taylor*, selected, arranged, and annotated by G. Homer Durham. Salt Lake City: Bookcraft, Inc., 1987.

———. *The Government of God*. Liverpool: S. W. Richards, 1852.

———. *On Marriage*. Salt Lake City, Utah: Deseret News Company, 1882.

Tucker, Pomeroy. *The Origin, Rise, and Progress of Mormonism: Biography of Its Founders and History of Its Church: Personal Remembrances and Historical Collections Hitherto Unwritten*. New York: D. Appleton and Company, 1867.

Tullidge, Edward W. *The Life of Brigham Young; or, Utah and Her Founders*. New York: n.p., 1876.

———. *The Women of Mormondom*. New York: [Tullidge and Crandall], 1877.

Turner, J. B. *Mormonism in All Ages; or, The Rise, Progress, and Causes of Mormonism: With the Biography of Its Owner and Founder, Joseph Smith Junior*. New York: Published by Platt and Peters, 1842.

Utah Compromise Club. *A Plan to Solve the Utah Problem*. Salt Lake City: s.n., 1880.

Utah Statehood. Reasons Why It Should Not Be Granted. Salt Lake City: Tribune Print, 1887.

Van Deusen, Increase McGee. *Startling Disclosures of the Wonderful Ceremonies of the Mormon Spiritual Wife System: Being the Celebrated "Endowment," as It Was Acted by Upwards of Twelve Thousand Men and Women in Secret, in the Nauvoo Temple, in 1846, and Said to Have Been Revealed From God*. New York: [s.n.], 1852.

———. *The Sublime and Ridiculous Blended: Called, the Endowment: As Was Acted, by Upwards of Twelve Thousand, in Secret, in the Nauvoo Temple, Said to Be Revealed From God as Reward for Building That Splendid Edifice, and the Express Object for Which It Was Built*. New York: The Author, 1848.

Van Deusen, Increase McGee, and Maria Van Deusen. *Spiritual Delusions: Being a Key to the Mysteries of Mormonism, Exposing the Particulars of That Astounding Heresy, the*

Spiritual Wife System, As Practiced by Brigham Young, of Utah. New York: I. and M. Van Deusen, 1854.

———. *Startling Disclosures of the Great Mormon Conspiracy Against the Liberties of This Country: Being the Celebrated "Endowment," As It Was Acted by Upwards of Twelve Thousand Men and Women in Secret in the Nauvoo Temple in 1846 and Said to Have Been Revealed From God.* New York: Blake and Jackson, 1849.

Vogel, Dan, ed. *Early Mormon Documents.* 5 vols. Salt Lake City: Signature Books, 1996–2003.

Waite, Mrs. C. V. *The Mormon Prophet and His Harem; or, An Authentic History of Brigham Young, His Numerous Wives and Children.* 5th ed. Chicago: J. S. Goodman and Company, 1868.

Ward, Artemus. *Artemus Ward: His Travels.* New York: Carleton, 1865.

———. "A. Ward Among the Mormons." *Artemus Ward in London: Comprising the Letters to "Punch" and Other Humorous Papers.* London: Hotten, [1870].

Ward, Austin N. *The Husband in Utah; or, Sights and Scenes Among the Mormons: With Remarks on Their Moral and Social Economy,* edited by Maria Ward. New York: Derby and Jackson, 1859.

———. *Male Life Among the Mormons; or, The Husband in Utah.* New York: Derby and Jackson, 1859.

———. *Male Life Among the Mormons; or, The Husband in Utah: Detailing Sights and Scenes Among the Mormons; With Remarks on Their Moral and Social Economy.* Philadelphia: John E. Potter and Company, 1863.

Ward, Maria [pseud.] *Female Life among the Mormons: A Narrative of Many Years' Personal Experience.* New York: J. C. Derby, 1855.

Ward, Maria. *The Mormon Wife: A Story of the Sacrifices, Sorrows, and Sufferings of Women.* Hartford, Conn.: Hartford Press, 1872.

Waters, William Elkanah. *Life among the Mormons, and a March to Their Zion. To Which Is Added a Chapter on the Indians of the Plains and Mountains of the West.* New York: Moorhead, Simpson and Bond, 1868.

Wells, Emmeline B., Diaries, 1844–1920. University of Utah, Special Collections Division.

Wells, Samuel Robert. *How to Read Character: A New Illustrated Handbook of Phrenology and Physiognomy for Students and Examiners: With a Descriptive Chart.* New York: Samuel R. Wells, Publisher, 1874.

Whitney, Helen Mar. *Why We Practice Plural Marriage.* Salt Lake City: Published at the Juvenile Instructor Office, 1884.

Woodhouse, W. W. *Mormonism an Imposture; or, The Doctrines of the So-Called Latter-Day Saints, Proved to Be Utterly Opposed to the Word of God.* Ipswich, N.Y.: N. Pannifer and J. M. Burton and Co., 1853.

Woodruff, Wilford. *The Discourses of Wilford Woodruff: Fourth President of The Church of Jesus Christ of Latter-day Saints,* edited by G. Homer Durham. Salt Lake City: Bookcraft, Inc., [1998].

———. *Wilford Woodruff's Journals, 1833–1898*. vol. 1, 6 vols. edited by Scott Kenney. Midvale, Utah: Signature Books, 1983–1984.

Woodward, Charles L., coll. and arr. *The First Half Century of Mormonism. Papers, Engravings, Photographs, and Autograph Letters*, vol. 1. New York: n.p., 1880.

Young, Ann Eliza. *Life in Mormon Bondage: A Complete Exposé of Its False Prophets, Murderous Danites, Despotic Rulers and Hypnotized, Deluded Subjects*. Philadelphia: Aldine Press, 1908.

———. *Wife No. 19: or, The Story of a Life in Bondage: Being a Complete Exposé of Mormonism, and Revealing the Sorrows, Sacrifices and Sufferings of Women in Polygamy*. Hartford, Conn.: Dustin, Gilman and Co., 1875.

Young, Brigham. *Brigham Young's Defence of Polygamy; or Marriage and Morals, in the Great Salt Lake City, with Six Reasons for a Plurality of Wives, as Delivered Before the Twelve Apostles of the Church of Jesus Christ, of the Latter-day Saints, at Utah*. London: C. Elliot, [1861].

———. *Discourses of Brigham Young*. Selected and arranged by John A. Widtsoe. Salt Lake City: Deseret Book Co., 1978.

———. *The Teachings of President Brigham Young*, vol. 3, compiled and edited by Fred C. Collier. Salt Lake City: Collier's, 1987.

Young, Brigham, President of The Church of Jesus Christ of Latter-day Saints, His Two Counsellors [*sic*], the Twelve Apostles, and Others. *Journal of Discourses*. 26 vols. 1855–1886. Reprint, [Salt Lake City: Deseret Book Co.], 1966.

GOVERNMENT DOCUMENTS AND COURT CASES

Ableman v. Booth, 62 U.S. 62 (1859).

Clawson v. United States, 114 U.S. 55 (1885).

Davis v. Beason, 133 U.S. 333, 341 (1890).

Late Corporation of The Church of Jesus Christ of Latter-day Saints v. United States, 136 U.S. 1 (1890).

Minor v. Happersett, 88 U.S. (21 Wall.) 162 (1875).

Murphy v. Ramsey, 114 U.S. 15 (1885).

Reynolds v. United States, 98 U.S. 145 (1879).

State of North Carolina v. William Frederick Rhodes, 61 N.C. (Phil. Law) 453 (1868).

In re Snow, 120 U.S. 274 (1887).

United States. Congress. *Congressional Globe*. Washington, D.C.: Blair and Rives, 1834–1873.

United States. Congress. *Congressional Record*. Washington, D.C.: United States Government Printing Office, 1979.

United States. Congress. *Congressional Serial Set*. Washington, D.C.: United States Government Printing Office, 1852–1896.

United States. Congress. House. *Journal of the House of Representatives of the United States*. Washington, D.C.: United States Government Printing Office, 1850–1896.

United States. Congress. Senate. *Journal of the Senate of the United States*, Washington, D.C.: United States Government Printing Office, 1850–1896.

United States. *United States Statutes at Large.* Washington, D.C.: United States Government Printing Office, 1860–1890.

United States. President. *A Compilation of the Messages and Papers of the Presidents 1789–1897.* Comp. James D. Richardson. Washington, D.C.: United States Government Printing Office, 1896–1899.

United States v. Cannon, 118 U.S. 355 (1886).

Utah. *Acts, Resolutions and Memorials Passed at the Several Annual Sessions of the Legislative Assembly of the Territory of Utah.* Salt Lake City: Joseph Cain, 1855.

Utah. *Compiled Laws of Utah.* Salt Lake City: Herbert Pembroke, 1888.

Secondary Sources

Adams, Arlin M., and Charles J. Emmerich. *A Nation Dedicated to Religious Liberty: The Constitutional Heritage of the Religion Clauses.* Philadelphia: University of Pennsylvania Press, 1990.

Alexander, Thomas G., ed. *Great Basin Kingdom Revisited: Contemporary Perspectives.* Logan, Utah: Utah State University Press, 1991.

Alexander, Thomas G. "An Experiment in Progressive Legislation: The Granting of Woman Suffrage in Utah in 1870." In *Battle for the Ballot: Essays on Woman Suffrage in Utah, 1870–1896,* edited by Carol Cornwall Madsen, 105–115. Logan, Utah: Utah State University Press, 1997.

———. *Mormonism in Transition: A History of the Latter-day Saints, 1890–1930.* Urbana: University of Illinois Press, 1986.

———. *Mormons and Gentiles: A History of Salt Lake City.* Boulder, Colo.: Pruett Publishing Company, 1984.

———. *Things in Heaven and Earth: The Life and Times of Wilford Woodruff, a Mormon Prophet.* Salt Lake City: Signature Books, 1991.

———. "Wilford Woodruff and the Mormon Reformation of 1855–57." *Dialogue: A Journal of Mormon Thought* 25 (Summer 1992): 25–39.

Allen, James B. "The Unusual Jurisdiction of the County Probate Courts in the Territory of Utah." *Utah Historical Quarterly* 36 (Spring 1968): 132–42.

Allen, James B., and Leonard J. Arrington. "Mormon Origins in New York: An Introductory Analysis." *BYU Studies* 9, no. 3 (Spring 1969): 241–74.

Allen, James B., Leonard J. Arrington, and Ronald W. Walker. *Studies in Mormon History 1830–1997: An Indexed Bibliography.* Urbana: University of Illinois Press, 2000.

Allen, James B., and Glen M. Leonard. *The Story of the Latter-day Saints.* Salt Lake City: Deseret Book Co., 1992.

Allen, James B., Ronald W. Walker, and David J. Whittaker. *Mormon History, 1830–1997: An Indexed Bibliography.* Urbana: University of Illinois Press, 2000.

Allison, Robert J. *The Crescent Obscured: The United States and the Muslim World, 1776–1815.* Chicago: University of Chicago Press, 2000.

Allred, Janice Merrill. *God the Mother and Other Theological Essays.* Salt Lake City: Signature Books, 1997.

Altman, Irwin, and Joseph Ginat. *Polygamous Families in Contemporary Society.* Cambridge: Cambridge University Press, 1996.

Anderson, Benedict. *Imagined Communities: Reflections on the Origin and Spread of Nationalism.* Revised edition. London: Verso, 1991.

Anderson, Lavina Fielding, and Maureen Ursenbach Beecher, eds. *Sisters in Spirit: Mormon Women in Historical and Cultural Perspective.* Urbana: University of Illinois Press, 1987.

Andrus, Hyrum L. *Doctrines of the Kingdom—Foundations of the Millennial Kingdom of Christ,* vol. 3. Salt Lake City: Bookcraft, Inc., 1973.

———. *Joseph Smith and World Government.* Salt Lake City: Deseret Book Co., 1958.

Armstrong, Nancy. *Desire and Domestic Fiction: A Political History of the Novel.* New York: Oxford University Press, 1987.

Arrington, Chris Rigby. "The Finest of Fabrics: Mormon Women and the Silk Industry in Early Utah." *Utah Historical Quarterly* 46 (Fall 1978): 376–96.

Arrington, Leonard J. "The Economic Role of Pioneer Mormon Women." *Western Humanities Review* 9 (Spring 1955): 145–65.

———. *Brigham Young: American Moses.* New York: Alfred A. Knopf, 1985.

———. "Crusade Against Theocracy: The Reminiscences of Judge Jacob Smith Boreman of Utah, 1872–1877." *The Huntington Library Quarterly* 24, no. 1 (November 1960): 1–45.

———. *Great Basin Kingdom: An Economic History of the Latter-day Saints, 1830–1900.* Lincoln: University of Nebraska Press, 1966.

———. "Mormon Origins in New York: An Introductory Analysis." *BYU Studies* 9, no. 3 (Spring 1969): 241–73.

———. "Persons for All Seasons: Women in Mormon History." *BYU Studies* 20, no. 1 (Fall 1979): 39–58.

———. "Religion and Economics in Mormon History." *BYU Studies* 3 (Spring and Summer, 1961): 15–33.

Arrington, Leonard J., and Maureen Ursenbach Beecher, eds. *New Views of Mormon History: A Collection of Essays in Honor of Leonard Arrington.* Salt Lake City: University of Utah Press, 1987.

Arrington, Leonard J., and Davis Bitton. *The Mormon Experience: A History of the Latter-day Saints.* 2nd ed. Urbana: University of Illinois Press, 1992.

———. *Mormons and Their Historians.* Salt Lake City: University of Utah Press, 1988.

Arrington, Leonard J., Feramorz Y. Fox, and Dean L. May. *Building the City of God: Community and Cooperation among the Mormons.* 2nd ed. Urbana: University of Illinois Press, 1992.

Arrington, Leonard J., and Jon Haupt. "Intolerable Zion: The Image of Mormonism in Nineteenth-Century American Literature." *Western Humanities Review* 22 (Summer 1968): 243–60.

Arrington, Leonard J., and Susan Arrington Madsen. *Sunbonnet Sisters: True Stories of Mormon Women and Frontier Life.* Salt Lake City: Bookcraft, Inc., 1984.

Bachman, Daniel W. "New Light on an Old Hypothesis: The Ohio Origins of the Revelation on Eternal Marriage." *Journal of Mormon History* 5 (1978): 19–31.

———. "A Study of the Mormon Practice of Plural Marriage before the Death of Joseph Smith." Master's thesis, Purdue University, 1975.

Backman, Milton V., Jr. *American Religions and the Rise of Mormonism.* Salt Lake City: Bookcraft, Inc., 1965.

———. *The Heavens Resound: A History of the Latter-day Saints in Ohio, 1830–1838.* Salt Lake City: Deseret Book Co., 1983.

Bagley, Will. *Blood of the Prophets: Brigham Young and the Massacre at Mountain Meadows.* Norman: University of Oklahoma Press, 2002.

Baker, Paula. "The Domestication of Politics: Women and American Political Society, 1780–1920." *American Historical Review* 89 (June 1984): 620–47.

Barkun, Michael. *Crucible of the Millennium: The Burned-Over District of New York in the 1840s.* Syracuse: Syracuse University Press, 1986.

Basch, Norma. "The Emerging Legal History of Women in the United States: Property, Divorce, and the Constitution." *Signs* 12, no. 1 (Autumn 1986): 97–117.

———. *In the Eyes of the Law: Women, Marriage, and Property in Nineteenth-Century New York.* Ithaca: Cornell University Press, 1982.

———. "Invisible Women: The Legal Fiction of Marital Unity in Nineteenth-Century America." *Feminist Studies* 5, no. 2 (Summer 1979): 346–66.

Bean, Lee L., Geraldine P. Mineau, and Douglas L. Anderton. *Fertility Change on the American Frontier: Adaptation and Innovation.* Berkeley: University of California Press, 1990.

Beecher, Maureen Ursenbach. "A Feminist among the Mormons: Charlotte Ives Cobb Godbe Kirby." *Utah Historical Quarterly* 59 (Winter 1991): 22–31.

———. "Inadvertent Disclosure: Autobiography in the Poetry of Eliza R. Snow." *Dialogue: A Journal of Mormon Thought* 23 (Spring 1990): 54–107.

Beecher, Maureen Ursenbach, Janath Russell Cannon, and Jill Mulvey Derr. *Women of Covenant: The Story of the Relief Society.* Salt Lake City: Deseret Book Co., 1992.

Beecher, Maureen Ursenbach, and Patricia Lyn Scott. "Mormon Women: A Bibliography in Process, 1977–1985." *Journal of Mormon History* 12 (1985): 113–28.

Beeton, Beverly. "Woman Suffrage in Territorial Utah." *Utah Historical Quarterly* 46, no. 2 (Spring 1978): 100–120.

———. *Women Vote in the West: The Woman Suffrage Movement, 1869–1896.* New York: Garland Publishing, Inc. 1986.

Beeton, Beverly, and G. Thomas Edwards. "Susan B. Anthony's Woman Suffrage Crusade in the American West." *Journal of the West* 21 (April 1982): 5–15.

Bennion, Janet. *Polygamy in Primetime: Media, Gender, and Politics in Mormon Fundamentalism.* Waltham, Mass.: Brandeis University Press, 2012.

———. *Women of Principle: Female Networking in Contemporary Mormon Polygyny.* New York: Oxford University Press, 1998.

Bennion, Lowell Ben. "The Incidence of Mormon Polygamy in 1880: 'Dixie' Versus Davis Stake." *Journal of Mormon History* 11 (1984): 27–42.

Bennion, Sherilyn Cox. "Enterprising Ladies: Utah's Nineteenth-Century Women Editors." *Utah Historical Quarterly* 49, no. 3 (Summer 1981): 291–304.

———. "The *Woman's Exponent*: Forty-Two Years of Speaking for Women." *Utah Historical Quarterly* 44 (Summer 1976): 222–39.

Bentley, Nancy. "Marriage as Treason: Polygamy, Nation, and the Novel." In *The Futures of American Studies*, edited by Donald E. Pease and Robyn Wiegman, 341–70. Durham: Duke University Press, 2002.

Bercaw, Nancy. *Gendered Freedoms: Race, Rights, and the Politics of Household in the Delta, 1861–1875*. Gainesville: University Press of Florida, 2003.

Bigler, David L. *Forgotten Kingdom: The Mormon Theocracy in the American West, 1847–1896*. Spokane, Wash.: Arthur H. Clark Co., 1998.

Bitton, Davis. "Mormon Polygamy: A Review Article." *Journal of Mormon History* 4 (1977): 101–18.

Bitton, Davis, and Gary L. Bunker. "Double Jeopardy: Visual Images of Mormon Women to 1914." *Utah Historical Quarterly* 46, no. 2 (Spring 1978): 184–202.

———. "Mesmerism and Mormonism." *BYU Studies* 15, no. 2 (Winter 1975): 146–70.

———. *The Mormon Graphic Image, 1834–1914*. Salt Lake City: University of Utah Press, 1983.

———. "Polygamous Eyes: A Note on Mormon Physiognomy." *Dialogue: A Journal of Mormon Thought* 12, no. 3 (Fall 1979): 114–19.

Bloch, Ruth. "The American Revolution, Wife Beating, and the Emergent Value of Privacy." *Early American Studies* 5, no. 2 (Fall 2007): 223–51.

Bloom, Harold. *The American Religion: The Emergence of the Post-Christian Nation*. New York: Simon and Schuster, 1992.

Boylan, Anne M. *The Origins of Women's Activism: New York and Boston, 1797–1840*. Chapel Hill: University of North Carolina Press, 2002.

Bradley, Don. "Mormon Polygamy before Nauvoo? The Relationship of Joseph Smith and Fanny Alger." In *The Persistence of Polygamy: Joseph Smith and the Origins of Nauvoo Polygamy*. Edited by Newell G. Bringhurst and Craig L. Foster, 14–58. Independence, Mo.: John Whitmer Books, 2010.

Bradley, Martha Sonntag. "Changed Faces: The Official LDS Position on Polygamy, 1890–1990." *Sunstone* 14 (February 1990): 26–33.

———. *Kidnapped From That Land: The Government Raids on the Polygamists of Short Creek*. Salt Lake City: University of Utah Press, 1993.

———. "Out of the Closet and Into the Fire: The New Mormon Historians' Take on Polygamy." In *Excavating Mormon Pasts: The New Historiography of the Last Half Century*, edited by Newell G. Bringhurst and Lavina Fielding Anderson, 303–22. Salt Lake City: Greg Kofford Books, 2004.

———. "Polygamy-Practicing Mormons." In *Religions of the World: A Comprehensive Encyclopedia of Beliefs and Practices*, 4 vols., edited by J. Gordon Melton and Martin Baumann, 1023–25. Santa Barbara, Calif.; Denver, Colo.; and Oxford, England: ABC-CLIO, 2002.

Bradley, Martha Sonntag, and Mary Firmage Woodward. "Plurality, Patriarchy, and the

Priestess: Zina D. H. Young's Nauvoo Marriage." *Journal of Mormon History* 20 (Spring 1994): 84–118.

Bringhurst, Newell G. *Saints, Slaves, and Blacks: The Changing Place of Black People Within Mormonism*. Westport, Conn.: Greenwood Press, 1981.

Bringhurst, Newell G., and Craig L. Foster. *Mormon Quest for the Presidency*. Independence, Mo.: John Whitmer Books, 2008.

Brodie, Fawn. *No Man Knows My History: The Life of Joseph Smith, the Mormon Prophet*. New York: Alfred A. Knopf, 1971.

Brooke, John L. *The Refiner's Fire: The Making of Mormon Cosmology, 1644–1844*. Cambridge: Cambridge University Press, 1996.

Brooks, Juanita. *John Doyle Lee: Zealot, Pioneer Builder, Scapegoat*. Logan: Utah State University Press, 1992.

———. *The Mountain Meadows Massacre*. Norman: University of Oklahoma Press, 1966.

Brown, Gillian. *Domestic Individualism: Imagining Self in Nineteenth-Century America*. Berkeley: University of California Press, 1990.

Brown, Samuel M. "Early Mormon Adoption Theology and the Mechanics of Salvation." *Journal of Mormon History* 37 (Summer 2011): 3–52.

Buerger, David John. *The Mysteries of Godliness: A History of Mormon Temple Worship*. Salt Lake City: Signature Books, 2002.

Buice, David. "A Stench in the Nostrils of Honest Men: Southern Democrats and the Edmunds Act of 1882." *Dialogue: A Journal of Mormon Thought* 21 (Autumn 1988): 100–113.

Burgess-Olson, Vicky. "Family Structure and Dynamics in Utah Mormon Families: 1847–1885." Ph.D. diss., Northwestern University, 1975.

———, ed. *Sister Saints*. Provo, Utah: Brigham Young University Press, 1978.

Burgett, Bruce. "On the Mormon Question: Race, Sex, and Polygamy in the 1850s and 1990s." *American Quarterly* 57, no. 1 (March 2002): 75–102.

Bush, Lester. "Mormon 'Physiology,' 1850–1875." *Bulletin of the History of Medicine* 56, no. 2 (Summer 1982): 218–37.

———. "A Peculiar People: 'The Physiological Aspects of Mormonism 1850–1875.'" *Dialogue: A Journal of Mormon Thought* 12, no. 3 (Fall 1979): 61–83.

Bushman, Claudia, ed. *Mormon Sisters: Women in Early Utah*. Cambridge, Mass.: Emmeline Press, 1976.

Bushman, Claudia, and Richard L. Bushman. *Building the Kingdom: A History of Mormons in America*. New York: Oxford University Press, 2001.

———. *Mormons in America*. New York: Oxford University Press, 1999.

Bushman, Richard L. *Believing History: Latter-day Saint Essays*, edited by Reid L. Neilson and Jed Woodworth. New York: Columbia University Press, 2004.

———. *Joseph Smith and the Beginnings of Mormonism*. Urbana: University of Illinois Press, 1984.

———. *Joseph Smith: Rough Stone Rolling*. New York: Alfred A. Knopf, 2005.

———. "Mormon Persecutions in Missouri, 1833." *BYU Studies* 3, no. 1 (Winter 1960): 11–20.

Butler, Jon. *Awash in a Sea of Faith: Christianizing the American People.* Cambridge, Mass.: Harvard University Press, 1990.

Campbell, Eugene E. *Establishing Zion: The Mormon Church in the American West, 1847–1869.* Salt Lake City: Signature Books, 1988.

Campbell, Eugene E., and Bruce L. Campbell. "Divorce Among Mormon Polygamists: Extent and Explanations." *Utah Historical Quarterly* 46 (Winter 1978): 4–23.

Cannon, Charles A. "The Awesome Power of Sex: The Polemical Campaign against Mormon Polygamy." *Pacific Historical Review* 43, no. 1 (February 1974): 61–82.

Cannon, Donald Q. "The King Follett Discourse: Joseph Smith's Greatest Sermon in Historical Perspective." *BYU Studies* 18, no. 2 (Winter 1978): 179–92.

Cannon, Donald Q., and Larry E. Dahl. *The Prophet Joseph Smith's King Follett Discourse: A Six Column Comparison of Original Notes and Amalgamations.* Provo, Utah: BYU Printing Service, 1983.

Cannon, Kenneth L., II. "Beyond the Manifesto: Polygamous Cohabitation among LDS General Authorities After 1890." *Utah Historical Quarterly* 46 (Winter 1978): 24–36.

Cannon, Mark W. "The Crusades Against the Masons, Catholics, and Mormons: Separate Waves of a Common Current." *BYU Studies* 3 (Winter 1961): 23–40.

———. "The Mormon Issue in Congress 1872–1882, Drawing on the Experience of Territorial Delegate George Q. Cannon." Ph.D. diss., Harvard University, 1960.

Carter, Thomas. "Living the Principle: Mormon Polygamous Housing in Nineteenth-Century Utah." *Winterthur Portfolio* 35, no. 4 (Winter 2000): 223–51.

Carter, Thomas, and Peter Goss, *Utah's Historic Architecture, 1847–1940.* Salt Lake City: University of Utah Press, 1988.

Casterline, Gail Farr. "'In the Toils' or 'Onward for Zion': Images of the Mormon Woman, 1852–1890." Master's thesis, Utah State University, 1974.

Catalogue of Books, Early Newspapers, and Pamphlets on Mormonism, Collected by the Late Mr. William Berrian. New York: V.H. Everson Print., 1898.

Chapman, Mary and Glenn Hendler. *Sentimental Men: Masculinity and the Politics of Affect in American Culture.* Berkeley: University of California Press, 1999.

Christensen, Carol W. *Mormons and Mormon History As Reflected in U.S. Government Documents, 1830–1907.* Washington, D.C.: Educational Resources Information Center, 1997.

The Church of Jesus Christ of Latter-day Saints. *Hymns of The Church of Jesus Christ of Latter-day Saints.* Salt Lake City: The Church of Jesus Christ of Latter-day Saints, 1985.

Chused, Richard H. "Married Women's Property Law: 1800–1850." *Georgetown Law Journal* 71 (June 1983): 1359–1425.

Clark, James Reuben, comp. *Messages of the First Presidency of The Church of Jesus Christ of Latter-day Saints 1833–1964.* 6 vols. Salt Lake City: Bookcraft, Inc., 1966.

Compton, Todd. *In Sacred Loneliness: The Plural Wives of Joseph Smith.* Salt Lake City: Signature Books, 1997.

Conway, Stephen, and Melvyn Stokes, eds. *The Market Revolution in America: Social, Political, and Religious Expressions.* Charlottesville: University Press of Virginia, 1996.

Cook, Blanche Wiesen. "Female Support Networks and Political Activism: Lillian Wald, Crystal Eastman, and Emma Goldman." In *A Heritage of Her Own: Toward a New Social History of American Women*, edited by Nancy F. Cott and Elizabeth Hafkin Pleck, 412–44. New York: Simon and Schuster, 1979.

Coontz, Stephanie. *The Social Origins of Private Life: A History of American Families, 1600–1900*. London: Verso, 1988.

Cornwall, Marie, and Laga Van Beek. "The Mormon Practice of Plural Marriage: The Social Construction of Religious Identity and Commitment." In *Religion and the Social Order*, edited by Marion S. Goldman and Mary Jo Neitz, 13–35. Greenwood, Conn.: JAI Press, 1995.

Cornwall, Marie, Camela Courtright, and Laga Van Beek. "How Common the Principle? Women As Plural Wives in 1860." *Dialogue: A Journal of Mormon Thought* 26 (Summer 1993): 139–53.

Cornwall, Rebecca Foster, and Leonard J. Arrington. "Perpetuation of a Myth: Mormon Danites in Five Western Novels, 1840–90." *BYU Studies* 23, no. 2 (Spring 1983): 147–65.

Cott, Nancy F. *The Bonds of Womanhood: "Woman's Sphere" in New England, 1780–1835*. New Haven: Yale University Press, 1977.

———. "'Giving Character to Our Whole Civil Polity': Marriage and the Public Order in the Late Nineteenth Century." In *U.S. History as Women's History: New Feminist Essays*, edited by Linda K. Kerber, Alice Kessler-Harris, and Kathryn Kish Sklar, 107–24. Chapel Hill: University of North Carolina Press, 1995.

———. *The Grounding of Modern Feminism*. New Haven: Yale University Press, 1987.

———. "Marriage and Women's Citizenship in the United States, 1830–1934." *The American Historical Review* 103, no. 5 (December 1998): 1440–74.

———. "Passionlessness: An Interpretation of Victorian Sexual Ideology, 1790–1850." In *A Heritage of Her Own: Toward a New Social History of American Women*, edited by Nancy F. Cott and Elizabeth H. Peck, 162–81. New York: Simon and Schuster, 1979.

———. *Public Vows: A History of Marriage and the Nation*. Cambridge, Mass.: Harvard University Press, 2000.

Cracroft, Richard H. "Distorting Polygamy for Fun and Profit: Artemis Ward and Mark Twain among the Mormons." *BYU Studies* 14, no. 2 (Winter 1974): 272–88.

Cross, Whitney R. *The Burned-Over District: The Social and Intellectual History of Enthusiastic Religion in Western New York, 1800–1850*. 2nd ed. New York: Harper and Row, 1965.

Davidoff, Leonore. "Regarding Some 'Old Husbands' Tales': Public and Private in Feminist History." In *Feminism, the Public and the Private*, edited by Joan B. Landes. New York: Oxford University Press, 1998.

Davidson, Cathy N., and Jessamyn Hatcher, eds. *No More Separate Spheres! A Next Wave American Studies Reader*. Durham: Duke University Press, 2002.

Davis, David Brion. "Some Themes of Counter-Subversion: An Analysis of Anti-Masonic, Anti-Catholic, and Anti-Mormon Literature." *Mississippi Valley Historical Review* 47, no. 2 (September 1960): 205–44.

Davis, Ray Jay. "Plural Marriage and Religious Freedom: The Impact of *Reynolds V. United States.*" *Arizona Law Review* 15, no. 2 (Spring 1973): 287–306.

Daynes, Kathryn M. *More Wives Than One: Transformation of the Mormon Marriage System, 1840–1910.* Urbana: University of Illinois Press, 2001.

———. "Mormon Polygamy: Belief and Practice in Nauvoo." In *Kingdom on the Mississippi Revisited: Nauvoo in Mormon History*, edited by Roger D. Launius and John E. Hallwas, 130–46. Urbana: University of Illinois Press, 1996.

———. "Single Men in a Polygamous Society: Male Marriage Patterns in Manti, Utah." *Journal of Mormon History* 24 (Spring 1998): 89–111.

Daynes, Kathryn M., and Sarah Barringer Gordon. "In-Laws and Outlaws: Criminal Prosecution of Mormon Polygamists in Utah Territory." Paper presented at the annual meeting of the American Historical Association, Philadelphia, Pennsylvania, January 2006.

Degler, Carl N. *At Odds: Women and the Family in America From the Revolution to the Present.* Oxford: Oxford University Press, 1980.

———. *In Search of Human Nature: The Decline and Revival of Darwinism in American Social Thought.* New York: Oxford University Press, 1991.

Degn, Louise. *Let the Women Vote.* Salt Lake City: KUED, 1997.

Denton, Sally. *American Massacre: The Tragedy at Mountain Meadows, September 1857.* New York: Alfred A. Knopf, 2003.

Derr, Jill Mulvay. "Eliza R. Snow and the Woman Question." In *Battle for the Ballot: Essays on Woman Suffrage in Utah, 1870–1896*, edited by Carol Cornwall Madsen, 75–90. Logan, Utah: Utah State University Press, 1997.

———. "The Lion and the Lioness: Brigham Young and Eliza R. Snow." *BYU Studies* 40, no. 2 (Winter 2001): 54–101.

———. "Woman's Place in Brigham Young's World." *BYU Studies* 18, no. 3 (Spring 1978): 377–95.

Dietz, Mary. "Context Is All: Feminism and Theories of Citizenship." *Daedalus* 116, no. 4 (Fall 1987): 1–24.

Douglas, Mary. *Purity and Danger: An Analysis of Concept of Pollution and Taboo.* Routledge Classics ed. London: Routledge, 2002.

Draper, Larry W., and Chad J. Flake, comp. *A Mormon Bibliography 1830–1930: Ten Year Supplement.* Salt Lake City: University of Utah, 1990.

DuBois, Ellen. *Feminism and Suffrage: The Emergence of an Independent Women's Movement in America, 1848–1869.* Ithaca: Cornell University Press, 1999.

———. *Woman Suffrage and Women's Rights.* New York: New York University Press, 1988.

DuBois, Ellen, and Linda Gordon. "Seeking Ecstasy on the Battlefield: Danger and Pleasure in Nineteenth-Century Feminist Sexual Thought." *Feminist Studies* 9, no. 1 (Spring 1983): 7–25.

Dunfey, Julie. "'Living the Principle' of Plural Marriage: Mormon Women, Utopia, and Female Sexuality in the Nineteenth Century." *Feminist Studies* 10, no. 3 (Fall 1984): 523–36.

Dwyer, Robert Joseph. *The Gentile Comes to Utah: A Study in Religious and Social Conflict (1862–1890)*. Rev. 2nd ed. Salt Lake City: Western Epics, 1971.

Edwards, Holly. *Noble Dreams, Wicked Pleasures: Orientalism in America, 1870–1930*. Princeton: Princeton University Press, 2000.

Edwards, Laura F. "'The Marriage Covenant Is at the Foundation of All Our Rights': The Politics of Slave Marriages in North Carolina After Emancipation." *Law and History Review* 14 (Spring 1996): 81–124.

Ehat, Andrew F. "'It Seems Like Heaven Began on Earth': Joseph Smith and the Constitution of the Kingdom of God." *BYU Studies* 20, no. 3 (Spring 1980): 253–79.

———. "Joseph Smith's Introduction of Temple Ordinances and the 1844 Mormon Succession Question." Master's thesis, Brigham Young University, 1982.

8: The Mormon Proposition. Directed by Reed Cowan. United States: David v. Goliath Films, 2010.

Elshtain, Jean Bethke. "Introduction: Toward a Theory of the Family." In *The Family in Political Thought*, edited by Jean Bethke Elshtain. Amherst: University of Massachusetts Press, 1982.

———. "Moral Woman and Immoral Man: A Consideration of the Public-Private Split and Its Political Ramifications." *Politics and Society* 4, no. 4 (1974): 453–73.

———. *Public Man, Private Woman: Women in Social and Political Thought*. Princeton: Princeton University Press, 1981.

Embry, Jessie L. "Grain Storage: The Balance of Power between Priesthood Authority and Relief Society Autonomy." *Dialogue: A Journal of Mormon Thought* 15 (Winter 1982): 59–66.

———. *Mormon Polygamous Families: Life in the Principle*. Salt Lake City: University of Utah Press, 1987.

———. *Mormons and Polygamy (Setting the Record Straight)*. Orem, Utah: Millennial Press, 2007.

———. "Ultimate Taboos: Incest and Mormon Polygamy." *Journal of Mormon History* 18 (Spring 1992): 93–113.

Embry, Jessie L., and Martha S. Bradley. "Mothers and Daughters in Polygamy." *Dialogue: A Journal of Mormon Thought* 18 (Fall 1985): 99–107.

Epstein, Barbara Leslie. *The Politics of Domesticity: Women, Evangelism, and Temperance in Nineteenth-Century America*. Middletown, Conn.: Wesleyan University Press, 1981.

Fales, Susan L., and Chad J. Flake. *Mormons and Mormonism in U.S. Government Documents: A Bibliography*. Salt Lake City: University of Utah Press, 1989.

Faragher, John Mack. *Women and Men on the Overland Trail*. 2nd ed. New Haven: Yale University Press, 2001.

Firmage, Edwin Brown. "The Judicial Campaign against Polygamy and the Enduring Legal Questions." *BYU Studies* 25 (Summer 1987): 91–113.

Firmage, Edwin Brown, and Richard Collin Mangrum. *Zion in the Courts: A Legal History of The Church of Jesus Christ of Latter-day Saints, 1830–1900*. Urbana: University of Illinois Press, 1988.

Flake, Chad J. *A Mormon Bibliography, 1830–1930: Books, Pamphlets, Periodicals, and Broadsides Relating to the First Century of Mormonism.* Salt Lake City: University of Utah Press, 1987.

———. *A Mormon Bibliography, 1830–1930: Books, Pamphlets, Periodicals, and Broadsides Relating to the First Century of Mormonism.* Edited by Chad J. Flake and Larry W. Draper, 2nd revision, revised and enlarged. Provo, Utah: Religious Studies Center, Brigham Young University, 2004.

Flake, Kathleen. "The Emotional and Priestly Logic of Plural Marriage." *Leonard J. Arrington Mormon History Lecture Series,* paper 15, 2009, 3, http://digitalcommons.usu.edu/arrington_lecture/15 (accessed September 25, 2010).

Flexner, Eleanor. *Century of Struggle: The Woman's Rights Movement in the United States.* New York: Atheneum, 1970.

Fliegelman, Jay. *Prodigals and Pilgrims: The American Revolution against Patriarchal Authority, 1750–1800.* Cambridge: Cambridge University Press, 1985.

Fluhman, J. Spencer. "An 'American Mahomet': Joseph Smith, Muhammad, and the Problem of Prophets in Antebellum America." *Journal of Mormon History* 34, no. 2 (Summer 2008): 23–45.

———. *"A Peculiar People": Anti-Mormonism and the Making of Religion in Nineteenth-Century America.* Chapel Hill: University of North Carolina Press, 2012.

Flynn, John J. "Federalism and Viable State Government—The History of Utah's Constitution." *Utah Law Review* 2 (September 1966): 311–25.

Foster, Craig L. "Doctrine and Covenants Section 132 and Joseph Smith's Expanding Concept of Family." In *The Persistence of Polygamy: Joseph Smith and the Origins of Mormon Polygamy,* edited by Newell G. Bringhurst and Craig L. Foster, 87–98. Independence, Mo.: John Whitmer Books, 2010.

———. "Victorian Pornographic Imagery in Anti-Mormon Literature." *Journal of Mormon History* 19, no. 1 (Spring 1993): 115–32.

Foster, Gains M. *Moral Reconstruction: Christian Lobbyists and the Federal Legislation of Morality, 1865–1920.* Chapel Hill: University of North Carolina Press, 2007.

Foster, Lawrence. "A Little-Known Defense of Polygamy from the Mormon Press in 1842." *Dialogue: A Journal of Mormon Thought* 9, no. 4 (Winter 1974): 21–34.

———. "Polygamy and the Frontier: Mormon Women in Early Utah." *Utah Historical Quarterly* 50, no. 3 (Summer 1982): 268–89.

———. *Religion and Sexuality: Three American Communal Experiments of the Nineteenth Century.* New York: Oxford University Press, 1981.

———. *Women, Family, and Utopia: Communal Experiments of the Shakers, the Oneida Community, and the Mormons.* Syracuse: Syracuse University Press, 1991.

Franke, Katherine. "Becoming a Citizen: Reconstruction-Era Regulation of African-American Marriages." *Yale Journal of Law and the Humanities* 11, no. 2 (Summer 1999): 251–309.

Freedman, Estelle. "Separatism as Strategy: Female Institution Building and American Feminism, 1870–1930." *Feminist Studies* 5 (Fall 1979): 512–29.

Garr, Arnold K. "Joseph Smith: Candidate for President of the United States." In *Re-*

gional Studies in Latter-day Saint Church History, Illinois, edited by H. Dean Garrett, 151–68. Provo, Utah: Department of Church History and Doctrine, Brigham Young University, 1995.

Gentry, Leland H. "The Danite Band of 1838." *BYU Studies* 14 (Summer 1974): 421–50.

Ginzberg, Lori D. *Women and the Work of Benevolence: Morality, Politics, and Class in the Nineteenth-Century United States*. New Haven: Yale University Press, 1990.

Givens, Terryl L. *By the Hand of Mormon: The American Scripture That Launched a New World Religion*. Oxford: Oxford University Press, 2005.

———. *The Latter-day Saint Experience in America*. Westport, Conn.: Greenwood Press, 2004.

———. *People of Paradox: A History of Mormon Culture*. New York: Oxford University Press, 2007.

———. *The Viper on the Hearth: Mormons, Myths, and the Construction of Heresy*. New York: Oxford University Press, 1997.

Godfrey, Kenneth W., Audrey M. Godfrey, and Jill Mulvay Derr, eds. *Women's Voices: An Untold History of the Latter-day Saints, 1830–1900*. Salt Lake City: Deseret Book Co., 1982.

Gordon, Sarah Barringer. "'The Liberty of Self-Degradation': Polygamy, Woman Suffrage, and Consent in Nineteenth-Century America." *Journal of American History* 83, no. 3 (December 1996): 815–47.

———. *The Mormon Question: Polygamy and Constitutional Conflict in Nineteenth-Century America*. Chapel Hill: University of North Carolina Press, 2002.

———. "'Our National Hearthstone': Anti-Polygamy Fiction and the Sentimental Campaign Against Moral Diversity in Antebellum America." *Yale Journal of Law and the Humanities* 8, no. 2 (Summer 1996): 295–350.

———. "The 'Twin Relic of Barbarism': A History of Anti-Polygamy in Nineteenth-Century America." Ph.D. diss., Princeton University, 1995.

———. "A War of Words: Revelation and Storytelling in the Campaign Against Mormon Polygamy." *Chicago-Kent Law Review* 78, no. 2 (2003): 739–72.

Greenawalt, Kent. *Religion and the Constitution, Volume 1: Free Exercise and Fairness*. Princeton: Princeton University Press, 2006.

Groberg, Joseph H. "The Mormon Disfranchisements of 1882 to 1892." *BYU Studies* 16 (Spring 1976): 399–408.

Grossberg, Michael. *Governing the Hearth: Law and the Family in Nineteenth-Century America*. Chapel Hill: University of North Carolina Press, 1985.

Grow, Matthew J. "The Whore of Babylon and the Abomination of Abominations: Nineteenth-Century Catholic and Mormon Mutual Perceptions and Religious Identity." *Church History* 73, no. 1 (March 2004): 139–67.

Habermas, Jürgen. *The Structural Transformation of the Public Sphere: An Inquiry into a Category of Bourgeois Society*. Trans. Thomas Burger. Cambridge, Mass.: MIT Press, 1989.

Hale, Van. "The Doctrinal Impact of the King Follett Discourse." *BYU Studies* 18, no. 2 (Winter 1978): 209–25.

Halttunen, Karen. *Confidence Men and Painted Women: A Study of Middle-Class Culture in America, 1830–1870*. New Haven: Yale University Press, 1982.

Hamilton, C. Mark. *Nineteenth-Century Mormon Architecture and City Planning*. New York: Oxford University Press, 1995.

Hanks, Maxine, ed. *Women and Authority: Re-Emerging Mormon Feminism*. Salt Lake City: Signature Books, 1992.

Hansen, Klaus J. "Mormon Sexuality and American Culture." *Dialogue: A Journal of Mormon Thought* 10, no. 2 (Autumn 1976): 45–56.

———. *Mormonism and the American Experience*. Chicago: University of Chicago Press, 1981.

———. *Quest for Empire: The Political Kingdom of God and the Council of Fifty in Mormon History*. Lincoln: University of Nebraska Press, 1967.

Hardy, B. Carmon. "Lords of Creation: Polygamy, the Abrahamic Household, and Mormon Patriarchy." *Journal of Mormon History* 20 (Spring 1994): 119–52.

———. *Solemn Covenant: The Mormon Polygamous Passage*. Urbana: University of Illinois Press, 1992.

Hardy, B. Carmon, and Dan Erickson. "'Regeneration—Now and Evermore!': Mormon Polygamy and the Physiological Rehabilitation of Humankind." *Journal of the History of Sexuality* 10, no. 1 (January 2001): 40–61.

Harline, Paula Kelly. "Polygamous Yet Monogamous: Cultural Conflict in the Writings of Mormon Polygamous Wives." In *Old West—New West: Centennial Essays*, edited by Barbara Howard Meldrum, 115–32. Moscow: University of Idaho Press, 1993.

Harper, Ida Husted. *The Life and Work of Susan B. Anthony*, 2 vols. Indianapolis: The Hollenbeck Press, 1898.

Hartog, Hendrick. *Man and Wife in America: A History*. Cambridge, Mass.: Harvard University Press, 2000.

Hatch, Nathan O. *The Democratization of American Christianity*. New Haven: Yale University Press, 1989.

Hayden, Dolores. *The Grand Domestic Revolution: A History of Feminist Designs for American Homes, Neighborhoods, and Cities*. Cambridge, Mass.: MIT Press, 1981.

Hayward, Barbara. "Utah's Anti-Polygamy Society 1878–1884." Ph.D. diss., Brigham Young University, 1980.

Hewett, Nancy. *Women's Activism and Social Change: Rochester, New York, 1822–1872*. Ithaca: Cornell University Press, 1984.

Higham, John. *Strangers in the Land: Patterns of American Nativism, 1860–1925*. 2nd ed. New Brunswick: Rutgers University Press, 1988.

Hill, Marvin S. *Quest for Refuge: The Mormon Flight from American Pluralism*. Salt Lake City: Signature Books, 1989.

Hobson, Barbara Meil. *Uneasy Virtue: The Politics of Prostitution and the American Reform Tradition*. New York: Basic Books, 1987.

Hofeling, Leland P. "Mormon Women and Woman Suffrage in an Era of Political Conflict in Territorial Utah, 1870–1896." Master's thesis, International University, 1977.

Hofstader, Richard. *Social Darwinism in American Thought*. Philadelphia: University of Pennsylvania Press, 1945.

Holland, Catherine A. *The Body Politic: Foundings, Citizenship, and Difference in the American Political Imagination*. New York: Routledge, 2001.

Howard, June. *Publishing the Family*. Durham: Duke University Press, 2001.

Hyde, Anne F. *Empires, Nations, and Families: A History of the North American West, 1800–1860*. Lincoln: University of Nebraska Press, 2011.

Irving, Gordon. "The Law of Adoption: One Phase of the Development of the Mormon Concept of Salvation, 1830–1900." *BYU Studies* 14, no. 3 (Spring 1974): 291–314.

Isenberg, Nancy. *Sex and Citizenship in Antebellum America*. Chapel Hill: University of North Carolina Press, 1998.

Iversen, Joan Smyth. *The Antipolygamy Controversy in U.S. Women's Movements, 1880–1925: A Debate on the American Home*. New York: Garland, 1997.

———. "A Debate on the American Home: The Anti-Polygamy Controversy, 1880–1890." *Journal of the History of Sexuality* 1, no. 4 (April 1991): 585–602.

———. "Feminist Implications of Mormon Polygyny." *Feminist Studies* 10, no. 3 (Fall 1984): 505–22.

———. "The Mormon-Suffrage Relationship: Personal and Political Quandaries." In *Battle for the Ballot: Essays on Woman Suffrage in Utah, 1870–1896*, edited by Carol Cornwall Madsen, 150–72. Logan, Utah: Utah State University Press, 1997.

Ivins, Stanley S. "A Constitution for Utah." *Utah Historical Quarterly* 25, no. 2 (April 1957): 95–116.

———. "Notes on Mormon Polygamy." *Western Humanities Review* 10 (Summer 1956): 229–39.

Jackson, Kenneth T. *Crabgrass Frontier: The Suburbanization of the United States*. New York: Oxford University Press, 1985.

Jacobson, Cardell K., and Lara Burton, eds. *Modern Polygamy in the United States: Historical, Cultural, and Legal Issues*. New York: Oxford University Press, 2011.

James, Kimberly Jensen. "'Between Two Fires': Women on the 'Underground' of Mormon Polygamy." *Journal of Mormon History* 8 (1981): 49–61.

Jensen, Andrew. *LDS Biographical Encyclopedia*, vol. 1. Salt Lake City: Published by the Andrew Jensen Memorial Association, and Printed by the Deseret News Press, 1936.

Johnson, Jeffery Ogden. "Determining and Defining 'Wife': Brigham Young Households." *Dialogue: A Journal of Mormon Thought* 20 (Fall 1987): 57–70.

Johnson, Paul E. *A Shopkeeper's Millennium: Society and Revivals in Rochester, New York, 1815–1837*. New York: Hill and Wang, 2004.

Johnson, Paul E., and Sean Wilentz. *The Kingdom of Matthias: A Story of Sex and Salvation in Nineteenth-Century America*. New York: Oxford University Press, 1994.

Jones, Megan Sanborn. *Performing American Identity in Anti-Mormon Melodrama* (New York: Routledge, 2009).

Kaplan, Amy. "Manifest Domesticity." *American Literature* 70, no. 3 (September 1998): 581–606.

Kelley, Mary. *Private Woman, Public Stage: Literary Domesticity in Nineteenth-Century America*. New York: Oxford University Press, 1984.

Kerber, Linda K. "Can a Woman Be an Individual?: The Discourse of Self-Reliance." In *Toward an Intellectual History of Women: Essays,* 200–223. Chapel Hill: University of North Carolina Press, 1997.

———. "A Constitutional Right to Be Treated Like American Ladies: Women and the Obligations of Citizenship." In *U.S. History as Women's History: New Feminist Essays,* edited by Linda K. Kerber, Alice Kessler-Harris, and Kathryn Kish Sklar, 17–35. Chapel Hill: University of North Carolina Press, 1995.

———. "The Meanings of Citizenship." *The Journal of American History* 84, no. 3 (December 1997): 833–54.

———. *No Constitutional Right to Be Ladies: Women and the Obligations of Citizenship.* New York: Hill and Wang, 1998.

———. "Separate Spheres, Female Worlds, Woman's Place: The Rhetoric of Women's History." *Journal of American History* 75, no. 1 (June 1988): 9–39.

———. *Women of the Republic: Intellect and Ideology in Revolutionary America.* Chapel Hill: University of North Carolina Press, 1980.

Kern, Louis J. *An Ordered Love: Sex Roles and Sexuality in Victorian Utopias: The Shakers, the Mormons, and the Oneida Community.* Chapel Hill: University of North Carolina Press, 1981.

Kettner, James H. *The Development of American Citizenship, 1608–1870.* Chapel Hill: University of North Carolina Press, 1978.

Kevles, Daniel J. *In the Name of Eugenics: Genetics and the Uses of Human Heredity.* Cambridge, Mass.: Harvard University Press, 1995.

Kidd, Thomas S. *American Christians and Islam: Evangelical Culture and Muslims from the Colonial Period to the Age of Terrorism.* Princeton: Princeton University Press, 2009.

———. "'Is It Worse to Follow Mahomet than the Devil?' Early American Uses of Islam." *Church History* 72, no. 4 (December 2003): 766–90.

Kimball, James L., Jr. "A Wall to Defend Zion: The Nauvoo Charter." *BYU Studies* 15, no. 4 (Summer 1975): 491–97.

Knobel, Dale T. *America for the Americans: The Nativist Movement in the United States.* New York: Twayne Publishers, 1996.

Krakauer, Jon. *Under the Banner of Heaven: A Story of Violent Faith.* New York: Doubleday, 2003.

Kunz, Phillip R. "One Wife or Several? A Comparative Study of Late-Nineteenth-Century Marriage in Utah." In *The Mormon People: Their Character and Traditions,* edited by Thomas G. Alexander, 53–73. Provo, Utah: Brigham Young University Press, 1980.

Lamar, Howard Roberts. *The Far Southwest 1846–1912: A Territorial History.* Rev. ed. Albuquerque: University of New Mexico Press, 2000.

Lambert, Frank. *The Founding Fathers and the Place of Religion in America.* Princeton: Princeton University Press, 2003.

Landes, Joan B., ed. *Feminism, The Public and the Private*. New York: Oxford University Press, 1998.

Larson, Gustive O. *The "Americanization" of Utah for Statehood*. San Marino, Calif.: The Huntington Library, 1971.

———. "An Industrial Home for Polygamous Wives." *Utah Historical Quarterly* 38, no. 3 (Summer 1970): 263–75.

———. "The Mormon Reformation." *Utah Historical Quarterly* 26 (January 1958): 45–63.

Larson, Stanley. "The King Follett Discourse: A Newly Amalgamated Text." *BYU Studies* 18, no. 2 (Winter 1978): 193–208.

———, ed. *Prisoner for Polygamy: The Memoirs and Letters of Rudger Clawson at the Utah Territorial Penitentiary, 1884–87*. Urbana: University of Illinois Press, 1993.

Lasch, Christopher. *Haven in a Heartless World: The Family Besieged*. New York: Norton, 1977.

Launius, Roger D. "The New Social History and the New Mormon History: Reflections on Recent Trends." *Dialogue: A Journal of Mormon Thought* 27, no. 2 (Spring 1994): 109–28.

LeSueur, Stephen C. *The 1838 Mormon War in Missouri*. Columbia: University of Missouri Press, 1987.

Lewis, Jan. "The Republican Wife: Virtue and Seduction in the Early Republic." *The William and Mary Quarterly* 44, no. 4 (October, 1987): 689–721.

Lieber, Constance L., and John Sillito, eds. *Letters from Exile: The Correspondence of Martha Hughes Cannon and Angus M. Cannon, 1886–1888*. Salt Lake City: Signature Books in association with Smith Research Associates, 1989.

Linford, Orma. "The Mormons and the Law: The Polygamy Cases." Parts 1 and 2. *Utah Law Review* 9, no. 2 (Winter 1964): 308–70; 9, no. 3 (Summer 1965): 543–91.

———. "The Mormons, the Law, and the Territory of Utah." *American Journal of Legal History* 23 (April 1979): 213–35.

Lister, Ruth. *Citizenship: Feminist Perspectives*. 2nd ed. New York: New York University Press, 2003.

———. "Dilemmas in Engendering Citizenship." In *Gender and Citizenship in Transition*, edited by Barbara Hobson, 33–83. New York: Routledge, Inc., 2000.

———. "Tracing the Contours of Women's Citizenship." *Policy and Politics* 21, no. 1 (January 1993): 3–16.

Ludlow, Daniel H., ed. *Encyclopedia of Mormonism: The History, Scripture, Doctrine, and Procedure of The Church of Jesus Christ of Latter-day Saints*, 4 vols. New York: Macmillan Publishing Company, 1992.

Lyman, Edward Leo. *Political Deliverance: The Mormon Quest for Utah Statehood*. Urbana: University of Illinois Press, 1986.

Lynn, Karen. "Courtship and Romance in Utah Territory: Doing Away With 'The Gentile Custom of Sparkification.'" In *A Sesquicentennial Look at Church History: Sidney B. Sperry Symposium, January 26, 1980, Brigham Young University Campus, Provo, Utah*, 211–23. Provo, Utah: Brigham Young University Church Educational System, 1980.

————. "Sensational Virtue: Nineteenth-Century Mormon Fiction and American Popular Taste." *Dialogue: A Journal of Mormon Thought* 14, no. 3 (Autumn 1981): 101–11.

Lyon, T. Edgar. "Doctrinal Development of the Church during the Nauvoo Sojourn, 1839–1846." *BYU Studies* 15, no. 4 (Summer 1975): 435–46.

Lystra, Karen. *Searching the Heart: Women, Men, and Romantic Love in Nineteenth-Century America*. New York: Oxford University Press, 1989.

Lythgoe, Dennis L. "Negro Slavery in Utah." *Utah Historical Quarterly* 39 (1971): 40–54.

MacKay, Kathryn L., comp. "Chronology of Woman Suffrage in Utah." In *Battle for the Ballot: Essays on Woman Suffrage in Utah, 1870–1896*, edited by Carol Cornwall Madsen, 311–18. Logan, Utah: Utah State University Press, 1997.

Madsen, Carol Cornwall. "'At Their Peril': Utah Law and the Case of Plural Wives, 1850–1900." *Western Historical Quarterly* 21 (November 1990): 425–43.

————, ed. *Battle for the Ballot: Essays on Woman Suffrage in Utah 1870–1896*. Logan, Utah: Utah State University Press, 1997.

————. "Decade of Détente: The Mormon-Gentile Female Relationship in Nineteenth-Century Utah." *Utah Historical Quarterly* 63, no. 4 (Fall 1995): 298–319.

————. Emmeline B. Wells: A Voice for Mormon Women." *John Whitmer Historical Association Journal* 2 (1982): 11–21.

————. "Emmeline B. Wells in Washington: The Search for Mormon Legitimacy." *Journal of Mormon History* 26, no. 2 (Fall 2000): 140–78.

————. "Emmeline Wells: 'Am I Not a Woman and Sister?'" *BYU Studies* 22 (Spring 1982): 162–78.

————. "'Feme Covert': Journey of a Metaphor." *Journal of Mormon History* 17, no. 1 (1991): 43–61.

————. "A Mormon Woman in Victorian America." Ph.D. diss., University of Utah, 1985.

————. "'Remember the Women of Zion': A Study of the Editorial Content of the *Women's Exponent*, A Mormon Woman's Journal." Master's thesis, University of Utah, 1977.

Madsen, Carol Cornwall, and David J. Whittaker. "History's Sequel: A Source Essay on Women in Mormon History." *Journal of Mormon History* 6 (1979): 123–45.

Mahajan, Gurpreet, ed. *The Public and the Private: Issues of Democratic Citizenship*. New Delhi: Sage Publications, 2003.

Mangrum, R. Collin. "Mormonism, Philosophical Liberalism, and the Constitution." *BYU Studies* 27, no. 3 (Summer 1987): 119–37.

Marquis, Kathleen. "Diamond Cut Diamond: Mormon Women and the Cult of Domesticity." Ph.D. diss., University of Michigan, 1976.

Marsh, Margaret. "Suburban Men and Masculine Domesticity, 1870–1915." In *Meanings for Manhood: Constructions of Masculinity in Victorian America*, edited by Marc C. Carnes and Clyde Griffin, 111–27. Chicago: University of Chicago Press, 1990.

Mason, Patrick Q. *The Mormon Menace: Violence and Anti-Mormonism in the Postbellum South*. New York: Oxford University Press, 2011.

Massie, Michael. "Reform is Where You Find It: The Roots of Woman Suffrage in Wyoming." *Annals of Wyoming* 62, no. 1 (Spring 1990): 2–22.

Matthews, Robert J. "The 'New Translation' of the Bible, 1830–1833: Doctrinal Development during the Kirtland Era." *BYU Studies* 11, no. 4 (Summer 1971): 400–422.

Mauss, Armand L. *The Angel and the Beehive: The Mormon Struggle With Assimilation.* Urbana: University of Illinois Press, 1994.

May, Dean. "A Demographic Portrait of the Mormons, 1830–1980." In *After 150 Years: The Latter-day Saints in Sesquicentennial Perspective,* edited by Thomas G. Alexander and Jessie L. Embry, 37–69. Midvale, Utah: Signature Books for Charles Redd Center for Western Studies, 1983.

Mazur, Eric Michael. *The Americanization of Religious Minorities: Confronting the Constitutional Order.* Baltimore: The Johns Hopkins University Press, 2004.

McConkie, Bruce R. *Mormon Doctrine.* Salt Lake City: Bookcraft, Inc., 1966.

———. *The Mortal Messiah: From Bethlehem to Calvary,* 4 vols. Salt Lake City: Deseret Book Co., 1981.

McDannell, Colleen. *The Christian Home in Victorian America.* Bloomington: Indiana University Press, 1986.

Mead, Rebecca J. *How the Vote Was Won: Woman Suffrage in the Western United States, 1868–1914.* New York: New York University Press, 2004.

Melville, J. Keith. *Highlights in Mormon Political History.* Provo, Utah: Brigham Young University, 1967.

———. "Theory and Practice of Church and State during the Brigham Young Era." *BYU Studies* 3 (Autumn 1960): 33–55.

Miles, Carrie A. "'What's Love Got to Do With It?': Earthly Experience of Celestial Marriage, Past and Present." In *Modern Polygamy in the United States: Historical, Cultural, and Legal Issues,* edited by Cardell K. Jacobson and Lara Burton, 185–207. New York: Oxford University Press, 2011.

Mintz, Steven, and Susan Kellogg. *Domestic Revolutions: A Social History of American Family Life.* New York: The Free Press, 1988.

Moore, R. Lawrence. *Religious Outsiders and the Making of Americans.* New York: Oxford University Press, 1986.

Moorman, Donald R. *Camp Floyd and the Mormons: The Utah War.* Salt Lake City: University of Utah Press, 1992.

Mulder, William. *Homeward to Zion: The Mormon Migration From Scandinavia.* Minneapolis: University of Minnesota Press, [1957].

Mulder, William, and A. Russell Mortensen, eds. *Among the Mormons: Historic Accounts by Contemporary Observers.* New York: Alfred A. Knopf, 1958.

Mulvay, Jill C. "Eliza R. Snow and the Woman Question." *BYU Studies* 16, no. 2 (Winter 1976): 250–64.

Muncy, Raymond Lee. *Sex and Marriage in Utopian Communities.* Chapel Hill: University of North Carolina Press, 1981.

The National Union Catalog: Pre-1956 Imprints. London: Mansell Publishing, 1979.

New York Public Library. *List of Works in the Library Relating to the Mormons.* New York: New York Public Library, 1909.

Newell, Linda King. "Emma Hale Smith and the Polygamy Question." *John Whitmer Historical Association Journal* 4 (1984): 3–15.

———. "The Historical Relationship of Mormon Women and Priesthood." *Dialogue: A Journal of Mormon Thought* 18, no. 3 (Fall 1985): 21–32.

Newman, Louise Michele. *White Women's Rights: The Racial Origins of Feminism in the United States.* New York: Oxford University Press, 1999.

Nichols, Jeffrey. *Prostitution, Polygamy, and Power: Salt Lake City, 1847–1918.* Urbana: University of Illinois Press, 2002.

Oaks, Dallin H. "Habeas Corpus in the State 1776–1865." *University of Chicago Law Review* 32 (Winter 1965): 243–88.

———. "The Suppression of the Nauvoo Expositor." *Utah Law Review* 9 (Winter 1965): 862–903.

Ostling, Richard, and Joan K. Ostling. *Mormon America: The Power and the Promise.* San Francisco: HarperSanFrancisco, 1999.

Pagliarini, Marie Anne. "The Pure American Woman and the Wicked Catholic Priest: An Analysis of Anti-Catholic Literature in Antebellum America." *Religion and American Culture: A Journal of Interpretation* 9, no. 1 (Winter 1999): 97–128.

Palmer, Grant H. "The Godbeite Movement: A Dissent against Temporal Control." Master's thesis, Brigham Young University, 1968.

———. *An Insider's View of Mormon Origins.* Salt Lake City: Signature Books, 2002.

Panek, Tracy E. "Search and Seizure in Utah: Recounting the Antipolygamy Raids." *Utah Historical Quarterly* 62, no. 4 (Fall 1994): 316–34.

Papanikolas, Helen Z., ed. *The Peoples of Utah.* Salt Lake City: Utah State Historical Society, 1976.

Pascoe, Peggy. *Relations of Rescue: The Search for Female Moral Authority in the West.* New York: Oxford University Press, 1990.

Pateman, Carole. *The Disorder of Women: Democracy, Feminism, and Political Theory.* Stanford: Stanford University Press, 1989.

———. *The Sexual Contract.* Stanford: Stanford University Press, 1986.

Peterson, Paul H. "The Mormon Reformation of 1856–57: The Rhetoric and the Reality." *Journal of Mormon History* 15 (1989): 59–87.

Peterson, Tarla Rai. "The *Woman's Exponent*, 1872–1914: Champion for 'The Rights of the Women of Zion, and the Rights of the Women of All Nations.'" In *A Voice of Their Own: The Woman Suffrage Press, 1840–1910*, edited by Martha M. Solomon, 165–82. Tuscaloosa: The University of Alabama Press, 1991.

Philips, Anne. *Democracy and Difference.* University Park: Pennsylvania State University, 1993.

———. *Engendering Democracy.* University Park: Pennsylvania State University Press, 1991.

Platt, Lyman D. "The History of Marriage in Utah, 1847–1905." *Genealogical Journal* 12 (Spring 1983): 28–41.

Pleck, Elizabeth. *Domestic Tyranny: The Making of Social Policy against Domestic Violence From Colonial Times to the Present.* New York: Oxford University Press, 1987.

Poll, Richard D. "The Legislative Anti-Polygamy Campaign." *BYU Studies* 26, no. 4 (Fall 1986): 107–19.

———. "The Mormon Question 1850–1865." Master's thesis, University of California, Berkeley, 1948.

———. "The Mormon Question Enters National Politics, 1850–1856." *Utah Historical Quarterly* 25, no. 2 (April 1957): 117–31.

———. "The Political Reconstruction of Utah Territory, 1866–1890." *Pacific Historical Review* 27, no. 2 (May 1958): 111–26.

———. "The Twin Relic: A Study of Mormon Polygamy and the Campaign of the United States for Its Abolition." Ph.D. diss., Texas Christian University, 1939.

Poll, Richard D., Thomas G. Alexander, and Eugene E. Campbell, eds. *Utah's History*. Provo, Utah: Brigham Young University Press, 1970.

Porter, Larry C., and Milton V. Backman, Jr. "Doctrine and the Temple in Nauvoo." *BYU Studies* 32 (Winter 1992): 50–54; (Spring 1992): 41–54.

Prince, Gregory A. *Power from on High: The Development of Mormon Priesthood*. Salt Lake City: Signature Books, 1995.

Pulsipher, John David. "The Americanization of Monogamy: Mormons, Native Americans, and the Nineteenth-Century Perception That Polygamy Was a Threat to Democracy." Ph.D. diss., University of Minnesota, 1999.

Quinn, D. Michael. "The Council of Fifty and Its Members, 1844–1945." *BYU Studies* 20, no. 2 (Winter 1980): 163–94.

———. *Early Mormonism and the Magic World View*. Salt Lake City: Signature Books, 1987.

———. "LDS Church Authority and New Plural Marriages, 1890–1904." *Dialogue: A Journal of Mormon Thought* 18, no. 1 (Spring 1985): 9–108.

———. "The Mormon Hierarchy, 1832–1932: An American Elite." Ph.D. diss., Yale University, 1976.

———. *The Mormon Hierarchy: Extensions of Power*. Salt Lake City: Signature Books in association with Smith Research Associates, 1997.

———. *The Mormon Hierarchy: Origins of Power*. Salt Lake City: Signature Books, 1994.

———, ed. *The New Mormon History: Revisionist Essays on the Past*. Salt Lake City: Signature Books, 1992.

———. "Plural Marriage and Mormon Fundamentalism." In *Fundamentalisms and Society: Reclaiming the Sciences, the Family, and Education*, edited by Martin E. Marty, R. Scott Appleby, Helen Hardacre, and Everett Mendelsohn, 240–93. Chicago: University of Chicago Press, 1997.

Regosin, Elizabeth. *Freedom's Promise: Ex-Slave Families and Citizenship in the Age of Emancipation*. Charlottesville: University Press of Virginia, 2002.

Riess, Jana Kathryn. "Heathen in Our Fair Land: Anti-Polygamy and Protestant Women's Missions to Utah, 1869–1910." Ph.D. diss., Columbia University, 2000.

Roberts, B. H. *The Life of John Taylor*. Salt Lake City: Bookcraft, Inc., 1963.

Romero, Lora. *Home Fronts: Domesticity and Its Critics in the Antebellum United States*. Durham: Duke University Press, 1997.

Rosenblum, Nancy L. "Democratic Sex: *Reynolds v. U.S.*, Sexual Relations, and Community." In *Sex, Preference, and Family: Essays on Law and Nature*, edited by David M. Estlund and Martha C. Nussbaum, 63–85. New York: Oxford University Press, 1997.

Rothman, Ellen K. *Hands and Hearts: A History of Courtship in America*. New York: Basic Books, Inc., 1984.

Russet, Cynthia Eagle. *Sexual Science: The Victorian Construction of Womanhood*. Cambridge, Mass.: Harvard University Press, 1989.

Ryan, Mary P. *Cradle of the Middle Class: The Family in Oneida County, New York, 1790–1865*. Cambridge: Cambridge University Press, 1981.

———. *The Empire of the Mother: American Writing About Domesticity, 1830–1860*. New York: Institute for Research in History and the Haworth Press, 1982.

———. "The Power of Women's Networks: A Case Study of Female Moral Reform in Antebellum America." *Feminist Studies* 5 (Spring 1979): 66–85.

———. "The Public and the Private Good: Across the Divide in Women's History." *Journal of Women's History* 15, no. 2 (Summer 2003): 10–27.

Said, Edward. *Orientalism*. New York: Pantheon Books, 1978.

Salmon, Marylynn. *Women and the Law of Property in Early America*. Chapel Hill: University of North Carolina Press, 1986.

Samuels, Shirley. *The Culture of Sentiment*. New York: Oxford University Press, 1992.

Scott, Patricia Lyn. "Mormon Polygamy: A Bibliography, 1977–92." *Journal of Mormon History* 19, no. 1 (Spring 1993): 133–55.

Sellers, Charles. *The Market Revolution: Jacksonian America, 1815–1846*. New York: Oxford University Press, 1991.

Sha'ban, Fuad. *Islam and Arabs in Early American Thought: The Roots of Orientalism in America*. Durham: The Acorn Press, 1991.

Sheingorn, Pamela, and Carol Weisbrod. "*Reynolds V. United States*: Nineteenth-Century Forms of Marriage and the Status of Women." In *History of Women in the United States, Volume 3: Domestic Relations and Law*, edited by Nancy F. Cott, 345–75. Munich: K. G. Saur, 1992.

Shipps, Jan. "An 'Insider-Outsider' in Zion." *Dialogue: A Journal of Mormon Thought* 15, no. 1 (Spring 1982): 138–61.

———. "Difference and Otherness: Mormonism and the American Religious Mainstream." In *Minority Faiths and the American Protestant Mainstream*, edited by Jonathan D. Sarna, 81–109. Urbana: University of Illinois Press, 1998.

———. *Mormonism: The Story of a New Religious Tradition*. Urbana: University of Illinois Press, 1985.

———. "The Principle Revoked: A Closer Look at the Demise of Plural Marriage." *Journal of Mormon History* 11 (1984): 65–78.

———. *Sojourner in the Promised Land: Forty Years among the Mormons*. Urbana: University of Illinois Press, 2000.

Shklar, Judith N. *American Citizenship: The Quest for Inclusion*. Cambridge, Mass.: Harvard University Press, 1991.

Short, Dennis R. *Questions on Plural Marriage, With a Selected Bibliography and 160 References.* Salt Lake City: Dennis R. Short, 1975.

Siegel, Reva B. "The Modernization of Marital Status Law: Adjudicating Wives' Rights to Earnings, 1860–1930." *Georgetown Law Journal* 82 (September 1994): 2127–211.

———. "'The Rule of Love': Wife Beating and Prerogative and Privacy." *The Yale Law Journal* 105 (June 1996): 2117–207.

Smith, George D., ed. *Faithful History: Essays on Writing Mormon History.* Salt Lake City: Signature Books, 1992.

———. *Nauvoo Polygamy: "But We Called It Plural Marriage."* Salt Lake City: Signature Books, 2008.

Smith, Joseph Fielding. *Answers to Gospel Questions,* compiled and edited by Joseph Fielding Smith, Jr. 5 vols. Salt Lake City: Deseret Book Co., 1957.

———. *Church History and Modern Revelation.* 4 vols. Salt Lake City: Council of the Twelve Apostles of The Church of Jesus Christ of Latter-day Saints, 1946–1949.

———. *Essentials in Church History.* 13th ed. Salt Lake City: Deseret News Press, 1950.

———. *History of the Church of Jesus Christ of Latter-day Saints.* 7 vols. 13th ed. Salt Lake City: Deseret Book Co., 1951; reprint.

Smith-Rosenberg, Carroll. "Dis-Covering the Subject of the 'Great Constitutional Discussion,' 1786–1789." *Journal of American History* 79, no. 3 (December 1992): 841–73.

———. *Disorderly Conduct: Visions of Gender in Victorian America.* New York: Alfred A. Knopf., 1985.

Somers, Margaret R. "Citizenship and the Place of the Public Sphere: Law, Community, and Political Culture in the Transition to Democracy." *American Sociological Review* 58, no. 5 (October 1993): 587–620.

Sonne, Conway B. *Saints on the Seas: A Maritime History of Mormon Migration, 1830–1890.* Salt Lake City: University of Utah Press, 1983.

Sorensen, Don. "Being Equal in Earthly and Heavenly Power: The Idea of Stewardship in the United Order." *BYU Studies* 18, no. 1 (Fall 1977): 100–116.

Speth, Linda E. "The Married Women's Property Acts, 1839–1865: Reform, Reaction, or Revolution?" In *Women and the Law: The Social Historical Perspective,* vol. 2, edited by D. Kelly Weisberg, 69–91. Cambridge, Mass.: Schenkman Publishing, 1982.

Stanley, Amy Dru. "Conjugal Bonds and Wage Labor: Rights of Contract in the Age of Emancipation." *Journal of American History* 75, no. 2 (September 1988): 471–500.

———. *From Bondage to Contract: Wage Labor, Marriage, and the Market in the Age of Slave Emancipation.* Cambridge: Cambridge University Press, 1998.

Stanton, Theodore, and Harriot Stanton Blatch, eds. *Elizabeth Cady Stanton,* 2 vols. New York: Arno and The New York Times, 1969.

Stapley, Jonathan A. "Adoptive Sealing Ritual in Mormonism." *Journal of Mormon History* 37 (Summer 2011): 53–117.

Taylor, P. A. M. *Expectations Westward: The Mormons and the Emigration of Their British Converts in the Nineteenth Century.* Ithaca: Cornell University Press, 1966.

Taysom, Stephen C. "A Uniform and Common Recollection: Joseph Smith's Legacy,

Polygamy, and Public Memory, 1852–2002." In *Dimensions of Faith: A Mormon Studies Reader,* edited by Stephen C. Taysom, 177–213. Salt Lake City: Signature Books, 2011.

Tompkins, Jane. *Sensational Designs: The Cultural Work of American Fiction, 1790–1860.* New York: Oxford University Press, 1985.

Toscano, Margaret, and Paul Toscano. *Strangers in Paradox: Explorations in Mormon Theology.* Salt Lake City: Signature Books, 1990.

Underwood, Grant. *The Millenarian World of Early Mormonism.* Urbana: University of Illinois Press, 1993.

University of Utah. Libraries. Manuscripts Division. *Utah Politics and Government: A Guide to Collection Materials.* [Salt Lake City]: Manuscripts Division, J. Willard Marriott Library, University of Utah, 1998.

Van Wagenen, Lola. "In Their Own Behalf: The Politicization of Mormon Women and the 1870 Franchise." *Dialogue: A Journal of Mormon Thought* 24, no. 4 (Winter 1991): 31–43.

———. "Sister-Wives and Suffragists: Polygamy and the Politics of Woman Suffrage, 1870–1896." Ph.D. diss., New York University, 1994.

Van Wagenen, Michael Scott. *The Texas Republic and the Mormon Kingdom of God.* College Station: Texas A and M University Press, 2002.

Van Wagoner, Richard S. *Mormon Polygamy: A History.* 2nd ed. Salt Lake City: Signature Books, 1989.

Vetterli, Richard. *Mormonism, Americanism, and Politics.* Salt Lake City: Ensign Publishing Company, 1961.

Vogel, Dan. *Joseph Smith: The Making of a Prophet (A Biography).* Salt Lake City: Signature Books, 2004.

Walker, Ronald W. "The Stenhouses and the Making of a Mormon Image." *Journal of Mormon History* 1 (1974): 51–72.

———. "The Godbeite Protests in the Making of Modern Utah." Ph.D. diss., University of Utah, 1977.

Walker, Ronald W., David J. Whittaker, and James B. Allen. *Mormon History.* Urbana: University of Illinois Press, 2001.

Walker, Ronald W., Richard E. Turley, and Glen M. Leonard. *Massacre at Mountain Meadows.* New York: Oxford University Press, 2008.

Warenski, Marilyn. *Patriarchs and Politics: The Plight of the Mormon Woman.* New York: McGraw-Hill Book Company, 1978.

Welter, Barbara. "The Cult of True Womanhood." *American Quarterly* 18 (Spring 1966): 151–74.

———. "The Feminization of American Religion, 1800–1860." In *Clio's Consciousness Raised: New Perspectives in the History of Women,* edited by Mary Hartman and Lois W. Banner, 137–57. New York: Harper and Row, Publishers, 1974.

White, Jean Bickmore. "Political Deliverance at a Price: The Quest for Statehood." *Journal of Mormon History* 12 (1985): 135–39.

———. "Woman's Place Is in the Constitution: The Struggle for Equal Rights in Utah in 1895." *Utah Historical Quarterly* 42 (Fall 1974): 344–69.

Whitney, Helen, Jane Barnes, and PBS Home Video. *The Mormons*. United States: PBS Home Video, 2007.

Whitney, Orson F. *History of Utah*. 4 vols. Salt Lake City: G. Q. Cannon, 1892–1904.

Whittaker, David J. "The Bone in the Throat: Orson Pratt and the Public Announcement of Plural Marriage." *Western Historical Quarterly* 18 (July 1987): 293–314.

———. "Early Mormon Pamphleteering." Ph.D. diss., Brigham Young University, 1982.

———. "Early Mormon Polygamy Defenses." *Journal of Mormon History* 11 (1984): 43–64.

Wiggins, Marvin E. *Mormons and Their Neighbors: An Index to Over 75,000 Biographical Sketches From 1820 to the Present*. Provo, Utah: Harold B. Lee Library, Brigham Young University, 1984.

Wilcox, Linda P. "The Mormon Concept of a Mother in Heaven." In *Sisters in Spirit: Mormon Women in Historical and Cultural Perspective*, edited by Maureen Ursenbach Beecher and Lavina Fielding Anderson, 64–77. Urbana: University of Illinois Press, 1987.

Willey, Angela, "'Christian Nations,' 'Polygamic Races' and Women's Rights: Toward a Genealogy of Non/Monogamy and Whiteness." *Sexualities* 9, no. 5 (2006): 530–46.

Williams, J. D. "The Separation of Church and State in Mormon Theory and Practice." *Journal of Church and State* 9 (Spring 1967): 238–62.

Williams, Joan C. "Domesticity as the Dangerous Supplement of Liberalism." *Journal of Women's History* 2, no. 3 (Winter 1991): 69–88.

Winn, Kenneth H. *Exiles in a Land of Liberty: Mormons in America, 1830–1846*. Chapel Hill: University of North Carolina Press, 1989.

Wood, Gordon S. "Evangelical America and Early Mormonism." *New York History* 61 (October 1980): 359–86.

———. *The Radicalism of the American Revolution*. New York: Alfred A. Knopf, 1992.

Wright, Gwendolyn. *Building the Dream: A Social History of Housing in America*. New York: Pantheon Books, 1981.

Wright, Stuart A., and James T. Richardson, eds. *Saints under Siege: The Texas Raid on the Fundamentalist Latter Day Saints*. New York: New York University Press, 2011.

Young, Kimball. *Isn't One Wife Enough?* New York: Henry Holt and Company, 1954.

Index

CHRISTINE TALBOT is an assistant professor of women's studies at the University of Northern Colorado.

The University of Illinois Press
is a founding member of the
Association of American University Presses.

Composed in 10.75/13 Arno Pro
by Jim Proefrock
at the University of Illinois Press
Manufactured by Thomson-Shore, Inc.

University of Illinois Press
1325 South Oak Street
Champaign, IL 61820-6903
www.press.uillinois.edu